The Critical Practitioner in Social Work and Health Care

Edited by
Sandy Fraser and
Sarah Matthews

The Open University

SAGE Publications
Los Angeles ▪ London ▪ New Delhi ▪ Singapore

The Open University
Walton Hall
Milton Keynes
MK7 6AA
United Kingdom
www.open.ac.uk

SAGE Publications Ltd
1 Oliver's Yard
55 City Road
London EC1Y 1SP

SAGE Publications Inc.
2455 Teller Road
Thousand Oaks, California 91320

SAGE Publications India Pvt Ltd
B 1/I 1 Mohan Cooperative Industrial Area
Mathura Road, New Delhi 110 044
India

SAGE Publications Asia-Pacific Pte Ltd
33 Pekin Street #02-01
Far East Square
Singapore 048763

Library of Congress Control Number: 2007926255

British Library Cataloguing in Publication data

A catalogue record for this book is available
from the British Library

ISBN 978-1-4129-4840-1
ISBN 978-1-4129-4841-8 (pbk)

Typeset by C&M Digitals (P) Ltd., Chennai, India
Printed in Great Britain by The Cromwell Press Ltd, Trowbridge, Wiltshire
Printed on paper from sustainable resources

The Critical Practitioner in Social Work and Health Care

NORTHBROOK COLLEGE SUSSEX BW

Further, Higher and Adult Education

Library and Information Services

Critical social work practice

This Reader forms part of the Open University course Critical Social Work Practice (K315) which is a 60-point, third-level practice course in the Degree for Social Work in England and Scotland and in Critical Social Work Practice (KZW315) in Wales.

Details of these and other Open University courses can be obtained from the Student Registration and Enquiry Service, The Open University, PO Box 197, Milton Keynes MK7 6BJ, United Kingdom: tel. +44 (0)845 300 6090, e-mail general-enquiries@open.ac.uk.

Alternatively, you may visit the Open University website at http://www.open.ac.uk where you can learn more about the wide range of courses and packs offered at all levels by The Open University.

Contents

Editors

Sandy Fraser

Sandy Fraser is a Lecturer in Social Work, Faculty of Health and Social Care at the Open University. He is the lead academic involved in the production of K315 Critical Social Work Practice, the course with which this book is associated. Sandy previously worked as a children and families social worker in South Wales and Devon.

Sarah Matthews

Sarah Matthews is a Staff Tutor in the Open University regional office in Manchester. Sarah worked as a social worker in the mental health field for over 20 years, latterly as a senior manager for Liverpool City Council. She is currently a mental health commissioner for the Department of Health and provides independent training and consultancy services to agencies in the public and private sectors concerning services to adults.

Contributors

Claire Ballinger

Claire Ballinger is a Reader in Occupational Therapy in the Faculty of Health and Social Care at London South Bank University. Her research interests include evidence-based practice, falls and falling and older people's perspectives of chronic illness and health care. She has recently co-edited a textbook on qualitative research methods for allied health professionals with Linda Finlay.

Sheila Barrett

Sheila Barrett is a Senior Lecturer in Organisational Behaviour at the Business School at Greenwich University. She has worked as a practitioner, an academic, an organisation development consultant and executive coach in health, social care and education. She is an Associate Fellow of the British Psychological Society and her research interests include leadership and happiness in the workplace.

James Blewett

James Blewett is a registered social worker who has worked in a variety of child-care settings. He currently teaches and researches in social work and is the research director of Making Research Count, a national research dissemination project, which in London is based at the Social Care Workforce Research Unit, King's College London. James also lectures on social work post-qualifying programmes at Royal Holloway, University of London and at the Open University.

Hilary Brown

Professor Hilary Brown is based in the Practice Consultancy Unit of the Centre for Social and Psychological Development, Canterbury Christ Church University. She works primarily in the field of disability rights, with an emphasis on safeguards and protection from abuse, in collaboration with a number of agencies including the Council of Europe. Her recent work has included projects on financial abuse, palliative care for people with learning disabilities and various aspects of the new Mental Capacity Act. She also chairs reviews and enquiries.

Mike Burt

Mike Burt worked in residential care before qualifying as a social worker in 1988. He has subsequently worked as a social worker in children's services. Mike became Deputy Head of Social Work at the University of Chester in 2003, having been the programme leader for the Diploma in Social Work at Warrington Collegiate Institute since 2000. He is particularly interested in the role of social work in society and in the history of social work.

Barry Cooper

Dr Barry Cooper is a Lecturer in Social Work at the Open University. He has previously worked as a child care and mental health social worker and as a social services training officer for practice teaching and post-qualification award programmes in Bristol. His Doctoral research studies at Bristol University focused upon constructivist assessment perspectives within social work practice and education and he has published a number of journal articles exploring these themes.

Celia Davies

Celia Davies is currently Director of the Research for Patient Benefit Programme in the National Institute for Health Research and is a Visiting Professor at the London School of Economics. Her most recent book (with M. Wetherell and E. Barnett) is *Citizens at the Centre: deliberative participation in healthcare decisions*, Policy Press, 2006.

Maureen Eby

Maureen Eby is a Senior Lecturer in the Faculty of Health and Social Care at the Open University. She is a nurse who works in both clinical practice and education. Her writing is born out of her research into whistle-blowing, accountability and her eighteen years as an expert witness within nursing clinical negligence cases. Currently she heads the post-registration initiatives of the Faculty's Nursing Programme.

Keith Edwards

Keith Edwards has a degree and a Masters in sociology and an MBA. He worked as a social worker for Lewisham and Barnardo's, and then taught on a CSS (Certificate of Social Service) course. In 1991, he became a development officer and trainer for Powys County Council. He moved to Warwickshire County Council in 2002, and is now Assistant Head of Service for Planning and Performance in the Children, Young People and Families Directorate.

Linda Finlay

Linda Finlay is a freelance academic consultant offering training and mentorship on how to apply qualitative research in health care. She also teaches and writes for the Open University in the Social Science and Health and Social Welfare faculties. Qualifying originally as an occupational therapist, she obtained a psychology degree and PhD. She has published widely, being best known for her textbooks on psychosocial occupational therapy, groupwork and qualitative research.

Ann Gallagher

Ann Gallagher is Senior Research Fellow in the Faculty of Health and Social Care Sciences at Kingston University and St George's University of London. She has a long-standing interest in, and concern with the promotion of, professional ethics. She has engaged in empirical work relating to dignity in health care, the arts in health and conflicts of interests in safeguarding children. Her theoretical work relates to virtue ethics, dignity, human rights, the teaching of professional ethics and transcultural ethics.

Ann Glaister

Ann Brechin, now Glaister, is retired but was formerly Senior Lecturer in the Faculty of Health and Social Care at the Open University, contributing to courses on disability, learning disability and health and social care.

Colin Guest

Colin Guest is a freelance consultant working in the education, social and health care fields. A former teacher, he has worked in the private, public and voluntary sectors as both practitioner and manager. He is on record as commenting that he feels fortunate to have worked as a manager through two decades of constant change. For a while he directed a private sector training company supporting social and health care organisations. His interests include training, change management and improving communications.

Chris Hallett

Chris Hallett is Head of Service for Children in Need with Warwickshire County Council. He is a registered social worker and also holds an MSc in Public Sector Management. He is an Associate Fellow at Warwick University. Previous publications include chapters on developing good practice in community care and children's services.

Celia Keeping

Celia Keeping MA, CQSW, works part-time as a social worker in a community mental health team where she worked as an Approved Social Worker for ten years. Her specialist practice area is now psychodynamic psychotherapy. Celia is also a Senior Lecturer in the Faculty of Health and Social Care at the University of the West of England, where she has a special interest in the effect of emotions on organisational life and social work practice.

Alun Morgan

Alun Morgan is a Lecturer in the Faculty of Health and Social Care in the Open University. His practice experience has been in child care and mental health social work, including senior local authority child care management. His research interest is in service-user participation through information technology and multi-media.

Barbara Prynn

Barbara Prynn qualified as a psychiatric social worker. Latterly she has worked in the field of adoption, particularly with adopted adults and their birth families. In her PhD she considered the characteristics of adopting families which might lead to positive or negative outcome. Her other research has been into the professional histories of former child care officers, and the later lives of people born between the World Wars who were adopted or fostered.

Phil Sawbridge

Phil Sawbridge is an Assistant Head of Service with Warwickshire County Council and holds responsibilities for Safeguarding Children, Quality Assurance and Service Development within the Children in Need Division. He is a registered social worker and holds an MSc in Child Protection Studies and an MBA.

Philip Scarff

Philip Scarff is a former Director of a large NHS health authority and has held senior management posts in Social Services. For the past fourteen years he has been an independent consultant specialising in the public and voluntary sectors, mainly in health and social care and related fields. He has broad experience of multi-agency working and strategic and business planning. His publications include training courses in financial management and tendering and contracting for public bodies.

Janet Seden

Janet Seden is a Senior Lecturer in the Faculty of Health and Social Care at the Open University. She has worked in probation and children and families social work. She has taught counselling in adult education and social work since 1990. Janet is the author of *Counselling Skills in Social Work Practice* (Open University Press, 2005) and has published on the assessment and provision of services for children in need and their families; social work theory, practice and processes; children and spirituality; practice teaching; and managing care.

Aidan Worsley

Professor Aidan Worsley is the Head of Social Work at the University of Chester. His research interests include practice education, community involvement in social work education and the nature of social work research. He has long been a keen supporter of practice teaching, and acted as chair of the National Organisation for Practice Teaching from 2001 to 2004. He qualified as a social worker in 1987 and his professional career was primarily with the Probation Service. After ten years as a probation officer and senior probation officer he joined a Social Services Department Staff Development Team. From there he moved into higher education, managing a Practice Teaching Award programme, before taking on a Head of Social Work role. He has been Professor of Social Work at Chester since January 2006.

Acknowledgements

Every effort has been made to trace all the copyright holders, but if any have been inadvertently overlooked the publishers will be pleased to make the necessary arrangement at the first opportunity.

Grateful acknowledgement is made to the following sources for permission to reproduce material in this book.

Chapter 1

Figure 1.1: Adapted from Barnett et al. (1997) *Higher Education*. Open University Press, p. 105. Reproduced with the kind permission of the Open University Press.

Figure 1.2: from Dutt and Ferns (1998) *Letting through the Light: A Training Pack on Black People and Mental Health*. Race Equality Foundation and Department of Health, p. 29. Reproduced with the kind permission of the Race Equality Foundation.

Chapter 12

Figure 12.2: Colebatch (1998) *Policy*. Open University Press, p. 38. Reproduced with the kind permission of the Open University Press.

Figure 12.3: Winstanley et al. (1995) 'When the pieces don't fit a stakeholder power matrix to analyse public sector restructuring', *Public Money and Management*, 15 (2): 21. Blackwell Publishers. Reproduced with the kind permission of Wiley-Blackwell.

List of Abbreviations

AI	Appreciative Inquiry
AMHP	Approved Mental Health Professional
ASW	Association of Social Workers
BASW	British Association of Social Workers
CAMHS	Child and Adolescent Mental Health Services
CBET	Competency-Based Education and Training
CCETSW	Central Council for Education and Training in Social Work
CCT	Competitive Compulsory Tendering
CCW	Care Council for Wales
CIPW	Creating an Inter-Professional Workforce
CPD	Continuing Professional Development
CPS	Crown Prosecution Service
CQSW	Certificate of Qualification in Social Work
CRB	Criminal Records Bureau
CSCI	Commission for Social Care Inspection
CSS	Certificate of Social Service
ECHR	European Convention on Human Rights
GSCC	General Social Care Council
HEI	Higher Education Institution
HRA	Human Rights Act
IMCA	Independent Mental Capacity Advocate
MSW	Medical Social Worker
NCVQ	National Council for Vocational Qualification
NHSP	Newborn Hearing Screening Programme
NICE	National Institute for Clinical Excellence
NISCC	Northern Ireland Social Care Council
NMC	Nursing and Midwifery Council
NOS	National Occupational Standards
OFSTED	Office for Standards in Education, Children's Services and Skills
PIPE	Promoting Inter-Professional Education
PREP	Post-Registration Education and Practice
PRTL	Post-Registration Training and Learning
PSW	Psychiatric Social Worker
RCT	Randomised-Control Trial
SCIE	Social Care Institute for Excellence
SIA	Spinal Injuries Association
SSCC	Scottish Social Care Council

SSSC	Scottish Social Services Council
TOPSS	Training Organisation for the Personal Social Services
UDHR	Universal Declaration of Human Rights
VFM	Value for Money

Introduction

Sandy Fraser and Sarah Matthews

Getting our social work or health care practice 'right' is crucial. Yet what constitutes good social work or health care is often a matter for contention. This book, *The Critical Practitioner in Social Work and Health Care*, sheds light on what underpins good practice. It is based on the understanding that practice in social work and health care is always problematic in some way. The practitioner always has to deal with changing demands and expectations and thus must be open to new knowledge and perspectives. The critical practitioner must then interrogate and analyse these new situations to arrive at 'best practice'. There is no final stock of knowledge that can permanently equip social work and health care professionals. Their job involves addressing uncertainty and being open to change.

We believe that the central quality and approach that a practitioner must have in addressing uncertainty is the possession of a critical stance. By critical we do not mean being negative or pessimistic. We do mean that the practitioner needs to be sceptical and evaluative about their own practice and of practice situations. This includes the policy and procedures that form the context for their practice. And this is not navel-gazing. A questioning approach to practice is essential if we are to avoid resource-led, rule-driven practice which pays little attention to what service-users want or need. While policies and procedures help guide our actions to what, we hope, generally 'works', practitioners have to be able to 'think outside the box'.

Uncertainty and a 'critical approach' may be mistakenly associated with an inability to focus on what is practical and needed. It may be incorrectly linked with a certain lack of personal and professional confidence. A distinction can be made between different types of confidence. On the one hand 'false confidence' in which a practitioner is defensive and bases their actions only on a bureaucratic rule – almost denying their professional autonomy and discretion. On the other hand 'real confidence' allows the practitioner to justify their actions based on their critical scrutiny of situations, on available evidence and a clear understanding of their role in the situation. This book is aimed at equipping practitioners to think about, to analyse and reflect upon their own practice and that of their employing agency, to enable them to justify their actions rather than being merely defensive of them. We hope readers will find that this book is a powerful tool in coming to terms with the various uncertainties they may face. Yet uncertainty means that this book cannot be exhaustive or comprehensive. What we can do is to deal with some of the major dimensions or challenges that practitioners confront.

This book should be useful to a range of professionals in the social work, social care and health care fields working in the UK and some related jurisdictions. Readers need to be aware, however, that it is also a Course Reader for an Open University course called K315

Critical Social Work Practice. This course is part of the Open University's Social Work Degree Programme and the book reflects some of the needs of this course. It should also be noted that the book is based on a previous publication, *Critical Practice in Health and Social Care* (Brechin, Brown and Eby, 2000). Some of the chapters in the current edition are updated and revised versions of those contained in the previous publication.

Review of contents

In Chapter 1 Ann Glaister introduces us to the idea that critical practice is an interdisciplinary concept. Following other authors she defines the components of an individual's critical practice as critical action, critical reflexivity and critical analysis. However, we learn that this can never be done in an isolated way, as critical practice involves constant discussion with peers and service-users to find the right approach to a given problem or issue. Critical practice must also be supported by a range of principles, firstly that of 'respecting others as equals', and secondly that practitioners must always be open to new knowledge, allowing challenge to their preconceptions. This also means being aware that sometimes the practitioner does not have knowledge appropriate to a given situation. Defining what we need to learn is a hallmark of good practice and not an admission of professional failure. However, it would be a professional failure were we not to act to obtain appropriate knowledge when our lack of knowledge becomes clear. Glaister also links critical practice with developments in critical theory and social constructionism. The author suggests that the focus of critical practice is ultimately on 'making a difference' by forging relationships to empower others; critical practice inherently involves addressing and opposing oppression and discrimination.

In Chapter 2 Mike Burt and Aidan Worsley consider professionalism in the context of the continued rise of regulatory frameworks. Using a sociological perspective, the authors debate what a profession is. They critique both the process and the traits of a profession and argue that the concept is complex and hard to pin down. Using some of the broad themes from this analysis the authors go on to relate them specifically to social work. In particular they do so in the context of what they see as the shift from specific therapeutic/intervention roles to broader roles. They question whether the growth of so-called bureaucratic or statutory social work actually distances the social worker from the community, and then consider not just how social work draws boundaries around itself, but how it differentiates itself from others. Today's social workers are expected to relate to other professionals and to work well in complex settings. The authors discuss whether the complementary or conflicting opportunities for social workers to embrace the complexity of people's relationships with other professions are at odds with the focus on service-users' relationships with others.

The remainder of the chapter identifies six main areas which explore the connection between regulatory frameworks and social work as a profession. The first area, registration and protection of title, considers the historical development of the call for registration and asks whether this strengthens social work as a profession. Other areas covered include the impact of codes of practice and the role of the different Care Councils, the value of the occupational role, the impact of the social work degree and, lastly, the various nation-specific reviews of social work. The authors conclude that the contested nature of social work is such that there will always be threats and opportunities. They draw together what they see as the pertinent issues in this debate and urge that as a profession social work has to be proactive.

In Chapter 3 Hilary Brown and Sheila Barrett consider the dynamic between people who use services, carers and professionals. The chapter explores what happens when user and carer movements develop enough momentum to engage with, and challenge, the knowledge on which professional interventions are based. The authors consider the impact which increased service users' skills and resources for dealing with problems and creating their own networks can have. They argue that this can, in turn, affect individual relationships, as well as strategic and operational aspects within social care agencies. The chapter is divided into three sections. In the first section the authors consider the theory generated by user groups and its practical implications, and offer a case example. In the second section they critique how feedback from people who use services and carers is listened to. Many professionals, they argue, are committed to increasing participation at an individual level, but this commitment can be compromised by resource limitations and the routine of procedural assessment designed to allocate such resources. The authors consider person-centred planning and decision making and compare this with consultation exercises. They introduce the reader to Winkler's principle of 'outside scrutiny' and that real partnership can only be based on equality. In addition, they analyse the role of complaints and, finally, discuss how services should be redesigned so that user involvement is enshrined in the decision-making structures.

Throughout Chapter 3 the authors show how complex the interaction of roles has become and argue that boundaries between people who use services, carers and professionals may become blurred. They debate the terminology used to describe the various protagonists, and point out a distinction between participation and involvement. In turn, they argue that organisations cannot 'do' participation without changing their own attitudes and structures.

In Chapter 4 Keith Edwards, Chris Hallett and Phil Sawbridge, consider the complexity of the workplace in social care and in particular the issue of how to allocate and manage workload. A key quality of the critical practitioner is to be able to anticipate the demands that may be placed on them by their managers. The ability to anticipate demands may be essential to 'surviving' in the workplace. The authors review tools for this job when they think through different ways to allocate workload. They reveal that this is not simply a technical issue – how workload is allocated is part of a culture and concerns an agency's approach to practice. Part of the complexity of workload concerns the quality of information available to practitioners and managers about service-users' needs and services. The chapter discusses the impact of Information and Computer Technologies (ICT) on how information about service-users is managed. The authors consider how ICT could have major beneficial effects in meeting service-users' needs; for example, posing a possible future dominated by freelance social work practitioners who engage with service-users via the Internet, more or less abandoning office-based work for some service-user groups. ICT is also seen as a key component in producing 'seamless' services that solve problems in disjointedness of service delivery. Workload and the management of information is key to 'surviving in the workplace' for the critical practitioner, but so too is an awareness of the policy context. The authors discuss 'Best Value', the nature of agency-based partnership, in the context of a general policy shift from 'professional autonomy' to 'corporate accountability'. They consider some of the underpinning knowledge needed to work with corporate complexity and multi-professional and multi-stakeholder partnerships. The chapter ends by considering some of the challenges that the critical practitioner will face or needs to anticipate from the perspectives of their managers or of the teams that he or she belongs to.

In Chapter 5, by Colin Guest and Phil Scarff, we are introduced to another important critical language; that of the basic concepts in financial accounting and budgets for practitioners in health and social care. The concepts the authors use have wide applicability both as tools in one's own practice and for analysing the practice of employing agencies. They consider a case study: 'Middlebrook' is a centre operated by a 'national charity', and we learn about financial issues that its manager 'Marjorie' has to tackle. They discuss Middlebrook's budget, offering us insight into accounting language that the critical practitioner can use in a variety of settings: there is explanation of 'revenue budgets', 'fixed and variable costs', 'unit costs', 'direct and indirect costs', 'overhead costs' and many other tools that improve critical practitioners' understanding of the financial basis of and for their practice.

In Chapter 6 by Barbara Prynn we change the pace and look at aspects of social work practice between 1948 and 1972. The author considers her own experience of social work in the 1960s and her research into the experiences of a number of practitioners who were social workers in the 1960s. The chapter considers the organisational context for practice both before and after the Seebohm/Kilbrandon Reforms which led to the professionalisation of social work. The author suggests that the key dimension that has changed is the nature of the relationship between the service-user and the social work practitioner. The author concludes that pressure from the political left and the political right since the early 1970s has diminished the centrality of the relationship between practitioners and service-users. Indeed, readers could revisit some of the previous chapters in the light of Barbara Prynn's reflections. A key issue is whether there are strengths in past practice which could contribute critically to better outcomes in the twenty-first century.

In Chapter 7, by Maureen Eby and Ann Gallagher, we are introduced to ethical practice. The authors distinguish between the concepts of 'values' and 'ethics'. Values are about what we hold dear, and concern what we believe to be the best way of acting towards others, either in our personal or professional relations. Ethics, on the other hand, concerns the systematic enquiry into the values we hold. It will note, for example, where our different values compete with one another. Ethical enquiry seeks to establish patterns of thoughts in relation to the values we hold. The chapter examines competing values in different practice contexts. It distinguishes between ethical issues and ethical problems. The authors also introduce the reader to a range of ethical approaches – approaches which underpin the development of 'ethical principles' such as are contained in 'Codes of Practice'. We also learn about the 'virtues approach', the 'duties approach', the 'consequences approach' and other moral philosophy approaches. The reader is invited to identify which approach best characterises their profession's ethical stance. Each ethical approach can become a critical analytical tool that can be used to challenge received wisdom – for example, questioning whether professional ethical codes, like the social work codes of practice, are ethically consistent or self-contradictory. Eby and Gallagher's chapter introduces us to some of the tools that practitioners need to examine critically and justify both their own and their profession's values and ethics.

In Chapter 8 Celia Keeping provides two focal points: first the understanding of research and its impact on social work practice and, second, the question of if, and how, a social work practitioner can be a researcher. The chapter is about the place of research in social work practice today. It allows the reader to explore how practitioners currently engage with research to inform their practice and to examine the question of whether or not research evidence should necessarily be the basis for all aspects of social work practice. The chapter begins by discussing the context and setting in which social workers currently operate. The author critiques 'trends' such as evidence-based practice, and considers developments such as the Social Care Institute for Excellence and Making Research Count. Evidence about how research informs social work practice is reviewed, alongside a discussion of the nature of practitioner research and how it differs from other types of research. Consideration is given to the benefits of research in practice, including whether research offers practitioners and people who use services empowerment and protection. The chapter considers the barriers to and enablers of the use of research in practice, including what kinds of organisational culture support research in practice. The author concludes that research in practice is possible, viable and valuable for critical, analytical and reflective practice.

In Chapter 9, Linda Finlay and Claire Ballinger discuss working in teams, particularly in multi-agency settings. Teamwork, they argue, is firmly on the government's agenda, driven by the findings of various enquiries and an increasing commitment towards integrated care. Section 1 starts by exploring what constitutes co-ordinated multi-disciplinary teamwork. The authors recognise that different models of teamwork operate in practice. Section 2 challenges the assumptions behind the commonplace view that teamwork is necessarily an effective way of working, and analyses the value and limitations of teamwork. Section 3 examines the challenges to teamwork and how the conflicts inherent in multi-disciplinary working can constrain attempts to collaborate. Finally, different strategies for fostering positive teamwork are explored in Section 4.

In Chapter 10, by Janet Seden, we are introduced to the fact that the organisational context in which we work affects our practice. This is both obvious and subtle. We learn about how organisational structures and organisational cultures can affect our performance. Following Charles Handy's ideas we are invited to try and characterise the culture of our own organisation; is it dominated by a 'power culture', a 'role culture', a 'task culture' or a 'person culture'? We are also invited to provide an 'image' of our organisation. Such images render a thumbnail picture of what it is like to live and work within a given organisation; common images are examined – for example, organisations likened to a 'machine', an 'organism', a 'brain', a 'psychic prison'. The image helps us towards critical awareness of how far our organisation is a 'learning organisation', that is, one which is like a critical practitioner – able to learn from the challenges of change either from government directives or from the demands of service-users. Janet Seden provides critical concepts that will help practitioners to articulate how well their agency operates organisationally. She gives the example of 'appreciative inquiry' as a process by which an agency can demonstrate that it is a 'learning organisation' and by which practitioners can collect evidence of the effectiveness of agency organisation and communicate that to agency policy-makers. The chapter also addresses inter-organisational working and provides tools to analyse issues and problems in this area.

In Chapter 11, by Maureen Eby and Alun Morgan, the focus is on accountability. Practitioners are not completely free agents; they cannot perform their jobs in a context of epistemological and professional anarchy. They have discretion to act within systems of bounded rationality; they must show how their actions relate to their prescribed role, and justify to a range of stakeholders their use of discretion. Eby and Morgan provide a framework for how to understand accountability: 'social accountability', in the sense of what is generally acceptable to one's colleagues; 'ethical accountability' in being clear about the ethical approach to one's actions; 'legal accountability' in being clear about one's powers and duties under legislation; and 'professional accountability' in being clear how one's actions accord with the rights and responsibilities of a profession.

Chapter 12, by Celia Davies, examines the policy process. First she considers some of the different answers that students of public policy have given to the question: 'How does policy get made?' Second, she explores the growing scope that new policy thinking is providing to help practitioners and others develop and share policies at local level. Davies argues that the model which assumed policy was a rational process taking place at the top of organisations and requiring tight control of implementation is being replaced by a model which recognises policy as a complex and altogether messier process with more participants, much experimentation and multiple feedback loops. Davies concludes that this is an important theme for all those who work in social work and health care and that a critical practitioner needs to be both willing and able to take part in the policy process, acknowledging the multiple perspectives that people will bring and welcoming opportunities to engage with policy development and make it relevant and supportive to practice.

In Chapter 13 Barry Cooper challenges us to think critically about what continuing professional development (CPD) means. He observes that the various regulatory bodies have required post-registration training and learning (PRTL) but their aims and requirements have been quite moderate. He argues that the way we approach CPD reflects our approach to practice in general – that is, the approach of both the individual practitioner and of their employing agency. The chapter also discusses the limitations of a competency-based approach to PRTL and CPD and offers some insights for the way forward. CPD is not merely a matter of technically updating our knowledge on recent events or legislation, although that is clearly necessary. Although regulatory bodies continue to base their PRTL and CPD requirements on competency-based teaching and learning there are significant limitations to this approach after professional qualification has taken place. It may be possible to mark out competencies which *prepare* the practitioner for workplace uncertainties, but those very uncertainties and the diverse knowledges that follow leave elaborate competency frameworks behind. Rather, current conditions mean that meeting the challenge of obsolescent knowledge becomes the responsibility of the critical practitioner. The critical practitioner should be not simply a map-reader but a map-maker. This is an aspect of the autonomy and agency of the critical practitioner. Such an approach cannot be isolated from other current themes in practice, such as the involvement of service-users. Practitioners may construct new knowledge by being 'practitioner researchers', for example, but the crucial dynamic will be between supervisor and supervisee. Exploring new inclusive ways to practise is not merely the responsibility of the individual practitioner but, as the codes of practice recognise, it is the responsibility of employers too.

In Chapter 14 James Blewett examines the future of social work for practitioners in terms of threats and opportunities. What do the changing organisational frameworks for social work practice mean for practitioners? Will social work survive as a professional discipline? Blewett reviews social policy developments leading up to the period of the New Labour governments. He then analyses how New Labour thinking has affected social work in relation to adult services, and to children and family services. He argues that there is a threat, arising from developments in social policy, that professional social work will face a diminished role and increasing marginalisation. Social work has already developed a culture of 'bureaucratisation and performance management', and it is likely that this will remain part of the picture for the foreseeable future. Social work will continue to face limited resources for its practice. Despite the various hazards, Blewett recognises that the picture is not simply one of an under-resourced, disempowered and stigmatised profession, strangled by bureaucracy and lacking a clear role or identity. There is a basis for optimism. He gives examples of excellent and innovative practice, in which service-users appreciate and value social workers and their services across a range of practice contexts. In a theme which is reminiscent of Barbara Prynn's chapter, Blewett reports that good social work is based upon the quality of the relationship with service-users. It is the relationship rather than resources that has transformational significance in social work. There is a concern that the configuration of current care services undermines the key component of relationship, but critical practitioners must find ways to promote their relationship with service-users as their key contribution. Nevertheless, Blewett ends his chapter with a warning that social work practitioners cannot take the existence of their profession for granted, and that critical practitioners must seek alliances with other professions but above all find ways to speak with greater clarity and confidence about their roles and tasks.

Throughout this book we challenge the reader to examine and reflect upon the world of the critical practitioner in social work and health care. Critical practice is not new. Rather, this book gives the opportunity to appreciate critical practice in the past, to consider its present incarnation and to contemplate its impact as we look ahead. Critical practice is a living thing. It is at the core of all activity undertaken with service-users, carers and their communities, and ultimately reflects the skills and values which are fundamental to the professional caring role.

Reference

Brechin, A., Brown, H. and Eby, M.A. (eds) (2000) *Critical Practice in Health and Social Care*. London: Sage.

Chapter 1

Introducing critical practice

Ann Glaister

The day-to-day experience of health and social care work is often one of fire-fighting; managing time constraints; dealing with conflicting demands; setting difficult priorities; managing tricky relationships; finding short cuts; dealing with stress and frustration (both internal and external); and struggling to hang on to simply doing the job. It is about operating within organisational and social constraints as an individual, feeling accountable and responsible, yet often powerless and lacking in any real autonomy (Fish and Coles, 1998).

The challenge is to find an approach which acknowledges the inadequacies as well as the difficulties of much current practice; recognises the major policy changes that have been taking place; welcomes moves towards greater inter-agency co-operation and the increasingly proactive role of service-users; but still values the positive motivation to provide support for others, which takes many practitioners into health and social care work in the first place. This chapter will develop a concept of 'critical practice' as a way of trying to engage with such challenges, particularly at a level appropriate to the experienced practitioner.

What is 'critical practice'?

The critical practitioner

The term 'critical' is used here to refer to open-minded, reflective approaches that take account of different perspectives, experiences and assumptions. It is not about being critical in the common parlance of being negative and destructive. Taking a constructive critical stance is not, of course, the prerogative of professionals. Here, however, it is discussed in the professional context with the implication that it encapsulates what experienced professionals and practitioners try, and indeed are called upon, to offer.

What is required increasingly is a capacity to handle uncertainty and change, as well as being able to operate in accordance with professional skills and knowledge. Practitioners must, in a sense, face both ways, drawing on a sound knowledge and evidence base on the one hand, but at the same time being continually aware of the discretionary and contextual basis of their practice. Most practitioners will recognise this sense of dilemma. Barnett (1997: 143–4) puts it like this:

> Professionals have the duty to profess. But professing in a post-modern age calls for the capacity to be open to multiple discourses and to engage, albeit critically, with them.

A critical approach implies no particular moral direction in itself. If, however, we agree that there is a fundamental assumption of social justice underpinning the provision of care for others, it follows that successful caring processes must be both empowering and anti-oppressive. And practitioners' purpose will be to achieve solutions that are at some level felt to be just by all parties. Kitwood, in his book *Concern for Others*, talks of 'the converging threads of integrity and integration' as desirable for one's own moral development and, therefore, necessarily for others,

> since there is a crucial sense in which all human beings are made of the same stuff, suffer the same kind of anguish, experience similar joys. It is to wish and hope for that same integrity for all persons, within their own particular cultural frame. In short, to seek an inner truth and integration for oneself is of necessity to desire integrity on the part not only of a few close others, but of a much larger circle of friends, colleagues and acquaintances. But if these, then why not all?

> (Kitwood, 1990: 211)

Three case studies are described over the next few pages. Each reflects the complexity of critical practice. They are not so much accounts of the expertise involved in knowing what to do; rather they tell the story of the expertise involved in being able to tolerate the 'not knowing' as practitioners negotiate their way around different opinions, beliefs and practices. They reflect Kitwood's 'converging threads of integrity and integration'. Being able to acknowledge uncertainty and recognise conflicting lines of argument and different perspectives, while staying true to one's own understandings, lies at the heart of much professional work.

Case Study   Jaqui – a physiotherapist

A young mother of three children has circulatory problems caused by diabetes, leading to progressive breakdown of tissue in one foot and leg. Amputation is inevitable and the surgeon sees his role as minimising the damage by removing as little as is clinically essential at each stage. An initial operation to remove the toes is followed six months later by a removal of half the foot and then the whole of the foot. Jaqui, the physiotherapist, sees from her vantage point the devastation this approach wreaks on the family and the mother's health generally. Each time the disease process reasserts itself to the point of tissue breakdown, with associated stress to other body systems. The procedure involves time in hospital, there is the stress of the operation itself, time off work for the young woman's husband, further separation for the children, followed by the period of recovery before any functional rehabilitation can begin.

Jaqui knows that the eventual picture will resolve itself as a below-the-knee amputation, at which point things are likely to stabilise. To move to that point at the outset would mean one traumatic event instead of multiple interacting traumas; it would lead to better health for the mother, rather than for her to be trapped in a cycle of illness and partial recuperation for years, and a satisfactory rehabilitation process with functional prosthesis.

With care and tact, Jaqui attempts to discuss it with the doctor, but to no avail. She considers ways in which she might raise it during a ward round with the doctor in front of the family, or even behind his back, but concludes that the potential damage from such an intervention might be worse for the family than the current position. She recognises that the likelihood of her arguments being accepted would be minimal. Without the doctor's backing, the family is unlikely to accept the idea of a major amputation.

Jaqui's decision not to intervene further flew in the face of what she felt to be the best outcome for the family, and was probably harder for her than to argue her case further. Her personal and professional analysis of the situation had to include awareness of the family's likely reactions and feelings as well as the context of the more powerful role of the doctor and the importance of the family's trust in him. The difficulties partly arose, she knew, from the unequal status and consequently limited communications between doctors and therapists.

Case Study   Adjoa – a community nurse

An experienced nurse working as part of a team attached to a large primary care practice, Adjoa finds the increasing use of agency nurses on temporary contracts very worrying. She has no management or supervisory role and yet is aware of her greater expertise in relation to their often unknown (at least to her) level of experience. As a black, female nurse, she is also conscious of the sensitivity of such tensions about roles and responsibilities when a white, male nurse is appointed on contract.

For a period the male nurse takes over some of Adjoa's excess workload. On subsequently revisiting one of her elderly patients (an 80-year-old Asian man) she finds that a lesion that had been healing well has begun to break down again because the wrong kind of cream has been used. She finds herself very angry and yet unable to remedy the situation. She confronts the contract nurse who is offhand about the matter, making her acutely conscious of her lack of any formal seniority. She feels her gender and racial and ethnic identity, and those of the client, make matters worse, but does not feel sure whether this is her problem or her colleague's. (Is he being racist and sexist or does she just anticipate that he will be?) Even angrier now, she takes up the matter with her senior, but is effectively made to feel that she is overreacting.

Unlike Jaqui, Adjoa acted on her initial feelings about the situation but ended up feeling that she had 'blown it' by getting so angry. A friend helped her to talk it through some weeks later and suggested that maybe she had every right to feel angry. What seemed to have happened, though, was that her anger had made it very difficult for her to really analyse the situation or reflect on her own reactions. When she could do this, the picture began to change. She could see the problems for the contract nurse, thrown in at the deep end without obvious lines of peer support being established; she could see the financial limitations forcing short-termism in appointments; she could see her own uncertainties, despite her experience, limiting her capacity to offer non-judgemental support to colleagues.

At this point she began to formulate a new strategy and approached her line manager to discuss how the team might support itself more effectively in the longer term.

Case Study   Martin – a residential care home manager

As manager of a care home for young people, Martin found himself faced with a difficult dilemma. Sophie, a 15-year-old, was persistently self-harming and heavily involved in substance abuse. For some time it had been clear that the home could not provide a safe environment for her and after a process of negotiation and consultation a specialist foster placement was found for her, which, combined with intensive support work, offered a good chance for her to make some progress towards recovery. But Sophie refused to go. She understood all the reasons and the arguments, but simply dug her heels in and refused to agree.

Existing legislation and Martin's training stressed the importance of the young person's right to choose. Yet here he was confronted with a situation where he knew the young person's welfare was seriously at risk. His decision, not taken alone or lightly, was to insist that she must go. He knew he was taking away a part of her autonomy, in the hope that she would gain more subsequently. He also felt strongly that insistence must be presented with explanation and acknowledgement of the conflict, conveying in essence 'I know this is not what you want, but these are the reasons why I believe it is what must happen.'

Martin's difficulty was that whatever action he took or did not take would be wrong in one sense or another. The best he could do was to be clear about the context of his decision and the value base he was drawing upon, and on that basis to make the best decision he could. His concern to maintain respect for Sophie's different view was an important part of the story for him. He did not pretend that her view did not matter or that his view was right and hers was wrong. He did not feel comfortable about it, but decided his primary concern must be to protect her welfare in this situation.

Practitioners, as these examples illustrate, cannot occupy some detached space from which vantage point they make clear-cut, evidence-based decisions about their clients. They are in there too, struggling to make sense of things, to communicate, and buffeted in the same way by winds of change, by personal and cultural influences, as are service-users and others. Practitioners face conflicting principles and a context that is complex and requires reflection, rather than the straightforward application of knowledge and skill.

These examples argue, then, for a professionalism involving not just the critical appraisal of knowledge and action – not just a critical handling of theory and practice – but also the importance of acknowledging personal involvement and discretion.

These three examples illustrate the importance of what Barnett (1997) describes as 'the three domains of critical practice'. Adapting his terminology previously (Brechin et al., 2000), we framed these as the domains of critical analysis, critical action and critical reflexivity. The domain of critical analysis can be seen as the critical evaluation of knowledge, evidence, policies and practice, with an in-built recognition of multiple perspectives and an orientation of ongoing enquiry. Critical action requires a sound skill base, but also calls for a recognition of power inequalities and structured disadvantage and seeks to work across difference towards empowerment. The third domain, critical reflexivity, presumes an aware, reflective and engaged self; the term 'reflexivity' implies that practitioners recognise their engagement with service-users and others in a process of negotiating understandings and interventions and are aware of the assumptions and values they bring to this process.

This chapter will argue that professional education and development need to draw out a capacity not only for critical analysis and critical action but also for critical reflexivity, combining to create an awareness of the circular and interactive processes by which the 'self' develops as a critical practitioner. An adapted version of Barnett's three domains of critical practice is shown in Figure 1.1.

In each of the case study examples, the practitioner was operating across these three domains. Each was drawing upon their professional knowledge and understanding to analyse the situation; each had been using a repertoire of skilful actions (including inaction); and each held a reflexive view about their own position and feelings. It is artificial, of course, to describe these as separate processes; the reality will be rather more integrated – 'joined-up practice', perhaps.

There seem to be some crucial aspects of the process those practitioners were engaged in which span or underpin the three domains. It may help to identify these in terms of two guiding principles: the principle of 'respecting others as equals' and the principle of an open and 'not-knowing' approach.

The principle of 'respecting others as equals'

Given the relatively powerful position of professionals in society, and the fact that health and social care practitioners are working explicitly with people in vulnerable positions, it is not surprising that built-in oppression is increasingly recognised. A substantial body of work in the form of research, papers, books, policy documents and practice experience addresses explicitly the problems of the imbalance of power and how attempts may be made to redress it. Not only that, but the concept of establishing a value base, which affords equal rights and respect to all, is at the core of all the vocational qualifications and occupational standards relevant to work in this field.

In the field of child care, the legislative and policy frameworks have shifted significantly towards upholding children's rights to be heard, but also towards the rights of children to be protected from harm (Scottish Executive, 2003; HMSO, 2004a). Against this backdrop, Martin understood the power he had and the responsibility he had to intervene in a life. Already a 'looked-after' young person, Sophie was now to be moved again against her

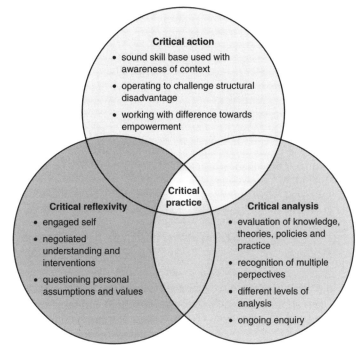

Figure 1.1 Three domains of critical practice
Source: Barnett, 1977: 105

wishes, and yet as far as could be foreseen 'in her best interests'. What he did to acknowledge this conflict was to respect her views and feelings, not in this case by accepting them, but by talking about them and allowing them to be different from his own. Respecting Sophie's rights did not lead Martin to abdicate his own rights and responsibilities.

Had Sophie been one year older, at 16 she would now be technically eligible to apply for direct payments to support herself, putting her in a much stronger position to make her own decisions. Legislation in England and Wales, Northern Ireland and Scotland has broadened the scope of direct payments to include eligibility for 16- and 17-year-olds (Department of Health, 2001; Northern Ireland Executive, 2002; Scottish Executive, 2003). There are exclusions, however, and in fact Sophie's known substance abuse, the risks she would run and the fact that she was in residential care as a looked-after young person would all be likely to exclude direct payments as a possibility. The continual evolution of such policies nevertheless highlights the shift in relationships in favour of greater equality and autonomy for service-users, and illustrates the degree of challenge to Martin and others like him and the delicate, ethical balancing act involved in managing such situations.

Respecting others as equals applies not only to working with service-users but also to working with colleagues, including supporting and being supported by them. Indeed, in the case of children's services, Martin is also required to work across agency boundaries co-operatively as the policies and principles driving the integration of children's services are implemented (see Scottish Executive, 2001; HMSO, 2004b; or for a review of this experience on the ground in Scotland, Glaister and Glaister, 2005). Power differentials between professions, hierarchies within professions, and different theoretical, structural and practice frameworks all contribute to major difficulties in communication between one practitioner and another. The cases of both Jaqui, in her relationship with the more powerful doctor, and Adjoa, in her ambiguous relationship with her colleague as well as the problems with her line manager, illustrate these difficulties. Interestingly, both of them looked for solutions that involved moving towards greater opportunities for learning and support through establishing more respectful and equal relationships.

This principle is well developed and has a good pedigree. It is not, however, easy to translate into practice. It does not mean denying or disparaging professional knowledge and expertise. Rather, it is about seeking to share skills and understandings and offer potential interventions or explanation. Such offers will not always be accepted, however, and critical practice will be about struggling to build and sustain respectful and equal relationships within which meanings and ways forward can be negotiated.

The principle of an open and 'not-knowing' approach

The second guiding principle for critical practice is openness. Accepting a degree of uncertainty about any intervention has to be part of the job. There will be conflicting needs and widely varying views about priorities and the desirability of different outcomes. Who is to say, for example, whether a half-leg amputation and remaining healthier and more active is more desirable than struggling on with less devastating surgery for a longer period? Who is to say whether insisting on a move to a foster placement will be for the best – and whose best? And if things go wrong, who is to say where the blame lies?

To take up a position of openness is to accept that professional practice is an evolving process within a social and political context. This is not to deny the importance of established thinking and evidence – far from it. Professional practice is rooted in theories, and keeping up with the latest research evidence will continue to be important. It is more like the adage, 'The more you know, the more you know what you don't know.' Openness and 'not-knowing' require engagement with the process of evolving knowledge.

Practice then, can be seen as part and parcel of a continual process of theorising and evidence building. Theories develop as attempts to make sense of how things seem (Howe, 1987; Thompson, 1995). They do not tell some absolute truth, but theorising is part of a human process of trying to make our experiences more intelligible (Argyris and Schon, 1974). Practitioners are, *par excellence*, theorisers, as Schon (1983) in particular has argued. Thompson suggests it is a mistake for practitioners to see themselves as concerned only with practice, while others attend to the theory. He argues that:

> we need to recognise the fallacy of theoryless practice so that we are not guilty of failing to review our ideas and lacking the flexibility to adapt or abandon them in the light of changing circumstances.

> (Thompson, 1995: 29)

Theories are always 'only theories', in the sense that certainty is always elusive, partial and seen from a particular perspective. Being 'only a theory', however, is also an essential feature of open-mindedness, in that theories are provisional and there to be tried and tested and debated in order to evolve. To accept 'not-knowing' is in the best tradition of philosophers and scientists down the ages. What is strange is how far professionals have been pushed (or have pushed themselves) into a defensive position of seeming to be the opposite – all-seeing and all-knowing. Acknowledging 'not-knowing' indicates, in contrast, a clear stimulus for further exploration and knowledge development and provides a climate for the development of defensible rather than defensive practice.

What is suggested here is that critical practice should be seen as an integral part of an ongoing shared and discursive process of theorising and knowledge development.

A theoretical context

Critical practice occurs in a theoretical context, although the influences may not always be very apparent to practitioners. The ideas behind the accounts and analyses of critical practice offered here can be seen as stemming from several interrelated theoretical traditions.

For some, particularly those who have studied sociology at some point, the most obvious link will be to critical theory – historically to the work of the Frankfurt School and more recently to variants of the work of a writer such as Habermas (1972). For others, critical practice will gel with an understanding they have developed of social constructionism in psychology or sociology, with its insistence that the social context in which we live is not extraneous reality, but is constructed by us as part of a process of creating that context. The language that we use is seen as part of a process of creating shared meanings and experiences. What this argues essentially is that humans are 'meaning-generating systems'. Such thinking has a long history, but has more recently been extensively debated – for example by Bateson (1972), Harre (1986), Shotter and Gergen (1989), Gergen (1991), McNamee and Gergen (1992), and Shotter (1993).

There are broader links too with feminist theory (see, for example, Maynard and Purvis, 1994) or with history from below (as in Porter, 1985) or with the implications of the social model of disability (for example Oliver, 1990 or Shakespeare and Watson, 1997), particularly in the sense that these challenge established ways of formulating and researching issues and insist that, from the standpoint of oppressed groups, there are new questions to be addressed and new ways of collecting data.

While it may be helpful and may enrich an understanding of critical practice to be able to make links such as these (see, for example, Layder, 1997; Porter, 1998), it is by no means necessary to do so. A critical practitioner needs to recognise that their work involves them in activities and relationships which are not adequately explained by theories and evidence drawn from the material world. The concept of critical practice is based on assumptions that:

- Social and organisational structures are not given and immutable.
- Individuals have agency in that they imbue situations with meaning and that these meanings have consequences.
- Interpersonal relationships and structures reflect and create power imbalances which can be uncovered and challenged.
- Alternative circumstances, strategies and outcomes can be envisioned and sometimes brought about.

This is to acknowledge that practitioners in health and social care need to work with a broader theoretical framework in their daily practice. Acknowledging different discourses cannot fail to bring the questioning stance which is at the heart of critical practice.

Critical practice in action

So how does any of this relate back to the three case studies? It was argued earlier that practitioners are engaged in theorising, but does it make any sense to suggest that they might think in such abstract terms as these? The exercise involves thinking about their arguments and dilemmas in relation to a theoretical framework which takes on board not just a sense of an individual in society but also a sense of how meanings and understandings may be socially constructed.

Jaqui was very clearly aware of the wider context in which both the family and the professional service operated. The issue was not just about physical rehabilitation after an amputation. It was about a young woman in the context of a family life and the particular roles and expectations she would expect and be expected to meet. Jaqui's own role as physiotherapist set her in a particular and subordinate relationship to the doctor in the context of wider professional and regulatory systems. What took her beyond this into the realms of critical practice was her recognition that different meanings could co-exist and have validity; that more powerful voices might hold sway, but that this did not mean they were right, or necessarily wrong, and most importantly that not knowing what was best to do in the circumstances was perfectly appropriate, although decisions had to be made and ways might be found for opening up some further dialogue around these meanings in the future.

Adjoa was similarly aware of the constraints of the system on how she and others worked. She also saw the potential of the more powerful white majority to discredit her voice as a black professional and identified her lack of formal status as making it difficult to support or know how to criticise her colleague. As she grappled with the issues, she began to take on a different perspective, realising that her view of things was not the only one or necessarily the most helpful and constructive one. She was able to blend together a view which respected her own agency as well as others, and to understand the power of existing structures to constrain or facilitate, in a way that provided her with a course of action for the future.

Martin knew the systems in which he and the young person were located; they could not be more clearly spelled out in policy documents in the child care field. He also understood the importance of the meaning that might be attached to his decision. Inevitably for the young person, it meant her wishes were overruled, at least on the face of it. He hoped that his explanations and respect for her views would create a more positive meaning for her; one that said she had been heard and understood, but that a decision genuinely thought to be more in her best interests had been taken. To have gone along with her wishes would not necessarily have been more respectful.

Where does this take us in terms of defining 'critical practice'? Drawing together all these elements, which address process, guiding principles and theoretical perspective, leads us to the following summary.

Critical practice entails:

- operating across the three domains of analysis, action and reflexivity;
- working within a value base that respects others as equals;
- adopting an open and 'not-knowing' approach to practice;
- understanding individuals (including oneself) in relation to a socio-political and ideological context within which meanings are socially constructed.

Having framed a concept of critical practice in this way, we now turn to consider what this means in terms of fundamental, everyday processes – what you actually do to engage in critical practice.

Becoming a critical practitioner

Forging relationships

What most practitioners are concerned with on a day-to-day basis is being a good enough practitioner, seeking to help and striving at least to do no harm, within increasingly tight budgetary constraints. The case studies offered some examples of what might be described as critical practice in action, where outcomes are not perfect, nor even satisfactory much of the time, but where, nevertheless, good enough decisions must be made on the best information and judgements available. In a sense, the professional has ownership of his or her working role and space and, within that, both experiences and creates professional practice (Kolb, 1995; Tsang, 1998). This second section will unpack those ideas just a little further, exploring what it means to 'respect someone as equal', for example, or to maintain an 'open mind'.

At the heart of health and social care practice, then, there is the first pillar of critical practice: forging relationships with people, whether as clients or colleagues. This requires sophisticated interpersonal skills. Being a good communicator and able to forge good relationships is a starting point, but it has to extend to include, for example, the capacity to establish a dialogue in difficult circumstances: to negotiate, mediate, set boundaries, challenge and influence. Constructive relationships may have to be developed with diverse and challenging clients, relatives, colleagues, managers, trainees, other professions, planners, politicians and often the media and the public. This requires, as we have argued, not only a good understanding of how others may operate but also a sensitive and well-tuned awareness of oneself.

This aspect of direct care work has been described in terms of emotional labour (Smith, 1992) and is beginning to be more widely recognised within training and support. As a professional develops, further emotionally demanding tasks arise. There is the process of balancing priorities in meeting the competing needs of many clients (including potential clients who are not accessing the service); the balancing of time and resource constraints; balancing statutory, interventionist and preventative work and the balancing of time for face-to-face work against time for administration, liaising, supervisory or personal development responsibilities, and a growing sense of responsibility for, or at least awareness of, the direction of the organisation and the professional roles within it on a wider scale. This wider political professional perspective may still remain connected with individual client work. As depth and breadth of understanding and skill grow, so the awareness and critical perspective on work and relationships with individuals has to evolve (Mann, 1998; Allen, 1997).

Within this broader critical framework, interpersonal skills remain central (Thompson, 1996). The professional will be handling communications with a wide range of people. This will involve multiple roles and among these we might identify the following relationships:

- professional–client relationships
- professional–team relationships
- inter-organisational relationships
- purchaser–provider relationships
- supervisor–learner relationships
- manager–staff relationships
- relationships with policy-makers or politicians
- relationships with the media or the public

Not all will be in agreement with each other and the capacity to create and maintain open dialogue while holding on to core principles and negotiating priorities demands sophisticated skills. Forging relationships is not just about being friendly, but about creating connections and channels through which real communications can occur, bringing opportunities to learn about other views and perspectives, and discovering ways of talking constructively about differences of opinion.

Fundamentally this is about establishing equity and mutual respect. The Rogerian emphasis on warmth, positive regard, genuineness, empathy and equality holds sway here and is hard to better as a foundation (Rogers, 1951). Recognising and respecting the other person's viewpoint and feeling positive and accepting towards them does not mean losing touch with your own beliefs and feelings. Dialogue and partnership essentially involve bringing yourself and your own ideas, principles and knowledge base to the relationship and communication. To do that without disempowering the other, to remain genuinely open to learning from them, to offer ideas without defensiveness or pressure, and to hear and receive in return – those are the sophisticated skills of constructive engagement with others.

Given the multiple differing roles, perspectives and power relations, this will seldom be straightforward. A capacity for mediation and negotiation is required when relationships threaten to break down or cannot easily be established in the first place.

Negotiation is the only way to achieve the best outcome for individuals or organisations who need things from each other ... You need to get people talking, keep people talking and work towards a better understanding of different parties' needs and wishes.

(Fletcher, 1998: 21)

The concept of working together in partnerships and across role boundaries towards goals which may have to be negotiated evokes a very different image from that of the individual autonomous professional fixing something that has gone wrong. The expectation that professionals should be able to work in such a way has increased significantly (Hornby, 1993; Loxley, 1997) and the relational aspect, or forging of relationships, within such work can be seen as central.

Seeking to empower others

The concept of empowerment is the second pillar of critical practice. Concepts such as oppression, discrimination, empowerment and equal opportunities have become part of the language in health and social care work (Dominelli, 1988; Braye and Preston-Shoot, 1995; Thompson, 1998). They have reflected a recognition that less powerful or minority groups tend to become oppressed and disadvantaged and that health and social care services and professionals are so much a part of the status quo that they inevitably and unconsciously play a part in this structured oppression. In recognising this, critical practitioners begin to understand oppressive forces and work to reconstruct power imbalances. What has been learned from disabled, feminist and black perspectives has valuable messages for all critical practice (Pinkney, 1999).

The concept of empowerment is often called into question, particularly when it is lightly bandied about without any real justification. Empowerment, as a term, also risks seeming to carry the implication that power is in the gift of the practitioner to bestow. It can also be in danger of focusing too much on individuals and overlooking structural disadvantages. Or it may ignore cultural differences in the perception of how power should be appropriately vested and deployed. Gomm (1993) rightly challenges naive and circular justifications of professional power in practice, but nevertheless allows, rather grudgingly, that the term 'empowerment' designates many excellent practices and it is hard to see, indeed, how striving towards clearer understandings of and better practice towards empowerment can be a bad thing.

Direct payments enabling recipients to choose and pay directly for whatever kind of support they feel they need, are now established as an alternative way of delivering services, and can be seen as a natural development of any strategy to empower. Following revised legislation and guidance (Department of Health, 2001; Northern Ireland Executive, 2002; Scottish Executive, 2003; National Assembly for Wales, 2000), it is now mandatory for local authorities to offer a direct payment option and individuals are enabled to draw directly on such payments to purchase support tailored to meet their needs as they see them, untrammelled by the opinions of professionals or the nature or accessibility of care service provision. The option is also now extended to include 16- and 17-year-olds, over-65-year-olds and carers, including young carers. It is also clear that advocates, whether parents or guardians, can act as supportive intermediaries for the receipt and deployment of direct payments. Buying in the support of personal assistants is a frequent use that is made of the payments and Spandler (2004: 187) offers a useful review, considering this trend critically within a wider context. She suggests:

> There are a number of factors that need to be addressed to ensure that direct payments continue to be a progressive strategy. These include reconciling conflicting ideologies such as those advocating individual choice and/or collective provision; the need for political action to secure adequate resources; and the development of alternative strategies such as cooperatives to address the collective needs of direct payment recipients and workers.

A push towards market forces and a shift away from the development of more broadly tailored responses to collective need has led to a plethora of voices welcoming the introduction of direct payments as significant and long overdue (for example, Morris, 1997; Campbell, 1997; Glendinning et al., 2000; Stainton, 2002). Concerns are raised not so much by individual recipients as by others, who note a longer-term concern about the drive towards cost-cutting; the difficulties of developing and evaluating new services; and the problems of ensuring that the needs of those who are most vulnerable and least able to articulate their requirements are well protected and can be met.

There has been a necessary shift in professional perception and understanding towards a broader and more politically framed arena. Such debates have now become central to professional codes of practice and to professional training, and have also featured strongly in relation to minority ethnic groups (Dominelli, 1988 and 1997; Culley, 1996 and 1999; Doyle, 1997; Pinkney, 1999). This seems to reflect a growing awareness among professionals that working alongside service-users in tackling oppression is an inherent aspect of critical practice (Dominelli, 1997).

Analyses have historically tended to polarise people according to particular attributes, whether gender, ethnicity or role (including the role of service-user). This can be seen as a form of 'essentialism' (see, for example, Clarke and Cochrane, 1998) in which social behaviour is ascribed to some particular 'essence' of the individual, such as 'blackness' or 'femaleness' or 'disablement' or 'neediness'. It is easy then to fall into the trap of assuming that all people who are socially constructed as 'black', 'old', 'disabled' or 'homosexual', for example, share similar experiences and aspirations (SSI, 1998; Pinkney, 1998; Culley, 1999). New developments, such as direct payments, increasingly challenge such limited ways of thinking and talking. For example, the firm line on anti-oppressive social work practice has been reformulated in terms of inclusivity and citizenship (Clarke and Cochrane, 1998; Saraga, 1998; Pinkney, 1999; Thompson, 1999). The polarising of characteristics by gender, particularly in relation to asserting women's capacity for caring, has been reframed, for example by Davies (1995 and 1998), who argues that these stereotypes represent 'cultural codes of gender' rather than gender attributes. The dependency relationships imposed on disabled people have been challenged by thinking emerging from the social model of disability (for example, Oliver, 1990) and, as we have seen, more recently by challenges to the delivery of 'care' through the increasing implementation of 'direct payments' (Morris, 1991 and 1997; Swain and French, 1998; Spandler, 2004).

All this impinges very directly on practice. For example, Pinkney suggests, in discussing 'same-race' adoption policies, that current reformulations see the child 'as an individual', with an identity which is multi-layered and complex, rather than one-dimensional. 'Race' is an important feature in this assessment, but so are other factors such as class, gender, health, friends, school, neighbourhood, the child's and the family's wishes, and so on (Pinkney, 1998).

Lewis (1996), in research with social workers, describes how race and gender relations emerge from 'situated voices' – in other words, from the way people talk about other people and each other, thus creating complex and shifting personal meanings about gendered and racial identities, but meanings which arise also from particular historical and social situations. We are all, in Lewis's sense, 'situated voices' playing a part in creating our own and others' understandings and experiences – using our own voices, but voices which carry a heritage, are embedded in a current context and anticipate a future. Such voices will have racial and ethnic elements, gender, sexual orientation, socio-cultural experiences, religious or ideological beliefs, family positions and experiences, and social role through work or other contexts.

For white Anglo-Saxons, ironically, owning and valuing ethnic and cultural identity and its influences can be problematic, in the first place because they are rendered almost invisible by being the norm in the UK context. The ethnocentric assumption is that it is others who are different, who have racial and ethnic identities, which are then seen as requiring special pleading. Owning a white cultural identity brings the discomfort of an implicit label of oppressor. Yet valuing and understanding one's own identity is fundamental to offering empowering help to others (Dutt and Ferns, 1998).

Seeking to empower individuals and to challenge oppression and discrimination may involve more than just recognising and challenging on the basis of rather simplistic models of identity and social relations. Increasingly, it becomes part of a wider project of critical practice aiming to facilitate more permeable boundaries, acknowledge more flexible roles and identities and develop more dialogic ways of working with others. It is about supporting the inclusion of service-users or recipients as equal – or indeed lead – participants within negotiations and decision making and in the control of service planning and delivery.

Making a difference

The third suggested pillar of critical practice is 'making a difference'. Practitioners assess, judge and intervene with the aim of making something better than before, whether by helping a wound to heal (physically or emotionally) or helping to improve somebody's circumstances or situation in some way. There is in this sense both a moral and a pragmatic or evidence-based dimension. In order to make, and continue to make, 'good enough' interventions, practitioners have to keep up to date with the latest practice and research evidence, weigh up that evidence in relation to their own working practice and situation, and act and evaluate outcomes accordingly.

Scientific method offers an approach to evolving knowledge and practice in this way by testing out beliefs to prove or, alternatively, to attempt to disprove them. The notion of evidence-based practice stems from this tradition (Muir Gray, 1997) and now forms the basis for policy planning and implementation, for professional practice and audit and for professional training and professional development.

The call for evidence-based practice reflects a rational and, what some would describe as, a Western frame of reference. That does not make it right – or wrong – but it does give it a particular cultural 'style'. Fernando (1991), in discussing mental health services, suggests that 'style' will affect the underlying assumptions and the nature of interventions:

> The goal of all Eastern religions and psychology is enlightenment, subjective experience and meditation. In general, the quest for understanding in Western thought is for facts, in the East, for feelings. The Westerner seeks knowledge, the Easterner seeks to know.

> (Fernando, 1991: 93)

Dutt and Ferns (1998), in their training pack on 'black people and mental health', draw upon Fernando's analysis to develop three dimensions of cultural style (see Figure 1.2).

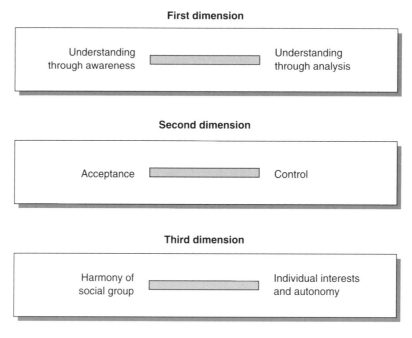

Figure 1.2 Three dimensions of cultural style
Source: Dutt and Ferns, 1998: 29

The first dimension is about achieving understanding: in 'rational' terms, through analysis of formal information; and in 'emotional' terms, through achieving greater self-awareness. The second dimension of cultural style concerns the response: whether by seeking to control or eradicate the symptoms, or by acceptance combined with a restoration of balance. The third dimension addresses assumptions about outcome – whether a concern with re-establishing the autonomy and interests of the individual or with the harmony of the social group to which the individual belongs.

In seeking to build partnerships and to empower, it is the professional, ultimately, who will be expected to 'know' and to be responsible for any decisions, advice or interventions. Yet professionals have their own ethnic and cultural origins and styles and, as with those they are working with, these will vary widely. To some extent such 'differences' will be overruled by a professional training, which privileges intellectually based arguments and views, and by the power of the professional to impose those views. And yet, increasingly, this power is called into question by the central importance of creating dialogue, partnership and respect.

As well as such concerns about whether practitioners should rely solely on rational analytic approaches, there are also reasons to doubt that professionals do, or even can, operate in a purely rational way. Theoreticians exploring how people make decisions have struggled to find models which account for how they do so. Typically, these have been cognitive and statistical models, describing the kinds of factors that may be taken into account in thinking rationally about the best decision to reach (Ranyard et al., 1997; Kahneman et al., 1982). Such a formulation would fit comfortably with the implementation of evidence-based practice.

Subsequent work in psychology, however, has suggested that in practice people do not actually operate in this rational way. We tend rather to 'base our choices on rules and strategies derived from past experience with similar problems' (Eiser and van der Pligt, 1988). We are also influenced by our attitudes and values and by the feedback loops from earlier decisions. Therefore, they argue, it is essentially a social process rather than a rational, individual one. In other words, belief systems and cultural style may have a powerful impact on practice.

From large-scale policy issues to specific practice decisions and the moment-to-moment decisions that are part of an ongoing process – how to respond to a request, how to initiate or conclude a conversation, the tone of voice, the interpretations placed on what is said or done – all will be influenced not just by formal evidence and analysis but by a host of other less formal understandings and feelings (Schon, 1992 and 1994; Lester, 1995; Schell and Ceverso, 1993). Rational, evidence-based practice can be powerfully effective, but it will always depend on what evidence is seen as relevant and what outcomes are seen as meaningful. It is inevitably limited in its range of vision, and the critical practitioner seeking to make a difference and also to value difference must draw on it as a tool and source of information, but not as the whole or only story.

Experience and expertise should not be devalued, nor, as Claxton (1998) argues, the power of human intuition. Neither should we ignore the importance of the value base operating alongside our own unconscious motivations and defences. In professions and organisations which are mediating human need and social justice, there is surprisingly little emphasis on the fundamental human processes involved. Kitwood (1990 and 1998) argues for the importance of moral space and draws upon 'depth psychology' to examine caring work. Smith (1992, 1999) talks of 'emotional labour'. Hornby (1993) discusses the essentials of 'self-responsibility and social integration'. Barnett (1997) suggests we cannot have genuine critical thinking and critical action without self-engagement.

We need to recognise these broader frames of reference in thinking about evidence-based practice and professional development. If the professionalisation of work in health and social care is ultimately of value, it must be because it enhances rather than dehumanises our capacity to value and understand ourselves and others as moral and sentient beings – and our capacity to treat others, especially vulnerable others, accordingly, in working to support and provide for health and social care.

Conclusion

The concept of critical practice developed here locates the practitioner within the frame as an active participant in a process of creating meanings and understandings and forging relationships and dialogue across difference. Rather than presuming a detached, objective and wholly rational role based on assumptions of passive compliance from others, the critical practitioner is seen as reflexive and engaged. Thus, in seeking to work in an empowering way, awareness of personal and socio-cultural origins and belief systems is seen as an essential basis for creating respectful and equal relationships and for challenging discriminatory barriers.

Critical practitioners must be skilled and knowledgeable and yet remain open to alternative ideas, frameworks and belief systems, recognising and valuing alternative perspectives. 'Not-knowing' and uncertainty need to be valued as an orientation towards openness and a continuing process of learning, even if, at times, it can be essential to act swiftly and confidently. This sense of critical practice with its dilemmas and conflicts, but also its sense of creative and developmental process, underpins and infuses the work of all health and social care practitioners today.

References

Allen, D. (1997) 'The nursing–medical boundary: a negotiated order?', *Sociology of Health and Illness*, 19 (4): 498–520.

Argyris, C. and Schon, D. (1974) *Theory and Practice*. San Francisco, CA: Jossey-Bass.

Barnett, R. (1997) *Higher Education: A Critical Business*. Buckingham: SRHE and Open University Press.

Bateson, G. (1972) *Steps to an Ecology of Mind*. London: Intertext Books.

Braye, S. and Preston-Shoot, M. (1995) *Empowering Practice in Health and Social Care*. Buckingham: Open University Press.

Brechin, A., Brown, H. and Eby, M.A. (eds) (2000) *Critical Practice in Health and Social Care*. London: Sage.

Campbell, J. (1997) 'Implementing direct payments: towards the next millennium', in S. Balloch and N. Connelly (eds), *Buying and Selling Social Care*. London: National Institute for Social Work. pp. 22–34.

Clarke, J. and Cochrane, A. (1998) 'The social construction of social problems', in E. Saraga (ed.), *Embodying the Social: Constructions of Difference*. London: Routledge.

Claxton, G. (1998) 'Investigating human intuition: knowing without knowing why', *The Psychologist*, 88 (May): 217–20.

Culley, L. (1996) 'A critique of multiculturalism in health care: the challenge for nurse education', *Journal of Advanced Nursing*, 23: 564–70.

Culley, L. (1999) 'Working with diversity: towards negotiated understandings of health care needs', in C. Davies, L. Finlay and A. Bullman (eds), *Changing Practice in Health and Social Care* (K302 Reader 1). London: Sage.

Davies, C. (1995) *Gender and the Professional Predicament in Nursing*. Buckingham: Open University Press.

Davies, C. (1998) 'Caregiving, carework and professional care', in A. Brechin, J. Walmsley, J. Katz and S. Peace (eds), *Care Matters: Concepts, Practice and Research in Health and Social Care*. London: Sage.

Department of Health (DOH) (2001) *Health and Social Care Act*. London: HMSO.

Dominelli, L. (1988) *Anti-racist Social Work*. London: British Association of Social Workers/Macmillan.

Dominelli, L. (1997) *Sociology for Social Work*. Basingstoke: Macmillan.

Doyle, C. (1997) 'Protection studies: challenging oppression and discrimination', *Social Work Education*, 16 (2): 8–19.

Dutt, R. and Ferns, P. (1998) *Letting through the Light: A Training Pack on Black People and Mental Health*. London: Race Equality Unit and Department of Health.

Eiser, J.R. and van der Pligt, J. (1988) *Attitudes and Decisions*. London: Routledge.

Fernando, S. (1991) *Race and Culture in Psychiatry*. London: Tavistock/Routledge.

Fish, D. and Coles, C. (1998) *Developing Professional Judgement in Health Care*. Oxford: Butterworth Heinemann.

Fletcher, K. (1998) *Negotiation for Health and Social Services Professionals*. London: Jessica Kingsley.

Gergen, K. (1991) *The Saturated Self*. New York: Basic Books.

Glaister, A. and Glaister, R. (eds) (2005) *Inter-agency Collaboration: Providing for Children*. Edinburgh: Dunedin Academic Press.

Glendinning, C. (2000) *Buying Independence: Using Direct Payments for Integrated Health and Social Services*. Bristol: Policy Press.

Gomm, R. (1993) 'Issues of power in health and welfare', in J. Walmsley J. Reynolds, P. Shakespeare and R. Woolfe (eds), *Health, Welfare and Practice: Reflecting on Roles and Relationships* (K663 Reader). London: Sage/Open University.

Habermas, J. (1972) *Knowledge and Human Interest*. London: Heinemann.

Harre, R. (1986) *The Social Construction of Emotion*. New York: Basil Blackwell.

HMSO (2004a) *The Children Act*. London: HMSO.

HMSO (2004b) *Every Child Matters: Change for Children*. London: HMSO.

Hornby, S. (1993) *Collaborative Care: Interprofessional, Interagency and Interpersonal*. Oxford: Blackwell.

Howe, D. (1987) *An Introduction to Social Work Theory*. Aldershot: Wildwood House.

Kahneman, D. Slovic, P. and Tversky, A. (eds) (1982) *Judgement under Uncertainty: Heuristics and Biases*. Cambridge: Cambridge University Press.

Kitwood, T. (1990) *Concern for Others: A New Psychology of Conscience and Morality*. London: Routledge.

Kitwood, T. (1998) *Dementia Reconsidered*. Buckingham: Open University Press.

Kolb, D.A. (1995) 'The process of experiential learning', in M. Thorpe, R. Edwards and A. Hanson (eds), *Culture and Processes of Adult Learning*. London: Routledge/Open University.

Layder, D. (1997) *Modern Social Theory: Key Debates and New Directions*. London: UCL Press.

Lester, S. (1995) 'Beyond knowledge and competence: towards a framework for professional education', *Capability*, 1 (3): 44–52.

Lewis, G. (1996) 'Welfare and the social construction of race', in E. Saraga (ed.), *Embodying the Social: Constructions of Difference*. London: Routledge.

Loxley, A. (1997) *Collaboration in Health and Welfare: Working with Difference*. London: Jessica Kingsley.

Mann, H. (1998) 'Reflections on a border crossing: from ward sister to clinical nurse specialist', in P. Smith (ed.), *Nursing Research: Setting New Agendas*. London: Arnold.

Maynard, M. and Purvis, J. (1994) (eds) *Researching Women's Lives from a Feminist Perspective*. London: Taylor & Francis.

McNamee, S. and Gergen, K. (1992) *Therapy as Social Construction*. London: Sage.

Morris, J. (1991) *Pride against Prejudice*. London: The Women's Press.

Morris, J. (1997) 'Care or empowerment? A disability rights perspective', *Social Policy and Administration*, 31 (1): 54–60.

Muir Gray, J.A. (1997) *Evidence-based Healthcare: How to Make Health Policy and Management Decisions*. Edinburgh: Churchill Livingstone.

National Assembly for Wales (2000) *The Community Care (Direct Payments) Amendment (Wales) Regulations Statutory Instrument No.1868*. London: HMSO.

Northern Ireland Executive (2002) *Carers and Direct Payments Act*. London: HMSO.

Oliver, M. (1990) *The Politics of Disablement*, London: Macmillan.

Pinkney, S. (1998) 'The reshaping of social work and social care', in G. Hughes and G. Lewis (eds), *Unsettling Welfare: The Reconstruction of Social Policy*. London: Routledge.

Pinkney, S. (1999) 'Anti-oppressive theory and practice in social work', in C. Davies, L. Finlay and A. Bullman (eds), *Changing Practice in Health and Social Care* (K302 Reader 1). London: Sage.

Porter, R. (1985) 'The patient's view: doing medical history from below', *Theory and Society*, 14 (2): 175–98.

Porter, S. (1998) *Social Theory and Nursing Practice*. Basingstoke: Macmillan.

Ranyard, R. Crozier, W.R and Svensen, O. (eds) (1997) *Decision Making: Cognitive Models and Explanations*. London: Routledge.

Rogers, C. (1951) *Client-centered Therapy: Its Current Practice, Implications and Theory.* Boston: Houghton Mifflin.

Saraga, E. (ed.) (1998) *Embodying the Social: Constructions of Difference.* London: Routledge.

Schell, B.A. and Ceverso, R.M. (1993) 'Clinical reasoning in occupational therapy: an integrative review', *American Journal of Occupational Therapy,* 47 (7): 605–10.

Schon, D.A. (1983) *The Reflective Practitioner.* London: Temple Smith.

Schon, D.A. (1992) 'The crisis of professional knowledge and the pursuit of an epistemology of practice', *Journal of Interprofessional Care,* 6 (1): 49–63 (originally published 1984).

Schon, D.A. (1994) 'Teaching artistry through reflection in action', in H. Tsoukas (ed.), *New Thinking in Organisational Behaviour.* Oxford: Butterworth Heinemann.

Scottish Executive (2001) *For Scotland's Children: Better Integrated Services.* Edinburgh: Scottish Executive.

Scottish Executive (2003) Protection of Children Act. Edinburgh: Scottish Executive.

Shakespeare, T. and Watson, N. (1997) 'Defending the social model', *Disability and Society,* 12 (2): 293–300.

Shotter, J. (1993) *Cultural Politics of Everyday Life.* Buckingham: Open University Press.

Shotter, J. and Gergen, K. (1989) *Texts of Identity.* London: Sage.

Smith, P. (1992) *The Emotional Labour of Nursing.* Basingstoke: Macmillan.

Smith, P. (1999) 'Logging emotions: a logbook of personal reflections', *Soundings,* 11: 128–37.

Social Services Inspectorate (SSI) (1998) *They Look after Their Own, Don't They: Inspection of Community Care Services for Black and Ethnic Minority Older People.* London: Department of Health.

Spandler, H. (2004) 'Friend or Foe? Towards a critical assessment of direct payments', *Critical Social Policy,* 24 (2): 187–209.

Stainton, T. (2002) 'Taking rights structurally: disability, rights and social worker responses to direct payments', *British Journal of Social Work,* 32: 751–63.

Swain, J. and French, S. (1998) 'Normality and disabling care', in A. Brechin, J. Walmsley, J. Katz and S. Peace (eds), *Care Matters: Concepts, Practice and Research in Health and Social Care.* London: Sage.

Thompson, N. (1995) *Theory and Practice in Health and Social Welfare.* Buckingham: Open University Press.

Thompson, N. (1996) *People Skills: A Guide to Effective Practice in the Human Services.* Basingstoke: Macmillan.

Thompson, N. (1998) *Promoting Equality: Challenging Discrimination and Oppression in the Human Services.* Basingstoke: Macmillan.

Thompson, N. (1999) 'Theory and practice in health and social care', in C. Davies, L. Finlay and A. Bullman (eds), *Changing Practice in Health and Social Care* (K302 Reader 1). London: Sage.

Tsang, N.M. (1998) 'Re-examining reflection – a common issue of professional concern in social work, teacher and nursing education', *Journal of Interprofessional Care,* 12 (1): 21–31.

Chapter 2

Social work, professionalism and the regulatory framework

Mike Burt and Aidan Worsley

Students of social work might be forgiven for occasionally wondering what they have let themselves in for. Certainly, when a social worker queries how free they are to practise in the way they feel best – as a professionally trained social worker – the question of the regulation placed upon them via legislation, employer's policy and procedure and the expectations of the profession itself, can feel quite challenging. It might appear that their knowledge, skills and experience enable them to make well-informed and accurate judgements about interventions, but these are circumscribed – if not compromised – by the many different forms of regulation that surround and constrain their actions. It could be argued that as levels of autonomy and discretion get eroded, the need for professional training lessens – the need for 'professional' social workers lessens. This chapter aims to explore these themes, particularly in relation to regulation around issues such as qualifying training, national standards, codes of practice and the regulatory role of the General Social Care Council (GSCC). It should be noted that the GSCC is an England body. The GSCC has partner organisations in Scotland (SSSC); in Wales, the Care Council for Wales (CCW); and in Northern Ireland, the Northern Ireland Social Care Council (NISCC). These types of regulation control entry to the profession and progression within it – yet they are not controlled by the profession itself. We will reflect on whether social work is a profession and, if so, what sort of regulation it is subject to and how the profession should respond to such regulation. It should not be taken for granted that social work, in itself, actually constitutes a profession.

When we think of a profession, or a 'professional job', our modern usage of these concepts blurs the boundaries between certain occupational roles that carry elements of status and power and, at the other extreme, the notion that doing something well, or effectively is 'professional'. We need to refine our concepts when considering the nature of social work's status as a profession and ask ourselves not just whether social work is a profession or not, but to what extent and in what ways it is a profession. We begin this chapter by offering some theoretical constructs drawn from the sociology of professions, to enhance our understanding of the concept. We will conclude by considering the issue of how social work can differentiate itself from other occupational groups within multi-professional settings, and how social work's values and ethically informed practice might assist in that process.

Social work as a profession

One approach to the question analyses the characteristics or traits that are exhibited by certain occupational groups. Many authors have employed a 'trait' approach as they attempted to delineate and isolate certain aspects of professions as distinguished from occupations (notably Parsons, 1954; Greenwood, 1957; and Friedson, 1994). Most authors begin with the concept of professional *knowledge*. There are three elements here that characterise a profession's knowledge; the deployment of a skill informed by theoretical knowledge, the conviction that such knowledge requires training and education and, finally, a requirement that professional competence is tested, normally by some form of examination, against criteria laid down by the professional training body. At first glance, we might assume that social work fits the bill here, but let us pause to ask the question: does social work have a distinctive knowledge base? The question is difficult to answer; social work itself has always been something of a contested activity and authors have frequently commented on its struggles to define its status, both in terms of an academic discipline as well as an arena of professional practice (Lovelock et al., 2004). There are, however, readily identifiable statements about social work knowledge. The social work qualifying degree is assessed against National Occupational Standards (TOPSS, 2002) and involves a standardised curriculum contained in statements from the Department of Health (DoH, 2002) and the Quality Assurance Agency for Higher Education (QAAHE, 2000) – yet all these statements are fairly general and it is hard to pick out aspects that are quintessentially social work, as opposed to any other profession. Social work draws on knowledge from a range of disciplines, notably law, social policy, psychology, sociology, and so forth. What social work struggles to find is its 'own' knowledge base, although one could argue that its distinctiveness is in its *value* base. The QAAHE Benchmarking statements for social work talk about the importance of dealing with inequality, social injustice, discrimination, and with uncertain and complex situations (QAAHE, 2000).

Thinking more broadly, there can be little doubt that what a student learns as they enter the social work profession has a profound effect, beyond knowledge learning. Greenwood, writing on social work as a profession some time ago observed that 'the professional is a person whose work becomes his life' (Greenwood, 1957: 15). Our identity as people is often defined by matters such as gender, class, and race but perhaps we might more readily see ourselves as best defined by the profession we have chosen. Hall, writing on this broad theme of identity, believes that we no longer possess simple identities, but rather fragmented, contradictory identities (Hall, 1996). Perhaps, as social workers, we are constructing a composite professional identity that draws in a similar way from different sources. The question this raises is one of consistency – how can social work be a unified profession under such circumstances?

This, in turn, leads us to a second professional trait: *organisation*, in the sense of cohesion. This would include how social work might distance itself from other occupations and maintain its exclusivity around some aspects of its role. For social work, this is perhaps less clear as there is no obvious unifying *body* or *agency*. The British Association of Social Workers (BASW) takes on aspects of this role and is certainly the largest association promoting high professional standards in social work but its membership is less than complete and it struggles to articulate a comprehensive professional voice. Furthermore, social work is becoming increasingly divided in the delivery of its service, splitting into areas of specialism – most broadly around children and adults – that some might argue have little to do with each other and are drifting further apart as the *Every Child Matters* (DoH, 2003) agenda links children's services work most closely to education, while adults lean towards health. One might conclude that this is a particular area of challenge and provides both threat and opportunity to social work as a profession. Payne (2004) suggests that the location of social workers in a range of different settings, and within multi- and inter-professional teams provides positive opportunities for individual social workers to develop skills and influence.

The third and final trait is related to how a *bond* is created and maintained within the profession. There are two elements commonly referred to: adherence to a professional code of conduct and a commitment to altruistic service. This would appear to be a more fruitful area, as the GSCC Code of Practice sets out a clear statement of guidance on conduct in the social care workplace (GSCC, 2002b). As social workers we are often said to possess a sense of 'vocation', a sense that what we are doing is making a difference to the lives of disadvantaged people and certainly, as we look at how the role of social worker has developed over the years, its background in charity work speaks to an altruistic foundation. However, this in itself can be contested from a conflict perspective which argues that the concept of 'profession' is a means of occupational control that benefits the practitioners rather than the public, and the image of public service and altruism is an ideology used to justify higher incomes and prestige of the profession. Johnson's (1972) analysis from this line of thinking throws light on one reason why there might be limits to the professional aspirations of social work, namely that it works with the 'undeserving'.

The traits that we have discussed represent the sociological make-up of a profession; they are acquired over time within a historical but non-linear development and can be exhibited to varying degrees within a wide range of characteristics. An illustration of the model in practice is the work of Etzioni (1969), who developed the concept of the 'semi-profession' – teachers, nurses and social workers, for example – which, according to the trait approach, would only be able to demonstrate *half* the required traits:

> Their training is shorter, their status is less legitimised, their right to privileged communication less established, there is less of a specialised body of knowledge and they have less autonomy from supervision or societal control than 'the' professions.
>
> (Etzioni, 1969: v)

Etzioni was the first writer to delineate social work in this way using the traits of the traditional, established professions as a gauge and seeing how it measured up. The importance of judgements of this kind is seen when we consider how much power each occupational group is able to exert in the workplace. Ask the question: who controls the workplace? Friedson, writing generally about professions, argued that the 'central issue of professional power lies in the control of work by the professional themselves, rather than control by consumers in an open market or by the functionaries of a centrally planned and administered firm or state' (Friedson, 1994: 44). Is it social workers who control the type of work they engage in, the methods of intervention and so forth? Or do those decisions tend to be made by managers within the bureaucratic structures of an organisation? Etzioni talked of the tensions that can exist between the profession's principles and the organisational ones, because 'the authority of knowledge and the authority of administrative hierarchy are basically incompatible' (Etzioni, 1969: viii). Following this line of argument we can reflect on the problems and tensions that can arise when a professional group, such as social work, with its particular knowledge and value base, works within an organisational structure. This might be a local authority or health service that, while sympathetic to the aims of the profession, has other competing agendas that arguably necessarily limit the level of discretion and autonomy that it wishes the profession to command. A local authority, for example, has many different professions working within its boundaries, tight budgets to manage and prioritise, and responsibilities over consistency and quality in the delivery of service that inevitably lead it to seek greater control over the workplace. At its simplest we can see this argument laid out in the competition between needs-led and resources-led assessment. A trained, qualified social worker deploying their knowledge of assessment might wish for the service-user's needs to be met regardless of cost. From the organisation's perspective it has to work within a budget and within procedures that govern equity and fairness (often through the development of criteria) and thus, inevitably, seek to impose a resource-led model. In this sense we see a broader nature of professional regulation and, from David Howe's analysis, the issues at the heart of it:

> Managers seek to create regular and predictable task environments so that routine responses can be prescribed in set situations. They attempt to define both the work and the way the organisation functionaries will react. Thus, in a predefined situation, the social worker is expected to act in a pre-programmed way. Work becomes both fragmented and standardised. By increasing rules, routines, procedures, the manager diminishes the area of professional discretion available to the social worker.

> (Howe, 1991: 124)

But does this sound like the reality of the situation? Inevitably, we are working in complex and dynamic work situations, within a broad range of types and scales of organisation, some more organic in their structure than hierarchical and 'mechanical'. A social worker's experience of these differences will vary. There is perhaps also a sense in which there is a *process* of professionalisation that social work is engaged with that fluctuates over time, and social work is perhaps not accurately seen as a perennial semi-profession. Macdonald (1997) talks of the 'professional project' that involves tackling the development of the 'traits' we have discussed above, and also establishing relationships with the state, competing occupational groups and educational institutions. He sees this as an ongoing, dynamic process and reminds us that professions and social work, in particular, are engaged in different struggles as they make their way. Professional workers are more likely to be employees than self-employed, to be working for large organisations and, in social work's case, often to have their levels of pay, conditions of service and general independence controlled by the state. Oppenheimar (1973) called elements of this process the 'proletarianisation of the professional', but James (2004), writing specifically about social work, talked more brusquely about the 'McDonaldization' of social work. He describes a process where principles of efficiency, predictability and control are brought to bear on a limited number of services, where training is focused on people learning how to intervene in a small number of limited ways and where the environment of social work loses its scope for innovation and creativity. He acknowledges that he may be pessimistic about the direction of social work but asks readers if his theory has the 'ring of truth' about it (James, 2004: 53).

Briefly considering the critical path taken by the profession towards its present location, we can see some significant staging posts along the way that have affected both the social work role and its context. James (2004) argues that during the 1960s social work enjoyed a highly individualised way of working, clearly focused on the relationship between social worker and client. He further suggests that the creation of social services departments in 1971 in England and Wales led to the bureaucratisation of social work and that the development of short-term, task-centred, contract-based and behavioural methods of intervention began to dominate practice (James, 2004). By the 1990s there was a clear perception that social workers spent a reduced amount of time working directly with service-users themselves. Harris (2003) argues that social work's future was placed in a different context as a result of the passing of the NHS and Community Care Act 1990, and the Children Act 1989. In particular he notes that the Act became the primary vehicle for accomplishing the transformation of the culture of social work and the establishing of the social work business: 'the role of the state as direct provider of services was to diminish to be replaced by the roles of enabler, subsidiser and regulator' (Harris, 2003: 40). With these shifts in role came the notion of case management. Rather than working primarily and directly with individuals, social workers became responsible for making more comprehensive assessments and subsequently integrating the whole range of activity and intervention connected with an individual. The corollary? That the social worker focuses on administrative, procedural and organisational aspects of the role (Lymbery and Butler, 2004).

Regulation and the road to the GSCC

Many observers (Howe, 1991; McLaughlin, 2006b) believe that social work practice is becoming increasingly regulated. For the purposes of this chapter we will look at particular aspects of regulation that are located within the broad frameworks of social work registration and professional education, attempting to understand them in terms of social work as a profession. The path taken towards registration for the profession is closely intertwined with the debate about whether a central council would enhance the development of social work as a profession. Should this central council be seen as an advocate for the profession, promoting its interests, or should it possess a more regulatory role? The new millennium started with plans to protect the title 'social worker' by legislation and to register all social workers who were entitled, by professional qualification, to use the designation. Yet, this was not a particularly new or novel idea. The registration of social workers was actually considered by a study committee of the Association of Social Workers (ASW) which met and reported in 1954. The questionnaire which the committee circulated suggested that the advantages of registration would include an ability to 'protect the public from treatment by unqualified people, give employers some reliable indication of competence, help to maintain and improve standards of work and training … ' (ASW, 1954: 32). It did not suggest that enhanced professional status would result.

The Report of the Working Party on Social Workers (Younghusband, 1959) led to the establishing of a Council for Social Work Training in 1962. However, it only covered training for social workers in health and welfare departments, and the Central Training Council in Child Care continued with its work. The establishment of the Central Council for Education and Training in Social Work (CCETSW) in 1971 brought together the separate training bodies at the same time as the creation of single social service departments and led to the introduction of two-year generic qualifying programmes with the award of a Certificate of Qualification in Social Work (CQSW).

Malherbe (1982) reports that in 1977 'The Future of Social Work', a discussion paper from a joint steering group on accreditation, which included representatives from the British Association of Social Workers (BASW) and CCETSW, recommended the establishing of a General Social Work Council. The paper suggested that, 'This Council would be responsible for: accreditation of courses of training in social work; the accreditation of social work practitioners; the regulation of social work practice through disciplinary procedures' (Malherbe, 1982: 31). In the mid-1980s the government rejected a proposal to develop a three-year qualification for social work (Payne, 1996). Bamford (1990) reports that in the 1980s BASW used the term 'new professionalism' to indicate not only the continuing importance of qualifications and expertise to the social work profession but also to signify that a different kind of relationship with the service-user was appropriate, one which empowered the service-user to exercise choice. The election of a Labour government in 1997 saw the introduction of a number of measures which together appear to have raised the profile of the social work profession, within the broader context of social care. The Care Standards Act 2000 provided for the establishing of the General Social Care Council (GSCC). The Council has seventeen members and is required by law to have a majority of lay members and a lay chairperson. This requirement also has to be met in respect of the Council's conduct panels and registration panels. Both these facets (of lay involvement) are worthy of note, given our questioning of the control exerted over the profession by those outside of it. In 2002 the GSCC published the first code of practice for social care workers and code of practice for employers. In April 2003 the first social workers began to be included in the register of qualified social workers. In that same year the GSCC, working with the Department of Health, produced requirements to shape a qualifying honours degree in social work to replace the previous Diploma in Social Work (DoH, 2002; GSCC, 2002a; GSCC, 2003). Together these developments established the profession alongside others that had had similar provisions for some considerable time. They also offer developments that clearly impact at the most fundamental level on issues of profession and regulation.

Protection of the title 'social worker'

Section 61 of the Care Standards Act 2000, which came into force on 1 April 2005, states that,

> if a person who is not registered as a social worker in any relevant register with intent to deceive another a) takes or uses the title of social worker; b) takes or uses any title or description implying that he is so registered, or in any way holds himself out to be so registered, he is guilty of an offence.

The legislation makes it a criminal offence to use the title 'social worker' with intent to deceive. The protection of the title 'social worker' is significant in that it delineates qualified social workers as a distinct professional group and creates a significant impetus for the profession to clarify its role and function. However, as we can see, the title is contingent upon registration. It must be acknowledged that the process of registration is controlled by the Councils, which are government-sponsored bodies, as opposed to the profession itself. The GSCC, although formed *in part* from the ashes of the CCETSW, is noticeably more distant from the professional worker than its predecessor, which is illustrated, for example, by its own minimalist approach to the development of the curriculum for the social work degree. The GSCC has a much broader remit, for example in respect of social care, and a clearer, more formal regulatory function. One cannot equate the profession with the regulatory body. Here they are two distinct entities and it would certainly not be true to say that the GSCC *fully* reflects the interests of the social work profession which it regulates. The GSCC's strategic objectives are established with central government and the Department of Health in particular, which is the sponsoring (funding) department of the GSCC responsible for the great majority of its income.

Registration

In order to be registered, social workers must meet the criteria laid out in Section 58 of the Care Standards Act 2000, demonstrating they are of good character, physically and mentally fit for the professional role, have completed an approved course and agree to abide by the Code of Practice. However, the GSCC's failure to define what physical and mental health issues might preclude one from joining the profession is problematic, perhaps even inconsistent with the ethical approach of the profession – demonstrating the difference between the GSCC as regulator and professional body:

> There is a rather distasteful paradox here in that whilst social work commits itself to user involvement in the provision of training, consultancy and service provision, at the same time it [the GSCC] is using a medical framework with which to preclude such users from actually *joining* the profession. Reasonable adjustments and a caring response rather than a bureaucratic, medically framed reaction would be more fitting with the values of the social work profession.

> (McLaughlin, 2006b: 6)

The social care register is itself a public document and can be accessed at www.gscc.org. The register records the geographical area within which a registered social worker practises. Re-registration is a further requirement of registration and must take place every three years. Social workers must undertake a minimum of ninety hours or fifteen days post-registration training and learning in order to re-register. This is an interesting development and follows a similar pattern to some health professions. It could be argued that the relatively low levels of time required to sustain registered status (five days of 'training and learning' a year) was a lost opportunity. How much stronger would it have been to require the achievement of a post-qualifying award within that time frame – or even within the first six years of practice? The emphasis, it appears, is on the control dimension of regulating the professional workforce rather than promoting its continuing professional development.

Codes of Practice

Everyone who joins the social care register has to agree to abide by the *Code of Practice for Employees* (GSCC, 2002b). There is also a Code of Practice for Employers which governs the agencies in which they work. The Codes of Practice are a critical part of regulating the social care workforce and contain criteria to guide practice and standards of conduct which workers have to meet across the four countries and their care councils (NISCC, GSCC, WSCC and SSSC). The GSCC requires that social workers must:

1. Protect the rights and promote the interests of service-users and carers;
2. Strive to establish and maintain the trust and confidence of service-users and carers;
3. Promote the independence of service-users while protecting them as far as possible from danger or harm;
4. Respect the rights of service-users whilst seeking to ensure that their behaviour does not harm themselves or other people;
5. Uphold public trust and confidence in social care services; and
6. Be accountable for the quality of their work and take responsibility for maintaining and improving their knowledge and skills.

   In general these codes appear to be a satisfactory attempt to define some of the ethics of the profession and institutionalise workers' commitment to the value base. However, one can see that regulation and standard-setting is also an integrated part of this agenda. For example, there are formal statements about upholding public trust and accountability; and of particular interest is one of the subsections of Code 5, which requires that social workers do not 'behave in a way, in work or outside work, which would call into question your suitability to work in social care services' (GSCC, 2002b: section 5.8). Some authors query whether how social workers conduct themselves in their private lives is any business of the GSCC, how well it is equipped to take on the role of moral arbiter and with what agendas it approaches that task (McLaughlin, 2006b). Interestingly, McLaughlin points out that there was surprisingly little criticism of the codes following their publication – or indeed since. Given that being struck off the register prevents social workers from future employment in that sector, one might have expected a more forceful response, yet in one survey most social workers believed registration would raise the profile and standards of the profession (McLaughlin, 2006b).

   The Code of Practice for employees also includes a requirement that social care workers are responsible for maintaining and improving their knowledge and skills. This should include undertaking relevant training towards that personal development as well as their contribution to the learning and development of others (Requirement 6). There is a matching requirement in the Code for Employers (Requirement 3), which states that employers must provide training and development opportunities to enable social care workers to strengthen and develop their skills and knowledge. Clearly, there is now a strong emphasis on ensuring that the social work/care workforce is equipped to do its job, by providing the education and training for each job role and ensuring that workers continue to learn and develop. The vision embodied in the Green Papers for both the child care and adult social care workforce (DoH, 2003; DoH, 2005) includes the idea that all staff should have personal development plans which identify learning and development needs and ways in which these needs will be met. Employers are expected to deploy a significant percentage of their staff-training budget on workforce development and individual employees are expected to contribute to the cost of their own development. Statutory inspectors will consider all these factors and the progress made will have significant impact on the 'star ratings' of employers.

Social work degree

The introduction of the three-year undergraduate degree as the basic requirement for social workers to become qualified and eligible to practise is a significant policy change and results from a long campaign to establish a degree qualification for social work. The social work degree was introduced in autumn 2003 and produced its first graduates in 2006. Its key characteristics include the removal of age restrictions for qualifications, the introduction of compulsory CRB and health checks for applicants, and literacy and numeracy standards required for entry. In terms of learning there were also requirements around preparation for placement, evidence-based practice, inter-professional learning and a greater amount of time spent in practice. The number of days on placement for qualifying students increased from 130 to 200 days on the degree, more days, but proportionately the same. To meet this demand, practice-learning opportunities are being created in agencies that have traditionally not taken social work students and a variety of new ways of offering practice-learning opportunities are being developed (Doel, 2005). Students on the degree can expect to undertake practice in more than one setting, working with different service-user groups, and have experience of statutory intervention (DoH, 2002).

National Occupational Standards

Social work students will be familiar with the National Occupational Standards (NOS) (TOPSS, 2002) for social work – they provide the criteria for the assessment of practice. The NOS for social work are, in one sense, the single, clearest statement of what it currently means to be a social worker. They are an attempt to analyse the essence of the professional task into key components and to deploy them as criteria to assess students and/ or practitioners in their work. They were written by the Training Organisation for the Personal Social Services (TOPSS), since replaced by separate training organisations for staff working with children (Children's Workforce Development Council) and those working with adults (Skills for Care).

As is the case with other competency structures, the National Occupational Standards indicate what workers should be able to do in order to demonstrate that they have met the standards set. The competence approach tries to be as objective as possible, but by its very nature social work does not have a scientific basis, being involved in human social situations which are complex and uncertain, and many see competency structures as the antithesis of social work (O'Hagan, 1997). They consist of broad statements of key functions or roles within social work as practised across a range of settings. There are six key roles in total. Functional analysis was employed to identify what workers must be able to do in order for the key roles to be performed across a range of settings. The analysis was completed in a series of stages with the levels of performance becoming increasingly more detailed and explicit at each stage. The key roles are thus split down into twenty-one units which are again subdivided into seventy-seven elements of competence. Each element is then expanded into performance criteria. To achieve an element of competence students should be able to demonstrate that they can do everything that is spelt out through the performance criteria. This can lead to a concentration on the minutiae and a loss of appreciation of the whole because the whole is often greater than the sum of its parts. Dominelli (1996) argues that it is a dogmatic and inflexible approach which reduces complex social interactions to snapshots and moves away from relationship-building which, she argues, is the fundamental core of the profession. Indeed, a significant debate has continued in social work education since the early 1990s about whether a competence-based framework should be applied to the complexities of the profession. Constructions such as the National Occupational Standards for Social Work include a range of skills and knowledge which learners must demonstrate and be able to evaluate critically and apply in practice. Failure to acquire the knowledge which informs competence could lead to robotic performance with little understanding of the reasons why intervention has gone well (or badly) and poor ability to justify actions and predict outcomes. In short, it could lead to robotic performance and a de-professionalising of the role. But by the same token, an overemphasis on performance criteria can lead to shallow, unimaginative and essentially unprofessional practice (Thompson, 2002: 153).

Differentiation, values and ethics

As noted above one of the 'traits' of a profession is to clearly establish, delineate and protect the sphere of activity within which it functions. Notwithstanding the problems of differentiation in multi-professional settings, social work has experienced difficulty in identifying specifically what its purpose is compared to other professions (Wickwar and Wickwar, 1949; Butrym, 1976; Barclay Report, 1982; Clarke, 1993; Clark, 2000). Stevenson (2004: 238) suggests that 'upon the notion of expertise, it can be argued the future of social work as a profession must rest. This is pertinent to education and practice.' The challenge for social work is to suggest and promote its area(s) of expertise, within the emerging, challenging context of the multi- and inter-professional approach to meeting service-user's needs. The challenge is clarifying exactly what its area of expertise is. The emerging professional context offers very different opportunities for the profession, depending on one's analysis. It could be argued that social work expertise should be negotiated between the professions, recognising that there are areas of overlap. If we pursue this line of thinking, we might need to question whether some of the broader claims about the primary focus of social work could only be achieved as a consequence of the integrated and connected work of a range of professions in the current context. It might follow that if the areas of expertise which are said to differentiate social work are those which at some point could be adopted or integrated by other professional groups, we would move towards a situation where social work becomes very differently constructed. Alternatively, in respect of working in a multi-professional context, Frost, Robinson and Anning (2005) suggest that perhaps social work's particular skills in dealing with complex situations, uncertainty and conflict perfectly equip them to be a, perhaps *the*, cohesive force within multi-professional teams. Does this turn the focus of the profession away from the service-users at the root of vocation and values, or would it allow social work a new foundation on which to build a stronger profession?

There are, of course, at least two sides to the coin of differentiation. One looks at what social work does to differentiate itself from others; the other side can be what social work does to prevent others from colonising its professional territory. One of the enduring observations in social work is that social workers intervene with people at the point at which the individual interacts with their environment (Younghusband, 1959; Hollis, 1970; Stevenson, 2004). Social workers are more likely to become involved if there are complex family issues that need to be addressed in respect of people's care; if there is conflict between people; or if an individual is at risk of being harmed physically or emotionally, or is at risk of causing harm to another. An ecological systems perspective is one of the models which are currently used to make a holistic assessment of complex social situations (Jack, 2003). Other professions, such as those located within health and education services, are increasingly suggesting that they also adopt a holistic perspective in their response to meeting people's needs. To maintain a sense of differentiation in this arena, social work might need to identify the particular way in which it adopts its holistic approach, especially in the context of an inter-agency approach. It may be useful to explore whether there is a contrast in the way that other professions increasingly work with individuals in the context of social and environmental factors, whereas social workers have the expertise to engage directly and in a sustained way with the complex and often conflicting relationships that exist in those networks.

It is also suggested that social work can be distinguished by its values (Shardlow, 1998). Indeed, the Green Paper 'Adult Services, Independence, Well-being and Choice' (DoH, 2005: 28) asserts that 'we want to create a different environment which reinforces the core social work values of supporting individuals to take control of their own lives and to make choices which matter to them'. However, Clark (2000: 34) conflictingly asserts that 'there is nothing fundamental in social work values that is not to be found in the mainstream of western societal values … ', and that 'the discourse on values in social work often seems vague and unsatisfactory' (2000: 41).

So, if the values of the professions are to be a source of effective differentiation from other professions, how can this be understood, given Clark's serious misgivings? The concept of and belief in *social justice* is a strong premise within the social work profession and is perhaps one starting point for comparison with other claims for a similar value base. A social justice perspective for social work practice has two strands which relate respectively to the empowering of individuals at the micro level and to the significance of structural disadvantage at the macro level. The first strand emphasises the basis of social morality which, it is suggested, should fundamentally inform social work practice. Bisman (2004: 109) suggests that, 'at its core, social work must respond to the moral imperative of caring for the neediest among us … values are pivotal in the conceptualisation and justification of the profession'. The second strand relates to the discourse of structural disadvantage. Garrett (2003) argues that anti-oppressive practice emphasises the importance of recognising the constraints that social structure imposes on an individual's capacity for action. Jordan (2004) takes this a step further, urging an emphasis on the social work role in the resolution of structural problems. Social work, in these ways, becomes a political practice, engaging with those confronted by unjust social relations, including those with social institutions (such as the state and the family) that are divergent from the norm (Butler and Pugh, 2004). It can therefore be suggested that social work, in its pursuit of social justice, must not only be concerned with individual empowerment, but with political activity in pursuit of that empowerment which is presented as an ethical endeavour.

There is a growing recognition that an understanding of the 'ethics of care' can contribute to our understanding of the needs of service-users in social work practice (Orme, 2002; Parton, 2003; Featherstone, 2006). It seems surprising, given our comments about social justice and professional values, that so little work has been done to develop a care ethics approach to social work, especially given that care is obviously a central concern in human life (Banks, 2006). Morris (1993) draws a distinction between independence as self-sufficiency and independence as having the capacity to have choice and control over one's life. Williams (2001: 487) also argues, taking a macro view, 'care is not only personal; it is an issue of public and political concern whose social dynamics operate at local, national and transnational levels'. Yet it can be argued that care (in its sense of virtue) does not *require* the social worker to connect with the person receiving the care (Banks, 2006). This is not to suggest that we are necessarily focusing on the relationship between the social worker and service-user. This form of intervention may also be mediated through the carers', the support workers', social workers' or other professionals' relationship with a service-user. Social workers have expertise in relationships not only in the traditional sense of between themselves and the service-user, but in respect of the way in which people are cared for, by others and by themselves, they facilitate those relationships. Social workers therefore have to develop expertise in communication skills to enable them to engage with service-users to empower people to maximise their potential. They can be expected to facilitate carers, service-users and significant others to care collaboratively and resolve conflict. For individuals who experience stress, there may be an impact on their ability to engage in the reciprocal social relationships which facilitate social functioning. Social workers can use their social sciences knowledge and practice experience to facilitate the achievement of individual goals for each service-user.

So here we see a number of themes coming together. The social work profession is concerned with the notions of relationships within care and caring for others and this can most readily be understood through the profession's value base and commitment to social justice at micro and macro levels. This, perhaps, is a unique aspect to its professional claim. The complex nature of relationships between and among members of a family, significant others, the broader community and society are all, in this analysis, within the frame of understanding and working with the service-user. We could therefore argue that there is a sense in which the focus of social work practice has moved not only from casework to case management but also from 'working with the individual client in his or her family and social context' to 'working with the impact for the individual of their family and social context'. The perception of social work as a profession which works only with individuals as a focus runs the risk of reinforcing a 'medicalised' rather than 'social' approach to meeting people's needs. Perhaps the social work profession is most able to differentiate itself from others within the broad field of the helping professions by asserting the need for the profession to engage directly with others in a service user's network and engage directly with people's relationships, not only with them as individuals.

The concern that this analysis leaves is the extent to which the development of the case-management role and the regulation of social workers' practice enable social workers to carry out the work described above. How far does the impact of bureaucracy allow the profession to develop its expertise in this area? If we consider the social worker as gatekeeper to services and as case manager, it could be argued that this has led to a distancing of social work from the individual, becoming less rather than more concerned with social justice and the ethics of care. The question we return to in this chapter is: 'How far is the social worker free to make these choices?'

Conclusion

It could be argued that individual autonomy has never been a particular feature of main-stream social work practice because it has developed almost exclusively within the public sector rather than in private practice. Nevertheless, the discussion earlier in this chapter suggests that there has been a change in the extent to which social workers have discretion in respect of how they deploy their knowledge, skills and values. We have particularly considered the regulation social work has recently experienced in relation to social work education, the codes of practice and the requirements of registration. These have been broad, legislative forms of regulation that have impacted in very real ways on the nature of training and the ethical base of the profession. The question remains whether these forms of regulation, with their concerns over quality, consistency and equity, allow the professional sufficient freedom to exert judgement and respond to the increasingly complex scenarios that make up professional practice. Can social workers assert, for example, a case for suitability for services, as opposed to eligibility? Flynn suggests that,

> Ultimately professionals assert the authority of expertise and claim disinterested integrity … knowledge and skills may be codified and systematized but they cannot be completely programmed; outcomes of intervention are to varying degrees uncertain, and the particularity of individual cases and clients requires professional discretion.

> (Flynn, 1999: 34)

The concern about the increasing influence of managerialism and regulation is that the nature and forms of control over what a professional does is so complete that professionals become de-skilled in respect of what they expect of themselves and what they can achieve with service-users. Social workers need to look beyond the specific requirements which are made of them in an organisational context and from a managerialist perspective, to develop a creative approach that maximises the use of social work knowledge and skills. Fook, Ryan and Hawkins (2000: 9) state that 'when professionals learn to practice, they must learn about a phenomenon, and knowledge about how to use that knowledge'. Nevertheless, social workers are themselves at different stages of their own professional development and the extent to which they are able to work in an increasingly autonomous way will depend on their current stage of professional development. Similarly, it could also be argued that different elements of the profession are at different stages of development. In conclusion, one might wonder whether the student of social work will have found the 'ring of truth' through any elements of these debates. The continued drive for regulation appears to have picked up pace although some elements clearly have beneficial outcomes for the profession. A complex picture is being drawn and some elements appear to be being erased. Social work, as Dominelli (2004) warns us, is a 'troubled and troubling profession' and these are uneasy times. Practitioners need to embrace fully the political and ethical dimensions of their practice and play a more proactive role in ensuring that both regulation and the professional role are shaped by the profession's values.

References

Association of Social Workers (ASW) (1954) *Report on the Registration of Social Workers*. London: Association of Social Workers.

Banks, S. (2006) *Ethics and Values in Social Work* (3rd edn). Basingstoke: Palgrave.

Bamford, T. (1990) *The Future of Social Work*. Basingstoke: Palgrave.

Barclay Report (1982) *Social Workers: Their Roles and Tasks*. London: Bedford Square Press.

Bisman, C. (2004) 'Social work values, the moral core of the profession', *British Journal of Social Work*, 34 (1): 109–23.

Butler, I. and Drakeford, M. (2005) *Scandal, Social Policy and Social Welfare*. Bristol: Policy Press.

Butler, J. and Pugh, R. (2004) 'The politics of social work research' in R. Lovelock, K. Lyons and J. Powell (eds), *Reflecting on Social Work – Discipline and Profession*. Aldershot: Ashgate.

Butrym, Z. (1976) *The Nature of Social Work*. London: Macmillan.

Carr-Saunders, A.M. and Wilson, P.A. (1933) *The Professions*. Oxford: Clarendon Press.

Clark, C. (2000) *Social Work Ethics*. Basingstoke: Macmillan.

Clarke, J. (ed.) (1993) *A Crisis in Care? Challenges to Social Work*. London: Sage.

Davies, M. (1991) (ed.) *The Sociology of Social Work*. London: Routledge.

Department of Health (DoH) (2002) *Requirements for Social Work Training*. London: Department of Health.

Department of Health (DoH) (2003) *Every Child Matters*. London: HMSO.

Department of Health (DoH) (2004) *Adult Services: Independence, Well-being and Choice*. London: HMSO.

Department of Health (DoH) (2005) *Independence, Well Being and Choice*. London: HMSO.

Department of Health and Social Security (DHSS) (1985) *Social Work Decisions in Child Care: Recent Research Findings and Their Implications*. London: HMSO.

Doel, M. (2005) *New Approaches to Practice Learning*. London: Practice Learning Taskforce.

Dominelli, L. (1996) 'Deprofessionalising social work: anti-oppressive practice, competencies and postmodernism', *British Journal of Social Work*, 26 (2): 153–75.

Dominelli, L. (2004) *Social Work*. Cambridge: Polity Press.

Etzioni, A. (ed.) (1969) *The Semi-Professions and Their Organisation*. London: Coller Macmillan.

Featherstone, B. (2006) 'Rethinking family support in the current policy context', *British Journal of Social Work*, 36 (1): 5–19.

Flynn, R. (1999) 'Managerialism, professionalism and quasi-markets', in M. Exworthy and S. Halrfod (eds), *Professionals and the New Managerialism in the Public Sector*. Buckingham: Open University Press.

Folgheraiter, F. (2004) *Relational Social Work*. London: Jessica Kingsley.

Fook, J., Ryan, M. and Hawkins, L. (2000) *Professional Expertise: Practice, Theory and Education for Working in Uncertainty*. London: Whiting & Birch.

Friedson, E. (1994) *Professionalism Reborn: Theory, Prophecy and Policy*. Cambridge: Polity Press.

Frost, N., Robinson, M. and Anning, A. (2005) 'Social workers in multidisciplinary teams: issues and dilemmas for professional practice', *Child and Family Social Work*, 10 (3): (August): 187–96.

Garrett, P.M. (2003) 'The trouble with Harry: why the "new agenda of life politics" fails to convince', *British Journal of Social Work*, 33: 381–97.

General Social Care Council GSCC (2002a) *Accreditation of Universities to Grant Degrees in Social Work*. London: GSCC.

General Social Care Council GSCC (2002b) *Code of Practice for Employees*. London: GSCC.

General Social Care Council GSCC (2003) *Statement of Commitment*. London: GSCC.

Greenwood, E. (1957) 'Attributes of a Profession', *Social Work*, 2 (3): 8–19.

Haines, J. (1976) *Skills and Methods in Social Work*. London: Constable.

Hall, S. (1996) 'New ethnicities' in D. Morley and K.H. Chen (eds) *Critical Dialogues in Cultural Studies*. London: Routledge.

Hallett, C. (1982) *The Personal Social Services in Local Government*. London: George Allen & Unwin.

Harbert, W. (1988) *The Welfare Industry*. Hadleigh: Holhouse Publications.

Harris, J. (1998) 'Scientific management, bureau-professionalism, new managerialism: the labour process of state social work', *British Journal of Social Work*', 28 (6): 839–62.

Harris, J. (2003) *The social work business*. London: Routledge.

Higham, P. (2006) 'The challenges of modernisation: how social work education is developing a new professionalism for social work', Keynote address, National Organisation for Practice Teaching Conference, 12 September 2006.

Hollis, F. (1970) 'The psychosocial approach to the practice of casework' in R.W. Roberts and R.H. Nee (eds), *Theories of Social Casework*. Chicago: University of Chicago Press.

Howe, D. (1991) 'Knowledge, power and the shape of social work practice' in M. Davies (ed.), *The Sociology of Social Work*. London: Routledge.

Jack, G. (2000) 'Ecological influences on parenting and child development', *British Journal of Social Work*, 30: 703–20.

James, A. (2004) 'The McDonaldization of social work – or "come back Florence Hollis all is (or should be forgiven)", in R. Lovelock, K. Lyons, and J. Powell (eds), *Reflecting on Social Work – Discipline and Profession*. Aldershot: Ashgate.

Johnson, T.J. (1972) *Professions and Power*. London: Macmillan.

Jordan, B. (2004) 'Emancipatory social work? Opportunity or oxymoron?' *British Journal of Social Work*, 34: 5–9.

Lovelock, R., Lyons, K. and Powell, J. (eds) (2004) *Reflecting on Social Work – Discipline and Profession*. Aldershot: Ashgate.

Lymbery, M. and Butler, S. (eds) (2004) *Social Work Ideals and Practical Realities*. Basingstoke: Macmillan.

Macdonald, K. (1997) *The Sociology of the Professions*. London: Sage.

Malherbe, M. (1982) *Accreditation in Social Work*. London: CCETSW.

McLaughlin, K. (2006a) 'A taste of their own medicine', Spiked Online 26/06/2006, http://www.spiked-online.com/index.php?/site/article/906/(accessed 20/01/07).

McLaughlin, K. (2006b) 'Regulation and risk: the General Social Care Council and the social work register in context', *British Journal of Social Work* Advanced Access published 24 July 2006, doi:10.1093/bjsw/bc1079.

Merton, R.K. (1968) *Social Theory and Social Structure* (3rd edn). Collier.

Morris, J. (1993) *Independent Lives? Community Care and Disabled People*. Basingstoke: Macmillan.

Noddings, N. (2002) Starting at Home, *Caring and Social Policy*. Berkeley and Los Angeles; University of California Press.

O'Hagan, K. (ed.) (1997) *Competence in Social Work Practice: A Practical Guide for Professionals*. London: Jessica Kingsley.

Oppenheimar, M. (1973) 'The proletarianisation of the professional', in P. Halmos (ed.), *Professionalisation and Social Change*, Monograph 20. Keele: University of Keele.

Orme, J. (2002) 'Social work: gender, care and justice', *British Journal of Social Work*, 32: 799–814.

Parkin, F. (1971) *Class Inequality and Political Order*. London: Paladin.

Parsons, T. (1954) *The Professions and Social Structure: Essays in Sociological Theory*.

Parton, N. (2003) 'Rethinking professional practice: the contributions of social constructionism and the feminist "ethics of care" ', *British Journal of Social Work*, 33: 1–16.

Payne, M. (1996) *What is Professional Social Work?* Birmingham: Venture Press.

Payne, M. (2004) *Teamwork in Multi-professional Care*. London: Palgrave Macmillan.

Pilisuk, M. and Hillier Parks, S. (1986) *The Healing Web, Social Networks and Human Survival*, Hanover, NH and London: University Press of New England.

Quality Assurance Agency for Higher Education (QAAHE) (2000) *Benchmarking Statements for Social Policy and Administration and Social Work*. Gloucester: QAAHE.

Sainsbury, E. (1977) *The Personal Social Services*. London: Pitman.

Shardlow, S.M. (1998) 'Values, ethics and social work', in R. Adams, L. Dominelli, (eds) and M. Payne, *Social Work: Themes, Issues and Debates*. London: Macmillan.

Skills for Care (2005) *The State of the Social Care Workforce 2004*, London: Skills for Care.

Stevenson, O. (2004) 'The future of social work', in M. Lymbery and S. Butler (eds), *Social Work Ideals and Practical Realities*. Basingstoke: Macmillan.

Thompson, N. (2002) *People Skills*. Basingstoke: Palgrave Macmillan.

Training Organisation for the Personal Social Services UK Partnership (TOPSS) (2002) *National Occupational Standards for Social Work*. Leeds: TOPSS.

Wickwar, H. and Wickwar, M. (1949) *The Social Services*. London: Bodley Head.

Williams, F. (2001) 'In and beyond New Labour: towards a new political ethics of care', *Critical Social Policy*, 21 (4): 467–93.

Younghusband, E. (1959) *Report of the Working Party on Social Workers in the Local Authority Health and Social Welfare Services*. London: HMSO.

Chapter 3

Practice with service-users, carers and their communities

Hilary Brown and Sheila Barrett

In this chapter we will be looking in more detail at the dynamic between users and professionals, as individuals but also collectively. When user and carer movements develop enough momentum they start to engage with, and challenge, the knowledge on which professional interventions are based. They also begin to challenge the gap between the status and rewards which accrue to professionals in comparison with their own, often precarious and marginalised, economic status. Increasingly, service-users argue that their own skills and resources should be mobilised and are locating solutions within their own networks. This changing emphasis impacts on individual relationships but also affects strategic and operational aspects of social care provision with knock-on effects for their leadership, structure, culture, policy and practice in areas such as recruitment, training and resource allocation.

Of course, not all of those who use health and social services identify themselves strongly as 'service-users'. Many people have contact with primary or acute health services on a more or less occasional basis – they visit their GP a few times a year, or are booked for day surgery or receive treatment over a short, contained period of time. These contacts with services are normative and tend to go unremarked; usually they do not lead to significant changes in social roles or economic status. For these 'users', the kind of involvement that matters most occurs at a *personal* level, for example through shared decision making about the specifics of their treatment and intervention. They may worry about *when* they receive treatment, wanting it to be at a time that least disturbs their work or family responsibilities, and/or be concerned, if in hospital, about the accommodation, privacy and the quality of the food. These concerns are often wrapped up in the rubric of 'consumerism', as these people 'consume' a discrete service for a limited period in their otherwise busy and valued lives.

But for those whose use of services is more protracted and pervasive, and who might belong to communities which are at risk of being marginalised, the relationship with 'services' is more problematical. These groups may come to be *defined by their use of services*, by themselves as well as by others. Moreover this identity as 'service-user' is stigmatised and seen as devaluing. As a result of it, they may find themselves squeezed out of other valued social roles, denied jobs, housing and decent incomes, and be subject to widespread discrimination. Assertive individuals may be able to defy these limitations and exert an impact in their day-to-day dealings with health and social care professionals, but it is *as collectives* – as user groups and movements (for example the disability movement, mental health survivors, people with AIDS and HIV, carers' groups and the Black pressure groups, women's and gay and lesbian networks within them) – that they can have the most influence. Their relationship to service providers has undergone major changes, to the point that these user-led organisations now *offer* services as well as *use* them. Groups have taken on more formal organisational identities in order to interact with statutory agencies, within a contract as opposed to a campaigning culture.

Moreover 'go-betweens', such as advocates and pressure groups, also find themselves operating in a more complex environment and holding services to account in, and through, more complex webs of accountability. More formal statutory roles have been put in place through the 2005 Mental Capacity Act, which has introduced Independent Mental Capacity Advocates (IMCAs) to support people who need help in decision-making about financial, health or welfare issues. It is likely that the Mental Health Act will also include formal advocacy in this vein.

The chapter is divided into three sections:

- Understanding the challenge to *theory* from people who use services.
- Listening to *feedback* through a range of channels, mechanisms and 'sound-barriers'.
- *Redesigning services* so that user-involvement is enshrined in decision-making structures.

Throughout the chapter we will show how complex the interaction of roles has become in terms of both individual *and* organisational relationships. Conflicts of interest and difficult boundary issues arise at every turn.

Terminology

The term 'user' is not ideal and, as Øvretveit (1996: 83) remarks,

> many of the commonly used terms fail to describe or connote the kind of relationship which some practitioners seek to create. 'Patient' is too passive for many roles, especially in rehabilitation. It is too medical for people with mental health problems and learning or physical disabilities. 'Consumer' and 'customer' are at the other end of the extreme, implying confidence, self-possession and certainty rather than a willingness to form a partnership to work together. Whilst 'user' may be appropriate in some settings where the aim is to discourage any dependency, it gives the impression of someone exploiting the practitioner and does not advance the idea of partnership.

Øvretveit coins the phrase 'co-service' for the collaborative style of work which he believes practitioners and service-users are aspiring towards in these long-term services.

But users are not the only ones with an axe to grind. Carers also lay claim to a body of expertise which challenges professional dominance, but their distinct and sometimes competing interests can place them at odds with their relatives and with the professionals who provide the services on which they also depend. It is ingenuous to ignore the extent to which carers' lives are also reliant on services and this makes them users in their own right as well as, and sometimes instead of, impartial advocates on behalf of their relatives. Brown, Orlowska and Mansell (1996) argued that service models that are framed exclusively in terms of choice for primary service-users often neglect carers' secondary reliance on services to enable them to work or attend to other family relationships or activities, and that this has the effect of disqualifying them from comment.

> Because the service is never explicitly acknowledged as being for the parent as well as for their son or daughter, their voices are easily silenced: they can be characterized as neither unbiased advocates for their relatives nor legitimate complainants on their own behalf.

> (Brown et al., 1996: 227)

Significantly, recent policies assert the need for positive outcomes for families alongside their disabled relatives, including participation in the workforce and income support to offset the costs of caring for their (disabled) child or adult relative.

Nevertheless, although lip-service is paid to providing an 'independent' assessment of their needs, the role of carers is often defined *by default* so that it grows to include those things which services *won't* provide, even if the rhetoric implies that it is shrinking to allow the service-user more independence. More 'flexible' or 'efficient' models of service often impose increased responsibilities on unpaid carers without any negotiation, as for example when old-fashioned but reliable day services for adults with learning disabilities are replaced by more targeted activities which occupy less time, or when hospitals discharge people home more quickly after surgery. These are rarely stated as potential conflicts of interest but they complicate the position of carers in relation to service agencies and create distrust. Carers come to be suspicious of high-sounding motives, especially when the implicit motivation for change is a financial one, shifting the share of care provided by social care agencies back on to the shoulders of unpaid carers, and thereby moving the responsibility from a public, shared sphere to a private and personal one. Carers who resist such moves can find themselves backed into a corner, arguing against progressive service development for their relative because it might have a negative impact on their own lives.

Glazer (1990) described how, in the USA, limits on acute hospital budgets forced through by insurance companies obliged carers to take on increasingly technical tasks when their relatives were discharged earlier from hospital. Glazer talked about this process as '*work transfer*' and used the shift towards self-service cafeterias and do-it-yourself and self-assembly strategies in other industries as parallels to what was happening in health and social care. When tasks change hands in this way they are often accompanied by a shift in language or ideology that demotes complex areas of care and reframes them as less difficult. Glazer emphasizes how 'change in one, paid work, prompts a change in the other, unpaid work' (1990). Tasks tend to be reassigned to the family solely because they are no longer paid for out of the public purse. Home then becomes not only a site of professional health care work but also a substitute for it, a '*provider unit*' in its own right.

Nor are these changes necessarily welcome to carers. When seriously ill patients are discharged early from hospital it is often assumed that family members will cope and little planning is done either around the caring work or the other responsibilities of those family members who are to take on this role. Visiting professionals may assume that carers have no other commitments and avoid discussing the implications for them of the caring tasks which they are being expected to take on. Bibbings reports that:

> Although the physical burden can be heavy, many carers would say that their worst problems are of an emotional nature. Carers feel isolated. They may also feel angry, resentful and embarrassed by the tasks they have to perform: they often feel a sense of loss for the person for whom they are caring, and in addition they feel guilty for having these feelings in the first place.
>
> (Bibbings, 1995)

High turnover and 'flexibility' among the workforce often militates against consistent partnership, leaving carers carrying the responsibility for continuity.

But relocation of the caring work also challenges the *legitimacy* of professional models and expertise and exposes the unfairness in pay structures when seen against the meagre rewards meted out to unpaid 'carers-as-substitute' workers. Passing on skills to unpaid carers becomes a new and contentious task for professionals and can be complicated by these underlying inequities and the resentments that can arise when the worker is seen as having more knowledge, but so much less ongoing responsibility.

Participation and involvement are not the same thing

Participation and involvement are not, however, the same. Begum (2006) describes how the terms 'participation' and 'user involvement' have 'become common currency'(p. 3), but she sees user involvement as being just one component of participation, saying that 'participation can be perceived as a journey to improve outcomes for service users, but instead of professionals being in the driving seat, service users and professionals travel together' (2006: 4).

The meaning of participation for children and young people in developing social care has also been elaborated by Wright et al. (2006: 9) using a whole-systems approach, identifying four essential components:

- Children and young people's involvement in individual decisions about their own lives as well as collective involvement in matters that affect them …
- A culture of listening that enables children and young people to influence decisions …
- Not an isolated activity, but a process by which children and young people are enabled to influence change within an organisation …
- Not a hierarchy where the 'aim' is to reach the top of the ladder … different levels of participation are valid for different groups of children and young people and at different stages of an organisation's development.

Understanding the challenges from people who use services

Organisational implications of increased participation

Organisations cannot 'do' participation without changing their own attitudes and structures: this is a prerequisite of involvement but also a consequence of interacting with people who are closer to those on the receiving end of their services. In order to facilitate meaningful roles for people who bring life experience and/or their experiences as service-users into professional structures, agencies have to be prepared for their agencies to come under scrutiny. A research study, *Looking on: Deaf People and the Organisation of Services*, conducted by Alys Young, Jennifer Ackerman and Jim Kyle in 1998, illustrated some of the barriers that stood in the way of more equal involvement of deaf people as workers in two mental health settings and in a school for deaf children. The authors articulated a series of tensions at three levels, theoretical, interpersonal and structural. Inequalities at one level were mirrored at another:

- theoretically, narrow interpretations of the problems faced by individual service-users led to inappropriate models of service;
- interpersonally, inaccessible environments (both physical and linguistic) reinforced feelings of exclusion; and
- structurally, employment practices were not sufficiently flexible to reward experience as fairly as more orthodox expertise.

These layers 'bled' into each other, making it difficult to translate an abstract commitment to equality between hearing and deaf workers into reality, when to do so would have required detailed attention to hierarchical structures, more flexible roles and responsibilities, training of both new and established workers and the creation of new routes for career progression. These themes are echoed in a range of other user-led initiatives and service settings and are explored below.

Broadening the knowledge base

Service-users have increasingly challenged the relevance and appropriateness of the knowledge base of the health and social care professions and are involved in generating theory about their position in the world, theory which rests on their analysis and lived experience. 'Theory' in this context is both explanatory and anticipatory: it is a body of knowledge that helps to locate causes and predict what might happen. Disabled people claim direct knowledge of how to cope in a culture which 'segregates and penalises differences' (Gillespie-Sells et al., 1998: 83) and argue for this to be translated into action at interpersonal and structural levels when devising new models of service and organisational forms.

Prior to this, biomedical theories have held sway with a very precise focus on individual impairment or disease at the level of the individual, but they do not 'explain' its interaction with social and economic factors to produce the limits and difficulties disabled people experience. Nor does a medical perspective address the reactions of others to disability or illness, or the persistence of barriers in the social and physical world. *Social models*, such as those developed by disabled academics and activists extend the scope of what is under examination, looking for broader, often interlocking explanations. A social model of disability looks beyond the causes and even the effects of an individual's impairment to the causes of their exclusion from, and disadvantages in, social and civic life, in housing, employment and culture (see, for example, Oliver, 1990). Within the social model disabled people differentiate between their impairment and the extent to which it is allowed, by society, to disadvantage them (that is, their disability). This 'social model' is mirrored in the movements of mental health survivors and people with learning disabilities who have developed their own understandings (Goodley, 1997) about mechanisms of exclusion and strategies for change.

In the services for deaf people referred to previously, the first challenge to orthodox practice rested on a redefinition of the 'problem' of deafness. The deaf community assert that it is not appropriate for them to be understood in terms of a medical model with deafness cast as an individual impairment, when instead their community can be located as a linguistic/cultural minority and their difficulties reframed as the result of social barriers to inclusion. The authors explain that deafness has traditionally been thought about in terms of what is missing, but that this alternative view

> emphasises what is *present* – a living language and a unique community. Deafness is defined in terms of a way of life, not in terms of a medical condition. Deaf people are valued for their own cultural identity … they are not seen as impaired versions of hearing people.
>
> (Young et al., 1998: 1)

This position has often been stated *in opposition* to biomedical models and to the power dynamics generated by a model whose only focus was on what was 'wrong' with the individual. Disabled people are not disputing the accuracy of a biomedical model (Shakespeare et al., 2006) but they say that it is *not enough*, because it leaves them in the role of 'tragic individuals' with no model of how to achieve change.

Any antagonism has been generated partly as a reaction to the fact that the medical establishment has been able to establish hegemony over other kinds of theorising and over spheres of intervention that their 'model' failed to address. For example, health professionals historically claimed the right to adjudicate beyond their initial rehabilitative remit into broader arenas such as sexuality, housing, benefits and employment. Doctors would often place themselves as arbiters in relation to ethical issues such as whether disabled people should be 'allowed' to have sexual relationships or bring up children. They often ended up directly or indirectly (through rationing practical assistance) exerting control over all aspects of the lives of individual disabled people, not only, or even, specific health-related issues. Most disabled people would seek active engagement in using and governing the use of advanced biomedical interventions but would argue that medical intervention at the time of an illness or injury should give way to social action and personal assistance (not care) when people come to (re)build their lives (Øvretveit, 1996).

The social model also leads to very different diagnoses as to what helpful interventions would entail. In relation to deafness, for example, the social model would question the prioritising of 'normalising' strategies such as 'publicly funding cochlear implant programmes over sign language and community education programmes' (Hogan, 1997), placing instead more emphasis on ongoing practical assistance and assistive technology than on time-limited professional assessments. One disabled woman responding to a survey reported that

> 'If I had had more help with my children I would not have felt so isolated. For instance, if I had been provided with a driver I would not have felt more disabled but more empowered as a disabled mother. They sent me an awful health visitor with very narrow views about disabled mothers.'

> (Cited in Gillespie-Sells et al., 1998: 114)

The solution proposed by the woman herself fundamentally challenged the role of professionals and the appropriateness of 'health' based interventions. The mother perceived the health visitor's role as starting from an assumption that she would not be able to cope rather than from a commitment to tailor practical help in such a way that it underpinned and extended her ability to manage. The social model shifts the focus from personal inadequacy to the availability and adequacy of assistance.

The benefits of user involvement

Given that user and carer involvement is not always easy to facilitate, it is helpful to dwell on the positive outcomes that arise out of it. In the study of services for deaf people a number of very tangible benefits were identified when deaf people were recruited as staff to work with deaf mental health service-users. The deaf workers fulfilled four important roles: in addition to their obvious *signing skills* and first-hand knowledge of deaf culture, deaf workers were thought to be able to *empathise* with the particular forms of exclusion experienced by deaf people, to provide *role models* for deaf people and to *educate their hearing colleagues* about deaf issues, thereby dispelling stereotypes. The visible presence of deaf adults in services for deaf children was particularly valued because the children's confidence rose through 'recognising themselves in some of the adults around them' (Young et al., 1998: 6).

These advantages of user involvement in service delivery can be extrapolated to other settings. Mental health service-users who return to work in services may be more sensitive to and tolerant of, other users who are experiencing distressing symptoms. This has been encouraged within a network of services which all sign up to a charter that enshrines user-involvement in running and managing service provision called the Clubhouse movement. Self-help groups, whether for survivors of abuse or people with alcohol problems, also work on this basis. There may be particular issues to be faced in facilitating user involvement in services for older people, which have yet to be articulated but the same principles clearly apply.

While the *presence* of people who use, or have used, services in caring and leadership roles may not in itself be enough to guarantee a good service, their *absence* certainly undermines any stated commitment to empowerment in mission statements or public rhetoric. It robs people who use services of valuable insights, it leaves them without role models and it prevents disabled adults from passing on their stories. One disabled activist remarked that she could see no way anyone could set up any kind of service … if there was no consultation or representation of that client group in the workforce. If there is no collegial equality, there is unlikely to be a feeling of respect for the client group, albeit on an unconscious level.

(Andri White, 1996, no page number)

Partnership Boards, introduced into learning disability services under the auspices of 'Valuing People' (Department of Health, 2001), operate on this basis to include both people with learning disability and their relatives and carers in the design, prioritisation, and management of services.

Listening to feedback

About individual service provision …

Most professionals are not content to involve users in these more global ways without also embracing a commitment to increasing participation in decision making at an *individual* level (Øvretveit, 1996), but the rhetoric of person-centred planning and individual budgets has to sit within a more objective commitment to equity and rationing which is often carried out on the basis of increasingly routinised assessment. The two systems risk developing in parallel without enough overlap. Person-centred planning is developing its own modus operandi, based on 'circles of support', which seek to galvanise members of the person's informal network into providing a broader range of activities and support than can be guaranteed through paid-for service provision. There are tensions in locating the engine of service planning in informal networks, and equity of provision may become the first casualty. Middle-class, well-resourced families may indeed be able to mobilise a helpful team, whereas other more beleaguered communities may struggle to become, or to stay, motivated. Moreover, the model pioneered with those who have more pervasive and/or multiple intellectual disabilities, works on the basis of relatives taking the lion's share of the responsibility, whereas many service-users do not necessarily want their parents or relatives to be closely involved in their lives – indeed some struggle to create appropriate boundaries and to keep their families from burdening them with *their* problems, or taking over their accommodation or benefits, not the other way around. These assumptions were recently laid bare in a small study of people with learning disabilities whose person-centred plans were being drawn up against a backdrop of abuse, a study which challenged the notion that communities are always supportive, and that it is 'always the vicar who features in the PCP literature and never the loan shark!' (Brown and Scott, 2006: xx).

Nevertheless, 'direct payments' and individual budgets enable disabled people to manage their own care and dismantle many of the 'givens' in the user/worker relationship. The 2003 Valuing People document and the 2006 Social Care Green Paper all signal that these new forms of funding are to be encouraged. But although new types of direct health care work/personal assistance place individual workers in a very different hierarchical relationship to their 'user/employer', there are still problems and a complex set of personal interactions to manage as boundaries are crossed and re-crossed, especially in the giving of personal care. Flynn's recent research (2005) showed that abuse was still a risk despite the fact that the relationship had been redefined as 'working *for'*, and constituted a challenge to the usual 'professional' knowledge-base and hierarchical ways of working. Service-users in these schemes employ their assistants directly, manage the worker directly, and cut across existing career paths and employment patterns. Nevertheless, 'the arguments in favour of cash are that people are placed in control and the money is symbolic of this control' (Doyle, 1995: 43). Black service-users in one study were shown to be even more in favour of direct payments than their white counterparts (1995: 43), perhaps reflecting their even greater disempowerment in relation to traditional service providers.

About broader service development issues ...

Clearly there is a distinction between running an organisation and being asked to give your views on the services offered to you – the difference between being a member of the board and a regular customer. Winkler remarked that consumer models tend to redefine 'structural problems as problems of communication', and that this

> vision of customer relations extends to reducing the waits at the check-out counter and exchanging faulty goods with the minimum of questions asked. It does not extend, even at Marks and Spencers, to inviting customers on to the board, nor to consulting them about investment or even about what should be on the shelves, let alone in their products. The supermarket model certainly does not mean that retailers help customers sue manufacturers of products that have caused harm.
>
> (1987: 1)

Barnes and Walker (1996: 379) also point out the problems of relying on individuals to act as 'consumers' when they may be 'mentally disabled, frail or vulnerable' and when they are not in a 'position to shop around or have any realistic prospect of exit'. Carpenter (1994) takes a similarly pessimistic view arguing that

> The new public management has no strategy for tackling the social causes of disadvantage because it largely takes for granted the wider social context of inequality in which public services operate ... it has no realistic strategy for dealing with the fact that inequalities of class gender, 'race', disability and age constrain the ability of people to act as informed consumers.
>
> (1994: 91)

Although the concept of social exclusion has been elaborated since that time, it is still the case that service-users come to the table occupying very disadvantaged roles and speaking of realities that are usually not voiced in public discourses.

Service-level consultation takes place in a range of meetings and forums (see London Boroughs Grants Committee, 1997), including residents' committees, user panels, individual representatives on management boards or committees, customer surveys, suggestion boxes and more formal complaints procedures. Disabled people tend not to be well represented on the governing bodies of agencies serving them and the proportion of disabled people is usually outweighed by non-disabled 'experts' (Brown et al., 1998) but there are some honorable exceptions including, for example, the Spinal Injuries Association which has embedded user control within their constitution, with 75 per cent of its management committee having to be a service-user and elected by the membership.

Conflicting assumptions tend to surface in these consultation exercises, which are often ill-defined and badly timed. Many service providers opt for high-profile public meetings in preference to ongoing involvement and consultation, but while commissioners often favour the concept of the public meeting, consultees feel particularly angry if they sense that decisions have already been made or that they are being invited to rubber-stamp a proposal and not help to shape it. Bodies are often set up that have contested remits and more or less 'teeth', with conflicts of interest when they seek to bite the hands which are often also feeding them. Moreover, they tend to give disproportionate space to more vociferous sections of the community.

If participation is to succeed it is important that there is an infrastructure that enables the views of all sections of a community – particularly the most vulnerable, including women and children, and Black and other minority ethnic service-users (see Campbell and Lindow, 1996) – and for arrangements to be in place so that their views can be reliably channelled through to decision makers. Hundal (2006) has questioned whether this is what happens, arguing that:

> One of the main barriers to an open discussion is the system of representation. When the first generation of African-Caribbean and Asian migrants came to this country, politicians did not make much effort to engage them or understand their concerns. In recent years, as the numbers have grown and socio-economic issues have come to the fore, politicians have changed tack. Rather than engaging with these communities locally and constructively, they want so-called community leaders to do the job for them.

This, he argues, is inherently problematic, particularly in relation to faith communities, as the organisations that governments and their agencies tend to rely on

> reflect a narrow range of predominantly conservative opinion. They generally ignore non-religious, liberal or progressive opinions and yet claim to represent everyone of their particular faith. Any criticism, from the outside or within, is portrayed as an attack on the religion itself, making it more difficult to hold the groups to account. Worse, they largely consist of first-generation, middle-aged men who are out of touch with second and third-generation Britons. (Hundal, 2006)

Begum (2006) has also commented on the tendency to consult through Black community leaders and professionals, commenting that there may actually have been a *decrease* in the participation of Black and minority ethnic service-users. She locates this reluctance in a number of myths that are held about them and their communities, including such mistaken assumptions as that they lack interest in participation; that their communities look after their own; that their agencies are already working with them; and that the broader user movement is competently addressing issues of diversity. Begum (2006) asserts that these myths deter direct consultation with people who use services and argues for more resources to facilitate properly coherent participation.

Other tensions and contradictions also hamper the usefulness of user groups when advocating for what are essentially 'minorities within minorities' (Shakespeare et al., 1996: 182). For example in the disability movement gender and/or sexual orientation may be as salient as (dis)ability in relation to some issues, and fractures may appear. Shakespeare, Gillespie-Sells and Davis remark on this potential for contradictory attitudes to inclusiveness:

> Within identity group politics, it has always to be remembered that ... there are multiple oppressions, and that being progressive about one issue does not automatically mean being progressive about other issues.
>
> (1996: 182)

Involvement therefore requires a critical approach to the issue of representativeness and its reverse face, 'tokenism'. At it simplest tokenism can be seen in situations where individuals are asked to represent others without being supported to engage in proper consultation from the ground upwards, so that it becomes unclear whether a representative is there for themselves or for others, and unclear if they are passing on raw material or filtering information through the lens of approved hierarchies within as well as between communities. Even where representativeness has been attended to, situations may be set up in such a way as to minimise a user's chance of being powerful. For example, they are often isolated on committees or management boards leading Campbell and Lindow (1996) to advise: 'Never place one or two service users in a position of being greatly outnumbered by professional people. This can be an overwhelming situation.' But there is also genuine confusion about what role individuals can play, and Beresford and Campbell identify a conflict between

> competing models and cultures of democracy. While movements of disabled people and other service users have placed an emphasis on a participatory model of democracy the service world is firmly located in a representative system of democracy and bases its efforts to involve service users on a representative model of democracy.
>
> (1994: 323)

Users who represent the movement may indeed not be 'representative' in the sense of being 'typical', because they need to be more forceful than other users and this may actually be used to challenge their legitimacy where, for example, a forceful hospital consultant would not be so challenged. Beresford and Campbell declare that users who do the representing rapidly turn into activists who challenge assumptions, commenting that

> getting involved may not only lead to change, but also change *us*. We become different. We become 'unrepresentative' in ways some service providers do not want. We become confident, experienced informed and effective.
>
> (1994: 317)

Supporting user groups and networks also requires funding because users are not normally financially advantaged and activism gives rise to direct costs. But this also risks creating conflicts of interest as funding may be seen to depend on toeing the line.

In a seminal paper Winkler (1987: 2) argued that 'the key to any serious concept of consumerism is the principle of outside scrutiny', and she looked forward to more real partnership arrangements between providers and users. She argued that the latter could only be achieved if structural change underpinned emerging partnerships by making the relationships between users and practitioners more equal.

Learning from complaints

So we have seen that inequalities form a pervasive backdrop to the operation of both informal and formal (statutory) complaints systems. A naive view of complaints procedures might assume that a lack of complaints means that all is well, but this needs to be challenged by urging service agencies to set up a context within which it is possible to complain. A service with no complaints is not necessarily a good service – merely one in which users feel unable to voice their concerns. Conversely, a service where people do complain is not necessarily a bad one. It may simply be an indication that people do feel free to assert themselves. Wood (1995) used Lukes' analysis of different levels of power as a framework to describe different patterns of complaint making and resolution in mental health services. She distinguished between services in which there were:

- many complaints but few upheld (in Lukes' model this is one dimensional power), in that one side has more resources – in this case credibility – and this enables them to prevail at times of conflict)
- few complaints (in Lukes' model two dimensional power) where power is used to create barriers to complaining which prevent complaints being made rather than to dismiss them once they have surfaced
- no complaints (in Lukes' model three dimensional power) which prevents people 'from having grievances by shaping their perceptions, cognitions and preferences in such a way as they accept their role in the existing order of things ... '

(Lukes, 1977: 24)

People may not complain about a service if their views have been consistently suppressed within it, and services which fail to make space for users to comment freely are more likely to make users compliant than to generate complaints.

So how does a service set out to help service users complain? Most Health Trusts have a PALs (Patient Advocacy and Liaison Service), which operates across and outside traditional line-management structures to facilitate complaints and to help resolve them at an early stage (NAHAT, 1996). This can be a difficult 'go-between' role to manage as it involves maintaining a distance in relation to one's professional colleagues. Often the role involves remedying misunderstandings and re-establishing communication (especially where insufficient allowance has been made for the distressed state of patients and relatives), but it can also involve troubleshooting between professions and departments. Sometimes the role extends to enabling patients to make formal complaints or seek legal redress, but from the Trust's point of view the remit is really to defuse complaints at an earlier stage through counselling and mediation. Some might argue that this neutralises legitimate anger and softens any challenges brought to bear on the traditional structures and practices of professional power, but others would accept that the presence of an advocate, albeit one employed by the body against whom the complaint is directed, may facilitate the acceptance of feedback since informal complaints are less likely to be dealt with in defensive mode. It will be interesting to see whether a formal statutory mandated advocacy service, such as the Independent Mental Capacity Advocates and the mooted Mental Health Advocates, will be able to prevail against these pressures.

Interpreters are another group who occupy this potentially ambivalent space and are tasked with providing a very specific and boundaried input at the interface between the primary user and the professional. Training, briefing and debriefing are essential to the process to counteract the potential for interpreters to slide into over-reliance on their own personal and cultural values to the point of biasing their literal account of the encounter. Practitioners report that at times service-users who belong to small communities fear that personal information will be circulated to their community with negative consequences for them, particularly in relation to domestic violence, mental health and other stigmatised issues. There can be added difficulties when meaning gets lost in translation and this is a fear for service workers just as much as for service-users (see Ravall and Smith, 2003; Ravall, 2005).

Redesigning services to take users into account

Inclusive organisational cultures

Achieving flexibility (see Barnes and Walker, 1996: 379) can be difficult, especially when it comes to employing people on the basis of their life experience instead of more orthodox qualifications. In the services for deaf people referred to earlier in this chapter, the researchers homed in on the mismatch between the low occupational status of deaf workers and the high intrinsic value they brought to service delivery. Few deaf people hold related professional qualifications, often because of educational barriers so, in these settings, they had been 'slotted into' ready-made but subsidiary posts which hearing people used to occupy, for example posts as nursing auxiliaries or teaching assistants. The researchers characterised this as trying to 'fit a square peg into a round hole, where the round hole would not change shape' (Young et al., 1998: 9). Hearing staff voiced concern about exploiting their deaf colleagues whose job descriptions usually failed to describe their jobs accurately. Should they ask them to do more than they were being paid for? Should they invite them to management meetings when others at their 'grade' would not be expected to attend? How could they be promoted when they had come in to the work through an untraditional route with skills which were not recognised or accredited? Young, Ackerman and Kyle (1998) argued that this low-status/high-value tension 'disrupts' the normal expectation that qualifications, skills and experience would be brought together in individual practitioners, leading them to suggest that their presence provoked uncomfortable questions for both deaf and hearing people ... People questioned the value of professional qualifications if those without them nonetheless had fundamental skills that enabled them to do the job ... if deaf staff's contribution was really so important why were the majority of them the ones who did the most menial jobs?

(1998: 7)

The researchers located these problems (and potential solutions) at a structural level, even though they tend to be expressed at an interpersonal one. They advocated breaking down traditional roles and placing more emphasis on competence than qualification. They concluded that:

Situations is created in which individual professionals, be they deaf or hearing, are unlikely to possess all the pieces of the jigsaw that would allow them to do their job: professional qualifications, deaf centred skills and experience. Rather these three elements are distributed between deaf and hearing staff – each making a vital contribution.

(1998: 30)

Developing organisational structures which facilitate user involvement

When it comes to running services it is clear that users operate on a continuum from complete control and governance of their own autonomous organisations through to more marginal forms of consultation and influence, and often it is the structure of these organisations that indicates the true commitment to user involvement not its rhetoric. Wright et al. (2006) describe four interlinked components that make up the whole system; these are an organisation's culture, structure, practice and review.

Whole-systems approaches such as appreciative inquiry (AI) (Bushe, 1995) have been used to foster inclusion by bringing all parts of the system into balance. As a methodology AI seeks to recognise and appreciate what is positive about the whole system and to build upon what works well. Reed et al. (2002: 37) applied this model to improving the lives of older people going home from hospital, and to further this they described an event which had representation from 37 different agencies, and they argued that such an approach 'offers much where interagency working is needed in a blame free environment' (2002: 45). They also highlighted the importance of recognising and addressing the conflicts across systems such as those between service-users and service providers, especially when service-users may not have a strong enough voice to feel that they can dissent.

Clubhouse mental health services also provide an alternative model for people with enduring mental health problems, and are explicitly designed to support user involvement rather than tacking it on as an afterthought. Clubhouse services belong to a federation which sets out standards designed to guarantee this high level of user involvement, stipulating that they work without a hierarchy between users (who are referred to as 'members') and staff. Internally, members sit on staff interviews and are involved in staff supervision:

all meetings are open to members and staff and all the space is equally accessible, with an 'open doors' policy so that members do not get the feeling that people are talking behind closed doors. All the day-to-day tasks such as providing lunch, administering the transitional employment programme, and so on, become opportunities for co-working.

Other organisations *of* (as opposed to *for*) disabled people function as independent agencies – they may provide services and information to their members (as descendants of the 'self-help' movement which pioneered user-led agendas and service provision) and/or contract with the statutory sector to provide services to clients of health and social care services. This is an important distinction and some commentators have suggested that by becoming service providers the voluntary sector has lost some of its independence when it comes to campaigning or challenging statutory services (Rickford, 1998: 20). Black voluntary organisations have been particularly affected by this shift, as they were often smaller and more local than the large charities that have moved wholesale into a service provider role.

Conclusion

In this chapter we have seen how user and carer movements have challenged professional practice at a number of levels. Disabled people and other user groups have theorised their position in broader social terms and have challenged both the rationales for the service models on offer and the way these are delivered. They have argued for different kinds of input to, and from, service agencies, namely involvement which allows them to control practical assistance in their own lives while contributing to wider societal changes. Within services users have moved into practitioner and management roles in their own organisations and have taken on the role of arranging their own care as individuals and collectives. In larger, more traditional service organisations users are routinely consulted and complaints encouraged and/or actively facilitated. This has necessitated new skills on the part of professionals as well as new organisational structures.

This is not to say that disabled people and other user groups have stopped wanting and needing 'professional' health and social care but that they wish to access it, shape it, monitor it and evaluate it for themselves and on their own terms. User-focused services rely on open channels for feedback, complaints and accountability. This is a fundamental challenge to organisational structures and professional interventions and has led to the integration of a broader knowledge base into health and social care services – one which seeks to combine specific 'professional' expertise with the resources and resilience which grow out of lived experience.

References

Alcohol Concern (1996) *Consulting People who Use Alcohol Services.* London: Alcohol Concern.

Barnes, M. and Walker, A. (1996) 'Consumerism vs empowerment: a principled approach to the involvement of older service users', *Policy and Politics*, 24 (4): 375–93.

Begum, N. (2006) *Doing it for Themselves: Participation and Black and Minority Ethnic Service Users,* Report 14. London: Social Care Institute for Excellence and Race Equality Unit.

Beresford, P. and Campbell, J. (1994) 'Disabled people, service users, user involvement and representation', *Disability and Society*, 9 (3): 315–25.

Bibbings, A. (1995) 'Carers and professionals – the carer's viewpoint', in A. Leathard, (ed.), *Going Interprofessional: Working Together for Health and Social Welfare*. New York: Routledge.

Brown, H. (2004) *Citizens not Patients: Developing Innovative Approaches to Meet the Needs of Disabled People.* Strasbourg: Council of Europe.

Brown, H. and Scott, K. (2006) 'Person centred planning and the adult protection process', in P. Cambridge and S. Carnaby (eds), *Person Centred Planning and Care Management for People with Learning Disabilities.* London, Jessica Kingsley.

Brown, H., Orlowska, D. and Mansell, J. (1996) 'From campaigning to complaining', in J. Mansell and K. Ericsson, *Deinstitutionalization and Community Living: Intellectual Disability Services in Britain, Scandinavia and the USA,* London: Chapman and Hall. pp. 225–78.

Brown, H., Croft-White, C., Stein, J. and Wilson, C. (1998) *Taking the Initiative: Supporting the Sexual Rights of Disabled People: a Service Agenda.* Brighton: Rowntree/Pavilion Publishing.

Bushe, G.R. (1995) 'Advances in appreciative inquiry as an organization development intervention', *Organization Development Journal,* 13 (3): 14–15.

Campbell, P. and Lindow, V. (1996) *Changing Practice: Mental Health Nursing and User Empowerment.* London: Royal College of Nursing with Broadmoor Patients Council.

Carpenter, M. (1994) *Normality is Hard Work: Trade Unions and the Politics of Community Care.* London: Lawrence & Wishart with Unison.

Croft, S. and Beresford, P. (1992) 'The politics of participation', *Critical Social Policy*, 35: 20–44.

Department of Health (2001) *Valuing People: White Paper on Services for People with Learning Disabilities.* London: HMSO.

Doyle, Y. (1995) 'Disability: use of an independent living fund in south east London and users' views about the system of cash versus care provision', *Journal of Epidemiology and Community Health*, 49: 43–7.

Dworkin, A. (1979) 'Look Dick Look. See Jane blow it', published in *Letters from a War Zone* (1988) New York: Secker & Warburg.

Flynn, M. (2005) *Developing the Role of Personal Assistants: A TOPSS Pilot Project Examining New and Emerging Roles in Social Care.* Sheffield: University of Sheffield, School of Nursing.

Gillespie-Sells, K., Hill, M. and Robbins, B. (1998) *She Dances to Different Drums: Research into Disabled Women's Sexuality.* London: Kings Fund.

Glazer, N. (1990) 'The home as workshop: women as amateur nurses and medical care providers', *Gender and Society*, 4: 479–500.

Goodley, D. (1997) 'Locating self advocacy in models of disability: understanding disability in the support of self-advocates with learning difficulties', *Disability and Society*, 12 (3).

Hogan, A. (1997) 'Issues impacting on the governance of deafened adults', *Disability and Society*, 12 (5): 789–803.

Hundal, S. (2006) 'This system of self appointed leaders can hurt those it should be protecting', *Guardian,* 20 November.

Lindow, V. and Rooke-Matthers, S. (1998) 'The experiences of mental health service users as mental health professionals', Rowntree Finding Series. York: Joseph Rowntree Foundation.

London Boroughs Grants Committee (1997) *A Guide to User Feedback Methods.* London: LBGC.

Lukes, S. (1977) *Power: A Radical View.* London: Macmillan.

Meyer, J. (1993) 'Lay participation in care: a challenge for multidisciplinary teamwork', *Journal of Interprofessional Care*, 7 (1): 57–66.

Morris, J. (1993) 'Gender and disability', in J. Swain, V. Finkelstein, S. French and M. Oliver. *Disabling barriers-enabling environments.* London: Sage, pp. 85–92.

NAHAT (National Association of Health Authorities and Trusts) (1996) *Complaints: Listening, Acting, Improving … Guidance on Implementation of NHS Complaints Procedures*. Leeds: Department of Health.

Oliver, M. (1988) 'The social and political context of educational policy', in L. Barton (ed.), *The Politics of Special Educational Needs*. Lewes: Falmer Press.

Oliver, M. (1990) *The Politics of Disablement*. London: Macmillan.

Oliver, M. (1992) 'Changing the social relations of research production', *Disability, Handicap and Society*, 7: 101–14.

Øvretveit, J. (1996) 'How patient power and client participation affects relations between professions', in J. Øvretveit, P. Mathias and T. Thompson (eds), *Interprofessional Working for Health and Social Care*. London: Macmillan, pp. 79–102.

Peck, E. and Barker, I. (1997) 'Users as partners in mental health – ten years of experience', *Journal of Interprofessional Care*, 11 (3): 269–77.

Rachmaran, P. and Grant, G. (1994) 'Setting one agenda for empowering persons with a disadvantage within the research process', in M. Rioux and M. Bach (eds), *Disability is Not Measles*. Ontario: Roeher Institute, pp. 227–45.

Raval, H. (2005) 'Being heard and understood in the context of seeking asylum and refuge: communicating with the help of bilingual co-workers', *Clinical Child Psychology and Psychiatry*, 10 (2) (April): 197–216.

Raval, H. and Smith, J. (2003) 'Therapists' experiences of working with language interpreters', *International Journal of Mental Health*, 32 (2) (Summer): 6–31.

Reed, J., Pearson, P., Douglas, B., Swinburne, S. and Wilding, H. (2002) 'Going home from hospital – an appreciative inquiry study', *Health and Social Care in the Community,* 10 (1): 36–45.

Rickford, F. (1998) 'Partner or put upon?' *Community Care (*29 Jan.–4 Feb.): 20–21. Posted 9 May 2000.

Shakespeare, T., Gillespie-Sells, K. and Davies, D. (1996) *The Sexual Politics of Disability: Untold Desires*. London: Cassell.

White, A. (1996) in 'Sexuality and Physical Disability', Report of a Conference held on 14 June, SE Regional Trainers Forum, c/o Health Promotion Department, Canterbury, Kent.

Williamson, C. (1992) *Whose Standards? Consumer and Professional Standards in Health Care*, Buckingham: Open University Press.

Winkler, E. (1987) 'Consumerism in health care: beyond the supermarket model', *Policy and Politics*, 15: 1–8.

Wood, D. (1995) *Complaint Procedures in Mental Health Services* (SETRHA).

Wright, P., Turner, C., Clay, D. and Mills, H. (2006) 'Participation of children and young people in developing social care', *Practice Guide*, No. 6. London: Social Care Institute for Excellence.

Young, A., Ackerman, J. and Kyle, J. (1998) *Looking on: Deaf People and the Organisation of Services*. Bristol: Policy Press.

Chapter 4

Working with complexity: managing workload and surviving in a changing environment

Keith Edwards, Chris Hallett and Phil Sawbridge

Today's social workers have to deal with complexity both within the social care task and within the organisation, while still retaining professional discretion. Balancing all these complexities is the guide to survival, meeting the needs of the service-user while also contributing to the needs for corporate accountability, all within a social care world in the midst of change.

The dimensions of complexity will be examined to provide social workers with the context of how to survive in the workplace. Both managers and social workers talk about surviving because it is recognised that social work is a stressful role and managing this stress is a key factor for both the individual and the organisation. A key factor in managing stress is the ability of managers and social workers working together to manage their workload. Often in the everyday life of social work agencies there will not be a neat balance between the tasks to be completed and the availability of social work time. Decision making will be constrained by a number of issues, including the volume of work, the level and urgency of need, and the level of staffing, skill and experience within the social work team.

The issue of workload and how to manage it is a perennial problem across the range of social work agencies, from the small voluntary to the statutory sector, whether involving groupwork, community work or work with individuals. It is not just about finding someone to do the work; it is about finding the right work for each worker. While examples of how to manage complexity within workloads will be given later, it is important to stress that the principles outlined in specific areas are transferable across the range of social work settings.

The complexity of workloads

In the Victoria Climbié Inquiry report Lord Laming, although referring to local authority children's teams, described the general principle for allocating work.

The proper and well-thought-out allocation of cases is a central component of the effective management of a social work team … there will be significant variations among a given group of social workers as to their respective levels of experience, training and expertise… Perhaps most important of all, some will have more available time than others by virtue of their current workloads. All of these factors are relevant to the decision of which social worker should be allocated a particular case.

(Department of Health, 2003b: 200)

We quote Laming because this has been an explicit and high-status recent reference to managing workloads in social work. For this to be effective the manager must know the ability and experience levels of the social workers in their team and the precise state of their current workloads. Laming also noted that workload is more than a list of cases, because some pieces of work require far more time and attention than others. Similarly, it is not just the cases being held, or the groupwork being run, or the projects under way, but the full range of other duties, work and responsibility the worker has for the agency.

Laming went on to make two further recommendations about local authority child care social work but the principles apply broadly across all social work practice.

- Directors of social services must ensure that no case is allocated to a social worker unless and until his or her manager ensures that he or she has the necessary training, experience and time to deal with it properly.
- When allocating a case to a social worker, the manager must ensure that the social worker is clear as to what has been allocated, what action is required and how that action will be reviewed and supervised.

(2003b: 200)

The importance of managing workload is further endorsed in the Welsh Assembly reviews of social work (Garthwaite, 2006), the Scottish *21st Century Report* (Scottish Executive, 2006) and the *Options for Excellence* review (DfES, 2006).

In a background paper to the *Options for Excellence* review, Statham, Cameron and Mooney (2006) reported a number of key findings on how social workers used their time or were forced to use their time.

- Many (social workers and managers) reported it was not possible to complete their work within their contracted hours and many did additional hours or completed paperwork at home.
- Field social workers in all authorities raised concerns about the small amount of direct work they were able to do with children and families, estimating that a quarter or less of their time was spent on this and that it was mostly in response to crises.
- When working with looked-after children a large proportion of time was taken up with finding suitable placements, and travelling to and from placements outside the authority.
- Social workers did things because of the level of administrative support and the inadequacy of IT systems that were not a cost effective use of their time. This was true of social workers across all client groups.

This is all consistent with our experience of social workers talking about the demands of record keeping, using electronic systems, and completing key documentation. Statham, Campbell and Mooney also suggest that different kinds of children's social workers have different approaches to practice. While front-line children's social workers may be wary about the use of assessments and plans, leaving-care social workers were much more positive. The difference in view was not about the documents in themselves, but about the approach of practice.

> The fundamental difference was that the leaving care workers approached the pathway plan as an assessment that was completed in consultation with the young person; completing the paperwork for the pathway plan and meeting with the young person were not viewed as discrete tasks. Instead of reducing the time available to undertake direct work with young people, the completion of the pathway plan was perceived as a means of supporting and structuring this work.
>
> (Statham et al., 2006, quoting from Holmes and Ward, 2004: 6–7)

This serves to illustrate that how social workers spend their time reflects their (and their agencies') approach to practice, and how practitioners engage with their service-users. Whatever the agency, whatever the client group, similar choices have to be made about how to focus social workers' time on doing direct social work with clients and how to provide the administrative support.

Managing workload

The table below illustrates the various considerations required of the manager and supervisee undertaking a workload management exercise. The priority given to each dimension will vary depending upon the particular circumstances of each case.

Experience has shown that if a workload management scheme is to be introduced, then there are fears to be allayed. Some managers fear that the introduction of a system that sets limits upon the activity expected from staff may mean that they will be unable to allocate work.

Conversely, practitioners may fear a limit being placed upon their discretion to act and the placing of further expectations upon them at a time when they feel stretched to breaking-point. If negotiated carefully by both parties, workload management provides protection for the practitioner by setting limits upon the demands on their time, and identifies when they have no capacity to take on more work. For the manager it ensures that clear expectations have been set and that activity has been prioritised to ensure the best use of the resources available. Effective workload management can, therefore, be seen to meet the needs of both manager and practitioner and is coherent with effective supervision practice.

The national vision for 2020 is that 'effective workload management systems will offer more support for workers, clearer information for managers, better safeguards for service users and reduce inefficiency' (DfES, 2006: 50).

Table 4.1   Checklist for workload management

Issue	Question	Further considerations
Priority/risk	What are the key tasks for the client/project at this point in time?	• If the priority is high, then these tasks might need to take priority over others, or over the work of others.
Focus	What is 'key' about the activity in terms of precision and skill required?	• Does this worker have the skill required? • Is there anyone in the team who is better placed to undertake the task, either in terms of skill, or relationship to the client? • Are there training or developmental issues to be addressed?
Managing volume and scheduling	Can the tasks be done in the time available in the next time period?	• Does the worker have the time in the coming period? • If not, can s/he do other tasks later? • If not, can someone else do these now?
Time management	Is the activity being organised and scheduled to maximum effect?	• Is this a reasonable amount of time for this worker to take on this work with this client?
Accountability	Is the work being completed to national and agency requirements?	• Are there national and local standards for the delivery of this service? • Are we aiming to undertake the work to that appropriate standard?
Quality assurance	Is the work purposeful? Are objectives clear and are those objectives being met?	• Is the work being organised in the right way to achieve what needs to be done? • How will we monitor the impact of what is done?
Resource management	Does the work represent the most efficient and cost-effective way of achieving desired outcomes?	• Is the work fairly distributed across the team? • Can any work be re-allocated in terms of volume, complexity or scheduling to make the distribution more equitable? • Or potentially more effective? • Is there a case for additional resources to be allocated to this work?
Stress	How does the worker manage the stress that this activity will generate?	

Approaches to workload management

There are three different approaches to workload management described in the literature (Orme and Glastonbury, 1993; Wingham, 2002). Essentially, an activity is given a numerical rating, and significance is apportioned to the different elements shown in Table 4.1.

Those approaches are:

1. Priority/complexity – based on the complexity/priority/risk of the work to be undertaken.
2. Case/work type – based on the amount of time required.
3. Hybrid – where there is some combination of 1 and 2.

In the first approach, the complexity of the case is determined against a graduated scale of complexity, typically a 5-point scale. The agency identifies an optimum number of points a worker should carry and cases are allocated to that level.

In the second approach, points or time in hours are allocated to work or a case, depending upon the focus or type – for example, a community care assessment would be assumed to take a certain number of points hours. The agency would identify an optimum number of points a worker should carry or hours that can be allocated to and work is allocated to that level.

The third approach would be some combination of the first two. Allan, Ward and Bekenn (1996) evaluated an approach used in one local authority in the early 1990s. This was a hybrid of 'time' and 'priority'; the time element involved using an analysis of the time taken to complete previous work tasks from data over a reasonable length of time to model and predict the time required for anticipated tasks. This was combined with a weighting based on priority, status and the vulnerability of the service-user to risk. The strength of the approach was that the implementation of change was carefully managed, and this included an explicit policy on workload. But the calculations were complex. The overall conclusion was that:

> Its impact on individual working agreements and supervision was variable. It echoed staff's experiences of supervision. Some staff used the schedule to work out approaches to work and altering priorities. Other staff continued to use supervision to concentrate on individual cases and not examine their workload as a whole.

> (Allan et al., 1996: 13).

The approach that has been adopted in Warwickshire County Council is a variation of the third approach, and is based on the experience of local managers and workers. It allocates time/hours based on the time required to complete tasks. The time allocated depends upon the time required and does not assume that workers will work with a standard approach or efficiency. This last approach was formally adopted by Warwickshire in 2004. It was chosen because it was the easiest to calculate and could respond to changing circumstances. The time allocated (to a case or to any piece of work) could/would be negotiated within each supervision session as the level of intensity of the work and the circumstances of the individual practitioner change. Other models assume an even distribution of effort throughout the lifetime of a case. The three models are compared in the table below.

Table 4.2   Approaches to workload management

Expressed in	Priority/Complexity Points or hours	Case/work type Points or hours	Hybrid Hours/units
Focus	Depends upon complexity or priority or risk – potentially any number of levels can be used but typically 4 or 5.	Depends upon the type or work or intervention – e.g. community care assessment, or child looked after.	Depends upon what needs to be done in the coming period and how long it will take.
How achieved	Allocation to complexity level – which continues until complexity changes.	Allocation to activity type – which continues until activity changes.	Allocation for estimated hours needed to complete work – which continues until the work is completed or changes.
Advantages	• Simplicity. • Allows for staff to work at different paces.	Simplicity.	• Fits with a supervision focus on what needs to be done and how, and so is mutually reinforcing. • This can vary from practitioner to practitioner depending upon their skills and experience or from case to case on basis of need.
Disadvantages	• Does not directly match day-to-day change in demands of the work.	• Does not directly match day-to-day change in demands of the work. • It assumes that it is reasonable and appropriate to expect all staff to work in a similar way.	• Weekly/daily variations mean that this approach requires capacity for 'events' to be negotiated in – if not needed then there is scope for lower-priority tasks to be completed.

Integrated information solutions

Social care services are required to deliver services that are person-centric, proactive and seamless, to the most vulnerable members of communities. An integrated solution for social care is the vision set out in the *Every Child Matters* (DfES, 2003) and *Our Health, Our Care, Our Say* (DoH, 2006) governmental reports. For practitioners this solution relies heavily on the management of information in order to perform the many varied tasks involved from initial referral through to care planning and the data management used in performance returns.

The early history of social work relied on paper-based systems. Initially these were quite rudimentary but developed into bulky volumes of case files for complex situations. However, paper-based systems will simply not provide the visibility, completeness of information and speed of response required to deliver the modern new vision for social care.

It was in the late 1970s that computers were first introduced into social care settings. The initial focus was to enable statistical information to be gathered to feed the various annual returns to different government departments. This was a stage when greater emphasis was beginning to be placed on performance measurement and comparison across authorities. The advent of the computer led to the need to develop information systems to gather the data in a common format. The designs and specifications of these information systems were to create structured records to measure performance, and have been perceived by many practitioners as a bureaucratic administrative task adding little value to the social work tasks. However, the development of information systems led to the gathering of data that could be utilised for functions other than just statistical returns. Workload management systems rely on data to analyse capacity and these also have moved from paper-based systems to those reliant on computer-generated information.

During the process of systems development, a number of national inquiries into social care failures in service delivery identified the lack of information held to enable decision making in the case. This lack of information has been exposed in the forms of holding information and also the failure to share it accurately with other agencies, the failure to collect information and the failure to record accurately. Several inquiries highlighted the fact that if the information had been to hand, it would have thrown a different light on the issues underpinning the case (Department of Health, 2003b; Birchard Report, 2004).

Thus information and information systems have become a focal point for change and the government has played a leading role in setting out more uniformity for social care recording. In England the children's services framework for the *Assessment of Children in Need* led to an *Integrated Children's System* (Department of Health, 2000; Department of Health, 2003a) and in adult care services the introduction of the single assessment process (Department of Health, 2002) have all led to information being utilised in a structured way within social care records.

These complex assessment tools have been designed to collect and collate more holistically data relating to the individual service-user. These information systems also support information collected from other agencies into a multi-disciplinary single assessment that leads to the production of care plans.

For social workers the introduction of these structured assessment tools has been challenging as it has moved their style of recording away from paper records to a growing reliance on electronic records. This new era of information being shared and moved across agencies is leading to the production of information-sharing protocols to ensure confidentiality and safety of information, as well as the need to ensure that the service-user has given informed consent for the information to be used in this way. The acceptance and use of new systems is not unique to social workers. 'People adapt systems to their particular work needs, or they resist them or fail to use them at all; and there are wide variances in the patterns of computer use and, consequently, their effects on decision-making and other outcomes (DeSactis and Poole, 1994: 122). Some social workers have struggled with these changes in styles of recording and, as is often the case in the introduction of new methods of working, the outcomes in the initial stages of development are low in comparison with the input involved in the loading of the data. Greater technological advances are making clearer the potential benefits for service-users. While these changes impact more fully on social workers within the statutory sector, social workers in the non-statutory sector will also need to adjust, especially as more work is commissioned of them by the statutory sector, and thus they will be subject to the same disciplines around recording.

In our opinion, the case studies below indicate some of the potential benefits. In future, service-users are likely to have higher expectations of health and social care and to express their views more forcibly about the standard and quality of service delivery. There will be an increasing and pressing need to pool the total resources and allocate them on a more integrated basis, involving multi-disciplinary teams working in and through local access centres. We anticipate that both managers and practitioners will have to give up their sectarian attitudes and defensive stances, which are all too common features of the present separate services. If health and social services are not to unite in statute, then they must be united in the same basic objectives.

Case Study   Information technology provides service-users with access and control

Looking to the future how might health and social services be provided in the next ten to twenty years? If I am a service user entering my old age I would envisage that my first point of contact for a service would be through the internet and an interactive discussion with a social worker about my needs and how they might be met. The local office will probably have disappeared some years ago, as an efficiency saving. The capital and revenue costs of running an office may have become so high as to no longer be economical. Most people now work from home with a communication network that is more efficient and rapid in response. So, having discussed my needs with the social worker who has treated me with dignity and respect, listened to my views, explained my rights and gone through the range of choices available to me, I will probably be able to view my care plan on the internet by using my personal identity number (PIN) for security access. I might then also be able to consider any implications for my health record maintained by my local GP and again accessible through the internet with my PIN number. My care plan would have been costed and authorised and my cash limit set for direct payment. I would now need to shop around for the best deal with providers, again using the internet. I would have to be wary of all the sales patter as I choose the ones to interrogate through my interactive button. The social worker has been really helpful with suggestions on the type of questions I need to ask and the quality of service I should be expecting. Still, if I have any problems I can seek further help from a consultation with my social worker.

Is this greater user participation through greater control of the resources and choices and how to utilise them? Is this real empowerment – being able to influence decisions and make informed decisions with further support, if required? It is the type of service that I would want to receive. I would want to feel that I am in charge or control and could organise services at my convenience in my own home.

Case Study   An integrated children's system

The Department of Health set out the challenge of integrating children's systems and in Warwickshire County Council work commenced on this goal in 2003. The proposals set out by the Department of Health for an integrated children's system envisage a seamless service across professions and agencies with effective management of information, with, for example, a single assessment process. Lyndon and Payne (2003), in their work on introducing this approach in Warwickshire, describe the integrated children's system as a joined-up way of working which is not an information technology project but needs information technology to make it work. It is not just a vision for social services but spreads across all agencies working with children. They outline their vision for the integrated children's system as:

- a system that is supportive, accessible, available, flexible, easy to use, and is in line with technologies that users are likely to be familiar with outside of the Social Services context.
- a system where users are better rewarded for the information they gather and in return are given further information as tools to enable better outcomes.
- a system where better information sharing across agencies and teams will reduce the need for repeated assessments but still increase the quality of work being done with children, young people and their families.

In short, for staff it would be about working smarter not harder.

In both these case studies it can be seen that the role that information technology will play in the management of workloads for social workers is significant. Social workers will need to adjust their working practices to embrace the advantages that slick technological advances will afford for them, making increasing time available to social workers to complete the tasks they are competent and trained for in delivering better outcomes for service-users. It is also a positive sign for service-users, as both case studies indicate the potential for greater user-empowerment in the delivery of services.

Surviving organisational change: the context

Understanding the perspective of social services management on workload is only one aspect of 'surviving'. Another aspect is understanding the recent and current drivers of environmental change in the social care workplace. If social workers wish to advocate a practice linked to either 'values-based' or 'relationship-based' practice, they will need to understand other workplace imperatives, for example 'Best Value' (see below) and the implications of *Every Child Matters* (DfES, 2003) and *Our Health, Our Care, Our Say* (DoH, 2006), which have already been mentioned. These are only two of the initiatives of the New Labour government which have had a direct impact in the social care workplace. Managers in health and social services have to implement proposals and regulations to these kinds of imperatives, and social workers will need to be aware that their own practice will be heavily influenced by such initiatives and programmes. In the 1980s the Conservative government under Margaret Thatcher attempted to reform the public sector through the introduction of competition. More recently the dominant theme has been the provision of better services through collaboration and partnership, Box 4.1 indicates some factors that may support collaboration and partnership.

A recognition of the roles of many individual organisations in delivering the complex range of public services demanded by modern society, many of which overlap, coupled with the need to achieve 'Best Value', has led to an increasing propensity for public sector organisations in the UK to become partners. The principles of Best Value are set out in the government White Paper – 'Modern Local Government – In Touch with the People' (Department for Transport, Local Government and the Regions, 1998).

Best Value is defined as follows:

Best Value arrangements exist to secure continuous improvement in the performance of functions by public service organisations. Continuous improvement seeks to balance quality and cost considerations, and is achieved with regard to economy, efficiency, effectiveness, the equal opportunities arrangements, and sustainable development.

(http://www.scotland.gov.uk/Topics/Government/14838/564, accessed 17/02/2007)

This definition was formalised in children's services by *Every Child Matters* (DfES, 2003), which precipitated the move away from social services departments towards new partnerships such as children's trusts. Children's trusts are formal arrangements which bring together all services for children and young people in a geographic area, and are underpinned by the Children Act 2004 duty to co-operate and focus upon improving outcomes for children and young people.

Box 4.1   Organisational propensity to partner with other agencies

Butler and Gill (2001) identify a number of variables which determine the propensity of organisations to partner:

Scarcity – a shortage of resources makes shared endeavour seem more attractive.

Interdependence – where two or more organisations can be seen as dependent upon each other – the shared responsibilities between social care, health and education in meeting the needs of children with disabilities, for example.

Ambiguity – where a number of organisations come together to share and benefit from the knowledge of each constituent agency.

Favourable experience of partnerships – where an organisation has had a positive experience of partnership activity there is an increased likelihood of the experiment being repeated.

Strategic fit – refers to the extent to which the notion of partnering fits in with other strategies an organisation may be pursuing in other parts of its domain.

Regulatory imperative – while children's trusts are not mandatory, it is clear that regulators will be expecting to see evidence that they are in existence when services are inspected

The Best Value initiative, introduced after the 1997 General Election, is the mechanism by which the government drives its objective of achieving better performance from public sector organisations. Local authorities are required to review key services periodically to ensure that services are needed, that they are delivered efficiently, that they are benchmarked against the best comparable services, that stakeholders' views are sought and considered and that the service could not be provided more efficiently by someone else.

The long-term success of any organisation depends upon its capacity to deliver the best possible balance of quality and efficiency in respect of its products or services from the perspective of all key stakeholders. Within the public sector this is particularly challenging due to the need to satisfy a wide-ranging set of interest groups. In a child protection case, for example, a number of competing perspectives may come in to play. Examples of these perspectives might include:

- the needs of the child for safety, balanced against the potential emotional harm of disruption to family life;
- the interests of the child's parent[s] even though they may not be coterminous, if, for example, one party is accused of causing harm to the child;
- the need for the local authority to manage the potential political risk of appearing to be either too interventionist or too laissez-faire;
- the interests of the police force in solving a crime;
- the pressure to provide efficient and effective solutions at a minimal cost to the taxpayer.

The development of Best Value follows a traditional pattern of policy implementation within local government. It requires conformity and compliance to external pressure backed up by legislation and guidance. Central government offers local councils increasing freedoms in managing their own affairs and finances, provided councils modernise their structures and meet centrally prescribed levels of performance. The aim has been to encourage local councils to take up the challenge of meeting central government objectives and aspirations. Underpinning this approach is the desire to increase the participation of external stakeholders such as local residents, community groups, local business groups, thereby reinvigorating interest in local politics, with a view to reversing the trend of decreasing voter turnout in local elections (currently 30–40 per cent is common).

The Best Value programme is underpinned by a modernisation of local government structures. The movement towards 'unitary' councils reflects a long-standing search for greater efficiency and economies of scale. Traditional committee systems have given way to smaller 'cabinets' of key councillors. These councillors are clearly becoming more managerial and 'strategic' in their roles. Best Value can be seen as delivering the agenda of New Labour in four key areas:

1. as a vehicle for democratic renewal;
2. as a quality assurance system;
3. as a system of measuring the effectiveness of local authorities through a set of performance indicators, allowing comparative performance to be assessed;
4. as a mechanism for keeping costs down without an apparent ideological bias towards either the public or the private sectors.

The six key components of Best Value apply across all areas of local government and shape the development and delivery of services.

1. A performance management framework consisting of national objectives, performance indicators and an inspection regime.
2. Local performance plans that link planning at all levels of the local authority and are subject to a programme of reviews.
3. Performance indicators, standards and targets, some of which are national and some of which are agreed locally.
4. Fundamental reviews of key services.
5. Audit and inspection programmes to determine whether Best Value is being obtained.
6. Government intervention where services fail. The position of last resort is that failing services can be taken over by external providers until such a time as it is deemed safe for the local authority to resume control.

From professional autonomy to corporate accountability

The drive towards partnering as a way of demonstrating public sector efficiency has made organisations more complex, and the Best Value regime has placed additional layers of bureaucratic demands upon both adult and children's services as they strive to demonstrate compliance with an ever expanding national performance management framework. For these reasons newly qualified social workers may hear complaints from experienced colleagues of a limitation upon the value that the organisation places upon their individual professionalism compared to the 1970s and 1980s coupled with a huge increase in paperwork. It is our opinion that the emphasis has moved away from professional autonomy to corporate accountability.

Not only have new processes been imposed, but they are increasingly unlikely to be processes tailored to the social work profession. For example the *Every Child Matters* agenda requires integrated information systems for integrated service delivery. In turn that means that the professional knowledge of social care needs to be adapted and translated into a common language accessible across the whole sector. The social worker needs to develop and employ new technological skills accordingly, and ensure that they contribute towards the achievement of performance indicators in support of the corporate whole.

Working within a more complex environment than that of the old-style social services department presents both huge challenges for practice and new opportunities to simplify the experience of the service-user. The emerging partnerships to do with children's issues are designed to ensure that those dependent upon the services are offered clear choices, single points of contact for many services, and personalised and locally delivered care.

There are a number of characteristics of successful partnerships, without which ambiguity will prevail and the benefits of the partnership will be at best neutralised; in some cases the partnership will be detrimental to effective working (see Box 4.2).

Box 4.2   Characteristics of effective partnerships

- The added value of the partnership is recognised by all involved parties.
- Shared values, respect and an ability to work with a range of professional cultures. Without the ability of professionals from all disciplines to find ways of working together effectively, potential benefits to service-users will not be secured.
- Interpersonal requirements – equity, honesty, respect and open communication.
- Self interest – there must be something in it for every individual organisation and professional.
- An imperative to partner. In the case of the *Every Child Matters* agenda the imperative is legislation and regulation but there may be other drivers such as more efficient use of resources.

This sets the context for individual practitioners but they are both dependent upon and contributory to effective partnership. It has been argued that the realisation of social policy was very different from the theory or rational themes behind it. Implementation is not a rational activity governed by experts using scientific knowledge. Rather it is an irrational process dominated by petty political concerns and local interpretation. In spite of everyone's best efforts, the interdependent outcomes expected from partnership may remain aspirational. This is partly because the various interest groups involved, for example in delivering children's services, could compete with each other for the resources. Each interest group could implement what they see as the requirements placed upon their particular part of the partnership. This process will also reflect each interest group's competitive position through the pursuit of some kind of ideological pre-eminence among the various rival interest groups.

The attainment and the inclusion agenda within children's services is a prime example of this kind of tension and possible 'irrationality'. Does the state have a role in promoting the emotional well-being of children? After all, this is traditionally left to families. Should the state limit its attentions to developing a well-educated, well-qualified workforce? This is the view of Charles Lindblom (1965), who claims that public policy is actually accomplished through decentralised bargaining in a free market and a democratic political economy. He describes this as policy development by 'partisan mutual adjustment' or disjointed incrementalism. By that he means that whatever the government wants for its citizens, it is how staff on the front line deliver that policy which will determine its success. If, for example, the state wants every child to make a positive contribution, and we deliver services in such a way as to deter young people from accessing them, then the outcome will not be achieved.

Surviving in a changing environment: the challenge

We started this chapter by discussing workload and systems to manage workload. This was necessarily because of the contextual complexities we have outlined indicating how important it is to manage workload. We have moved a long way from the era of the Seebohm Reforms in which social work caseloads could be a lot higher than at present; and via generic working be more diverse in a milieu in which the *relationship* between the service-user and social worker was emphasised rather than consistency in the quality of the service delivered. Now, in contexts of high expectations of service delivery from multi-stakeholder partnerships the need for management for workloads and clarity in role boundaries is essential to emotionally and practically 'surviving'. This is as true for individual practitioners and their managers as it is for groups like the teams and organisations of which they are a part.

Clarity of role boundary immediately affects the issue of professional discretion; partnership working inherently limits some aspects of professional autonomy and discretion. Studies undertaken in the 1970s (Parsloe and Stevenson, 1978, for example) suggested that social workers then enjoyed a substantial degree of discretion and autonomy in managing their work with service-users. Social workers could decide the style and content of their direct work, and their work was not determined by bureaucratic procedures but by views of what constituted good professional practice established through the process of supervision. This process gave social workers considerable discretion to define problems and decide the priority given to the use of their time and control over their workload. Supervision consisted of a meeting between two colleagues of the same profession often to problem-solve cases, rather than demonstrate a superior–subordinate style of management.

Professional autonomy and discretion was particularly pertinent in casework which underpinned their workload. This discretion was about the method of intervention, the case plan, the frequency of contact and in many instances the decision to close a case. This discretion pervaded the profession until the start of the Thatcherite reforms led to massive contextual changes continuing through to New Labour reforms under Blair. The previous role of the social worker as advocate was weakened within the purchaser/provider era, as was the importance of discretion. Harris (2003) in *The Social Work Business* identifies the role that managers developed that focused on standardisation and compliance in service construct through rigorous procedures and supervising checks. He outlines this as the impact of managerialism, as a result of which the nature and role of social workers changed.

Constraints on expenditure were achieved through managing the assessment process, removing elements of discretion practised by social workers. In addition, high-profile national inquiries into failures within social work practice increased scrutiny and a drive for consistency. Regulatory bodies also increased their scrutiny of social work, focusing on ever-increasing close management of social work decisions. The implication of this was increased control and oversight and a reduction in the use of discretion enjoyed by social workers. Harris identified that:

> Much of this control is expressed in manuals, directions and guidelines that limit professional discretion and set up standardised and repetitive systems: tightly defined criteria for eligibility of services; standardised assessment tools; interventions which are often determined in advance from a limited list; minimisation of contact time; micro-case management and pressure for throughput.
>
> (Harris, 2003: 75)

In our opinion these changes have led to a more mechanical role for social workers in the statutory sector. It is possible that the voluntary sector has managed to retain more flexibility. The control over workloads, and therefore casework management, has also become more standardised and this fits the greater move towards performance management and meeting performance indicators. The loser in this new performance-dominated culture is the extent of discretion previously enjoyed by social workers.

Into this context steps the new social work graduate with expectations of critical practice and the professional discretion that the term implies. Above all practitioners, whether newly qualified or not, need to be conscious of the nature of the challenges for *all parties involved* if they are to 'survive and prosper' in their workplace.

Challenges for the practitioner

For the social work practitioner recent organisational change may appear to have been externally imposed with little input from or reference to the profession. Social work training programmes, at least until recently, appear to leave newly qualified staff ill prepared for the bureaucratic demands that are placed upon social workers within the statutory sector.

The potential benefits of partnership work are often highlighted but there is little preparation for the level of tactical subtlety required to make best use of the opportunity. An example of this is the tensions between health and social care staff over discharge arrangements from hospital. From a health perspective there is a pressure to free up hospital beds once any medical benefits have been achieved, while from a social care perspective hospital discharge may mean that a vulnerable adult is placed back in the community where their vulnerability is exacerbated. Practitioners who fare best in this environment are those who take the trouble to understand the 'social construct' of their partner and who can learn to create 'win–win' situations in their everyday negotiations. In this case, staff from both sectors working together in intermediate care teams have the opportunity to co-operate to deliver the 'right care in the right place at the right time'.

Often processes seem to be developed in order to meet performance or contract compliance reporting requirements rather than from the need to support front-line practice. Effective practitioners will look for opportunities to become involved in process developments to ensure that their perspective is not marginalised. Organisations wanting to make the best of their employees need to understand the values and belief systems that motivate them and to find ways to make administrative requirements unobtrusive and as supportive of practice as possible.

Challenges for the manager

The role of the manager is to ensure that policies, procedures and strategic objectives are delivered. Within an increasingly complex environment this means that they will be spending more and more time on performance management and monitoring, and this will be coupled with the challenge of maintaining up-to-date knowledge within their working environment. The manager in an integrated setting involving four agencies will suddenly be faced with four sets of knowledge bases to keep up with at a time where government policy output is more prolific than ever. Managing the cultural differences which occur within and between the sectors is perhaps the greatest challenge of all. New behaviours, such as collaborative working, knowledge and skill sharing, need to be valued; new ways of doing things need to be developed – processes that are acceptable to all, and not simply those of the dominant group superimposed upon the rest.

Challenges for the multi-professional team

Within the team context there will be a number of challenges to overcome. These challenges will be lessened if structural issues such as pay and conditions are sorted out before integration, but often these issues are 'parked' to be resolved once the structure is settled. Human resources, finance and organisational development activity could differ for any of the different professional groups represented within an integrated team. Pay and conditions could vary considerably between the staff groups working on similar tasks, thereby causing considerable tensions within the workplace.

Challenges for the organisation

The traditional bureaucracy of the public sector does not sit well with the devolved way of working required to meet the new agenda. New structures need to be devised which allow for flexibility and are less hierarchical that previously if new partners, in particular the voluntary sector, are to be encouraged to join in.

Partnerships set up around funding arrangements should be driven by the needs for those on whom the money will be spent. Where one partner is driven by values and the other mainly by the allocation of resources, conflict is inevitable and can only be avoided if open communication and trust are promoted.

Conclusion

It is clear that the complexity of working in the social care world and within organisations struggling to meet service-users' needs with limited resources requires considerable ingenuity to survive. Workload management is in its infancy in social care and there is no nationally agreed scheme. The different models outlined at the beginning of this chapter have both advantages and disadvantages, and the best schemes need a degree of flexibility to take on board the unpredictability of service-users' reactions to situations in their lives.

Newly qualified social workers will also face a myriad of information systems in the management of their work. Organisations are going through rapid change, with the advent of electronic systems gradually replacing the reliance on paper. The pace of change and the complexity of systems varies greatly throughout the UK. The one sure fact is that further change is on the horizon to embrace the evolving technological advances – hence, for example, in the social work degree the obligation for graduates to meet the requirements of the European Computer Driving Licence (ECDL).

The organisational bases of social work are also changing and this poses another layer of complexity. The dominant theme is that collaboration and partnership will secure better public services. Previously, the social work task was identified through professional autonomy within a framework of a code of ethics, but this has been superseded as the emphasis moves from professional autonomy towards corporate accountability. The future social work role and task offers many challenges and the critical social work practitioner will need constantly to update their knowledge and skills to meet these challenges.

References

Allan, D., Ward, C. and Bekenn, A. (1996) *Workload Management: A Report of the Results of a Pilot Scheme Introduced at Brierley Hill Area Office*. Dudley: Dudley Social Services Department.

Birchard Report (2004) *The Birchard Inquiry Report*. London: The Stationery Office.

Butler, R. and Gill, K. (2001) 'Formation and control of public–private partnerships: a stakeholder event', in G. Johnson and K. Scholes (eds), *Explaining Public Sector Strategy*. Harlow: Pearson Education.

Department for Education and Skills (DfES) (2003) *Every Child Matters*. London: The Stationery Office.

Department for Education and Skills (DfES) (2006) *Options for Excellence – Building the Social Care Workforce of the Future*. London: Department of Health.

Department of Health (DoH) (2000) *Framework for the assessment of children in need and their families*. London: Department of Health.

Department of Health (DoH) (2002) 'Guidance on the single assessment process for older people', Health Service Circular, HSC 2002/001. London: Department of Health.

Department of Health (DoH) (2003a) *The Integrated Children's System*, CD-ROM.

Department of Health (DoH) (2003b) *The Victoria Climbié Inquiry – Report of an Inquiry by Lord Laming*. London: Department of Health and the Home Office.

Department of Health (DoH) (2006) *Our health, Our Care, Our Say: A New Direction for Community Services*. London: The Stationery Office.

DeSactis, G. and Poole, M.S. (1194) 'Capturing the complexity in advanced technology use: adaptive structuration theory', *Organization Science*, 5 (2): 121–47.

Garthwaite, T. (2006) *Social Work in Wales: A Profession to Value*. London: ADSS (Association of Directors of Social Services).

Harris, J. (2003) *The Social Work Business*. London: Routledge.

Holmes and Ward (2004) 'How social workers spend their time', unpublished paper prepared at request of DfES.

Johnson, G. and Scholes, K. (2001) *Explaining Public Sector Strategy*. Harlow: Pearson Education.

Lindblom, Charles E. (1965) *The Intelligence of Democracy: Decision Making Through Mutual Adjustment*. New York: Free Press.

Lyndon, P. and Payne, M. (2003) *Warwickshire Integrated Children System*. Warwick: Warwickshire Social Services Department. Unpublished internal report.

Orme, J. (1995) *Workloads: Measurement and Management*. Aldershot: Avebury.

Orme, J. (2002) 'Managing Workload', in R. Adams, L. Dominelli and M. Payne (eds), *Critical Practice in Social Work*. Basingstoke: Palgrave.

Orme, J. and Glastonbury, B. (1993) *Care Management – Tasks and Workloads.* Basingstoke: Palgrave.

Parsloe, P. and Stevenson, O. (1978) *Social Services Teams: The Practitioner's View.* London: HMSO.

SCIE (Social Care Institute for Excellence) (2003) *Practice Guide 1: Managing practice* http.//www.scie.org.uk/publications/practiceguides/bpg1/index.asp. Published January 2003.

Scottish Executive (2006) *Changing Lives: Report of the 21st Century Social Work Review.* Edinburgh: Scottish Executive.

Statham, J., Cameron, C. and Mooney, A. (2006) 'The tasks and roles of social workers: a focused overview of research evidence', prepared for *Options for Excellence,* Task Group 3, Thomas Coram Research Unit, Institute of Education, University of London.

TOPSS (2002) *National Occupational Standards for Social Work.* Leeds: Training Organisation for the Personal Social Services UK Partnership.

White, V. and Harris, J. (2001) (eds) *Developing Good Practice in Community Care.* London: Jessica Kingsley.

White, V. and Harris, J. (2004) *Developing Good Practice in Children's Services.* London: Jessica Kingsley.

Wingham, G. (2002) 'Caseload management', *Care and Health*, 17 May.

Chapter 5

Counting the costs

Colin Guest and Philip Scarff

Successive governments have been accused of starving essential public services of the money they need to improve the well-being of people and communities. Critics of the public services say they have plenty of money: they just need to stop wasting it and use it better. Finance managers used to take much of the blame for this: they were seen as the 'Abominable No-Men', who refused to see the merit of new approaches and so stifled good ideas at birth. Practitioners who could see a better way of doing things became frustrated at their seeming inability to influence how resources were allocated and used.

In recent years both practitioners and finance staff have 'grown up' in relation to financial management. Practitioners have become skilled in controlling budgets and using them creatively, while finance staff are now much more part of the team, helping practitioners to use resources flexibly and effectively, while still complying with the labyrinthine rules governing the use of public money. And yet, despite extra investment in public services since 2000, we still hear pleas for more money and reports of services being cut because of lack of funds. The need for practitioners to be highly skilled in understanding and managing their money to the best effect is therefore as important as ever.

At the core of this chapter there is a single case study that aims to bring to life a series of important concepts associated with the management of budgets and to show their importance not only for specialised finance staff but also for those who are more directly involved in delivering services. These themes are set in the context of a transformation of the financial regime in public services and of questions about its implications.

New regimes – new roles

In the years after the Conservative victory in the general election of 1979, there were moves towards more active management and new strategies for objective-setting and performance management in the public sector. Local authorities became enablers of services while private and voluntary organisations became service-providers on a larger scale than ever before.

Since Labour came to power in 1997 they have greatly increased spending in several areas, notably education and health, but the 'price' for local government and other service-providers has been more central direction, control and monitoring. This is typified by:

- a series of national strategies, for example for services relating to children, adults, housing, learning disability, drugs and alcohol;
- target-setting, often linked to increased funding and 'flexibilities' through Public Service Agreements between the government and local authorities;
- centralised regulation and inspection regimes, for example Ofsted for schools, nurseries and childminders and the Commission for Social Care Inspection (CSCI) for residential and domiciliary care;
- the national drive to recruit and retain a competent social care workforce, co-ordinated by Skills for Care;
- Direct payments, introduced to create more flexibility and choice in the provision of social services;
- the Best Value regime, described later; and
- directions on the structure of service delivery, for instance integrated NHS/local authority mental health teams, joint social services/NHS equipment services for people with disabilities and the integration of children's social services with education (following the report on the death of Victoria Climbié).

The government has required greater partnership working between agencies, for example in the planning and delivery of services for adults with learning disabilities, child and adolescent mental health and physical disability. 'Section 31 Agreements' under the Health Act 1999 allow local authorities and NHS bodies to work together in a formal legal framework: this often involves the pooling of budgets to enable an integrated service to be provided, while avoiding the inter-agency wrangling that sometimes characterises efforts by public bodies to work together. Greater public participation in service delivery and planning has been encouraged, best demonstrated perhaps by the introduction of Direct Payments to allow service-users to plan and purchase their own care.

Case Study 1 gives accounts of the adjustments those working in social care have had to make as they started to take more responsibility for resources.

Case Study 1   Mike's story – managing social services

Up to the early 1990s almost all our services for children, elderly and disabled people were provided in-house. I was both a purchaser and a provider of services. By 1992 only about 10 per cent of our budget was used to buy services from the private or voluntary sectors. Budgets were not of paramount importance to us because we were primarily practitioners who expected most of the budgeting to be done by finance specialists.

Each year we gave grants to local organisations which provided day-care or home-help services but there was very little objectivity in the way we spent the grant money and we

(Continued)

(Continued)

didn't specify how much service we wanted or lay down any quality standards. We had no objective means of looking back at their performance so that we could compare them or judge value for money. The result was a cosy status quo.

There were dramatic changes following the implementation of the NHS and Community Care Act. From 1992 I had to learn a new range of competencies. I had a budget for purchasing services. I could choose where I bought the services from by referring to a list of approved in-house or external providers who met minimum standards of cost and service quality. Some of our in-house providers closed or were privatised. My role became very different: I managed my budget by making choices and balancing priorities, costing the care of each service-user.

Nowadays we still assess need and purchase services in much the same way, but within a far tougher regime. We have to work more closely with colleagues from the NHS and meet a whole range of quality standards and time limits. These are either laid down by the government or enforced through inspections. We have a target to reach for the number of people receiving Direct Payments and we have to contribute to the broader targets set for the council in our Public Service Agreement. If we cause delayed transfers from hospital by failing to make effective arrangements for care, we can be fined by the hospital. This can affect the rating the service receives from CSCI.

On the positive side, the new frameworks do help to provide consistency in service delivery and we have a clearer understanding of what is expected of us. Collaboration with other agencies has improved – though the number of partnership meetings has increased – and by pooling our resources, either formally or informally, we are able to make better use of our budgets to improve services and cost effectiveness.

The implications of Mike's story are that financial management of social services could no longer be hidden away in a separate finance department. The era of 'the treasurer', probably something that a respectable accountant liked to be called in 1948, no longer has contemporary relevance (Masters, 1993; Tonge and Horton, 1996). The skills in drawing up contracts and service-level agreements needed to be shared effectively with those who were managing and delivering services at the front line. Local authority social workers, as care managers, found themselves among those in charge of a budget, making decisions about what care services in the community to purchase for individuals and groups. Hospital clinicians were soon handling devolved budgets, embroiled in the business of calculating what a particular service or operation cost and thinking in altogether new ways about inputs and outputs. Mike (see above) was upbeat when he looked back. Others have been less so, focusing on broader aspects of the reforms, pointing to the insecurities and job losses that contracting has entailed, concentrating on the speed of implementation, the imposition of too rigid a notion of the market, the many things that have gone wrong and the fear sometimes of speaking out about this (Hadley and Clough, 1996).

The new financial regime certainly exposed the finance function to new ways of working on a rapid timetable when information systems and IT support were not in place. Social work training did not traditionally include subjects like financial management, and social work values often emphasised a distance from 'money' issues. Social workers have struggled with the new language of economic thinking (Mackintosh, 2000); they have often had poor information and support (Lewis et al., 1996). There have been new providers from the private or independent sector, whose balancing of costs, quality and profit need to be understood. There have been major adjustments of culture and style for those in the voluntary sector, who have had to balance their new provider roles with their older commitments to demonstration projects and to campaigning for change (Deakin, 1996). In all, a great deal of 'juggling and dealing' has clearly needed to happen to make a reality of services in the new system (Leat and Perkins, 1998).

Has this new financial regime clarified the true costs of service provision? Or has it, to use a classic phrase, produced 'people who know the cost of everything and the value of nothing'? Do national strategies and target-setting ensure fairness, consistency and high quality in service delivery or do targets lead to a tick-box culture, reducing the scope for practitioners to make professional judgements? Do they cause more conflict between managers and practitioners? It is worth bearing such questions in mind while working through the next Case Study in this chapter. It follows Marjorie as she prepares and manages her budget for Middlebrook, a fictional residential facility for people with learning difficulties.

Case Study 2   Managing resources – the case of Middlebrook

Middlebrook is one of five centres operated by a national charity. Until a few years ago it was run by a local authority social services department, topped up by some health trust funding. Middlebrook has twelve service-users, who have daily supported employment in the neighbouring town. The centre has five staff: Marjorie (the centre manager), two support workers, a job coach, and a cleaner/handyperson.

Marjorie returned to paid work in her thirties after bringing up a family, and became a social work assistant in her local authority. Three years later, she was sponsored by her employer to train as a social worker and, three years on from that, she became the registered manager at Middlebrook. Her duties included the day-to-day operations of the centre, ensuring cover and supervising staff. She has had to learn to operate in a new environment in which Middlebrook has had to become competitive, tendering annually for local authority and health authority contracts. This has meant careful attention to how resources are used. Each month Marjorie spends a few hours monitoring the budget and forecasting what the end-of-year expenditure is likely to be.

Marjorie's revenue budget is a key working tool. Revenue budgets are used to meet day-to-day costs of services, such as staff, materials, fuel and relatively inexpensive equipment, and they are usually allocated for just one year at a time. (The other type of budget – the capital budget – is used to pay for expensive purchases, which have a longer lifetime, such as building works or equipment. Capital budgets are planned with a rolling programme, over several years.) The income and expenditure figures for Middlebrook's revenue budget are shown in Table 5.1. They are 'cash limits': Marjorie must not spend more than the amounts shown and must also achieve the stated income figure. In practice, there is usually scope for *virement* – variations between the different items in a budget as long as the net expenditure is within its cash limit. Senior managers, such as Marjorie's line manager, who may have responsibility for several centres, may have similar discretion across all the services for which they have budgetary responsibility.

The overall cash limits in a budget ultimately reflect political or corporate decisions about the funding that will be made available to a service year on year. They also reflect decisions taken locally by senior managers about the funding of individual services and the relative priority they attach to them. In a private organisation, adherence, or not, to cash limits can make the difference between staying in business or going into liquidation. Public sector organisations do not go bankrupt (although private and voluntary organisations certainly can), but overspending in one service means less money for another and, intentionally or not, can change the priorities set by senior officers or elected members. It is a brave, or foolish, service manager who ignores the cash limits set for his or her service!

Table 5.1   Revenue budget for Middlebrook

	£000	£000
Expenditure		
Staff	107.3	
Premises	10.0	
Transport	15.3	
Food	24.3	
Supplies and services	10.1	
Miscellaneous	4.0	
Total gross expenditure		171.0
Income		
Social services	35.0	
Primary care trust	12.5	
Staff meals	6.0	
Client charges	31.5	
Total income		85.0
Net expenditure		86.0

Managing a revenue budget

Table 5.1 shows that the centre has been allocated a cash limit of £171,000 for the financial year (see total gross expenditure). Not surprisingly for a service specialising in providing care, a large proportion of this – in practice over 60 per cent – has been allocated to pay the staff. There are five other types of expenditure, and together these six categories of approved costs are the 'total gross expenditure'.

Income plans are set out in the lower half of the table, showing the sums that are planned to be collected from social services, from the primary care trust, from staff who eat their meals at the centre, and from service-users who pay for their care. The total of

£85,000 represents the annual income Marjorie must collect to set against her gross expenditure, leaving a net expenditure of £86,000, a deficit which the charity meets centrally. Reductions in Middlebrook's income are sometimes caused by short-term vacancies when service-users stop using the services. These vacancies have a double effect as, when a service-user leaves, both the social services income and service-user charges are temporarily lost. It is not possible to catch up on lost income by increasing the number of service-users beyond the approved level of twelve, for which Middlebrook is registered.

How, then, can Marjorie cut costs? Her accountant will supply a monthly report of the expenditure incurred and income collected. To get the most from that report, and to make it more accurate, she needs to be prompt in paying bills and sending invoices to social services and the health authority. The report does not tell her what her future expenditure commitments are, so she keeps her own record of her spending plans. By then combining the actual expenditure shown on her reports with her local record of commitments, Marjorie has a better picture of the financial situation.

The accountant comments:

If you have any reductions in Middlebrook's income you'll have to reduce your expenditure to cover the losses. Look for flexibility in your budget. Separate your fixed costs from your variable ones and concentrate on reducing the variable costs.

Understanding costs

To do what the accountant suggests and to ensure she is getting the best value from the limited resources available to her, Marjorie needs a clear understanding not only of the concepts of fixed and variable costs but also of several other related ideas.

Fixed and variable costs

As a general rule, fixed costs are those which do not change in the short term, even if levels of activity vary (in this context, the term 'activity' means work or services). Variable costs, though, as the term implies, do change as levels of activity vary. However, it is often difficult to make a distinction between these two types of costs and, in reality, they tend to be semi-fixed or semi-variable. Middlebrook's budget table illustrates how the distinction can become blurred. Take staffing costs: most of these costs are fixed because they relate to permanent staff, on contracted hours. Marjorie is committed to spending these fixed costs, but knows that there can be some variability in her staffing costs, as the job coach and one support worker are sessional staff, who work as and when required. This means she can regard the staffing budget as having both fixed and variable elements, and she could have some flexibility within the monies allocated for sessional staff. For example, she can offset some of the income losses caused by service-user vacancies by reducing the hours worked by sessional staff until those vacancies are filled, but she needs to budget for deploying her sessional staff to cover sickness, training and holiday absences, too.

Looking further down Middlebrook's budget table, costs can be categorised as follows.

Premises – this is a fixed cost to meet a head office contractual payment.

Transport – this contains a fixed element of £8,000 for the lease payment for Middlebrook's minibus. The £7,300 balance is variable, as it pays for staff mileage, which fluctuates as the number of service-users travelling to supported employment placements changes. Marjorie can avoid the need for additional staff mileage whenever she has two or more service-user vacancies, as the minibus, which can carry ten people, will then accommodate them all.

Food – technically, these costs are variable, as Marjorie manages the food budget according to a weekly cost per resident. However, some of the economies of buying in bulk are lost when she buys for fewer residents, producing little or no savings.

Supplies and services – little flexibility is found here, as the budget meets the costs of electricity, gas, water and minibus fuel, which remain predominantly fixed when activity reduces.

Miscellaneous – Marjorie 'inherited' this budget allowance when she arrived at Middlebrook, and uses it to meet the costs of minor repairs to the building, replacing equipment and improving facilities. The costs are largely fixed, because they pay for the essential, planned repairs and replacements which keep Middlebrook up to registration standard. She has to keep something in reserve for emergencies, however.

Unit costs

A key concept that Marjorie has learned to use with good effect, as we shall see below, is unit costs – that is, the costs of an individual unit of service, for example, one week of care for one resident in a home or an hour of domiciliary care. By calculating unit costs she knows how much is being spent on Middlebrook's activities and services. Unit costs are increasingly used to assess whether value for money is being given by one provider compared with another. They can equally be used internally, to see whether costs are stable or changing. Sometimes, a manager like Marjorie will calculate unit costs herself, as a local management tool. However, it is also likely that target unit costs will be set by others, such as senior managers, auditors or those who commission services. Since the 1980s it has been government policy to set a range of performance indicators, including unit costs, for health and social care services.

The arithmetic for calculating unit costs is not complicated – you add up all the costs incurred in providing a service and divide them by the number of units of service provided. Thus:

$$\text{Unit cost} = \frac{\text{All the costs of providing a service}}{\text{The number of units of service provided}}$$

Problems can arise, however, in getting agreement about which costs are to be included in the calculations. For example, some resources, such as equipment, staff or accommodation, may be shared between providers, and 'ownership' of such costs may be uncertain. This issue is touched on below, when we look at direct and indirect costs and overheads. Working from the revenue budget for Middlebrook and her monthly expenditure reports, Marjorie calculated unit costs for the Centre's three main categories of service.

1. The unit cost for the overall support provided to service-users, produced by adding up all Middlebrook's costs for that month and dividing them by the number of service-users supported in that same period.
2. A unit cost for Middlebrook's supported employment services, produced by separating the costs of staff time, transport, administration, etc., that were put into the service that month and dividing them by the number of days of supported employment provided in the same period.
3. A unit cost for the meals prepared in the Centre's kitchen – Marjorie calculated these to help her manage the kitchen more effectively and to see whether the information would help reduce waste. The monthly costs of staff, food, fuel and materials were separated and divided by the number of meals provided during that period.

Up to this point, the revenue budget has been taken as given, but those accountable for resources need to be aware of direct and indirect costs and of overheads that may be allocated. Understanding these, and successfully challenging them, may make a dramatic difference to budgets, unit costs and the amount available to spend on services.

Direct and indirect costs

These two terms are used to signify where a cost belongs, how it is to be allocated, or which budget it belongs to. A cost is called direct if it is clear who is responsible for it. For example, at Middlebrook the costs of salaries, food and transport are clearly the responsibility of the Centre and are 'direct'. Indirect costs, however, are harder to pin down. These are costs that are shared and apportioned between budgets – often using a formula that can be related to the level of activity. For example, the costs of putting clean linen into a hospital ward have a range of elements, including the actual laundry costs (probably contracted out), porters and administration. One arrangement for allocating these costs would be to charge them to each ward according to the number of occupied bed-days on each ward. If it is not entirely clear how indirect costs are comprised or who is responsible for them, they might be apportioned wrongly, or neglected. When they are neglected, indirect costs tend to produce winners and losers, because somebody ultimately picks up the cost and it may be by default, causing a budget problem.

Middlebrook is a relatively small organisation with a self-contained budget, sharing no facilities or activities with other organisations. Its revenue budget shows that Marjorie meets the direct costs of her services. Marjorie would be well advised, however, to find out from her line manager whether she will be expected to pay for any hidden indirect costs. These could, for example, be a commitment on the Centre's 'miscellaneous' expenditure heading shown on the budget table. 'Indirect' costs need to be watched very carefully and minimised or eliminated wherever possible!

Overhead costs

Sometimes called 'on-costs', 'overheads' is a loose term used to describe the range of costs associated with making a service possible, but not directly connected with front-line activity. There is no strict convention or rule defining what should be included in overheads, but common examples are the administrative functions such as personnel, finance, and legal and property services which support organisations. In the 1990s new public sector overhead costs were created in developing the internal market and purchaser and provider functions. During that time, however, some internal overhead costs were 'externalised' through contracting out. Overhead costs are a perennial preoccupation, usually coming to the fore during the major budgeting exercises which follow financial crises or budget cuts, the aim being to reduce 'non-essential' expenditure by targeting the activities which surround and support practitioners. It can be an exceedingly problematic process to decide what (and who!) constitutes an overhead cost, where the cuts will be made, and how the remaining costs should be shared.

Understanding fixed and variable costs and being able to calculate unit costs in these ways does not mean that a budget-holder is then entirely free to allocate spending as he or she sees fit. Marjorie's employers have limited her spending authority to £1,000 on any new items, and she must obtain three written quotations before going to her line manager for permission to spend more. Most organisations impose constraints on their employees, limiting their authority, to ensure that financial probity is maintained, as well as accountability to shareholders, elected representatives or the public at large. In the fields of health and social care, too, practitioners and managers are constrained by limits to their individual authority to spend money, or vary from service plans, as a means of ensuring that resources are used only for the purposes for which they were intended.

Budget plans and business plans

So far we have been considering Middlebrook's revenue budget simply as a table of figures, giving Marjorie a set of parameters for the activity of the Centre, only some of which she can change. A budget is not just a set of figures, however. To be most useful, a budget should be part and parcel of a written plan, describing what the service or business priorities are, what staff are going to do and the resources that are to be used, expressed in financial terms.

This brings us to the concept of business planning. The practice has its roots in commercial businesses, which have seen the process as an effective means for defining and meeting their objectives. In cases where the creation of the business plan remains the firm prerogative of senior managers and accountants and is not clearly understood and accepted by front-line managers and staff, there is considerable research to suggest that budgets will be resented and perhaps subverted (Williams and Carroll, 1998: 65–6). An alternative is to engage the workforce in:

- determining what the organisation is in business for – its mission
- analysing the organisation's strengths, weaknesses, opportunities and threats
- setting specific business objectives
- devising a plan for implementing the objectives
- clarifying who is accountable for the implementation
- agreeing how and when the plan will be reviewed.

The motivator for business planning seen in this way is the sense of ownership which the workforce can develop by taking part in the planning process, the greater understanding of their roles and of the resources available to them in going about their work.

During the 1990s, business planning – or what some people prefer to call service planning – became an increasingly accepted and developed discipline in non-profit-making organisations which competed for contracts. Most health and social care providers produce some form of annual business plan, for internal and external consumption (see, for example, CPS, 1993). Effective business planning should connect with and involve key people at all levels, enabling them to influence the outcome and communicate the message across the organisation. In larger organisations business plans at unit level should be compatible with each other: they should be consistent with and contribute to achievement of the organisation's wider goals, as expressed in directorate plans and the community strategies that all local authorities are required to prepare.

Some agencies take business and service planning still further, involving customers and service-users in the planning process, and seeing this as very much part of their strategy for quality. If the budget is a plan then, like all plans, it should be open to change, if circumstances alter. The amounts of money available, or service priorities, may change during a financial year and the budget plan provides a point of reference to check progress against targets, aims and objectives, or to see whether new service choices or priorities are possible. Some organisations incorporate their budget plan inside their business plan and use them as a management tool, in a continuous process of service delivery and control, changing the plan when necessary, using their resources flexibly to respond to threats and opportunities. In the next sub-section we show how Marjorie, working in this way, turned a potential crisis into an opportunity.

Responding to budgetary problems

Last year Marjorie organised a business planning workshop for members of Middlebrook's team and the charity's board. The workshop produced a mission statement for the Middlebrook Centre:

> To provide high quality care and guidance which enables disadvantaged people to maximise their potential and lead rewarding lives in the community.

During the workshop, board members confirmed two rumours that had been circulating:

* that the social services department had changed its funding rules for people with a learning disability – this would produce a 15 per cent drop in Middlebrook's social services income next year, amounting to £5,250.
* that the charity which operates Middlebrook was in financial difficulties and would be forced to reduce the deficit funding it provides (see Table 5.1) by 10 per cent – this would amount to £8,600 in a full year.

The total loss of funding for the next year was thus predicted to be £13,850.

Marjorie was able to set out a plan for Middlebrook which could potentially replace the income losses, reduce the financial risks caused by short-term service-user vacancies and also provide surpluses which could be used to improve the Centre's placement capacity. She explained that she had been invited to put in a bid to a trust which would provide

£65,000 over three years if Middlebrook would provide additional supported employment opportunities for service-users with neighbouring organisations. The financial case that Marjorie successfully put to the charity's board was as follows.

Twelve service-users attend supported employment placements in town each weekday. Under present working practices, the direct costs of the supported employment services are mostly fixed, consisting of payments to staff who transport service-users to town and back, plus sessional payments to a job coach who arranges placements and monitors and records progress. These costs do not change in direct proportion as the numbers of placements rise and fall. The other major cost is for transport, using the minibus and staff cars. These costs are fixed, unless the number of service-users travelling falls to ten or less, when only the minibus is needed. In working out her proposal, Marjorie calculated the daily unit cost of providing supported employment from Middlebrook. Here is the formula she used:

Direct costs plus	**Indirect costs**	divided by	**Number of days'**
(staff and	(percentage of management,		**service provided**
transport)	administration, insurances,		
	etc. that go in to supported		
	employment)		

Here is that formula again, this time with the figures included:

$$\frac{£35,000}{2,940} \begin{array}{l}\text{(total direct and indirect costs for} \\ \text{a full year, before proposed savings} \\ \text{implemented)} \\ \text{(12 service-users} \times 245 \text{ days supported} \\ \text{employment days each)}\end{array} = \begin{array}{l}£11.90 \text{ unit cost} \\ \text{per service-user} \\ \text{per day}\end{array}$$

On the basis of these calculations, Marjorie explained, the trust would contribute £65,000 over three years in equal instalments, in return for the provision of ten more supported employment placements. These ten service-users would be available from three local day centres. Marjorie persuaded the charity's board that she could take on the extra workload and further reduce the unit costs of Middlebrook's supported employment service by making changes to the way in which service-users travel to their placements in town. The aim would be to go ahead with person-centred planning goals for a number of service-users who wished to use public transport to and from their supported employment. This preparation could be achieved without additional costs, using existing staff. For a minority of service-users, public transport would not be possible, as they worked away from bus routes or would be unlikely to achieve the necessary competency. For this minority, transport would be provided by contract with a local taxi company. The plan, however, would replace the current costly practice of deploying two staff to travel with twelve people. Very importantly, at the same time it would address the mission – enhancing service-users' independence and achievements. Marjorie calculated that, after taking into account a small increase in the job coach's hours, the new travel-to-work practice could produce salary and mileage cost savings of £8,000 in a full year. Further savings of £5,000 a year could be produced by disposing of the minibus and hiring one when necessary.

Marjorie calculated that when next year's income losses (£13,850) were offset by new income and costs savings (£21,666, £5,000 and £8,000), an annual surplus of £20,816 could be achieved. She proposed that a new business plan should be developed, investing the surpluses in Middlebrook to increase the Centre's placement capacity and sustain the supported employment service once the trust funding finished in three years' time. The trust offering the funding had indicated that they were impressed by the quality of Middlebrook's services and would see their services as giving good value for money to the trust, particularly as the Centre could provide services immediately, without funded development time. Marjorie calculated the unit cost to the trust of supported employment for the additional ten service-users as follows:

$$\frac{£21,666}{2,450} \quad \begin{array}{l}\text{(all costs} - £65,000 \text{ divided by 3)} \\ \text{(10 service-users} \times 245 \text{ days supported} \\ \text{employment days each)}\end{array} \quad \begin{array}{l}= £8.84 \text{ unit cost} \\ \text{per service-user} \\ \text{per day}\end{array}$$

Marjorie also calculataed the *overall* unit cost to Middlebrook of providing supported employment for the 22 service-users:

$$\frac{£22,000}{5,390} \quad \begin{array}{l}\text{(all costs)} \\ \text{(22 people working 245 days each)}\end{array} \quad = \begin{array}{l}£4.08 \text{ unit cost} \\ \text{per day}\end{array}$$

This represented a dramatic reduction in present costs. The new proposals would need to be explained to all Middlebrook's staff and there would have to be discussions with the staff affected by the new travel-to-work arrangements. The board, however, felt that the arguments for going ahead were overwhelmingly strong and that staff would see that there were longer-term benefits. The accountant commented that the previously fixed costs to Middlebrook would be drastically reduced. The partnership with the trust would, he said, provide excellent value for money for all parties. He would help prepare a five-year business plan.

Value for money and value for mission?

The previous sections have demonstrated what might be achieved in a service-delivery agency such as Middlebrook through embedding the revenue budget in the overall business or service plan and through better understanding of the components of the budget and the extent to which they could be changed. Financial information, however, cannot stand alone. It needs to be set alongside information on the quality of the service to be achieved.

In following her accountant's advice to look at fixed and variable costs, for example, Marjorie noted that there was some flexibility as far as the deployment of sessional staff was concerned. In principle, she could offset some of the income losses by reducing their hours. But should she do this? On the face of it, it was more economical. She would certainly save money. However, she might run the risk of reducing staff morale, causing resignations at a time when social care providers are finding it increasingly difficult to recruit and retain their workforces. Even should Middlebrook succeed in recruiting, there would be associated costs. In the long run therefore, the cost savings might disappear, so it might not be efficient. Then there is the consideration of the quality of support service-users are receiving from long-standing sessional staff and the extent to which their satisfaction with the service is based on the familiarity and continuity that the present system offers. Marjorie needs therefore to bear in mind that reducing hours could mean a lower-quality, less effective service.

The three Es – Economy, Efficiency and Effectiveness (see Box 5.1) – became something of a mantra in the public sector as services became subject to competition. The Conservative governments of the 1980s and early 1990s encouraged numerous Value for Money (VFM) studies to question practices in social and health care. In 2000 the Labour government replaced the previous government's competitive compulsory tendering (CCT) regime with 'Best Value'. It is administered by the Audit Commission which carries out regular Best Value inspections on council services, from waste disposal to corporate strategy. The aim of Best Value was to ensure that within five years all council services achieved performance levels that were only achieved by the top 25 per cent of councils at the start of the five years. The emphasis of the initiative is on continuous improvement. It replaced the three Es with the four Cs:

- Challenge – Why do we do this? Can we do it a better way?
- Consult – What do local people think? How do the council's employees think they could do things better? What do other organisations that could provide the service think?
- Compare – Do other councils or similar organisations give a better service?
- Compete – Could the work be done better or more cheaply by another contractor? Do opportunities exist for partnerships with other public bodies, businesses or voluntary organisations?

Box 5.1   The three Es

Economy

The utilisation of resources of appropriate quality at the lowest possible price.

Efficiency

The relationship between goods and services provided and the resources used to provide them. An efficient activity produces the maximum output for any given set of resource inputs; or it has minimum inputs for any given quality and quantity of service provided.

Effectiveness

The extent to which an activity or programme achieves its intended objectives. It will often be examined in terms of the nature and severity of unwanted side effects.

(Glynn et al., 1996: 246–7)

Are VFM and Best Value just synonyms for cost reduction? Providing that all three Es are taken into account, the answer is no. When VFM is seen more narrowly, however, the results can be thoroughly counterproductive. Case Study 3 provides an example of this, where management action to tackle cost reduction had a series of negative consequences. It threw other equally important performance indicators off balance. As a result, the quality and quantity of social work service was adversely affected. The next two case studies, however, illustrate more positive outcomes. Case Study 4 tells a story in the statutory sector of costing activities, utilising business planning, involving staff and developing targets which were achievable and shared. Case Study 5, from the voluntary sector, had a similarly positive outcome and a crucial one for an organisation that needed to continue to attract contracts.

Case Study 3   Unforeseen consequences

A busy social work department in a large hospital introduced a computerised case-management system, which depended on social workers completing a form for each service-user, for prompt input to the computer. The administration manager became concerned about the amount of time spent by expensive social workers in completing the forms, and concluded that the practice constituted poor value for money. Consequently, the staff budget was adjusted to allow clerical staff to be recruited to complete the forms, reduce social work costs and free up time for other tasks.

However, problems arose when the clerical staff, understandably limited in their specialist knowledge, constantly needed to refer to the social workers with queries arising from the forms. New service-users also objected that they were being denied access to social workers and many of them logged formal complaints, which of course needed proper administration, involving the customer service unit and the hospital social work team. Health practitioners also confirmed that a backlog of referrals had been created. The management action had achieved reductions to the payroll costs of the social work team, but simultaneously lowered the quality of the service and increased administration costs elsewhere. The administration manager was advised that service quality had been reduced unacceptably and that social workers should resume the form-filling until the training needs of the clerical staff had been addressed.

Case Study 4   Bringing in business planning

A county council had a central unit to provide occupational therapy services – major and minor adaptations to enable disabled people to continue to live in their own homes rather than a care home. The unit's revenue budget, covering staff and running costs and minor adaptations, was £4 million and its capital budget, for major adaptations such as lifts and bathroom extensions, was £5 million. In 1993 the unit overspent its revenue budget by £500,000 and underspent its capital budget by £2.5 million – effectively denying service to those who needed it. Council members were asking 'Why are we employing all these staff when they are not delivering the service?' There was a real danger that the unit's budget would be cut and its staff reduced. An investigation revealed that:

- None of the unit's managers had any experience of budget management or business planning.
- There were no systems in place to record or forecast expenditure or activity.
- Approval of a major adaptation took several months and often money allocated in one year was not spent – replacement funding had to be found in the following year.
- There was no process of planning for the coming year's activities.

The unit gave up an occupational therapist post to meet the cost of a new business manager. All the unit's staff had an opportunity to contribute to and comment on a business plan for the coming year. The plan set out the current year's activity and budget as a basis for the coming year, for which targets for major and minor adaptations were set. The cost of the staff and other running costs were calculated accurately and systems were introduced to monitor both revenue and capital expenditure each month. Realistic forecasts were made of the time-scales for individual major adaptations so that money could be allocated to the financial year in which it would be needed. Links were formed with the finance staff to make sure the unit had timely and accurate information about its expenditure. At the end of the first year of this process the capital budget was 85 per cent spent, and there was only a very small overspend on the revenue budget. The unit had reached its targets on the number of minor adaptations to be provided. Other benefits included a rational basis for allocating resources to meet competing demands and resolving conflicts about resource allocation, and a new spirit of partnership between the unit and colleagues in the finance section. By demonstrating its ability to manage its budget and plan its activity the unit gained credibility and was able to attract additional capital and revenue funding to expand its activities. Since then it has taken over responsibility for other services. Its revenue and capital budgets have doubled and the services it provides are a major component in the county's community care strategy.

Case Study 5   Calculating the real costs of a service

A voluntary organisation (VO), which was providing meals on wheels on behalf of social services and running a lunch club for elderly people with funding from the district council, was finding it difficult to meet increasing costs and demand within fixed budgets. The meals on wheels and the lunch club meals were cooked at the VO's kitchen using the same food and staff. The VO's with social services for the meals on wheels was based on unit costs for each meal. The unit cost included the cost of the fresh ingredients from which the meals were prepared, the cooks' wages and a proportion of the running costs of the kitchen, as well as mileage payments to volunteers who delivered the meals using their own cars. The lunch club was partly funded by a grant from the district council which had not been increased for some years.

The unit cost for meals on wheels had been calculated some years before and stood at £3 per meal. When this cost was reviewed it was found that:

- The ratio of lunch club meals (which the district council funded) and the meals on wheels had changed – as a result social services were not meeting their full share of the food and premises costs and staff wages.

- The unit cost had not been increased to reflect increased mileage payments to volunteers.
- The costs of the staff who administered the meals-on-wheels service had never been included.
- Unused food worth approximately £7,000 was being thrown away each year due to poor ordering practices and lack of portion control.

When these points were taken into account the true unit cost was £3.95 per meal. The councils were unable to increase their contribution so the VO decided to put the service out to tender. A private company offered to supply frozen meals for both the lunch club and the meals-on-wheels service at £2.50 each. The VO was able to reduce the kitchen staff at the lunch club, as the frozen meals simply required reheating.

There were, however, some additional costs to be met in the first year of the new arrangements – £15,000 to purchase special ovens to reheat the meals and adapt the kitchen to accommodate them and redundancy payments of £5,000. A good deal of time had to be spent negotiating with the district council, which was eventually persuaded to pay for the ovens, while the other additional costs were met by an increase of £1 in the cost of each meal – a decision that caused some soul-searching. But the other, ongoing, savings reduced the unit cost to £2.80 per meal, which kept it within the funding provided by social services and allowed scope for future growth in demand.

The final case study in this section brings in the topic of external partnership funding – something that we saw Marjorie use to good effect for Middlebrook. Partnership funding is currently important and can often seem to offer a way forward: supplementing an organisation's own budget by attracting funds from other sources, such as the UK government's Single Regeneration Budget or various European Funds. Another recent innovation is the introduction of Health Action Zones to fund projects to increase the overall health of people living in deprived areas. These funds, however, often have strict eligibility criteria and may not always be relevant. Almost all require close working between organisations in different sectors and increasingly competitive applications. Grant sources change constantly according to changing regional, national and European priorities, so will require close monitoring on websites and in the media to seize opportunities. Case Study 6, however, shows how a small voluntary organisation secured funding to continue a successful pilot project.

Case Study 6   Partnership working for more effective use of limited resources

A voluntary organisation which provided treatment and rehabilitation services for drug misusers had run a pilot 'arrest referral' scheme. Under this scheme a trained worker visited drug-misusing offenders immediately after their arrest or remand by the courts and offered them the opportunity to be treated for their addiction. The project involved close liaison between the worker, the police and the probation service and its aim was to provide treatment for people who had not previously had that opportunity and so improve their lifestyle and reduce the chances of their reoffending.

The pilot project was successful but the organisation, a charity, had no money to continue it. They then had the chance to join a partnership of public and voluntary organisations that was bidding for money from European funds. The grant programme provided 40 per cent of the cost of the project: the balance was 'match funding' (which can be existing expenditure that contributes towards achieving the project's aims).

The charity needed £80,000 per year to employ and support the worker, which they had to fund fully from the grant. Match funding was found by calculating the value of the time spent by police officers in dealing with arrested drug misusers and by the probation service in dealing with those remanded or convicted of an offence. This amounted to some £120,000 per annum and provided sufficient match funding to enable the grant to be obtained.

As a result, the charity was able to continue its successful project for the next three years, dealing with some 200 drug-misusing offenders per year. Many of them received treatment that would not otherwise have been offered to them, breaking their cycle of offending and reoffending, with consequent benefits to themselves and the community and reductions in cost for the criminal justice system. Lasting partnerships were formed between the police and the probation and drug treatment agencies, which have aided the development of similar collaborative working in the future.

What can be concluded from this series of case studies around the theme of achieving better value for money? First, dialogue between team members, across teams and between teams is essential, if unacceptable, unforeseen consequences of value for money initiatives are to be avoided or overcome (Glynn, et al., 1996). Finance specialists, service managers and practitioners need to work together to ensure issues of quality and cost are considered together, rather than either one dominating the other. Marjorie's travel solution demonstrated this – it was value for money because it was value for mission too. Secondly, however, there is what we might call the missing stakeholder problem. Notably absent in all the examples here, including the Middlebrook example, is the involvement of service-users in issues of financial planning and management. Yet service-users are stakeholders just as much as the service-providers are. If financial thinking can be extended to practitioners and service-providers in the ways this chapter has shown, can it not and should it not be extended to the users of those services too? There is research to show that learning disability service-users can be very effectively involved in evaluating residential services in the community and that, when they are, the thinking about service priorities changes (Whittaker, 1994).

Finally, we need to draw attention to some of the hurdles and the constraints the case studies tend to neglect. Financial management and budget handling are not always as straightforward as the positive examples here might seem to suggest. Financial accounting systems, designed to meet the needs of specialist finance staff, have sometimes not been able to produce the timely, rapid, detailed and easy-to-use information that service managers need.

Even when good information is available choices may not be clear-cut, and it may be difficult to make the kinds of judgements that are needed in the complex case, for example, of creating a care package for someone in need of care in the community (Leat and Perkins, 1998). Sometimes, too, there is just not enough money available to keep services going for certain service-user groups or to fund important new developments, especially for smaller organisations which do not have the flexibility in the use of their budgets that larger organisations have. There are limits to creative thinking and active financial management if the purse is just too small.

Conclusion

Greater transparency in the financial management process, as some of the material in this chapter has demonstrated, can bring considerable benefits – aligning goals and resources more closely, clarifying policy choices, bringing more stakeholders into the policy process and sometimes, indeed, allowing more service or better services with fewer resources.

Since 2000 the government has made more money available for health and social care but has also demanded much more from local authorities and service providers. Best Value, national strategies for major areas of social care provision, national inspection regimes – these all represent a centralising tendency. Managers have undoubtedly become more skilled and creative in the use of money and, through inter-agency collaboration and pooled budgets, should be able to obtain better value for money and provide higher quality and more seamless services. Yet the ability to count the cost is no panacea. Budget managers, as this chapter has also emphasised, have to work within constraints and may not be able to reach the happy solutions that Marjorie found for the Middlebrook Centre. Purchasers and providers still need to negotiate over contracts, debating the amount and quality of service and watching how shared costs will fall. Despite pooled budgets and formal agreements inter-agency collaboration can still be hard work. With year-on-year demands to find cost savings, the argument that the total resource has become insufficient sometimes needs to come to the fore. Certainly it must be acknowledged that, however well they manage budgets and forecast expenditure, people at all levels in social care will continue to work with limited resources, and hard choices need to be made. Being able to work with the basic concepts outlined here is thus a key requirement for critical practice as discussed in this book, but it is by no means the only one.

References

Centre for Public Services (CPS) (1993) *A Detailed Handbook for the Public Service and Business Plans*. Sheffield: CPS.

Deakin, N. (1996) 'The devil's in the detail: some reflections on contracting for social care by voluntary organisations', *Social Policy and Administration*, 30 (1): 20–38.

Glynn, J., Perkins, D. and Stewart, S. (1996) *Achieving Value for Money*. London: W.B. Saunders Co. Ltd.

Hadley, R. and Clough, R. (1996) *Care in Chaos: Frustration and Challenge in Community Care*. London: Cassell.

Leat, D. and Perkins, D. (1998) 'Juggling and dealing: the creative work of care package purchasing', *Social Policy and Administration*, 32 (2): 166–81.

Lewis, J., with Bernstock, P., Bovell, V. and Wookey, F. (1996) 'The purchaser/provider split in social care: is it working?', *Social Policy and Administration*, 30 (1): 1–19.

Mackintosh, M. (2000) 'Flexible contracting? Economic cultures and implicit contracts in social care', *Journal of Social Policy*.

Masters, S. (1993) 'Financial management in the NHS', *Public Money and Management*, 13 (1): 4–5.

Tonge, R. and Horton, S. (1996) 'Financial management and quality', in D. Farnham and S. Horton (eds), *Managing the New Public Services*. London: Macmillan.

Whittaker, A. (1994) 'Service evaluation by people with learning difficulties', in A. Connor and S. Black (eds), *Performance Review and Quality in Social Care*. London: Jessica Kingsley.

Williams, J. and Carroll, A. (1998) 'Budgeting and budgetary control', in J. Wilson (ed.), *Financial Management for the Public Services*. Buckingham: Open University Press.

Chapter 6

Reflections on past social work practice: The central role of relationship

Barbara Prynn

It is interesting in a discipline in which personal histories are of crucial importance, that statutory social work agencies seem uninterested in their own history. Perhaps it is simpler to be untrammelled by historical ways of doing things. It is easy when thinking about social work in the past to see everything in black and white. If the past was a golden age then what has followed has been a decline: or the new is by definition, better. But there was good and bad practice in the past as there is good and bad practice now. The central question that I want to address is whether or not practice in the past, in our case between 1948 and 1972, has any practical relevance to the twenty-first century.

My professional social work experience began in the 1960s in mental health. I worked in psychiatric hospital settings, child guidance clinics and a local authority mental health department. Following the Seebohm reforms (Seebohm, 1968), I happily moved to medical social work and later to child care. The latter part of my career has been in fostering and adoption. In this chapter I will use some illustrations from my own experience. I have interviewed people who were adopted or fostered and who grew up between the wars (Prynn, 2001) and I will use material drawn from my subsequent research[1] into the reminiscences of social workers active between 1948 and the 1970s. Between 1996 and 2003 I interviewed more than thirty people who had been child care officers during this period. Some of them worked in other social work agencies or hospitals. The social workers described what it was like to work in social care before and after the Seebohm reorganisation, together with their reflections on social work practice.

The discussion and examples given will be drawn chiefly from local authority welfare services in England and Wales, with reference to hospital social work and social work in voluntary agencies. In Scotland, the Kilbrandon Report (1964) recommended changes which came into force in 1968 to set up social work departments, absorbing the former

---

[1] Pseudonyms are used for all research participants.

children's departments and other personal social welfare departments. Most significant was the introduction of children's hearings, which 'are one of our most remarkable institutions' (Fraser of Carmyllie, 2003). And Northern Ireland 'has had an integrated system of health and personal social services since 1973; through a structure of four Health and Social Services Boards and nineteen Hospital and Community Trusts' (Heenan, 2004: 799).

The contrasts between the nations of the UK were and are important, but many of the themes which social work practice exhibited in England and Wales between 1948 and 1972 could also be found in other parts of the UK.

I do not intend to provide a history of social policy as it relates to social work. My main concern is with the experience of being a social worker during the period. Nevertheless some context-setting is required before dealing directly with practice. We need to examine the organisational structures which delivered social work services. What did social workers do, and how were they part of the departments in which they worked? There will be discussion of the language and style of social work, showing the difference between social worker–client relationships during the period 1948–1972 and service-user–social worker relationships now.[2] I want to argue that while there were many deficiencies in social work practice between 1948 and 1972, the centrality of the personal relationship between social worker and service-user was more pronounced then as compared to now. Arguably in current-day statutory social work, there is a preoccupation with case or care management, which exhibits greater emotional distance between social worker and service-user than was the case during the period under discussion.

The context for practice

The structure of welfare provision following the Second World War was part of the social reconstruction of the Welfare State 'which marked the end of the Poor Law in this country' (Pugh, 1968: 3). Services were set up to deal with basic needs, making use of what had been learned during the war about the effects of deprivation on children (Pugh, 1968).

Social workers aimed to improve people's lives with relatively minor adjustments, especially in the late 1950s when the Prime Minister, Harold Macmillan, at a Tory Party rally in Bedford in 1957, advised people to 'go around the country, go to the industrial towns, go to the farms and you will see a state of prosperity such as we have never had in my lifetime – nor indeed in the history of this country … Indeed let us be frank about it – most of our people have never had it so good.'

Generally speaking, social workers did not challenge the established social and political order or the various structures for the provision of welfare services. Yet during the 1960s there was growing unease with the notion that Britain had 'never had it so good'. One aspect of this unease was with the existing 'specialised' or perceptibly 'fragmented' organisation of social services. Concern was expressed by policy-makers and social

---

[2] Although it is anachronistic, 'clients' (the term used during the period under discussion) will mainly be referred to as service-users in the chapter.

workers that problems which arose for individuals of whatever age could not be separated from their family situation, and that to seek help from separate agencies which did not work together in a formal way was unhelpful. The idea of having one social service agency in each local authority with one door through which the public might go to seek help culminated in the Seebohm reforms, which were supported by the professional social work associations.

Social work agencies and training for social work between 1948 and 1972 were concentrated on maintaining relationships between social workers and service-users, often for long periods of time. There was tension, which increased during the 1960s and 1970s, between some social workers who chose to concentrate on interpersonal needs and others who thought about service-users in a more political way. These perspectives are not incompatible as Rustin (1991) suggests, but the tension continued after the inception of social services departments.

The pre-Seebohm work experience for social workers

Local authority social workers between 1948 and 1972 were involved in the provision of services through teams which worked with clearly defined service-user groups. A child care officer would have worked in a children's department; a mental welfare officer would have worked in a mental health department. The separate departments had existed in each local authority area since 1948. Social workers were employed in hospitals, either with people who had mental health problems in a psychiatric social work department, or with people with physical illness as medical social workers. Until 1974, when hospital social workers came under the umbrella of Social Services departments, both psychiatric social workers (PSWs) and medical social workers (MSWs) in hospitals (who were called lady almoners until 1964 when their training body, the Institute of Almoners, changed its name to the Institute of Medical Social Workers) were employed by hospital management committees.

There were social workers in voluntary agencies for children such as Dr Barnardo's and the Children's Society. Voluntary agencies for adults or families – for example the Family Welfare Association (http://www.fwa.org.uk/about_hist.html [last accessed 06/02/2007]), Family Service Units[3] and the Liverpool Personal Service Society (http://www.pss.org.uk/module_images/ACCTS%20Fin%20Rep0304.pdf [last accessed 06/02/2007]) also employed social workers.

Although the first 'generic' course had been established as early as 1954 (Stevenson, 2005: 570), generally speaking social work training reflected the specialisms outlined above. Entrants to social work saw themselves becoming 'child care officers' or 'medical social workers', rather than social workers in a general sense. The disadvantage of this was that social workers tended to see their own specialism as overarching. An extreme example might be that a medical social worker would make a plan for a patient without

---

[3] Family Service Units were an independent charity but they have now merged (01/06/2006) with the Family Welfare Association.

having sufficient regard to the needs of the patient's family; or a child care officer might consider the needs of the children of a family without much regard to the needs of a father with mental health problems. An advantage in belonging to a specific working group was being able to learn from one's colleagues as well as learning by working in the same field all the time.

Polly Gordon, an occupational therapist until 1964, said about becoming an assistant child care officer:

> I think that the greatest input that I had was [learning] by 'sitting next to Nelly'. There was a very good, supportive, atmosphere in the office and I remember that. And you learned because you listened to other people's telephone conversations. You read other people's files. And people were very helpful to you.

> (Interview, Polly Gordon, 2002)

In hospitals MSWs were members of medical teams, and some felt that their status derived from the medical staff with whom they worked. MSWs carried out tasks such as arranging financial services for hospital patients, booking convalescent homes and ensuring that patients could manage in their own homes. The major part of their work was assisting patients and their families with difficult diagnoses or bereavement. One of the tensions for MSWs related to their position as professionals with expertise in relationships with ill people and the 'hand-maiden' status, which some medical staff accorded them. This was one reason why it was particularly important for MSWs to belong to a professional group, while at the same time locating their 'professional identity' within the hospital (Carter, 1971: 268). Notwithstanding this ambiguity, the MSW was an integral part of the hospital professional community, and could have profound influence on how patients and their families were thought about (Davis, 2006).

The situation today is different. McLeod (as described in Bywaters and McLeod, 2002: 141) undertook an 'action research consultancy with 2 hospital-based elderly service teams' in the late 1990s. She found that 'over seventy per cent of the patients did not know that there were social workers on site' and that

> a substantial minority of patients with requirements for the input of a modest level of social work services to ward off situations which threatened a serious collapse of health on discharge were not being referred by other colleagues.

Psychiatric social workers (PSWs) were unlike other pre-Seebohm social workers in that they worked in a variety of settings.

> I think [the] APSW [the Association of Psychiatric Social Workers] was very much a professional association in the strict sense that entry was by holding a particular professional qualification. People went into various different fields of social work adult mental health work, quite a lot of APSW members had moved into other fields. It

was to a certain extent generic, people had done the Mental Health Course [the PSW training] after having done something else.

(Interview, Kevin Barker, 2002)

In hospitals PSWs were in a position similar to medical social workers in being members of a multi-disciplinary team. They worked in both general and psychiatric hospitals, and in local authority mental health services, where in the 1960s they tended to be in a minority. PSWs also worked in prisons, the probation service, so-called 'maladjusted schools' and in universities or university counselling services, as well as in voluntary agencies such as the NSPCC and in local authority departments other than mental health.

Psychiatric social workers were involved differently with medical teams than medical social workers. This may be because of the psychodynamic bias of social work in the post-war period. The relationships of the service-user and his or her internal world were paid acute attention by the social worker, in tune with the thinking of psychiatrists; and because in the 1960s, following the work of Laing (1960), people with mental health difficulties were beginning to be treated in their families, an area in which PSWs were experienced. From 1948 until the 1980s PSWs worked in Child Guidance Clinics. The clinics changed their title to Child and Family Clinics in the 1980s and are now generally known as Child and Adolescent Mental Health Services (CAMHS).

There was a division of labour in the clinics. The child psychiatrist or psychotherapist would see the child and the PSW would see the child's parents. Today there would be regular family meetings with both professionals, whereas then the professionals would meet without the family. This approach excluded the parents from important discussions and plans for their child's future as well as limiting the child's (or young person's) own input.

One part of the local authority social worker's role, whatever the specialism, was to do home visits. PSWs differed from MSWs in that they more often visited the homes and families of hospital patients. Since local authority social workers did the majority of their work in clients' homes, they were compelled to think about the family as a whole even if their specialist perspective was narrower. This practice raised other problems in regard to confidentiality, not allowing the service-user a choice of meeting place, and considerations regarding social workers' safety.

By the early 1970s, in line with Seebohm, the work and its location changed completely. Most field social workers in Social Services departments in England and Wales worked in 'generic' social work teams where usually each worker would work with *all* service-user groups.

[T]he 1970 Local Authority Social Services Act abolished the Children's Departments. The departments were amalgamated with welfare departments, mental health departments and sections of other educational, housing and health services into SSDs [Social Services Departments].

(Holman, 2001: 63)

The role of the manager

In the hierarchy of management in the pre-Seebohm departments, continuing into the later 1970s, the second tier were called 'senior social workers' and the third tier were 'area officers'. Present-day terms like 'team manager' suggest something different. Arising out of psychodynamic practice in social work, supervision of practice has always meant something emotionally warmer than the process of ensuring that a worker has met organisational or regulatory goals. While it was part of the function of the senior social worker to manage the members of a team and the work it did, the title stressed practice knowledge and experience rather than the different task that 'manager' implies. Supervision of social workers was seen to be performed by an experienced peer rather than a 'boss'. Although this may not have implied less scrutiny, Holman (2001: 53) describes the detailed overview taken by Barbara Kahan when she was children's officer in Dudley between 1948 and 1951, which emphasises her personal approach: 'Dudley was responsible for 72 children in care plus supervision of private fosterings and those placed for adoption. Barbara was interested in every one of these children.'

The function of the chief officer was commented upon by Sarah Leslie, a child care officer in the 1960s.

> In terms of the examination of work the Children's Officer and the Deputy Children's Officer would read every case; they had duplicate files in area offices. The Children's Officer would read everything over the year's period; and the very strict adherence to Boarding Out Regulations checking that they had done visits.
>
> (Interview, Sarah Leslie, 2003)

Alison Ball described how in the late 1960s the Chief Officer

> would see every single piece of post in the morning. And she would often write comments on top of the post expecting some sort of answer to whatever question she was making about the piece of the correspondence. You got wise to it afterwards; you thought 'well she'll never remember all this' so you just forgot about it. But to see every single piece of post that came in, and, more or less, a lot of it that went out too!
>
> (Interview, Alison Ball, 2002)

The all-seeing eye of the chief officer continued in new Social Services departments. Although social workers had a relative degree of autonomy in terms of their daily work, the letters they wrote were signed by the chief officer, who also read the letters they received. Since most communication was by post, this meant that all the social worker's correspondence with service-users or other agencies was open to criticism and amendment by their head of department.

Satyamurti (1981: 30–31) describes how correspondence was managed in a Social Services department in 1970.

Every morning at 9.00 a.m. the Director, Assistant Director and Group Controllers (each being responsible for one of five areas of the Department's work) met in (the Director's) room for what was referred to as the 'morning post meeting'. This could last for up to one-and-a-half hours … The meeting had no agenda, but consisted in the ad hoc discussion of what seemed a random selection of the department's mail. The letters were simply read by everyone, and put aside to be passed to the appropriate area team.

Professional identity

The professional associations were important for social workers pre-Seebohm in a way that the British Association of Social Workers (BASW) today is not. Each professional group had an association. There were heated discussions in the 1960s as members debated whether or not untrained social workers should belong to BASW. There was a fear of 'dilution', the loss of professional values and specialised experience, which were seen to be integral to the role of a social worker. Stevenson (2005: 570) believes that

the decision of BASW to remove qualification as a criteria for membership of the association gravely weakened its capacity to engage in constructive dialogue with other comparable associations and government.

This perspective suggests that a professional association consisting of members who have followed an agreed course to attain professional status, comparable perhaps to the British Medical Association, can take a powerful stand when negotiating with central or local government. In this sense the professional associations were pressure groups, and they published journals, although there were journals such as Case Conference for a general social work readership. The organisations held annual conferences where current issues were introduced by prominent people in the field. The conferences emphasised the importance of the identity of a worker as belonging to a specific association.

Practice

Each social worker had a caseload, and the numbers were very high compared to today. Gail Jackson (interview, 2002) 'had a caseload of ninety' in 1969. The essence of the work was 'casework' which would now be called 'counselling'. 'Casework' was influenced by psychodynamic thought. The work of Bowlby (1953) and Winnicott (1957) influenced children's departments as well as social work in child guidance clinics and elsewhere. Froggett (2002: 138) says that:

Casework is an intrinsically biographical method, where the intersections of the narratively structured experience of practitioners and clients informs the process of therapeutic reflection, and indeed the momentum and modality of the work.

An earlier definition (Bowers, 1949, quoted in Biestek, 1961: 1) of casework, was as

> an art in which knowledge of the science of human relations and skill in relationship are used to mobilise capacities in the individual and resources in the community appropriate for better adjustment between the client and all or any part of his total environment. The casework relationship is a form of treatment.

The Children and Young Persons Act 1963 created a family casework service in children's departments, so that the 'art' and 'skill in relationship' were also used in work with families. Timms (1964: 183) discussed the ambiguities in the term 'family casework' and confusion between practitioners and families about its meaning. He suggested that the definition came from:

> The idea of service to the family unit and the encouragement of 'good' or 'healthy' family life [which] provides a point of entry into the family and the beginnings of an agency programme that can be presented to the community.

Pugh (1968: 18) says that:

> This present tendency amongst social workers to see the family as the unit of casework treatment is of course rooted in psychoanalytic concepts of the importance of family relationships for the inner emotional life of the individual.

And Heywood (1959: 182) comments, in relation to casework in child care:

> It is the relationship – found in the foster home or Children's Home – provided by the case worker which is the healing factor in the child's life … The caseworker has the very skilled job of interpreting the needs of the child to the carefully chosen foster-parent or housemother, and helping them also to contain and overcome their real anxieties in the new situation.

The relationship between child and caseworker was undoubtedly significant – in my opinion much more so than the present relationship between a child and a social worker, which tends to feature less frequent contact. However the suggestion that the casework relationship was the primary therapeutic agent, rather than the combined effort of the caseworker and the foster carer, for example, tends to deny the helpfulness of the provision of positive alternative family life. Casework, or counselling as we'd call it now, had always been criticised by some as insufficient (Wooton, 1959: 296). During the early 1970s it came under growing pressure from the political left.

> Casework, the commonest form of social work practice is under mounting attack from the political left … The case against casework consists of the proposition that as casework leads to the adjustment to social norms, it tends to conceal the very ills in society which allegedly cause social malfunctioning in the first place.

(Robinson, 1972: 475)

Casework required a context of professional autonomy (Pugh, 1968: 109–10; Parsloe and Stevenson 1978: 134) and this permitted moves *away* from the psychodynamic practice that had originally underpinned casework. From the late 1960s radical perspectives including Marxism and feminism began to have an influence on social work practice in general (Hobsbawm, 1994: 298–301; 310–19). While Seebohm brought a profession together organisationally, in intellectual terms and its day-to-day practice the social and emotional distance between social worker and service-user tended to increase gradually; a process which developed further under the influence of the New Right in the 1980s and early 1990s via such processes as 'marketisation' (Gregory and Holloway, 2005).

The relationship between worker and client – which might continue for years – sometimes crossed the difficult boundary between a professional relationship and friendship. One of the questions I asked the former child care officers whom I interviewed, was about friendships with service-users or foster carers. Only one of them insisted that friendship would have been unprofessional. Almost all the others continue, decades later, to have friendly relationships with former service-users and their descendants. One of the basic dilemmas for social workers, now as then, concerns how to manage the psychological distance and boundary between themselves and the people with whom they are working.

In this connection, one of the issues often discussed in supervision was that of 'dependency' (Froggett, 2002). A long-term close relationship between social worker and service-user was more likely to occur when the latter was living at home than in a hospital setting. The worker could become more deeply involved with the family situation. Dependency was not encouraged, as it was perceived to reflect the social worker's own need rather than that of the service-user. The current definition of 'service-user' implies a relationship where dependency would be unlikely, and the present emphasis on short-term work also diminishes the possibility of relationships which might be thought unprofessional developing.

While social workers were busy during the day, they also had to do night and weekend emergency duty. They were paid extra for this. They could take time off later if they were called out in the middle of the night, but they had to turn up for work the following morning. One of the difficulties for welfare officers and child care officers following reorganisation was having to take on the onerous and regular task of mental health duty calls:

> And of course the other thing was the emergency duty that you had to do because you were on duty from five o'clock one night until nine o'clock the next morning. Or it was a weekend all Saturday or all Sunday and you could get paid for it but you could also after a time, I think there was so much objection that they eventually decided that if we did five sessions we could get time off in lieu. But of course the question of taking it off was not easy and even if you'd been called out say at five o'clock in the morning to a mental health case, I mean you were expected to be at work at nine o'clock in the morning.
>
> (Interview, Alison Barnes, 2002)

The service-user for whom the crisis occurred did not always know the emergency social worker, but there was more likelihood that they would, or that the social worker would know something about them, than is the case with present-day emergency duty teams.

In terms of day-to-day work, regardless of the department in which workers were employed, social work in local authorities was delivered in similar ways in the 1960s. Many operated a 'patch' system, that is, individual social workers were responsible for definite geographical areas, much like a police 'beat'. This arrangement often continued some time after the Seebohm reorganisation (Stevenson, 2005: 275). A worker might get to know a wide range of different kinds of service-users in the patch very well. Workers in different departments were closely involved with others who worked the same patch. Some agencies had a patch system for foster families, which facilitated the growth of positive working relationships between practitioner and foster parents. Tom Grant, talking about practice in 1966, said:

> Each [worker] had a patch which was their own. And they also doubled up for another patch and there were two men and two women and so the men tended to take on the boys who were in care [and] the women tended to take the girls who were in care, and on supervision orders. So we would double up for each other's office area, but it was very satisfying having your own patch, and developing it and being encouraged to develop it so that one became very much involved in the *community work* [my emphasis] in the particular patch that you were covering.

> (Interview, Tom Grant, 2002)

Statutory social workers, had opportunities via the 'patch system', to develop a position within a community, defined on a geographical basis. It is reasonable to ask if the role of case or care managers today would allow for this possibility.

A child care officer's life was busy. While the specified intervals between visits to a child in the care system or for child care reviews have changed little since the Children Act 1948, these were seen as a minimum, not a maximum, during the era of the children's departments. A report had to be written on each contact. It was necessary that time was accounted for and actions taken, or thought about, recorded. In reading through case files for the 1960s and 1970s, one becomes aware of the agonising decisions that social workers had to make, and the heart-searching which went into making those decisions. Would case recordings today capture what a social worker felt emotionally about service-users and the associated decisions and dilemmas surrounding their care or service delivered? I think this would be quite rare.

In my own experience in the period under discussion, recording casework was handled in the following way. An interview with a service-user would be recorded in detail and this was central to the theory of casework. In my first job in a hospital psychiatric unit in the early 1960s, I was expected to complete a detailed account of *everything* that happened between the initial greeting with the service-user and our parting.

An initial interview would be to record a social or family history. The social worker would have an agenda for the interview. How to conduct interviews, and how social workers should conduct themselves in interviews, was an integral part of social work teaching.

Recording continues to be central to the social work task, but the way in which it is done has altered. So-called 'open records' did not appear until the 1980s (BASW, 1980). There was no question before that of service-users reading – let alone adding to or changing – what was written about them. The relationship between worker and service-user was seen as the key to the future of the work, and *process recording* was used by social workers as an aide-memoire for themselves and for supervision.

> 'process recording' [was] used by 'caseworkers' in the 1950s and 1960s when a psychodynamically informed diagnosis was reached only in the context of the

relationship between client and worker, and which required the supervisor to read a 'blow by blow' account of their interaction.

(Prince, 1996: 27)

Every service-user interview could not have been written up as a process recording. It would have taken too long to do. Recordings were generally handwritten, typewriters being few and far between even in the 1980s. Yet in most settings a worker would be expected to produce process recordings regularly. Otherwise, recordings were shorter, while still fuller than would usually be the case today.

By the middle of the 1950s the purpose of case records reflected a professional concern with diagnosis, as social work adopted the medical model of examination, diagnosis, treatment and prognosis. Such 'professionalism' required records to be read by supervisors concerned not only with the accuracy of diagnosis but with the worker's own development as a caseworker.

(Prince, 1996: 13)

There would have been rather less emphasis in supervision on fulfilling statutory or other 'managerial' requirements. A social worker was expected to do all the necessary work with a service-user's family, perhaps alongside other social workers, without the assistance of other agencies. Ownership of records lay with the individual worker and the agency; the possibility of further scrutiny by service-users as a result of a complaint was barely a consideration.

Complaints procedures have traditionally been seen as somewhat alien to the world of personal social services but many social service departments now [between 1989 and 1991] offer a separate complaints service for children and young people in their care.

(Prince, 1996: 25)

Language and style

Parton and O'Byrne (2000) and Gregory and Holloway (2005) discuss the language of social work. Gregory and Holloway

look[ed] at how the *recipient* of social work intervention, the *social worker* and the *social work task* have been constructed and reconstructed from both inside and outside the profession as it responds to the exigencies of the prevailing social context.

(2005: 49)

Since the early 1970s the words for people in social work and their jobs have changed significantly. People who would now be called 'service-users' were 'clients'. Hospital social workers in the 1960s and 1970s, like their medical colleagues, referred to 'patients' rather than 'clients.'

These words represent disparate ideas about the people with whom social workers are engaged. The words and names we use are a function of social or emotional 'distance'. Management of this distance between social worker and service-user is a significant part of social work. 'Client' puts social workers on a par with lawyers, for example, in a professional relationship. 'Service-user' implies *agency,* and not being 'done to' by the social worker. The earlier 'client' and the present 'service-user' signify different distances.

While the term 'client' is no longer thought appropriate, a text used in social work training in the 1960s, *The Casework Relationship* (Biestek, 1961: 103), suggested a meaning of the word which is close to the definition of 'service-user'.

The principle of client self-determination is the practical recognition of the right and need of clients to freedom in making their own choices and decisions.

While there is overlap between the concepts of 'client' and 'service-user', different social and emotional distances are implied by each term. The closer relationship between social worker and client can be demonstrated by someone talking about 'my clients'. Perhaps it is possible to say 'my service-user', but it seems a strange and slightly awkward thing to say. Perhaps 'client' implies paternalism and possessiveness, yet being able to say 'my client' did indicate personal as well as professional responsibility on the social worker's part. Arguably the change in the 1990s from 'foster parent' to 'foster carer' and the similar change from a 'link (social) worker' to 'supervising social worker' (for foster carers) implies further increase in the emotional and social distance between social workers and the people who care for looked-after children.

While in some ways the pre-Seebohm departments were less formal and less structured places than twenty-first-century local authority social services, in a sense they were more formal. While colleagues might call each other by their first names, it was by no means standard that everyone in the department would be on first-name terms. The same applied to service-users who were called by their titles, and who called social workers by their titles. In this respect statutory social work agencies differed from smaller agencies such as Family Service Units. As Margaret Wills said, when speaking of practice in the voluntary sector in the 1950s – and this has echoes in current practice:

The idea was that you worked alongside families instead of doing it to them as it were and we were on Christian [*sic*] name terms which a lot of [local authority] social workers found very difficult, you know. We were familiar, too emotionally involved, that sort of thing.

(Interview, Margaret Wills, 1996)

Even when workers and foster carers had known each other well for years, they continued to use each other's titles. This may be seen as a sign of respect on both sides. Use of first names may mask a real difference in power, and in social and emotional distance between social worker and service-user. Using everyone's first name may seem democratic, but it suggests a spurious equality. Even if workers in a department are on first-name terms with the director, everyone knows where the power lies. The same applies to using first names with service-users. They and social workers do not have an equal relationship. The social worker has the power to call the service-user to account, and to agree or refuse the delivery of a service. Elders may or may not relish being called by their first names by people of their grandchildren's age. Using someone's title is part of a relationship which can convey respect. It does not mean that the relationship is not friendly. It might be a good idea to return to a degree of formality, perhaps because it is difficult to convey fully the idea of respect without it; and because both worker and service-user may find it easier then to deal with difficult issues.

Relevance of the past for the present

What relevance does all this have for current social work practice? Social work does need to take heed of how things were done in the past, though some of it may seem quite alien, mystifying and not a good idea at all. Other aspects may seem intriguing and worth a second glance. Social work services are frequently reorganised as the result of internal or external pressure, for example as a result of tragedy (Ryden and Smith, 2000). Such reorganisations may be a useful time to ponder past practice.

In the late 1960s at a time when some social workers and particularly social work students (Hobsbawm, 1994: 298–301) were becoming more political or radical, the accepted version of the social work role was challenged by, for example, 'The Case Con Manifesto':

Every day of the week, every week of the year, social workers (including probation officers, educational social workers, hospital social workers, community workers and local authority social workers) see the utter failure of social work to meet the real needs of the people it purports to help. Faced with this failure, some social workers despair and leave to do other jobs, some hide behind the façade of professionalism and scramble up the social work ladder regardless; and some grit their teeth and just get on with the job, remaining helplessly aware of the dismal reality.

http://www.radical.org.uk/barefoot/casecon.htm (last accessed 10/02/2007)

Sheila West, a former child care officer, recalled:

[T]his was the era [the 1950s and 1960s] when we believed in casework; and its efficacy. I think it was just before the rise of 'Case Con' and before kind of … Marxist perspectives came along or reality hit the scene. I think the sixties were a time when we really believed that social workers could make an important contribution and difference, through casework.

(Interview, Sheila West, 2002)

As the service-user population changed, for example with increased immigration in the 1960s onwards, problems arose because of a lack of understanding of new varieties of family forms (Hobsbawm, 1994: 321). This change powerfully threatened the certainties with which social work was supported in the 1950s and 1960s, central to which were the casework relationship and respect for the individuality of service-users.

While in many English local authority areas Social Services departments continued to be the primary social work agency, their existence began to be threatened almost as soon as they were set up (Holman, 2001: 196). By the late 1970s there were experimental linkages with other local authority departments such as housing, for example in the London Borough of Bexley. More recently, in many areas there have been amalgamations with other local authority departments such as education.

Social workers and their organisations frequently have to work with those sections of society who are deemed difficult or dangerous or vulnerable. This will not change, despite the structures designed to deal with the problems, because, as Parton and O'Byrne (2000: 171) point out, the difficulties are socially constructed. It can never be possible for social work to get it absolutely right, partly because of the

> ambiguity [that] arises from its commitment to individuals and families and their needs on the one hand and its allegiances to a legitimation by the state in the guise of the court and its 'statutory' responsibilities on the other.
>
> (Parton and O'Byrne, 2000: 37)

Even the title 'social worker' may be contentious. When social workers with adults became 'care managers' in the 1990s (Froggett, 2002), to an extent they ceased to be social workers. The role could be performed without social work training. Social workers in child care are now becoming more like care managers, co-ordinating other workers who carry out different activities with looked-after children. These roles are essential given the way that welfare services are delivered, but are they social work? What is social work for? Do Social Services departments, or the combined departments or trusts which they are becoming, exist for the benefit of the service-user or for some other purpose?

> The aim in defending professional social work practice is not to protect our own social status but to defend the users of the service. The people who turn to social workers for help are complex bundles of feelings, thoughts and hopes. It requires skill, knowledge and training to understand them and provide an effective service. They deserve a high standard of care and this can only be achieved if we recognise their individual needs and values, without trying to turn them into two-dimensional characters that fit tidily into flow charts and information systems.
>
> (Munro, 2000: 10)

Perhaps it is positive for social workers' morale to consider themselves 'managers' in the sense of 'care' or 'case managers', who gather together groups of people to meet the variety of needs of a service-user family. It may be that some people become social workers in order to become managers. It is more likely that people become social workers because they want to make a difference in a personal way – as the recruitment literature suggests – and to know that something they have done could improve someone else's life.

The trend for the worker to perform a case-management role, whatever the specialism, increases the emotional distance between service-user and social worker. The attempt to mechanise the delivery of a service is in part a defence against the feelings engendered by the often intractable nature of the problems with which social workers have to deal, and the anxieties arising from feelings of inadequacy (Menzies-Lyth, 1988). Since to be human is to feel, better work will be done if social workers are open to the feelings of their service-users and aware of their own.

Professionalism … may allow the individual worker, faced with the unfathomability of a client's disturbance, or the responsibility of removing a child from its family, to disavow the emotional impact of the work and retreat into an omniscience which appears to be sanctioned by a rigid adherence to role.

(Froggett, 2002: 59)

It will not be possible to return to smaller departments. But it is suggested that people work better when they know where they are in their organisation, and when decisions about them or their work are not handed down from several tiers above. Child care officers may have felt overwhelmed by the attention they received from children's officers, but they respected the interest taken in the day-to-day work of the departments and understood the sound social work basis for the strong views children's officers held. Barbara Kahan 'argued that the Children's Departments "turned a minimalist Public Assistance service into a much more personalised and child-centred service"' (Holman, 2001: 59).

Perhaps the recent restructuring of Social Services departments into more specialised teams and multi-disciplinary trusts is a good thing. Multi-disciplinary working is not without its difficulties in terms of disparate hierarchies and professional jealousies. In order for all team members to work as they wish in their area of expertise there must be mutual respect.

In my view there should be a return to the primacy of the casework relationship, which 'has the potential to respond to the complex and highly individual ways in which people negotiate their relations with the outside world' (Froggett, 2002: 59). This would benefit service-users and increase job satisfaction for social workers. In the past much was taken for granted in regard to the efficacy of casework interventions. Evidence-based practice suggests that actions be based on research, rather than a feeling about the appropriateness of an approach. Does this invalidate casework? Not according to Newman et al. (2005: 25) who say that:

Evidence-based practice, in both challenging authoritarian views, and demanding that sources of authority justify their positions, is part of a long and honourable radical tradition in social work.

It is relevant to point out that evidence may be used both to challenge authoritarian views and to support them.

One of the issues for social work in the past (Stevenson, 2005) was how to work with service-users within the context of their daily lives. Criticism of casework centred on an assumed lack of recognition of societal needs and structural pressures. Both the internal and external worlds of service-users must be thought about. Knowledge of personal relationships and the dynamics of family life is, in my view, an essential ingredient, indeed the true generic ingredient, of social work.

It may be argued that life was simpler for social workers in the immediate post-war period, before the impact of child protection issues, for example. They had distinct and more homogeneous groups of service-users to work with, and less legislation and administration to think about. Perhaps social work is not fundamentally about structural social or political change. Perhaps it is more about ensuring that people's lives and their differences are safeguarded and made better than before social work intervention. If so, it has to be about getting to know service-users well, and helping them find their way out of difficulties. Social work should be broad enough to encompass the majority of service-users' relationship needs. This requires that time, thought and energy be put into the task. Cooper (2002: 8) describes how

> as a young newly qualified worker [he was taught] how to be properly present in the room with the client or family, how to use [him]self in the here and now, and how to properly trust a colleague in the therapeutic process.

Conclusion

Social workers between 1948 and 1972 may have been insufficiently aware of structural and cultural issues; they may have been frequently enmeshed in a culture of paternalism. But they held that a personal relationship with service-users was central to their professional identity and role. Practice and the supervision of social workers of that time reflected this contention. Critiques of casework and personal social service in the 1970s and 1980s from the political left and political right led to a diminution of the central role of relationship in social work. This is reflected in the current language and style of social work practice and in the increased prominence of the managerial function in supervision. If study of the recent past in social work offers us pause for thought, it might lead to consideration of how twenty-first-century social workers could offer a more relationship-based practice.

References

BASW (1980) *Clients are Fellow Citizens*. Birmingham: BASW Publications.

Berry, J. (1959) 'The car and child care', *Accord* (Spring).

Biestek, F.P. (1961) *The Casework Relationship*. London: Unwin University Books.

Bowers, S. (1949) 'The nature and definition of social casework', *Social Casework* (October).

Bowlby, J. (1953) *Child Care and the Growth of Love*. London: Penguin Books.

Bywaters, P. and McLeod, E. (2002) 'Tackling health inequalities', in J. Harris, L. Froggett and I. Paylor (2002) *Reclaiming Social Work: The Southport Papers*, Vol. 1. Birmingham: Venture Press.

Carter, D.T. (1971) 'Attitudes of medical social workers towards reorganisation', *British Journal of Social Work*, 1 (3): 155–76.

Carter Hood, P., Everitt, A. and Runnicles, D. (1998) 'Femininity, sexuality and professionalism in the children's departments', *British Journal of Social Work*, 28 (4): 471–90.

Cooper, A. (2002) 'Keeping our heads: therapeutic values in a time of change', *Journal of Social Work Practice*, 16 (1): 7–13.

Davis, A. (2006) 'Whatever does the social worker do? Reflections on 60 years of social work in the NHS', Lecture given to the Social Work History Network, 27.3.06.

Fraser of Carmyllie (2003) *The Kilbrandon Report*. Edinburgh: H.M.S.O.

Froggett, L. (2002) *Love, Hate and Welfare*. Bristol: Policy Press.

Gregory, M. and Holloway, M. (2005) 'Language and the shaping of social work', *British Journal of Social Work*, 35 (1): 37–54.

Heenan, D. (2004) 'Learning lessons from the past or re-visiting old mistakes: social work and community development in Northern Ireland', *British Journal of Social Work*, 34 (6): 793–810.

Heywood, J. (1959) *Children in Care*. London: Routledge & Kegan Paul.

Hiddleston, V. and Colvin, D. (2006) 'The unification years', Lecture given to the Social Work History Network, 3 November.

Hobsbawm, E. (1994) *Age of Extremes*. London: Abacus.

Holman, B. (2001) *Champions for Children*. Bristol: Policy Press.

Kilbrandon Report (1964) *Report by the Committee Appointed by the Secretary of State for Scotland*. Edinburgh: H.M.S.O.

Laing, R.D. (1960) *The Divided Self*. London: Tavistock Publications.

Menzies-Lyth, I. (1988) 'The functioning of social systems as a defence against anxiety', in I. Menzies-Lyth, *Containing Anxiety in Institutions*. Selected essays, vol. 1. London: Free Association Books.

Munro, E. (2000) 'Defending professional social work practice', in J. Harris, L. Froggett and I. Paylor (eds), *Reclaiming Social Work: The Southport Papers*, vol. 1. Birmingham: Venture Press.

Newman, T., Moseley, A., Tierney, S. and Ellis, A. (2005) *Evidence-based Social Work*, Lyme Regis: Russell House Publishing.

Packman, J. (1968) *Child Care: Needs and Numbers*. London: Allen & Unwin.

Parsloe, P. and Stevenson, O. (1978) *Social Services Team: The Practitioner's View*. London: HMSO.

Parton, N. and O'Byrne, P. (2000) *Constructive Social Work*. Basingstoke: Macmillan.

Pearson, G. (1973) 'Social work as the privatized solution to public ills', *British Journal of Social Work*, 3 (2): 209–28.

Perlman, H.H. (1957) *Social Casework: A Problem-solving Process*. Chicago: University of Chicago Press.

Prince, K. (1996) *Boring Records*? London: Jessica Kingsley.

Prynn, B. (2001) 'Growing up alone', *Oral History*, 29 (2): 62–72.

Pugh, E. (1968) *Social Work in Child Care*. London: Routledge & Kegan Paul.

Robinson, J.N.G. (1972) 'The dual commitment of social work', *British Journal of Social Work*, 2 (4): 471–81.

Rolph, S., Walmsley, J. and Atkinson, D. (2002) 'A man's job?: gender issues and the role of mental health welfare officers, 1948–1970', *Oral History*, 30 (1): 28–41.

Rustin, M. (1991) *The Good Society and the Inner World*. London: Verso.

Ryden, N. and Smith, F.H. (2002) 'Best Value – future choices for social workers', in I. Paylor, L. Froggett and J. Harris (eds), *Reclaiming Social Work: The Southport Papers*, vol. 2. Birmingham: Venture Press.

Satyamurti, C. (1981) *Occupational Survival*. Oxford: Basil Blackwell.

Seebohm Report (1968) *Report of the Committee on Local Authority and Allied Personal Social Services*. Cmnd. 3703. London: HMSO.

Sharkey, P. (2002) 'Community care, community work and social exclusion', in I. Paylor, L. Froggett and J. Harris (eds), *Reclaiming Social Work: The Southport Papers*, vol. 2. Birmingham: Venture Press.

Sims, D. (2000) 'The joint practitioner – a new identity', in J. Harris, L. Froggett and I. Paylor (eds), *Reclaiming Social Work: The Southport Papers*, vol. 1. Birmingham: Venture Press.

Stevenson, O. (2005) 'Genericism and specialization: the story since 1970', *British Journal of Social Work*, 35 (5): 569–86.

Timms, N. (1964) *Social Casework*, London: Routledge & Kegan Paul.

Winnicott, D.W. (1957) *The Child and the Outside World*. London: Tavistock Publications.

Wooton, B. (1959) *Social Science and Social Pathology*. London: Allen & Unwin.

Chapter 7

Values and ethics in practice

Maureen Eby and Ann Gallagher

Living and working in today's complex society raises all sorts of questions about the rights or wrongs of decisions and actions that confront us on a daily basis. These questions are asked not only about the larger issues such as abortion, consent, euthanasia, or resource allocation but also each day by individuals of themselves. Did I do the right thing? Should I have looked the other way? Was I wrong? Was there another way of looking at this? These are the sorts of questions that lead to the process of critical practice.

Often these questions remain unanswered, perhaps because life is too short to ruminate over past decisions. But unanswered questions do leave a legacy that lingers, surfacing with each new difficult encounter or decision. Living with this tension is hard for anyone who is trying to exercise responsibility creatively and with integrity. The challenge we face is to find ways of ensuring that ideas and aspirations are not totally lost, while being utterly realistic about existing constraints.

In this chapter we reflect on how individuals can creatively juggle and balance the constraints and opportunities found in current practice contexts for the benefit of all stakeholders. But what may be desirable for the practitioner may not be for the service-user, for his/her family, for the organisation or for the other employees. These multiple perspectives can at times conflict, but can also lead to new ways of thinking. This chapter focuses on the main approaches to the understanding of ethics. It will enable practitioners to recognise these alternative perspectives when faced with the unanswered questions and enable potentially helpful options within the decision-making process.

Values terminology

Values are essentially a set of beliefs, ideas and assumptions that individuals and groups hold about themselves and their society. Values should not be considered in a superficial and unreflective way. Pattison (2004: 1) puts it this way:

> the concept 'values' is one of those portmanteau concepts which chases after meaning, like 'community'. It derives its popularity and legitimacy from the fact that it is

an apparently simple, universally accessible concept which has a simple unexceptional primary meaning (a value is something people value) which conceals a large number of secondary meanings and understandings … The notions of value and values can easily slip, chameleon-like, between users and utterances, delighting all and offending none because most people do not take the trouble to think about what they actually mean in their own lives and those of others.

It is important for critical practitioners to distinguish between different types of values. There are *ethical values*, which indicate whether an action is 'right' or 'wrong'. *Aesthetic values* relate to views of what is good or beautiful in relation to, for example, art, nature or architecture. There may, of course, be overlap between these values. The architecture, colour scheme and ambience of a mental health unit, for example, have the potential to benefit or harm and to make people feel more or less valued. There are also *professional values* which are learnt and internalised via professional education. Professional values may be explicit or implicit, that is, they may be articulated verbally, or in professional codes, or they may be implied by everyday actions, for example by the way in which a practitioner appears to respect the rights and needs of colleagues and service uses.

Everyone holds their own *personal values*. As values are personal to the individual, sometimes they may never be articulated or shared. People may also belong to different social groupings, such as work, leisure or religion, which generally also share a common set of values that may or may not separate that grouping from others. Values not made explicit can be deduced from behaviour, but people may also claim to hold a set of values which is not evident by their behaviour, such as a person who believes in the sanctity of confidentiality yet breaks any confidence at the first opportunity.

People generally have a set of values, which may have one or more framework holding them together derived, for example, from religion, culture, class or profession. However, one value may conflict or compete with another value and different people may prioritise different values thus creating a sense of dissonance within that individual as shown in the scenario in Case Study 1.

Case Study 1   Mr Papadopoulos

Mr Papadopoulos is 73 years old and has recently been admitted to hospital for investigations. He is very breathless and has lost a good deal of weight over the last two months. On admission, his son and daughter tell all the professionals involved – nurses, doctors and social workers – that they do not want their father to have the results of the tests if the news is not good, for example, if cancer is diagnosed. They say that their father would 'lose the will to live'. A few days after admission Mr Papadopoulos raises the question of his diagnosis with one of the nurses as she helps him to wash. He explains that he would like to know the results as soon as possible as he is keen to 'put his affairs in order'.

The family of Mr Papadopoulos have made it clear that they believe that bad news, such as a diagnosis of cancer, would be harmful to their father resulting in his losing the will to live. Mr Papadopoulos, on the other hand, has asked the nurse about his diagnosis pointing out that he would like the information to be in a position to make arrangements. There is, therefore a conflict of ethical values, presenting a challenge to professionals, with the family wishing to protect their father, emphasising the value of non-maleficence (to do no harm) and Mr Papadopoulos' discussion with the nurse suggesting the value of self-determination or autonomy. These two values – autonomy and non-maleficence – are competing with each other. The professionals involved need to consider the views of Mr Papadopoulos and his family: the potential harms (non-maleficence) and benefits (beneficence) that ensue from breaking bad news and the significance of respect for a service-user's autonomy. Autonomy, beneficence and non-maleficence are principles used in health, social care and social work practice, and are discussed later in this chapter.

If a person is faced with two or more competing values, as in Case Study 1, then they will need to weigh and consider different values. This may lead to a feeling of disharmony or dissonance while the person involved decides which value will override the other.

Case Study 2   Rebecca

Rebecca, a social worker, has been invited to join her local residents committee. She has recently moved to a new housing development, Greenacres. A percentage of the housing on the site has been designated 'affordable'. A rehabilitation unit on the site continues to provide services to people with mental health problems. One of the committee members shares a concern that those who move to the affordable properties will have social problems, they will 'cause trouble', and bring property prices down. She says that residents have a 'right to know' what 'sort of people' are being offered accommodation on the site. Another member shares his concern about the people in the rehabilitation unit. He worries that they may be dangerous and that his children may be at risk.

Rebecca's personal and professional values are challenged by the discussion. She is aware that she is a new committee member and may be unpopular if she expresses values that are different from those of the majority. She also feels that she is being dishonest if she does not express values she holds dear relating to social justice, rights and non-discrimination. She is aware of a disconcerting and contrary personal value relating to her own situation. She has saved long and hard for her new home and thinks of it as an investment. She would, therefore, prefer to avoid a situation where it decreases in value.

This situation has arisen in Rebecca's personal life. She is a member of the committee because she is a resident of Greenacres and not because she is a social worker. Should the values she holds in her professional life be implicit to her personal life? Rebecca sees the potential to have an advocacy role in the committee, giving 'voice' to the interests of those with social and mental health problems. She could also challenge the idea that the committee has a 'right to know' information about new residents by highlighting the right to privacy. This may, however, alienate her from other members of the committee.

So for Rebecca there are three levels of conflicting values operating: personal values, professional values and values of the group (residents committee). How does the individual separate out and prioritise these competing values? Developing an understanding of ethics will help in dealing with these issues.

Ethics is that branch of philosophy concerned with the systematic study of human values and the principles and methods for distinguishing right from wrong and good from bad. Ethics is 'thinking and reasoning about morality' (Rowson, 1990: 3). But ethics is also about being human and living in today's world, as Verena Tschudin, an ethicist, describes:

> Ethics is not only for philosophers. Ethics is something which is done every day. It is not only about long words and dilemmas, but ethics is first and foremost about people: people with different views, values and experiences. It is not a question of who's right and who's wrong, but of how you can know what you believe is valuable, and stand by that value, and respect other people's values. It is about understanding how your feelings and society's norms relate to each other, and how you decide for yourself and others.
>
> (Tschudin and Marks-Maran, 1993: 3)

Ethics terminology

How do ethics and values intersect? When two or more values or moral principles are present within a situation, and they are not creating any problems or conflicts for the people involved, then an *ethical issue* has arisen. However, when these values or moral principles are in conflict, which poses a challenge about what to do, then an *ethical problem* has occurred (Purtilo, 1993). For instance, if Mr Papadopoulos in the example in Case Study 1 and his family had the same view regarding information-sharing, the value of autonomy would not be in conflict with the value of non-maleficence. It is not uncommon for families to wish to protect service users from distress and harm and they may not always fully appreciate the importance of information disclosure in enabling and empowering people to make decisions towards the end of life. Professionals encounter a moral problem when the values of families and service-users come into conflict.

An *ethical dilemma* occurs either when there is a choice between two courses of action that are both morally right but only one choice can be made (Purtilo, 1993) or when either course of action, if chosen, would lead to the compromise of values or principles (Beauchamp and Childress, 2001). Ethical dilemmas can occur between competing personal and professional values as well as between personal and organisational values. On a personal level, the value of autonomy or individual freedom can often conflict with the value of non-maleficence. This is usually seen as a conflict over personal lifestyles such as between one's beliefs and behaviours over smoking or drinking alcohol, but dilemmas can also occur between other values such as veracity (truth-telling) and non-maleficence. For example, if you are aware your friend is going out with someone you know is married, do you tell her, realising that it might cause her great pain, or do you not tell her and risk losing the friendship if she finds out later that you knew?

Conflict between veracity and non-maleficence can also occur at a professional or an occupational level. For example, a homeless man has come to the Accident and Emergency Department because it is cold and wet outside. Both the doctor and the nurse, not wanting to cause further harm by sending him outside again, admit the 'patient' for observation of his blood pressure, ensuring that he will have at least one warm, dry night with a hot meal before he is discharged. At an organisational level, individuals may have to decide between upholding their professional code – or in the case of many health and social care professionals their registration to practise – in situations where the organisation has compromised on quality and service due to financial constraints.

Ethical or moral distress occurs when barriers prevent a course of action perceived as right by the individual from happening (Purtilo, 1993). It has also been described as 'the psychological disequilibrium and negative feeling state experienced when a person makes a moral decision but does not follow through by performing the moral behaviour indicated by that decision' (Wilkinson, 1987/88: 16). In Rebecca's situation, her personal values may favour her supporting the committee in campaigning against certain 'sorts of people' moving to Greenacres. However, not expressing her deeply held professional values relating to human rights and anti-discrimination would leave Rebecca feeling compromised ethically.

An individual may also experience *moral or ethical unpreparedness* where she lacks the knowledge, experience and wisdom to respond appropriately to the complexities of ethical situations. It is not uncommon to hear practitioners and others say, 'I never thought of that as an ethical issue!' *Moral or ethical blindness* results in people not recognising ethical issues or problems as such, perceiving them instead as technical or clinical problems. A more challenging problem is that of *moral or ethical fanaticism*, whereby an individual adheres firmly to certain ideals and 'uncritically and unreflectingly makes moral judgements according to them' (Johnstone, 2004: 99). Other problems that people are more likely to observe in others than in themselves are: *moral indifference*, where people are unconcerned or uninterested in ethical matters; *amoralism*, where people reject ethics altogether; and *immoralism*, where people are aware of ethical norms or standards and deliberately breach them (2004: 99).

The study of ethics goes beyond the identification of ethical problems. Ethics is also about developing skills – the cognitive skills of reasoning, reflection, analysis and logic. These are essential skills for individual development and add considerable meaning to the critical practice of health and social care. Becoming more aware of ethical and value choices will enable the health and social care practitioner to have critical distance – space to embrace or change ways of thinking or acting and, importantly, to justify their actions on ethical grounds.

Approaches to understanding ethics

Ethics can be approached in a variety of ways, from the principle-based approach often found in health care ethics (Edge and Groves, 1994), or the theory-based approach such as deontology or utilitarianism found in most philosophy texts on ethics (Frankena, 1973), to the practical approach such as Seedhouse's ethical grid (Seedhouse and Lovett, 1992) or Niebuhr's response ethics (Niebuhr, 1963) found in the many 'how-to' books on ethics. Ashcroft et al. (2005) write of more recent approaches to ethics such as hermeneutic, phenomenological and empirical ethics. A few of the most common approaches to an understanding of ethical issues are described below. This is by no means meant to be a definitive discussion of these approaches but rather a synopsis that will enable you to engage in the many differing debates that surround the ethical issues in everyday practice. Table 7.1 summarises these approaches (see pp. 120–1).

Principles approach

Principles are general guides that have become so fundamental in everyday thinking that they are no longer questioned (Beauchamp and Childress, 2001). For example, the principle of retribution established in the biblical phrase 'eye for eye, tooth for tooth' originated in the Code of Hammurabi in 2100 BC, which stated, 'If a man destroy the eye of another man, they shall destroy his eye' (Infopedia, 1995: 1). A variety of principles can be found in ethics textbooks, but fundamental to health and social care ethics there are four basic principles: respect for autonomy, beneficence or doing good, non-maleficence or avoiding harm, and justice (Banks, 2001; Beauchamp and Childress, 2001). These four principles, described in further detail in Box 7.1, form the foundation of ethical practice and conduct which underpins professional workers' decision making.

Box 7.1   Principles of health and social care ethics

Respect for autonomy – asserts the basic right of individuals to participate in and make decisions about and for themselves. Three basic elements are incorporated within this principle: the ability to decide, the power to act upon choices and decision, and respect for the individual autonomy of others.

Beneficence – asserts the duty of practitioners to seek the good for service-users under all circumstances.

Non-maleficence – asserts the duty to avoid or prevent harm to individuals. If the practitioner cannot do good for the service-user, then at least the practitioner should not harm the service-user.

Justice – asserts that it is not enough to do good and avoid harm, but that some effort must be made to distribute the good and bad resulting from action which is distributed equally or according to need, effort, contribution, merit, ability or decided by some other means.

(*Source*: based on Edge and Groves, 1994: 28–9, 36–7, 39–40)

These principles can be seen in Case Study 1. The principles approach is widely used because it is based on apparently simple truths. However, basing ethical decisions on these four principles can seem too simplistic for today's complex world. Not every situation can be reduced to just these four principles.

Virtues approach

The virtues approach suggests that if people were encouraged to be virtuous then there would be no need for problem-solving methods for moral dilemmas because individuals would act according to their innate goodness. Aristotle (384–322 BC) (1976, 1992), a Greek philosopher, talked about the cardinal virtues of wisdom, courage, temperance and justice. Virtues not only move the individual into right action but also specify what that right action ought to be (Pellegrino and Thomasma, 1993). However, virtue ethics has been criticised for relying too heavily on precedent and tradition rather than on reason. Relying too

Table 7.1   Six approaches to understanding ethics

Approach	Major assumptions	Critique of assumptions
Principles approach	• Easy to understand as it is based on simple words or statements, e.g. the right to life, or justice, truth telling • Even though it is based on logic, it still incorporates the emotive aspects • Flexible and adaptable approach which applies universally to all groups • Can resolve a variety of conflicts	• Too simplistic for modern life • Difficult to question due to historical precedent • Narrowing life's conflicts into four or five principles is too rigid
Virtues approach	• Attempts to create a good or virtuous person • There can be both a virtuous act and a virtuous person • Stresses moderation in both feelings and actions • Encourages freedom within the virtuous individual to know and do the right things	• Assumes that virtues are naturally inherent in all human beings • Who decides what constitutes a virtue? Is happiness a virtue? • Does not provide a specific direction in ethical decision making • Relies too heavily on the past and traditional practice
Duties approach	• Goodwill is the most important human attribute, followed by reason • There are absolute moral rules that are established through reason that are obeyed out of a sense of duty in order to be a moral person • Individuals are never used as a means to another's ends • Right act will always be guided by moral duties, responsibilities and rights	• Too rigid for real life and very difficult to just derive morality from reason as pain and pleasure also make up our sense of right and wrong • Fails to take account that the consequences of an action can have disastrous results • Duties can clash – duty to your family, your employer, your profession • A sense of duty tends to lead to a blind acceptance of and obedience to authority • There are no exceptions to the rules
Rights approach	• A familiar discourse within health care and can be seen as the flipside of duties, that is, people have duties or obligations when other people have rights • Rights have ethical and legal status • They have universal application, for example, the UDHR	• They may conflict with each other • They are often used in a rhetorical manner with insufficient attention to their meaning
Consequences approach	• Apparently a simple and clear doctrine to understand and use in practice • The concept of happiness is far easier to grasp than that of natural rights or duties	• Difficult to know what all of the consequences of an action will be • How do you measure happiness and how do you compare the

Table 7.1   (Continued)

Approach	Major assumptions	Critique of assumptions
	• Maximising happiness offers a decisive and accurate procedure for decision making • Very attractive as a method of public decision making • Achieving the end does justify the means necessary	happiness of one with that of another? • Individuals value other concepts besides happiness, such as justice and equality • Confuses morality with expediency since the good of one person can be sacrificed for the good of many • Does not take into account motive when weighing up the consequences of an individual's actions
Emotive approach	• In making moral judgements the individual is expressing without stating or declaring their feelings and attitudes • Reason is and ought only to be the slave of passions • All moral statements attempt to persuade others to share one's own attitudes about the rightness or wrongness of certain acts • Care must be taken of the emotive meanings of ethical terms used and individuals need to distinguish their evaluative function from their descriptive function	• Stating something is good or bad does not always mean the individual is stating their own opinion or attitude • There is more to life than just right and wrong • Excludes rationality from moral arguments • Fails to distinguish serious moral arguments from irrational or non-rational propaganda
Feminist approach	• Ethics of care offers a new and vital direction of enquiry • Stresses that everyone is vulnerable to oppression and abandonment • Challenges traditional approach's denial of women's moral agency and the devaluation of women's experiences • Refuses to dominate or to be dominated • Ethics ceases to be an instrument of restraint and constraint, instead it empowers women with meaning	• Justice and care are not different approaches but are complementary, equally necessary components of morality • Glorifying care as normative for women only worsens the position of women • Caring can be abusive • Has yet to develop a substantial moral theory • Women are not morally perfect creatures • Seems to assert feminist values as superior to masculine values

Source: Adapted from Brechin et al. (2000) *Critical Practice in Health and Social Care*. London: SAGE. pp. 124–5

heavily on precedent and tradition may thwart creative solutions or personal autonomy (Edge and Groves, 1994). Virtue ethics has also been criticised for generally not providing a specific direction in ethical decision making: the fact that the virtuous person will know the right action does not always hold true.

Truth-telling (veracity) is a virtue that is enshrined in most professional codes. Is it always ethically right to tell the service-user the truth, even though the truth might cause pain or further suffering? Is there ever any justification for withholding the truth from the service-user? One line of argument is that it is sometimes in the patient's best interest for the truth to be withheld. This is seen as a paternalistic attitude which relies on the ethical concept of beneficence or doing good. But what about the service-user's own sense of autonomy and respect for people? What if the service-user does not want to be told the truth? Is telling the service-user the truth in these circumstances, or even lying to service-users, respecting them as autonomous individuals?

Duties approach

The duties approach concerns the principle of doing good – beneficence. It is generally felt that doctors, nurses, social workers and others have a duty to do good. Nurses and doctors are told they have a duty to care and this duty is embodied within the principles of negligence as stated by Lord Hewitt in the case of R. v. Bateman (1925): 'If a person holds himself out as possessing special skill and knowledge, and he is consulted, as possessing such skill and knowledge, by or on behalf of a patient, he owes a duty to that patient ...' (Korgaonkar and Tribe, 1995: 2; Dimond, 1997).

This duty to care is an obligation which spells out what ought to be done in a given situation, based on two assumptions: first that the person can actually do or perform the appropriate action; and second, that there is a choice of whether to act or not (Fletcher et al., 1995). However, it can be argued that professional codes actually prevent individuals from fulfilling their obligations because they prevent choice.

The duty-based approach forces a person to be a moral agent. In other words, 'a person is good when their only motive for doing something is that it is their duty to do it' (Palmer, 1999: 108). The ability to reason allows the moral agent to reflect upon and determine their duty. This approach stems from the work of Immanuel Kant (1724–1804), whose philosophy, known as deontology, makes the concept of duty central to morality. Kant firmly believed that the right act would always be guided by moral duties, responsibilities and rights; thus, some actions will always be considered immoral, regardless of their positive benefits (Fowler and Levine-Ariff, 1987).

Yet it is very difficult to derive morality just from reason alone. Pleasure and pain often form the basis of what we think of as 'good' and 'bad'. Should we base our ideas of 'right' and 'wrong' along similar lines? This is something that deontology appears to avoid (Edge and Groves, 1994). Not looking to the consequences of our actions can also lead to disastrous results. It is also possible to be faced with a conflict between two duties, such as the case of a young single mother who, despite being on full benefits, is moonlighting as a barmaid to make ends meet. The social worker's duty is to respect the service-user's confidences but the social worker also has a duty to the state to report fraud. So which duty takes precedence?

Rights approach

Generally, although not always, where rights are identified there are corresponding duties (Beauchamp and Childress, 2001: 359). Rights have been defined as 'justified claims which individuals or groups can make upon other individuals or upon society; to have a right is to be in a position to determine, by one's choices, what others should do or need not do' (2001: 357). The Human Rights Act 1998 in the United Kingdom has urged a renewed consideration of moral and legal rights. 'Human rights' have a long history but their existence also reminds us of human potential for cruelty (Lifton 1986, 1988; Steppe 1997; Glover 1999: 3). Rights have a central position in the *Code of Ethics* of the British Association of Social Workers. The Code refers to rights in the definition of social work (BASW, 2002: 2), as does the International Council of Nurses (http://www.icn.ch/pshumrights.htm accessed 12/12/06).

Speaking out about human rights violations is not an easy matter and it requires the moral qualities or virtues of courage and prudence. Good conduct, on a rights-based view, consists then of respecting the rights of others. There may not be agreement as to what these rights are or about what they mean – for example, in specifying what rights mean in different contexts.

Consequences approach

In the consequences approach, moral significance is given to the results of an action, not to the reasons given for the action. An action is right or wrong depending on the consequences produced, as measured against a specific end that is sought, for example pleasure or utility (Fowler and Levine-Ariff, 1987). One form of consequentialism is Utilitarianism, an ethical theory proposed by Jeremy Bentham (1748–1832) and later refined by John Stuart Mill (1806–1873). Utilitarians identified the goal of morality as the greatest happiness for the greatest number, and in consequentialist fashion claimed that an action is right in so far as it tends to promote that goal. As a philosophical theory, Utilitarianism is hampered by the fundamental difficulty of comparing quantitatively the happiness of one person with that of another, even though Bentham devised a method for calculating the quantity of pain or pleasure and called it the hedonic calculus (Box 7.2).

Box 7.2   Hedonic calculus

The amount of pleasure or pain is calculated by an individual based on the cumulative value that the individual places on the following seven dimensions:

- intensity
- duration
- certainty or uncertainty
- propinquity or remoteness
- fecundity or the chance it has of being followed by sensations of the same kind
- purity or the chance it has of not being followed by sensations of the opposite kind
- extent, that is the number of persons to whom it extends or who will be affected by it

(*Source*: based on Palmer, 1999: 69–70)

Utilitarianism is particularly attractive as a method for public decision making and it is strongly opposed to deontology that is, the view that the worthiness of an action depends upon its conformity with duty. Deontologists characteristically complain that consequentialism leads to a confusion of morality with expediency, since consequentialism seems to allow that the good of one person may be sacrificed for the good of many (Johnstone, 2004).

Allocation of resources, which is established on the principle of justice and fairness, is often based on the consequences approach. Does society treat individuals randomly, as in a lottery, or on a first come, first served, basis? Would you treat two individuals with liver transplants or give ten people hip replacements?

Emotive approach

The emotive approach claims that moral judgements do not state anything that is capable of being true or false, even subjectively, but merely express emotions. Emotivism is based on the belief that moral decisions have nothing to do with reason or rationality but that morality is all about feelings. According to the US philosopher Charles Stevenson (1908–1979):

> The emotive meaning of a word is the power that the word acquires, on account of its history in emotional situations, to evoke or directly express attitudes, as distinct from describing or designating them.
>
> (Stevenson, 1944: 33)

Stevenson argues that all moral statements are essentially an attempt to persuade others to share one's own attitudes about the rights or wrongs of certain acts. 'The reason we can't define "good" in purely descriptive terms is that "good" is emotional' (Gensler, 1998: 62). Emotivism is criticised for its exclusion of rationality from moral arguments and its failure to distinguish serious moral arguments from irrational propaganda. Not all moral judgements are emotions – some are unemotional (Gensler, 1998). Emotivism is seen by its critics as having trivialised ethical debate, for, in the main, it 'is not much different from simple common sense!' (Harmon, 1977: 39–40)

Emotional responses to developments in health and social care are not uncommon. People's first response to issues such as face transplants, the prospect of transplanting animal organs to humans, cloning, older mothers, or embryo research may well be an emotional one or, as some bioethicists have put it, the 'Yuck Factor' (Rifkin, 2001) where people experience feelings of squeamishness or repugnance. A recent debate regarding chimeras (combining the cells of two different species) led to an interesting blog discussion (see http://peasoup.typepad.com/peasoup/2005/04/chimeras_and_th.html), focusing on questions such as: What role, if any, ought the 'yuck factor' play in ethical discourse? And how might we distinguish repugnance from other emotions that play a role in ethical positions we take?

Relying purely on our emotional responses or experience of the 'yuck factor' is insufficient, as such responses may as likely emanate from prejudice as from a sense of injustice. Reflection and reasoning drawing on a range of ethical approaches are, then, also necessary.

Feminist and care-focused approaches

Feminist and care-focused ethics have different methods and priorities but the development of these two strands of thought are interlinked. Both of these approaches render visible the realities and structures previously obscured in Western and/or patriarchal ethical perspectives. As philosopher Betty Sichel writes:

> 'Feminine' at present refers to the search for women's unique voice and, most often, the advocacy of an ethics of care that includes nurturance, care, compassion, and networks of communication. 'Feminist' refers to those theorists ... who argue against patriarchal domination, for equal rights, a just and fair distribution of scarce resources, etc.

> (Sichel, 1991: 90)

The care-focused approach identifies the failure of those perspectives based on duty and utility to understand the attitudes and insights of women, whereas a feminist approach searches out the oppressive elements of society, rendering the invisible visible.

Carol Gilligan and Nel Noddings, both feminist moral theorists, write about the care-focused approach. Gilligan's work (1982) was an empirical study of the ways in which children look at moral issues. She concludes that girls tend to approach moral issues by examining the relationships involved, rather than searching out moral rules as boys did. Noddings (1984) attempted to base ethics upon natural caring rooted in receptivity, relatedness and responsiveness. This approach contrasted sharply with an ethics built upon moral rules, rights, duties and principles found in the other approaches. When a caring relationship succeeds, the cared-for person actively receives the caring thoughts and deeds of the carer, who spontaneously shares her or his aspirations, appraisals and accomplishments with the cared-for person.

Not all approaches to care-focused ethics rely on a feminist perspective. Gastmans (2006), for example, while acknowledging the origins of care-focused ethics in feminism, focuses on the meaning of care and on the process of ethical decision making. Gastmans emphasises the significance of relationships, the importance of interpreting different viewpoints and of incorporating institutional and societal contexts.

The feminist power-focused approach to ethics asks questions about male domination and female subordination before it asks questions about whether an instance or an object is morally good or evil or just or unjust. In Alison Jaggar's (1991) view, feminist ethics must articulate moral critiques of actions and practices that perpetuate women's subordination, prescribe morally justifiable ways of resisting such actions and practices, and envision morally desirable alternatives that will promote women's emancipation (Tong, 1997).

Feminist and care-focused approaches to ethics expand the voices heard within ethical debate. Broadly speaking, feminist ethical approaches value and render visible the following elements, which are often ignored in other approaches to understanding ethics:

- the importance and effect of power relationships
- connectedness rather than individualistic autonomy
- lived human experience

- varieties of human communication and interpretation, including those that are not based on literacy and rational expression, such as stories, gossip, anecdotes, touch and gesture
- communities and collectivities rather than individualism
- the significance of different viewpoints
- different ways of knowing
- the importance of the everyday and the ordinary

Critics of feminist approaches question the absolute adherence to values of trust and non-oppression situated against the realities found within the present system of patriarchal power in today's society. However, the ethical approaches discussed in this chapter have embedded values and presuppositions within them, and often their protagonists are a good deal less willing to look critically at these, seeing themselves as having access to reality in the form of reason, while seeing others as based on non-rational systems of myths and magic. The care-focused feminist approach is also criticised for perpetuating its own brand of stereotyping, which 'can lead to an absolute equation that woman = caring, and man = instrumental' or active (Porter, 1998: 192).

Values and ethics in practice

An understanding of the different approaches to ethics can assist in deconstructing the multiple meanings in problematic situations in health and social care and help to broaden the choices available. However, knowing about different perspectives does not by itself help an individual arrive at a decision. What else is needed? Hussey (1996: 251) believes that a professional is 'someone who has: a heightened sensitivity to the presence of a moral issue; an improved ability to reason and decide on moral questions ... of their work; enhanced skills in implementing moral decisions and acting in morally demanding situations; and the motivation to use these attributes and abilities.' To facilitate this process, both professional codes and ethical decision-making frameworks are tools that can help with decision making.

Challenging professional codes

Professional codes can be seen as framework statements of the values and beliefs of a particular professional group, which are designed to serve the interests of the profession and to protect the public. Generally, professional codes contain ethical principles which underpin the approach of professional practice such as autonomy, respect for people, promotion of welfare; ethical rules, the do's and don'ts of each code; and practice rules which are specific to each profession, such as not advertising or declaring a bequest from a client's will (Banks, 1998). Professional codes have several functions, which are described in Box 7.3.

Box 7.3   Functions of professional codes

1   Guidance – codes serve to remind professionals of their duties and obligations, to guide practice and to facilitate their work.
2   Regulation – codes prescribe the standards of behaviour and moral responsibility expected of professionals.
3   Discipline – codes identify areas of transgression, which enables the governing body to justify the use of penalties to sanction its code.
4   Protection – codes protect the public through the setting of standards of conduct of its practitioners.
5   Information – codes inform the general public of the standards of that profession, thus encouraging trust and confidence.
6   Proclamation – codes proclaim to the general public that in fact its members are professionals who have moral respectability and autonomy.
7   Negotiation – codes can be used as a tool of negotiation in disputes between colleagues and/or professionals and can serve as the justification for taking a particular course of action.

(*Source*: based on Hussey, 1996: 252)

Given these functions, just how useful are professional codes? They tend to be fairly brief, often stating broad and general principles; for example, 'must ... respect the patient or client as an individual' (NMC, 2004: 3). How are individuals to know what respect means? Codes can often be contradictory – for example, exhorting a practitioner to work with families, clients and patients as well as other professionals. Yet the interests of these differing groups are not the same; in fact they may well be at odds with one another.

Professional codes place great emphasis on the duties approach to understanding ethical issues. Codes often look like a list of duties that need to be fulfilled. These lists of duties, reinforced through the discipline function of codes (see Box 7.3), require individuals to follow the code's set of rules and obligations – see for example the social care code of practice for workers in Wales (http://www.ccwales.org.uk/ last accessed 23/02/2007). Some codes are fairly bald assertions and lists of duties to be performed without any indication of how the actions can or should be performed. Other codes are more helpful, offering interpretations of how the duties could be performed satisfactorily, for example the *Code of Ethics for Social Work* (BASW, 2002) and the nurses' *Code of Professional Conduct* (NMC, 2004).

Another difficulty with imbuing professional codes with a duties approach is that the world in which large organisations, such as the National Health Service or local authorities, operate is the world of the utilitarian; and as such is concerned about communities rather than individuals – the greatest good for the greatest number. The reality is that professionals working according to code that fosters duty and virtue are in fact working in a world where utility overrides duty and virtue. This disjuncture is responsible for a great deal of ethical distress and dilemma.

Furthermore, professionals may want to keep their personal and working lives separate. They feel that what they do in private is private and of no concern to their employer or their profession. A recent example involved a nurse who, in her spare time, was also a prostitute (Payne, 1999). As reported in the nursing press, she was fired from her Trust, yet the nurse's regulatory body took the view that 'The evidence wasn't such that she could be removed from the register' (1999: p. 10). This is in contrast to a recent case where the GSCC suspended a social worker from the GSCC register for two years because the social worker had advertised herself as an escort on a website associated with prostitution (http://www.gscc.org.uk/News+and+events/Media+releases/2006+archive/ last accessed 20/02/2007).

For a range of reasons, then, professional codes have perhaps not enhanced the morality of today's society but rather have placed an unreasonable burden of obligations on individuals. Professional codes may not serve those who are conscientiously raising questions about standards of practice and allocation of resources. In the past, individuals such as Graham Pink who were involved in 'whistle-blowing' have said professional codes were unsupportive;

> 'it [the UKCC's (now NMC) *Code of Professional Conduct*] should be scrapped. I have upheld the Code religiously, and as a result I face losing my job ... I see it as a very negative force at the moment. If you break it you get struck off, but it certainly doesn't do any good for patients ...'
>
> (Cole, 1991)

Nevertheless, professional codes can act as aide-memoires for the essentials of a value-based practice (Banks 1998: 29; Norman, 1998: 21). They help practitioners apply general principles in practice settings; professional codes become a resource to aid decision. Codes

- offer practical guidance on behaviour, especially those professional codes containing interpretative or explanatory statements;
- delineate and identify professional boundaries and are very useful in setting standards by which agency policy and practices can be judged;
- give an overriding responsibility to the public above that of an individual or employee when resources are scarce and standards are slipping;
- remind practitioners that they possess particular knowledge and skills that are used to benefit vulnerable individuals and that 'they have a duty to inform governments and agencies of inequities, lack of resources or the need for policy changes' (Banks, 2001: 110).

Ethical decision making

Almost everything we do has an ethical dimension. The decisions we make about the food we eat, the clothes we wear, the way we travel to work or the way we respond to service-users, colleagues and students have both ethical and non-ethical dimensions. Food, clothing and travel may, on the one hand, be viewed as matters of personal or aesthetic preference, but they also have ethical implications for other humans, for animals and for the environment. Similarly, in health and social care, practices fundamentally concerned with relationships, there are few decisions that do not have an ethical dimension.

Having some framework for ethical decision making is helpful for social workers or nurses beginning their careers. Frameworks exist and provide some structure and a process to enable practitioners to work systematically through a situation. If a practitioner is asked why she made one decision rather than another, she can provide some justification based on her working according to a framework. There are a number of ethical decision-making frameworks to choose from, for example Verena Tschudin (1994) and/or Megan-Jane Johnstone (2004: 110). The philosopher David Seedhouse (2006) has developed a web-based 'decision-support' framework, the 'values exchange' (http://www.values-exchange.com/ last accessed 23/02/2007). This enables participants to work through an ethical problem on-line and to give value-based responses based on ethical decision-making tools. The 'values exchange' renders people's values transparent and enables them to compare their responses with those of other people. Seedhouse's 'ethical or values grid' is designed to help health and social care professionals in their decision making. The website is free to use.

Conclusion

One of the fundamental goals of the study of ethics is to help practitioners develop practical reflective skills that can be used on a day-to-day basis to consolidate and reinforce ethical awareness and analysis as a vital, interesting and enriching part of everyday practice. An understanding of the various philosophical approaches to ethics and some sort of decision-making framework will enhance individuals' ability to work through their thinking on these issues and contribute to the decision-making process. However, it is equally important to recognise that understanding ethics as an isolated individual process will only lead to sterile decision making, often to no one's gain or understanding. The main thing is to get other people in on the thinking and decision making, as this is the first step towards effective ethics, which essentially is a social activity oriented to how people should live with and regard each other. It therefore makes sense to do ethics with other people and not on one's own, both as a means as well as to attain a desired end.

References

Aristotle (1976) *The Ethics of Aristotle: The Nicomachean Ethics*, Introduction by Jonathon Barnes. London: Penguin.

Aristotle (1992) *Eudemian Ethics*, Books I, II and VIII, Commentary by M. Woods, 2nd edn. Oxford: Clarendon Press.

Ashcroft, R., Lucassen, A., Parker, M., Verkerk, M. and Widdershoven, G. (2005) *Case Analysis in Clinical Ethics*. Cambridge: Cambridge University Press.

Banks, S. (1998) 'Codes of ethics and ethical conduct: a view from the caring professions', *Public Money and Management* (January–March): 27–30.

Banks, S. (2001) *Ethics and Values in Social Work.* 2nd edn. Houndsmill: Macmillan.

BASW (2002) *The Code of Ethics for Social Work*. Birmingham: British Association of Social Workers.

Beauchamp, T.L. and Childress, J.F. (2001) *Principles of Biomedical Ethics* (5th edn). Oxford: Oxford University Press.

British Broadcasting Corporation (BBC) (1998) 'Health: doctors reconsider transplant stance', BBC News, 28 December: http://news.bbc.co.uk/hi/english/health/newsid_243000/243500.stm (accessed 12.07.99).

British Medical Association (BMA) (2001) *The Medical Professional and Human Rights: Handbook for a Changing Agenda*. London: Zed Books in association with the BMA.

Cole, A. (1991) 'Upholding the code', *Nursing Times*, 87 (27): 26–9.

Dimond, B. (1997) *Legal Aspects of Care in the Community*. Basingstoke: Macmillan.

Davis, A.J., Tschudin, V. and de Raeve, L. (eds) (2006) *Essentials of Teaching and Learning in Nursing Ethics*. Edinburgh: Churchill Livingstone/Elsevier.

Eby, M.A. (1994a) *The Law and Ethics of General Practice*, Beckenham: Publishing Initiatives.

Eby, M. (1994b) 'Competing values', in V. Tschudin (ed.), *Ethics: Conflicts of Interest*, London: Scutari Press, pp. 85–109.

Edge, R. and Groves, J. (1994) *The Ethics of Health Care: A Guide for Clinical Practice*. Albany, NY: Delmar Publishers.

Fletcher, N., Holt, J., Brazier, M. and Harris, J. (1995) *Ethics, Law and Nursing*. Manchester: Manchester University Press.

Fowler, M. and Levine-Ariff, J. (1987) *Ethics at the Bedside*. Philadelphia, PA: J.B. Lippincott.

Frankena, W. (1973) *Ethics* (2nd edn). Englewood Cliffs, NJ: Prentice-Hall.

Gastmans, C. (2006) 'The care perspective in healthcare ethics', in A.J. Davis, V. Tschudin and L. Raeve (eds), *Essentials of Teaching and Learning in Nursing Ethics: Perspective and Methods*. Edinburgh: Churchill Livingstone Elsevier. pp. 135–48.

Gensler, H.J. (1998) *Ethics: A Contemporary Introduction*. London: Routledge.

Gilligan, C. (1982) *In a Different Voice*. Cambridge, MA: Harvard University Press.

Glover J. (1999) *Humanity – a Moral History of the Twentieth Century*. London: Jonathan Cape.

Harmon, G. (1977) *The Nature of Morality*. New York: Oxford University Press.

Hunt, G. (1998) 'Whistle-blowing and the crisis of accountability', in G. Hunt (ed.), *Whistle-blowing in the Social Services*. London: Arnold, pp. 1–15.

Hussey, T. (1996) 'Nursing ethics and codes of professional conduct', *Nursing Ethics*, 3 (3): 250–58.

Infopedia CD-ROM (1995) 'Punishment', in Merriam Webster's *Dictionary of Quotations*. London: SoftKey.

International Council of Nurses (2006) *Nursing and Human Rights: A Position Statement*. Geneva: ICN.

Jaggar, A.M. (1991) 'Feminist ethics: projects, problems, prospects', in C. Card (ed.), *Feminist Ethics*. Lawrence, KS: University of Kansas Press, p. 366.

Johnson, A. (1990) *Pathways in Medical Ethics*. London: Edward Arnold.

Johnstone, M.-J. (2004) *Bioethics: A Nursing Perspective* 4th edn. Sydney: Harcourt Brace Jovanovich.

Korgaonkar, G. and Tribe, D. (1995) *Law for Nurses*. London: Cavendish Publishing.

Lifton R.J. (1986) *The Nazi Doctors: A Study of the Psychology of Evil*. London: Macmillan.

Lifton R.J. (1988) *The Nazi Doctors: Medical Killing and the Psychology of Genocide*. New York: Basic Books.

McHale, J., Fox, M. and Murphy, J. (1997) *Health Care Law: Text and Materials*. London: Sweet & Maxwell.

New, B., Solomon, H. Dingwall, R. and McHale, J. (1994) *A Question of Give and Take: Improving the Supply of Donor Organs for Transplantation*. London: King's Fund Institute.

Newdick, C. (1995) *Who Should We Treat? Law, Patients and Resources in the NHS*. Oxford: Clarendon Press.

Niebuhr, H.R. (1963) *The Responsible Self*. New York: Harper & Row.

Noddings, N. (1984) *Caring: A Feminine Approach to Ethics and Moral Education*. Berkeley, CA: University of California Press.

Norman, S. (1998) 'Are we reading the same code?', *Nursing Times*, 94 (48): 21.

Nursing and Midwifery Council (NMC) (2004) *The NMC Code of Professional Conduct: Standards for Conduct, Performance and Ethics*. London: NMC.

Palmer, M. (1999) *Moral Problems in Medicine*. Cambridge: Lutterworth Press.

Pattison, S. (2004) 'Understanding values', in S. Pattison and R. Pill (eds), *Values in Professional Practice: Lessons for Health, Social Care and Other Professions*. Oxford: Radcliffe Medical Press.

Payne, D. (1999) 'Prostitution poser raises prospect of UKCC referendum', *Nursing Times*, 95 (1): 10.

Pellegrino, E. and Thomasma, D. (1993) *The Virtues in Medical Practice*. Oxford: Oxford University Press.

Pilgrim, D. (1995) 'Explaining abuse and inadequate care', in G. Hunt (ed.), *Whistle-blowing in the Health Service*. London: Edward Arnold, pp. 77–85,

Porter, S. (1998) *Social Theory and Nursing Practice*. Basingstoke: Macmillan.

Purtilo, R. (1993) *Ethical Dimensions in the Health Professions* (2nd edn). Philadelphia, PA: W.B. Saunders Company.

Rifkin, J. (2001) 'shopping for humans', *The Guardian*, 29 March, http://education.guardian.co.uk/higher/news/story/048519,00.html, accessed 13/01/07.

Rowson, R.H. (1990) *An Introduction to Ethics for Nurses*. Harrow: Scutari Press.

Seedhouse D. (2006) *Values Based Decision-Making*. Chichester: John Wiley & Sons.

Seedhouse, D. and Lovett, L. (1992) *Practical Medical Ethics*. Chichester: John Wiley & Sons.

Sherwin, S. (1992) 'Feminist and medical ethics: two different approaches to contextual ethics', in H.B. Holmes and L.M. Purdy (eds), *Feminist Perspectives in Medical Ethics*. Bloomington, IN: Indiana University Press, pp. 17–31.

Sichel, B. (1991) 'Different strains and strands: feminist contributions to ethical theory', *Newsletter on Feminism*, 90 (2): 90.

Steppe, H. (1997) 'Nursing under totalitarian regimes: the case of National Socialism', in A.M. Rafferty, J. Robinson and R. Elkan, *Nursing History and the Politics of Welfare*. London: Routledge.

Stevenson, C.L. (1944) *Ethics and Language*. New Haven, CT: Yale University Press.

Tadd, V. (1994) 'Professional codes: an exercise in tokenism?', *Nursing Ethics*, 1 (1): 15–23.

Tong, R. (1997) *Feminist Approaches to Bioethics*. Boulder, CO: Westview Press.

Tschudin, V. (1994) *Deciding Ethically*. London: Baillière Tindall.

Tschudin, V. and Marks-Maran, D. (1993) *Ethics: A Primer for Nurses*. London: Baillière Tindall.

Warren, R.C. (1993) 'Codes of ethics: bricks without straw', *A European Review of Business Ethics*, 2 (4): 185–91.

Wilkinson, J. (1987/1988) 'Moral distress in nursing practice: experience and effects', Nursing Forum, 23 (1): 16–29.

Chapter 8

Practitioner research

Celia Keeping

This chapter is about the place of research in social work practice today. It will have two focal points: firstly, an understanding of research and its impact on social work practice; and secondly, the question of whether social work practitioners can undertake research themselves and if so, how. I am a social worker with seventeen years' experience of working in a statutory child protection service and latterly as an Approved Social Worker in a community mental health team. I draw on my personal experiences as they serve to illustrate a journey I have undertaken in recent years to 'de-mystify' research, and hope it may in turn help other practitioners (and would-be practitioners) to understand the place of research in present-day social work practice.

The emergence over recent years of the imperative to engage with research has been just one of many changes within social work. As practitioners, my peers and I have experienced resistance to many of these changes, including the rise of the evidence-based practice movement. In the spirit of 'reflective practice' (Schon, 1983) I hope to explore the relevant issues here in order to examine possible resistances and potential benefits for the social work practitioner.

The context: modernisation and research

Changes in the delivery of welfare services

As social care professionals we operate in a very different world from that of twenty years ago. Processes of globalisation are impacting on practice and policy and making new demands on welfare professionals, who are consequently being required to operate in increasingly uncertain and complex environments. Economic changes associated with globalisation have resulted in an increase in competition (Dominelli, 1996), which in its turn has led to a modernisation and rationalisation of welfare delivery. In Britain the modernising agenda of New Labour has initiated the rise of managerialism with its emphasis on economy, effectiveness and efficiency and this has had major implications for social workers, not least in the demand for effective and efficient targeting of resources. Practitioners must know who most needs their help, what sort of help is required and what sort of help works best.

A further change is related to the role of professionals. The move towards managerialism and technocratisation within welfare services has had an impact on the dominance of the professions. Professionals have seen their roles undermined by the breaking down of their knowledge and skills into more task-specific roles and delivered either by less qualified people or by machines, resulting in more cost-effective delivery of services. Traditional respect for professional knowledge has likewise been subject to challenge as post-modern thinking brings into question the nature of knowledge and the right of the professional to define what is legitimate knowledge (Fook, 2004). The move for professionals to be more transparent and accountable in their work is another change and reflects the current challenge to 'professional dominance' (Friedson, 1970) in health and welfare services.

This breakdown in confidence in the, hitherto unchallenged, role of the professional has led to calls for the development of a body of evidence which is not directly related to professional knowledge and which is more readily verifiable and objective.

The new setting for social workers

More specifically, the professional status and the role and function of social workers has undergone fundamental changes over recent years. Three areas in particular have had a significant impact: the development of market-led approaches to the delivery of care; the related introduction of the care-management approach; and the integration of health and social care (Adams et al., 1999). Significant questions regarding the essential role and nature of social work and what distinguishes social workers from other professional groups continue to be raised by practitioners and public alike. Sheppard (1995) argues that social work's failure to defend itself from the prevailing ideologies of managerialism and consumerism, and the profession's inability to protect its traditional practice areas, have resulted from a historical failure to establish a coherent and robust knowledge base and specialist and effective skills. Social work's survival as a legitimate and effective force thus depends on an ongoing engagement with the best available evidence in order to strengthen and validate practice.

This situation has been recognised by a series of recent major reviews which aim to strengthen and improve the quality of social care throughout the UK. *Changing Lives: Report of the 21st Century Social Work Review* (Scottish Executive, 2006) in Scotland, *Options for Excellence* (DoH, 2006) in England and *Social Work in Wales: a Profession to Value* (Social Services Improvement Agency, 2005) all attempt to clarify and strengthen the position of social workers and recognise that in order for the profession to flourish social workers must be supported to build on their existing skills and knowledge.

The changing face of welfare services therefore calls for a way of creating certainty, legitimacy and economy. Interest in research within the personal social services reflects this process, and practice which is underpinned by the best possible evidence is seen as essential if the profession is to account for itself to policy-makers and public alike.

But what is the part played by research in my life as a busy practitioner? Is the business of research relevant to me or does it really only have relevance for academics and policy-makers?

The impact of research on social work practice

To what extent are social workers engaged with research?

A recent report produced for the Social Care Institute for Excellence (SCIE) (Marsh and Fisher, 2005) argues that research is a key factor in the delivery of best practice. But do practitioners use research? And if not, why not? A leading proponent of evidence-based practice, Brian Sheldon, found in a survey of over 1,000 social workers in England, that practitioners, despite enthusiasm for evidence-based practice, do not make good use of research, having poor knowledge of research findings and lack of appraisal skills. The study puts this down to social workers' poor understanding of the important place of research and their failure to read, implement and produce research themselves (Sheldon and Chilvers, 2001). Certainly, from my own experience I have to admit to putting the area of research very low down on my list of priorities. The idea that I could undertake research myself never even occurred to me, so little did it figure on my picture of development opportunities. What are the reasons for my lack of engagement and that of many other social workers? Can it be because of the personal inadequacies of myself and other individual social workers, or can we identify failings on a structural level? Marsh and Fisher (2005) identified two causal factors: a lack of a co-ordinated overview of social care research; and the irrelevance of many research programmes to practice.

Research needs to be managed

At present social work and social care lack an overall framework for the organisation of research. Piecemeal attempts have been made in the past to address this problem (see Marsh and Fisher, 2005, for a description) but the modernisation of the personal social services demands a new strategy for the development of a publicly funded research infra-structure relevant to social care. This lies in sharp contrast with the situation in the health service. For instance, in primary care a strategic framework has been developed in order to expand the knowledge base for the improvement of services. This has in turn attracted a significant increase in funding which, when compared with investment in research activity in social care, provides shocking figures illustrating the lack of equity in research investment between health and social care. For instance, as a percentage of the total service expenditure, the amount spent directly by central government on research and development in health is 16 times higher than that spent on social care. Over 100 times more is spent on individual staff members in health than that spent on each member of the social care workforce. As a social worker you can presently expect to have about £60 allocated to your research development needs, in sharp contrast to a GP who can expect £1,466, around 24 times more.

> The spending on social work as the key research discipline underpinning social care is so far below that in healthcare that it is difficult to see how they can share the same commitment to evidence-based policy and practice ... The level of resources devoted to relevant and applicable social care research is well below sensible levels for a workforce of this size, for service expenditures at this level, and for the importance of the service to millions of service users and carers.
>
> (Marsh and Fisher, 2005: 24)

A national strategy accompanied by appropriate levels of funding would raise the profile of research within social care, increasing social workers' awareness of the benefits of research and providing opportunities for individual practitioners to pursue their own developmental needs.

Is research relevant to practice?

The SCIE report makes the point that a significant number of academic researchers (by far the largest group undertaking social-care-related research) are reluctant, if not unwilling, to collaborate with practitioners and fail to engage with the way that those in the front line of service delivery use knowledge in practice. As a consequence much research, although informative and important, addresses more general issues relating to the delivery of social care policy rather than specific practice-based ones. While being invaluable in policy-making, research needs to be more focused on practice in order to take on a greater significance for front-line practitioners. Much academic research tends to address the causes of problems rather than their possible solutions in terms of effective practice interventions. Marsh and Fisher argue, however, that effective intervention in social care needs research that is relevant to the everyday concerns of those on the front line of services. Research therefore needs to be derived from practice concerns and must be easily translated into practice, otherwise social workers will be reluctant to spend their precious time seeking out knowledge that impacts only indirectly on their practice.

In order for research to take on greater meaning to social workers and thus become more integral to front-line delivery, the SCIE report argues that practitioners need to become more involved in the production of research. At present, the nearer you are to practice the less research you will do, and vice versa, with those furthest away from the front line undertaking the bulk of the research. The report recommends that this situation needs to be reversed, stating that closeness to practice is a 'major strength' that is not being utilised at present in social care.

By contrast to the situation in social care, health services are much further ahead in the move to involve front-line workers in the production of knowledge. For instance, in general practice a major investment has been made to support practitioners to undertake research and development activities, as it is recognised that high-quality R & D requires the contribution of not only academics but also NHS service providers. This support is still awaited in social care. My own research opportunity came through my associations with health rather than through social care, because of my position of being seconded by social services to the local NHS Mental Health Trust. All funding and support thus came via health – a definite advantage of interprofessional working!

How does research benefit the practitioner?

Research has an important part to play in the empowering of both users of services and social workers themselves. As the Audit Commission (2002) testified, social workers are leaving their jobs in the public sector as they are feeling overwhelmed, demotivated and undervalued. The connections between social work values, lived experience and the managerialist 'new world' of targets and policy initiatives has been broken, and social workers are finding meaningful practice increasingly difficult to sustain. In a climate where links between values and practice have become fragmented and marginalised social workers need to be able to develop room for a creative 'space' (Preston-Shoot, 2003) where practice can be thought about and be assigned meaning. Preston-Shoot suggests that the engagement by practitioners with research would create such a space, whereby evidence derived from research about effective practice can not only be utilised to enrich practice but also to challenge the configuration and delivery of services. Research can thus be seen as a tool for the reinvigoration of social work practice as well as a way of providing social work with an authoritative voice in modern welfare.

Research can also protect the social work practitioner against allegations of poor practice. Stephanie Tierney (2005) argues that the conscientious and explicit use of evidence should make social work less open to criticisms of incompetence and irresponsibility, and sees it as a way of empowering social workers. She also points out the protection it will offer service-users and carers from ineffective or damaging interventions.

The incorporation of research activity into the daily life of social workers requires that they open themselves up to new concepts and new ideas. The world of research has developed its own language and set of meanings, and newcomers can feel shut out from this seemingly baffling world full of unfamiliar concepts provoking bewilderment, anxiety and guilt. If we are to challenge the considerable resistance that I for one have encountered in my journey to becoming a research-literate practitioner, we need to develop a critical awareness of basic concepts used in research.

Basic ideas in research: what do we mean by evidence?

Research produces evidence and we need evidence to back up good practice. On the face of it this appears to be a straightforward assertion but this statement needs some critical attention. For a start, is the kind of evidence we find from research, even if it is practice-focused, the most helpful and relevant sort of knowledge to inform our practice? What do we mean by evidence anyway, and how does the way it is sought influence what 'evidence' is actually found? Different research methodologies produce different forms of evidence, the posing of research questions alone never being a neutral undertaking. Some forms of evidence carry a greater legitimacy than others, but how do we, as practitioners, decide what forms are most effective for us? Is research the only way of producing evidence? Are there different ways of finding what works, other than formal research activity? Has research taken over from practitioner wisdom and experience and is this yet another way of undermining the professional skills of the front-line practitioner? And what about the meaning derived from research findings – is this a purely objective exercise or are there factors which may influence not only the interpretation of findings but also their application? And lastly, how do we as practitioners make that link between research and practice?

Evidence-based practice: origins

Over the last few years central government has placed evidence-based practice firmly on the health and social care agenda. In 1996 it made a significant investment in evidence-based practice when it awarded £1.5 million to the Centre for Evidence-based Social Services at the University of Exeter, a body created to help fifteen local authority social services departments develop evidence-based practice. Another government-funded scheme was led by the University of Salford in 1997 and aimed to 'strengthen and cultivate' evidence-based practice in health and social care. Various documents relating to improvements in health and social care have also promoted evidence-based practice: for example DoH, 2001; and TOPSS, 1999. In addition, the National Institute for Clinical Excellence (NICE) as well as the Social Care Institute for Excellence (SCIE) have been set up with the specific intention of reviewing and making available research findings and best-practice guidelines.

The term 'evidence-based practice' has thus emerged over recent years and has become something of a catchphrase within health and social care. The term has seeped into my mind, as a practitioner, and has become associated in an unquestioning way with the idea of 'research'. However, given the current elevated status of evidence-based practice and its influence over our lives both as professionals and as users of services ourselves, we need a more critical understanding of this latest buzz-word. What do we mean by evidence-based practice and is it the best way of producing the kind of knowledge required for effective practice?

Although social work has some historical association with scientific research in its own right, the rise of the evidence-based practice movement in social care largely originated in response to developments in health care. Evidence-based medicine developed in order to bridge the gap between clinical practice and research through the dissemination of knowledge about best practice (Reynolds, 2000). The transfer of this idea to social care has involved a transfer of concepts commonly held in medicine into the field of social care.

Evidence-based practice: implications for professionals

Research in medicine usually assumes a scientific, rational basis for its understanding of health-related phenomena and will influence research within the field of social care to be more positivistic and measurement-based. The kind of data constituting acceptable 'evidence' will therefore more likely be drawn from studies which address quantifiable issues which can be easily measured, such as data produced by the randomised-control trial

(RCT). A hierarchy of acceptable evidence exists whereby this form of research holds pre-eminence because of its reputation as the most reliable research method due to its alleged avoidance of bias and error (Gray, 1997).

Brian Sheldon, the former director of the Centre for Evidence-based Social Services in Exeter, has adapted a commonly held definition of evidence-based medicine as a way of defining evidence-based practice in social work:

> Evidence-based social care is the conscientious, explicit and judicious use of current best evidence in making decisions regarding the welfare of those in need.
>
> (Sheldon and Chilvers, 2002)

This definition significantly omits any reference to the skills of the practitioner and the evaluation of experience, all 'evidence' coming from external sources (Taylor and White, 2005). Hollway (2001) criticizes this approach, accusing it of assuming a 'seriously reductive definition of what counts as evidence' (p. 10) and claiming for scientific evidence 'an authority, a basis for certainty, which it does not deserve, especially not when applied to human phenomena' (p. 10). She claims that evidence-based practice is a way of re-authorising scientific method within the human services and is a way of imposing reductive and standardised interventions on professional caring relationships.

Rolfe (2000) likewise argues that the adoption of evidence-based practice by social care is part of the move to make professional practice more technologised, and that it minimises the skill and wisdom of the practitioner. Hollway argues that it implies that practice was not based on evidence before the invention of 'evidence- based practice', and that the practitioner can only learn from external knowledge rather than from their own experience.

Hollway (2001) argues that the evidence that the randomised control trial and other quantitative methods produce is lacking in congruence with front-line social work practice which she describes as being characteristically complex, multi-faceted, changing and value-laden. She objects to this concept of evidence on several different counts. Firstly, from this perspective, objects of knowledge are seen as static and predictable and call for certainty. Secondly, questions which are too complex to answer by quantitative methods are excluded or over-simplified, thereby reducing complex psychosocial phenomena and fragmenting the individual subject. Hollway claims that the randomised control trial is generalised knowledge pooled and then averaged from many different respondents, and as such leaves no room for individual characteristics.

The nature and use of knowledge is addressed by Michel Foucault who believed that knowledge as an objective 'truth' does not exist, but is produced by those in power who hold particular beliefs and assumptions about the nature of truth. He said that knowledge can be used selectively to further the political ends of certain groups and this is picked up on by Trinder (2000), who notes that opponents of evidence-based practice have suggested its use is a 'covert way of rationing resources' (p. 2). In referring to the work of F.W. Taylor and his study of management principles at the beginning of the last century, Hollway suggests that scientific evidence has been used in the past in a way which devalues the experience-based knowledge and skills of workers. In so doing, it undermines their power and autonomy in the interest of legitimising managerial control over working practices. She suggests that evidence-based practice, relying as it does on the scientific collection and analysis of knowledge about welfare practices, is likewise being used to undermine the power and autonomy of health and social care professionals through the imposition of codified and proceduralised, efficiency-related knowledge.

From evidence to practice?

The concept of evidence-based practice makes the assumption that the move from evidence to practice is straightforward and that social workers are rational agents who apply logical principles derived from relevant research findings to their practice. The only possible problem could be the availability of that evidence to practitioners who, once armed with the 'truth', will automatically adjust their practice accordingly. However, not all agree. Webb (2001) believes that the decisions social workers take on a daily basis are subject to complex processes reaching beyond the availability of concrete evidence, and that evidence-based practice is imposing a simplistic, restrictive and authoritarian regime on to their practice. Webb believes that the process of decision making is never a neutral act, is always subject to cultural influences and is heavily influenced by inter-subjective relations. Thus practitioners are bound to be influenced by factors other than research evidence.

> A more complex relationship exists between social work interventions and decisions made by social work agencies which is governed by imperatives which fall outside the workings of a rational actor, such as the politics of inter-agency relations, internal organizational interest groups and managerially led initiatives aimed at enhancing 'productivity statistics'.

> (Webb, 2001: 63)

I would argue that in addition to the above external influences on our ability as practitioners to make informed decisions, is the fact of our own subjectivity and our own, often unconscious, needs. Despite our most assiduous attempts at self-reflection and reflective practice our own internal psychological forces, which often remain out of our conscious awareness, will impact on our practice, affecting what evidence we choose to utilise, in which circumstances, and indeed whether we utilise research at all in our practice.

Evidence-based practice – quantitative versus qualitative

As we have seen, the kind of evidence most commonly seen in evidence-based medicine, and by association in social care, is that derived from research which uses quantitative methodologies. In response to criticism of the dominance of this form of investigation the Cochrane Foundation, which promotes and represents evidence-based practice, formed a qualitative methods group (Trinder, 2000: 37). This type of research design derives evidence from smaller groups of research subjects, and thus is able to address issues in more depth. Unlike its quantitative counterpart with its view of the individualised, biological subject, qualitative methodology takes into account the influence of society, seeing its research respondents as products of their social circumstances. As such it is using a model likely to produce results that are more congruent with the way that social workers see the world. The evidence produced would thus be more accessible and meaningful to the practitioner, with the result that research and practice could become natural partners, informing and enhancing each other and thus leading to the development of the individual social worker.

The place of evidence

Thus the question of what 'evidence' is used, and how it is used, is complex and the use of evidence-based practice is possibly not the all-time panacea proclaimed by some. However evidence derived from research findings is a crucial ingredient in the development of social work practice. In their report for SCIE on the use of evidence in social work and social care, Marsh and Fisher agree that we need to be more circumspect in our use of 'evidence'. They draw on the work of Janet Lewis, the former Director of Research at the Joseph Rowntree Foundation, who proposes that the kind of knowledge required for social care practitioners consists of three, equally important elements: evidence produced from research; practice wisdom; and service-user and carer experiences (Lewis, 2001). This more balanced view respects and validates the enormous importance of practitioner experience, as well as pointing to the central role of users and carers as recipients and dictators of care. Marsh and Fisher suggest that the involvement of practitioners, users and carers in research activity, especially in leading research, is one way of ensuring their voices get heard.

Service-users and research

The modernisation agenda with its emphasis on the marketisation of welfare services is demanding a much greater level of citizen participation and democratic decision making within the provision of public services. The slow, yet increasing involvement of service-users in the production of knowledge within all areas of the welfare state is a reflection of the rise of consumerism, where users are seen as active and selective agents within the market-place of care. This movement requires a radical re-evaluation of the relationship between user and practitioner, whereby relationships are seen less as a site for the enactment of 'care' with all of its attendant moral and ethical connotations, and more as a site for the delivery of goods and services (Hoggett, 2006). Some writers consider this new form of relationship strips the practitioner/user encounter of meaning, diminishing both professional and user in the process, and prefer to frame the user according to the liberalist view of the human subject which promotes the link between professional and client. For instance, Wengraf and Chamberlayne (2004) accuse the Joseph Rowntree Foundation of taking an 'anti-professional' consumerist approach to service-users in the way they prioritise the place of the user in research production. They argue this serves to minimise and break down the therapeutic alliance between practitioner and user, thereby also severing any potential political alliance between the two.

However, despite misgivings from some quarters, the involvement of service-users and carers in research is very firmly on the national agenda. Fundamental to the founding principles of SCIE is the idea that users should be central to the setting of the research agenda and should be involved in all stages of research projects. But although most research undertaken in social care concerns itself with the needs of service-users and the meeting of those needs, we might ask how involved users actually are in research production. Although there are growing numbers of user-led research projects (see for example, Beresford and Turner, 1997; Evans and Fisher, 1999), evidence of the impact of user involvement on the quality of research is scarce (Fisher, 2002, is an example). Although funding bodies often require evidence that end-users will benefit from the research project, this often only refers to academics, policy-makers or commercial bodies, and rarely to service-users. Notable exceptions to this are the above-noted Joseph Rowntree Foundation, who, along with the Nuffield Foundation, stipulates that users must be involved in research proposals.

Increasingly, however, service-users are reacting to their hitherto marginalised position with respect to the research agenda and are demanding greater involvement in the production of research. For instance, the disability movement has criticised research for not involving disabled service-users and for failing to consider the place of social circumstances in the disabling of users (for instance, Oliver, 1992; Lindow and Morris, 1995; Barnes and Mercer, 1997). The resulting call for 'emancipatory' research has emphasised the need for research projects to have as their goal an improvement in the quality of life for service-users and a focus on issues prioritised by users.

Tierney (2005) suggests that involvement in research will empower service-users. She points to the need for transparency in work with users, who she feels are entitled to know the evidence pointing to the efficacy of any interventions the social worker may be suggesting. The resulting partnership between professional and user, she argues, would thus enhance their relationship. Through a familiarity with the 'language' of research users would be in a stronger position to argue their case.

In order to strengthen the alliance between the research community and service-users and carers, the Marsh and Fisher report for SCIE suggests that an up-to-date review and summary of user-produced research should be undertaken in order for future development to be planned. They also propose that ethical issues relating to research and user involvement need to be addressed in order for users and carers to become involved in all areas of knowledge production. They believe that users must also become involved in the commissioning and production of systematic reviews.

The researcher-practitioner

Necessary conditions for the research-active practitioner

We have argued that in order for research activity to become embedded in practice, practitioners themselves need to get involved in the production of research. We have also seen that without a national strategy to organise and promote front-line research activity, accompanied by the funding to make this happen, practitioners are unlikely to engage in the production of research in sufficient numbers to make a difference. Another essential ingredient in the promotion of the research-active practitioner is the kind of organisational culture which promotes the development of its workforce.

As we have seen, engagement with research can create the kind of creative space necessary for the promotion of good practice and a positive re-engagement with the principles of social work. This requires that the practitioner takes a more active and less reactive role in their own development. However, just as in policy and practice users of welfare services need to be seen in their social and economic situation, so practitioners need to be understood in their organisational and political context. The extent to which change is possible by both users and social workers is constrained by their social and economic environment (Frosch, 1987), and any change needs to take account of systemic considerations as well as individual ones. To quote Humphreys et al., (who cite Chapman, 2002):

> Knowledge-based practice is reliant upon stimulating innovation, enthusiasm and learning within organisations to acknowledge the multiple sources of knowledge, both new and old, which can create a more sensitive and informed practice. It potentially represents a challenge to top-down approaches to organisational change and professional development. This too frequently occurs within the 'command and control' style of new managerialism where fear of being shamed in the national league tables and blamed for practice shortcoming can undermine learning and inhibit creative change processes.

> (2003: 4)

The kind of environment which promotes change and development fosters supportive relationships, shared decision-making, understanding of change principles and creates a culture which values and accommodates questioning and reflection as well as valuing existing skills and knowledge. These qualities were identified by Senge (1992) as being necessary conditions for the 'learning organisation'. If research is to become meaningfully connected with practice both in terms of a critical examination of existing research by social workers and in their actual 'doing' it for themselves this kind of facilitative atmosphere must prevail.

Benefits of doing research in practice

Reflective practice demands that we take the time to link our experience in the field with theory and empirical knowledge, thus developing the 'knowledge-in-action' referred to by Schon (1991). McLeod (1999) states that the main point of research undertaken by practitioners is the improvement of their practice. Not only can doing research themselves have a direct impact on social workers' practice, but it can also help them to break down any barriers to research they may have and help tackle its mystique. As we have seen, evidence-based research can often mean 'statistics-based research' undertaken by 'experts' far from practice, and this can create distance and despondency for the practitioner who may feel (as I once did) shut out from this world. It will also help in the more effective evaluation of the validity and reliability of other research studies as workers experience first hand the dilemmas and debates of producing an ethically sound and methodologically stringent study for themselves.

Practitioner research versus academic research?

We have already established that most research in the UK is undertaken by academics. But what, if any, are the differences between practitioner research and academic research?

Different forces drive research in academia and research in practice. Ian Shaw (2005) makes the point that the organisational imperatives of practitioner research promote inquiry that focuses on service development and delivery and is maybe less likely to encourage research of a more general or esoteric nature, which academics are possibly better placed to undertake. A recent study undertaken in Wales (Keane et al., 2003) found that almost all topics focused on by practitioner-researchers were about direct practice or service delivery issues. This research highlighted three areas of concern for practitioner-researchers. Firstly, the position of the practitioner who is undertaking research is somewhat ambiguous, being 'inside' the practice arena yet 'outside' in terms of research activities. Secondly, and linked to the first point, is the issue of marginalisation of the practitioner-researcher. In my own experience I certainly experienced a degree of isolation from my colleagues while undertaking my research project, and one cannot dismiss the potentially damaging presence of envy within teams. Not only can the practitioner feel marginalised from their team, but they can also experience a degree of isolation from the academic world of research, with implicit suggestions that, as a social worker in practice, you cannot be doing 'serious' research. But are they right? Is practitioner research as valid as academic research?

The emphasis on the practical application of practitioner research implies that such research cannot contribute to a broader policy or academic forum and is limited to the practice arena. However, Shaw (2005) argues that the distinction between practice and theory is complicated and not as straightforward as some may believe. Conventional thinking holds that theory is a purely mental activity whereas practice is the straightforward application of ideas in the real world. However, practice derives the ideas it uses from sources other than pure theory and is a more complex process than meets the eye. For instance, the ideas derived from the tacit knowledge of practitioners refers to the kind of knowledge that, while not written down and formalised, is very often passed between practitioners and can be revealed through good practitioner research. This kind of 'practice wisdom' can be more readily accessed by practitioners themselves and has much to offer the social work world in all its forms. The unspoken and potentially elitist myth that practical knowledge is somehow inferior, or at least secondary, to theoretical knowledge can serve to alienate the social worker and undermine their confidence in embarking on their own research endeavours.

Do practice and research fit together?

Let us look more closely at the question of whether practice experience actually does lend itself to research production. What is the relationship between practice and research? Are they the natural allies we have suggested they might be? Do they inform and build on each other or are they, as some suggest, mutually exclusive?

Padgett (1998a, 1998b) believes that there are ethical and scientific reasons why practice and research should not be brought together. She argues that they have different goals which she sees as mutually incompatible: the objective of research is that of the pursuit of knowledge and scholarship, whereas practice is primarily concerned with the complex idea of 'helping'. Padgett feels that research within practice is unethical, posing insurmountable dilemmas regarding confidentiality, informed consent and withdrawal from research/treatment (Padgett, 1998a: 376). On a scientific front she claims that when a practitioner is also the researcher, particularly when utilising qualitative methodology with its

Table 8.1   Similarities between researchers and practitioners in social work

Social work processes	Research processes
1. Social worker is presented with a problem or issues.	1. Researcher is presented with a problem or question.
2. Social worker collects facts which illuminate the nature and purpose of the issues.	2. Researcher searches the literature on the problem or question.
3. Social worker designs a plan of action with service-user.	3. Researcher designs a study.
4. Social worker attempts to carry out plan, monitoring progress.	4. Researcher collects and collates material.
5. Social worker reviews work and may make make new plans.	5. Researcher analyses material and produces conclusions and possibly recommendations for future action.

incorporation of the idea of subjectivity, the issue of 'critical distance' required by the researcher arises, whereby dynamics within the social worker/client relationship may impede objective scientific enquiry. The argument regarding methodological rigour relating to the use of qualitative research methods within practice arises from other sources too, with criticisms of the 'anti-intellectual' approach of practitioners, along with their 'lack of scholarship' (Atkinson and Delamont, 1993: 210). These criticisms would appear to confirm the insularity and exclusivity of certain professional groups.

So, is there any affinity between research and practice? Commentators from the USA have been more vocal than those in the UK in exploring the relationship between the two. Jane Gilgun (1994) believes that qualitative research methods in particular share certain key features with practice and advocates their use within practice areas. She argues that there are three areas of compatibility. Firstly, the usual person-centred approach of social work practice is congruent with the focus within research on how respondents understand their world. Secondly, the social worker takes into account the environment of the client, while qualitative research likewise gives attention to the context of their data; and lastly, the individualisation of the social work client by the practitioner resonates with the use of individual case studies within this type of research.

Further similarities between researchers and practitioners were identified in a report commissioned by the Department of Health concerning what research had to say about child placements (DoH, 1991). The report found that both disciplines required careful observation and patient enquiry, accurate recording of findings, organisation of the information obtained, and careful analysis and weighing up of evidence. The parallel processes identified are summarised in Table 8.1.

The skills of reflection and awareness of self so intrinsic to practice can also make an important contribution to qualitative research in terms of understanding the dynamics within the researcher/respondent relationship and can add valuable data. For instance, Hollway and Jefferson (2000) have developed a qualitative research method known as the 'free association, narrative interview method', which proposes that within the process of gathering and analysing data the researcher is affected by their own feelings, both conscious and unconscious, as well as those of the respondent. If not understood these feelings can distort research findings, yet if, through a process of reflection, they are understood and applied to the research setting, they can serve as a rich and valuable source of data.

The skills that social workers use in their everyday practice, therefore, can enhance their research capacity. Conversely, the development of research skills can be a potentially rich source of practice enhancement. For instance, Lang (1994) recommends that techniques utilised by qualitative researchers for data gathering and analysis can be used in practice, enabling social workers to derive their own theory from their practice data and take action accordingly, rather than relying on existing theory. This integration of qualitative research skills within practice can therefore release the potential of social workers for theory-building and result in a more research-minded practitioner.

Where is the service-user?

I finish this section with a word of warning. As Shaw (2005) notes, within the literature about practitioner research there exists very little mention of ways in which service-users can become involved in research production, either through identification of research questions or commissioning of research. The current emphasis on the development of practitioner as researcher marginalises the position of the service-user and ways must be found to incorporate their views.

> Genuine involvement of service users [cannot] be taken forward if the focus remains on the researcher-practitioner relationship. There is a clear danger that in focusing on the modes of researcher-practitioner collaboration the voice of the service user is less prominent or simply outnumbered.

(Fisher, 2002: 306)

Conclusion

The relatively recent emergence of research within the field of social care and, more specifically, social work, is a potentially major force for the renewal of the profession as a site of sound critical, analytical and reflective practice. However, the research agenda, as with all developments within contemporary professional practice, needs to be understood within its political context and the influence the changing environment of welfare delivery has over the definition and use of knowledge. Questions need to be asked about whose knowledge counts and whose voice can be heard. As practitioners we need thus to adopt a critical approach to the use and production of research, particularly bearing in mind how far the research in question promotes an anti-oppressive agenda.

At present, as we have seen, production of knowledge tends to be driven by academics, far from practice, thus potentially marginalising both practitioners and service-users alike. An initiative known as 'Making research count' (Humphreys et al., 2003) has recently emerged, which aims to link research with practice through developing the interface between research, social work, social care and health. A national framework is being developed consisting of regional alliances between universities, local authorities, health trusts, primary care trusts and independent agencies. The organisation introduces the notion of 'knowledge-based practice', which incorporates a triangle of research, practitioner wisdom and service-user perspectives with the aim of strengthening the development of social work practice. By incorporating academic, practitioner and service-user within a context which values and accommodates different ways of 'knowing' this initiative will, I hope, serve to heal some of the splits which serve to hinder the development of a practical and useful research agenda based on equal access to all interested parties.

References

Adams, A., Heasman, P., and Gilbert, L. (1999) 'Opportunities and constraints to practitioner research in the personal social services', *Research, Policy and Planning: The Journal of the Social Services Research Group*, 17 (1). http://www.ssrg.org.uk/publications/rrp/1999/issue/article4.asp

Atkinson, P. and Delamont, S. (1993) 'Bread and dreams or bread and circuses? A critique of case study research in evaluation' in M. Hammersley (ed.), *Controversies in the Classroom*. Buckingham: Open University Press.

Audit Commission (2002) *Recruitment and Retention – a Public Service Workforce for the 21st Century*. London: HMSO.

Barnes, C. and Mercer, G. (eds) (1997) *Doing Disability Research*. Leeds: Disability Press.

Beresford, P. and Turner, M. (1997) *It's Our Welfare: Report of the Citizen Commission on the Future of the Welfare State*. London: NISW.

Chapman, J. (2002) *'System Failure: Why Governments Must Learn to Think Differently*. London: Demos.

Department of Health (DoH) (1991) *Patterns and Outcomes in Child Placement – Messages from Current Research and Their Implications*. London: HMSO.

Department of Health (DoH) (2000) *A Quality Strategy for Social Care*. London: Department of Health.

Department of Health (DoH) (2001) *Assessing Children in Need and their Families: Practice Guidance*. London: HMSO.

Department of Health (DoH) (2006) *Options for Excellence: Building the Social Care Workforce of the Future*. London: Department of Health.

Dominelli, L. (1996) 'Deprofessionalising social work', *British Journal of Social Work*, 26: 25–38.

Evans, C. and Fisher, M. (1999) 'Collaborative evaluation with service users: moving towards user-controlled research', in I. Shaw and J. Lishman (eds), *Evaluation and Social Work Practice*. London: Sage.

Fisher, M. (2002) 'The role of service users in problem formulation and technical aspects of social research', *Social Work Education*, 21 (3): 305–12.

Fook, J. (2004) 'What professionals need from research: beyond evidence-based practice', in D. Smith (ed.), *Social Work and Evidence-Based Practice*. London: Jessica Kingsley.

Friedson, E. (1970) *The Profession of Medicine*. New York: Dodd Mead.

Frosch, S. (1987) *The Politics of Psychoanalysis*. London: Macmillan.

Gilgun, J. (1994) 'Hand in glove: the grounded theory approach and social work practice research', in E. Sherman and W.J. Reid (eds), *Qualitative Research in Social Work*. New York: Columbia University Press.

Gray, J.A.M. (1997) *Evidence-Based Healthcare*. London: Churchill Livingstone.

Halton, W. (1994) 'Some unconscious aspects of organizational life: contributions from psychoanalysis', in A. Obholzer and V. Zagier Roberts (eds), *The Unconscious at Work*. London: Routledge.

Hoggett, P. (2006) 'Conflict, ambivalence, and the contested purpose of public organizations', *Human Relations*, 59 (2): 175–94.

Hollway, W. (2001) 'The psycho-social subject in "evidence-based practice"', *Journal of Social Work Practice*, 15 (1): 9–22.

Hollway, W. and Jefferson, T. (2000) *Doing Qualitative Research Differently: Free Association, Narrative and Interview Method*. London: Sage.

Hornby, S. and Atkins, J. (2000) *Collaborative Care: Interprofessional, Interagency and Interpersonal* (2nd edn). Oxford: Blackwell Science.

Humphreys, C., Berridge, D., Butler, I. and Ruddick, R. (2003) 'Making research count: the development of "Knowledge-Based Practice"', *Research Policy and Planning*, 21 (1).

Keane, S., Shaw, I. and Faulkener, A. (2003) *Practitioner Research in Social Work and Social Care: An Audit and Case Study Analysis*. Cardiff: Wales Office for Research and Development.

Lang, N. (1994) 'Integrating the data processing of qualitative research and social work practice to advance the practitioner as knowledge builder: tools for knowing and doing', in E. Sherman and W. Reid (eds), *Qualitative Research in Social Work*. New York: Columbia University Press.

Lewis, J. (2001) 'What works in community care?', *Managing Community Care*, 9 (1): 3–6.

Lindow, V. and Morris, J. (1995) *Service User Involvement: Synthesis of Findings and Experience in the Field of Community Care*. York: Joseph Rowntree Foundation.

Marsh, P. and Fisher, M. (2005) *Developing the Evidence Base for Social Work and Social Care Practice*. Bristol: Social Care Institute for Excellence Policy Press.

Masterson, A. (2002) 'Cross-boundary working: a macro-political analysis of the impact on professional roles', *Journal of Clinical Nursing*, 11 (3): 331–8.

McLeod, J. (1999) *Practitioner Research in Counselling*. London: Sage.

Molyneux, J. (2001) 'Interprofessional teamworking: what makes teams work well?', *Journal of Interprofessional Care*, 15 (1): 29–35.

Oliver, M. (1992) 'Changing the social relations of research production', *Disability, Handicap and Society*. 7 (2): 101–14.

Padgett, D. (1998a) 'Does the glove really fit? Qualitative research and clinical social work practice', *Social Work*, 43 (4): 373–81.

Padgett, D. (1998b) *Qualitative Methods in Social Work Research*, Thousand Oaks, CA: Sage.

Preston-Shoot, M. (2003) 'Changing learning and learning change: making a difference in education, policy and practice', *Journal of Social Work Practice*, 17 (1): 9–23.

Reynolds, S. (2000) 'The anatomy of evidence-based practice', in L. Trinder (ed.), *Evidence-based Practice*. Oxford: Blackwell.

Rolfe, G. (2000) *Research, Truth and Authority: Postmodern Perspectives on Nursing*. Basingstoke: Palgrave Macmillan.

Salter, E., Floyd, S. and Mistral, W. (2003) *Integration of Health and Social Care within Avon and Wiltshire Mental Health Partnership NHS Trust: Social Worker Views*. Mental Health Research and Development Unit, Avon and Wiltshire Mental Health Partnership NHS Trust and University of Bath.

Schon, D. (1983) *The Reflective Practitioner*. New York: Basic Books.

Schon, D. (1991) *The Reflective Practitioner – How Professionals Think in Action*. Aldershot: Avebury.

Scottish Executive (2006) *Changing Lives: Report of the 21st Century Social Work Review*. Edinburgh: Scottish Executive.

Senge, P. (1992) *The Fifth Discipline: The Art and Practice of the Learning Organisation*. London: Century Business.

Shaw, I. (2005) 'Practitioner research: evidence or critique?', *British Journal of Social Work*, 35 (8): 1231–48.

Sheldon, B. and Chilvers, R. (2001) *Evidence-based Social Care: Problems and Prospects.* Lyme Regis: Russell House.

Sheldon, B., and Chilvers, R. (2002) 'An empirical study of the obstacles to evidence-based practice', *Social Work and Social Sciences Review*, 10 (1): 6–26.

Sheppard, M. (1995) *Care Management and the New Social Work: A Critical Analysis.* London: Whiting & Birch.

Social Services Improvement Agency (2005) *Social Work in Wales: a Profession to Value.* Cardiff: Social Services Improvement Agency.

Taylor, C. and White, S. (2005) 'What works about what works? Fashion, fad and EBP', in A. Bilson (ed.), *Evidence-based Practice in Social Work.* London: Whiting & Birch.

Tierney, S. (2005) 'Reframing an evidence-based approach to practice', in A. Bilson (ed.), *Evidence-based practice in social work.* London: Whiting & Birch.

TOPSS (1999) *Modernizing the Social Care Workforce*, Consultation Document. Leeds: TOPSS.

Trinder, E. with Reynolds, S. (2000) *Evidence-Based Practice: A Critical Appraisal.* Oxford: Blackwell.

Webb, S. (2001) 'Some considerations on the validity of evidence-based practice in Social Work', *British Journal of Social Work*, 31 (1): 57–79.

Wengraf, T. and Chamberlayne, P. (2004) Editorial, *Journal of Social Work Practice*, 18 (3): 275–81.

Chapter 9

The challenge of working in teams

Linda Finlay and Claire Ballinger

Teamwork is firmly on the agenda as government policy-makers, consumer groups and the range of people working in health, social and voluntary sectors all call for greater commitment towards integrated care. Alongside calls for multi-professional working comes the breaking down not only of traditional professional boundaries, but also of the boundaries and identities of discrete teams. Individual teams increasingly comprise members working within a number of different agencies, who may have alliances with multiple groups (for example, professional, service-based and sector-based). Thus, individual practitioners face the challenge of holding on to their own knowledge or skill base while entering into the work of other professionals and services. This inevitably means developing new team relationships, modes of working, and ways of viewing the context of one's working environment.

All these developments suggest that teamwork is desirable, essential even, for providing effective interventions. Yet is this always the case? What constitutes good teamwork? Can a teamwork approach ever be counterproductive? Is it an effective way of patching up fractures within or between different services? What factors constrain teamwork and how might positive collaboration be fostered? In this chapter we aim to answer these questions by taking a critical look at teamwork and examining how it works in practice. The focus here will be on how practitioners with different areas of expertise work together in a team, rather than looking at inter-agency collaboration.

1 Exploring the concept of 'the team'

Payne (2000) highlights the multiple meanings of both 'team' and 'teamwork', and suggests that a useful activity for promoting enhanced teamworking is for a group's members to reflect on their individual understandings of the meaning of 'team'. In this chapter, a team is defined as a group of individuals, with varying backgrounds, perspectives, skills and training, who work together towards the common goal of delivering a health or social service. Ideally, team members collaborate and value one another's different contributions.

'Co-ordinated profession' or 'collective responsibility' teams?

Within the broad definition given above, teams can be organised in many ways, with different degrees of co-operation and collaboration. Consider Boxes 9.1 and 9.2: they describe the way two different teams operate in practice.

Box 9.1   A consultative team

Team members

1 consultant, 3 junior doctors, 15 nurses and nursing assistants, 2 physiotherapists, 1 occupational therapist and 1 helper, 1 part-time social worker, associated students.

The way the team is organised/functions

The consultant has overall medical responsibility for individual patients and (through the junior doctors' efforts) oversees all admissions, discharges and treatment decisions. The nurses implement the patients' treatment, much of which is prescribed by the doctors. Written referrals are made to the allied health professionals who are line-managed by their respective professional leads, and who have a degree of professional autonomy to decide on their particular interventions. Otherwise, decisions about treatment strategies are largely made by the consultant on the weekly ward round consisting of the junior doctors and senior nurses on duty. The routine format is that the nurses and doctors give a verbal report to the consultant on a patient's progress. The consultant outlines the next step for treatment after listening to the reports and conferring with the patient. The senior therapists and nurses also meet together on a weekly basis to discuss the overall management of particular patients' treatment. It is in this forum that therapists make their reports and recommendations, and it is the responsibility of the senior nurse to pass these on to the consultant. The allied health professionals meet together with their professional leads and other members of the same profession in their monthly, department-based meetings. Broader policy decisions regarding changes to ward practice are generally imposed by management.

Closeness of team relationships and degree of interaction

Relationships tend to be formal, with interactions generally task-focused and little socialising together as a team, for example during breaks or outside working hours. Uniforms and badges depicting the various names and roles ease interactions as members have clear expectations about different professional tasks and activity within the team. Some team members work more closely together than others – for instance, warm relationships can be found within the nursing staff as a whole. The three therapists also liaise closely as they negotiate a relevant division of labour.

Box 9.2   A multidisciplinary team

Team members

1 team leader (qualified nurse), 1 social worker, 4 community psychiatric nurses, 1 occupational therapist, 1 psychologist, 1 support worker, 1 part-time consultant psychiatrist, associated students.

The way the team is organised/functions

The team members gather at a weekly referral meeting to allocate newly referred clients to the most suitable team member, who will act as the key worker to co-ordinate care. Thereafter the key worker sees the client for an initial assessment and negotiates goals for intervention. The staff team meets regularly to review the progress of the clients in each key worker's caseload. In this meeting each key worker discusses his or her clients and gains advice from the other members. The key worker can also refer the client to other team members for specific interventions as appropriate. The team leader chairs the meetings and is the manager with overall responsibility. Policy decisions regarding day-to-day team practice are created jointly by all the team members and reviewed regularly.

Closeness of team relationship and degree of interaction

The team members work closely together and collaborate on several initiatives (for instance, joint interventions and peer supervision). In general, their relationships are close and informal, and many members of the team socialise together outside work hours. The team's work often involves a blurring of traditional role boundaries, so that it can be hard to distinguish the different professionals within the team by looking at their daily activities and interventions. Occasionally tensions arise within the team relating to insecurity around individual team members' contributions or feelings of not being sufficiently valued by others. From time to time, team members also clash in terms of their professional beliefs – for instance, about the role of medication. In general, however, team members feel united through the pursuit of a common objective.

In the example in Box 9.1, the sense of unity of purpose among team members is implicit rather than expressed, with professionals carrying out parallel interventions specifically relating to their role: the physiotherapists focusing on mobility, the occupational therapist on function, the social worker co-ordinating packages of care to facilitate discharge, and so forth. The consultant takes responsibility for all the key decisions within the context of a meeting where the allied health professionals' perspectives are presented by the senior nurse. Because interaction between team members is generally focused on patient-related tasks and is strictly bound by professional codes of conduct, there are rarely serious disputes between team members. It is notable that nursing and therapy assistants do not play a part in decision making and that patients also have a limited voice (see Box 9.3).

Box 9.3   The service user as a team member?

Ideally, patients/clients/service-users (hereafter referred to as 'service-users') and their carers should be considered as members of the team in so far as they are centrally involved in carrying through any treatment or care plan. The degree to which this happens in practice can be limited, particularly if they have problems such as cognitive impairment or communication difficulties. Service-users may be asked to express their 'problem' or to give their perspective, but often they do not take part in the actual decision making. The traditional practice of ward rounds in hospitals is a good illustration of this: patients may be asked how they feel now and whether they are ready to go home, but the clinical decision about when to discharge them is left to the professionals involved.

In the example in Box 9.2, the regular team meetings attended by all the key workers give them a strong sense of team membership, with closeness and loyalty to each other. The fact that there are also conflicts within this team does not unduly damage the sense of team identity and approach, although the resolution of differing and strongly held perspectives about client care sometimes takes time. The value that team members attach to their positions as autonomous professionals also means that the team leader needs to be a skilled facilitator in order to reach a solution where opinions are divided.

Øvretveit (1997a) picks up the contrast between such examples of teamwork in Boxes 9.1 and 9.2 by distinguishing between a 'co-ordinated profession team' and a 'collective responsibility team'. The former consists of a loose network which acts as a focus for referral and communication but then delivers separately organised and accountable services. The latter involved a close working group which pools its resources, for instance in team meetings and joint case notes. Team members take shared responsibility for use of resources (even where individuals take clinical decisions separately). In a co-ordinated profession team individual members are likely to be bound by the policies and priorities of their own profession or agency, whereas in collective responsibility teams, individual team members are more accountable to the team for the way they deploy their own time and resources.

In the reality of twenty-first-century health and social care practice, it is likely that professionals will belong simultaneously to a number of different teams which function in a variety of ways, in part dependent on the priorities and needs of the different services and their users.

Models of teamwork

Boon and colleagues (2004) describe seven different models of team working, ranged along a continuum from non-integrative to fully integrative care. The *parallel* team can best be described as a group of individual professionals who work in a common setting, usually with differently prescribed scopes of practice. Within *consultative* teams, practitioners who work independently share information about service-users, usually through indirect means of communication, as described in Box 9.1. Moving towards more integrative modes of service delivery, *collaborative* teams share information about common clients through informal means, such as shared breaks. In contrast, *co-ordinated* teams meet regularly for the purpose of sharing information, with an identified individual taking responsibility for passing information between the team and the client. *Multidisciplinary* teams, as illustrated in Box 9.2, comprise groups of individuals who express their own professional decisions which are then integrated by the team leader. Such teams tend to be non-hierarchical. and could move to the *interdisciplinary* position, where group decisions based on consensus start to predominate. The fully *integrated* team is united by a shared philosophy in which prevention of client problems is prioritised along with solutions, and each member of the team is valued for their particular contribution.

In practice, teams often operate a combination of these models. Also, the type of teamwork engaged in can change according to the task in hand and to the composition of team members at the time. For instance, while the example of a team in Box 9.1 mostly closely resembles a collaborative team, the allied health professionals may work in a more integrative way within their own smaller profession-specific teams. Øvretveit (1997b) reviewed the way a community mental health team functioned and found a range of practices. For instance, day centre staff collaborated as a sub-team, but in terms of links between them and the other services they operated as parallel teams and contact was largely ad hoc or dependent on personalities.

The work of most health and social care teams is too complex to be easily classified. However, it is useful to distinguish between different models to help us understand the structure and processes of a working team more closely. Table 9.1, based on the work of Boon et al. (2004), contrasts the seven different types of teams in terms of philosophy/values, structure, process and outcomes.

Having distinguished between different models, the question remains: which type of team and teamwork is best? In practice, each has a role depending on the demands of the situation and the function of the team. An interdisciplinary/integrative team or well co-ordinated multidisciplinary team would probably be the choice to provide a long-term, holistic package of care to a group of clients who have multiple and complex needs (such as those with enduring mental health problems, social needs or problems of addiction/dependency). In such a context, care would need to be taken to ensure team members value each others' different professional interventions and so avoid unnecessary duplication. In situations requiring quick decision and intervention (for example, acute orthopaedic wards), a hierarchical structure might be more appropriate. However, in this context care would need to be taken to ensure that professionals do not feel disempowered by the hierarchy, and hence inhibited about contributing. This again could result in clients not getting the best service.

The issue for teams, then, is not that some ways of operating are 'good' and others 'bad'. Instead, the working of the team should be appropriate to its purpose and function in terms of the services it is supposed to offer and the decisions it needs to take. The challenge for all teams and team leaders is how best to organise themselves to achieve these ends. In practice, teams do not necessarily operate as effectively as they might do.

2 The rhetoric and the reality

Challenging assumptions

That teamwork is desirable and an efficient, effective way of delivering health and social care is often taken as self-evident. Practitioners have consistently been exhorted to

Table 9.1   Comparison of models of teamworking in terms of philosophy/values, structure, process and outcomes

	Parallel/consultative teams	Collaborative/ co-ordinated/ multidisciplinary teams	Interdisciplinary/ integrative teams
Philosophy/ values	Reductionist models of service delivery e.g. biomedical model.	Accommodation of multiple dimensions of service delivery e.g. biopsychosocial model.	Holistic philosophies accommodating environmental and social/cultural context of service delivery.
Structure	Clear role definitions, formal hierarchical structure.	Acknowledgement of multiple perspectives, and requirement for 'facilitation' rather than leadership.	Egalitarian, with respect for diversity. Trust and respect underpin structure.
Process	Communication is delimited by need to inform the main decision maker.	Increased number of people involved in decision making, and acknowledgement of differing contributions.	Consensus decision making, recognition of client as team member.
Outcomes	Focus on single outcome such as improved health or social well-being.	Increased complexity and diversity of outcomes.	Focus on multiple aspects of well-being. Cost effective, and incorporating client defined outcomes.

Source: adapted from Boon et al. (2004)

collaborate and work within teams by government, professional bodies, management, user groups and the media, among others. The latest review of progress in implementing the National Service Framework for Older People, *A New Ambition for Old Age* (Department of Health, 2006a), for example, identifies 'joined-up care' involving effective working both within and across teams as one of the key principles for improving services for vulnerable older people. As Payne (2000: 27) comments: 'it is hard to find a policy or guidance document that does not promote coordination of services and collaboration of workers.'

With regard to professional education, the establishment of the CIPW (Creating an Inter-Professional Workforce) programme (Department of Health, 2006b) and funding of such projects as PIPE (Promoting Inter-Professional Education) (University of Reading, 2007) demonstrate the government's commitment to developing flexible workforces in health and social care that can work effectively together.

But to what extent do the assumptions match up to the reality? It is important to examine the claims and counter-claims. Three basic assumptions underpinning the rhetoric can be identified.

Do teams provide a more comprehensive service?

The first advantage claimed for teamwork is that it offers the possibility of delivering a comprehensive range of treatment and care services. The point of having team members from different disciplines and sectors is that each person can offer skills and knowledge arising from their own particular perspective. People with complex long-term health and social care needs require comprehensive and integrated services with input from a wide variety of different professionals (Department of Health, 2005). By combining the different areas of expertise and dovetailing contributions to ensure they are both timely and relevant, the service providers ensure users can be treated more holistically.

In practice, the quality of care delivered is sometimes less than ideal and different problems emerge. First, from the point of view of the service-user, it can be confusing, even disempowering, to have many different disciplines offering a service. For example, the team can prove destructive if team members offer contradictory 'expert' advice. Øvretveit's study (1997b) of the work in one community mental health team reveals how some clients were given contradictory advice and how there was a failure to carry out a mutually reinforcing care programme.

Barnes, Carpenter and Dickinson (2000) have discussed some of the difficulties in interprofessional working within contexts, such as community mental health, where interventions may be based on mutually conflicting knowledge bases, and shown that professional stereotyping may be very resistant to change. Additionally, Marsh argues for a clearer specification of the type of interprofessional practice required in different circumstances, pointing out that 'the evidence base showing how the current models of joint working really benefit service users is remarkably thin' (Marsh, 2006: 135).

Secondly, and paradoxically, a negotiated division of labour between members can actually result in less holistic practice as each member concentrates on a narrow focus of intervention. From the client's/patient's point of view, the intervention received can feel fragmented, with no one attending to the overall package of care. In order to combat such fragmentation, teams may experiment with different ways of organising their workload (such as adopting a care management system). Indeed, many social care agencies have adopted the care manager model to such a degree that they have turned away from team approaches in favour of the 'generic worker'. The degree to which 'lead practitioner' systems are effective depends largely on (a) the skills of the individual workers concerned; (b) the extent to which the worker is supported by other team members; and (c) the extent to which the worker can draw on other team members' expertise when necessary (see Box 9.4).

Box 9.4   The case for and against care co-ordination

Care co-ordination, previously described as key working, is a principle which underpins the operation of teams within many different contexts, including services for children, older people, and people with mental health problems. Care co-ordinators have responsibility for individual service-users, and maintain regular contact with them. They ensure that the care plan in place for individual service-users is being implemented, and liaise regularly with other members of the team. The care co-ordinator role can be taken on by any member, and is

(Continued)

(Continued)

usually divided between different team members (Mind, 2007). The care co-ordinator is a key instigator of the single assessment process, successfully implemented in older people's services, and now currently being extended to include other groups including people with longer-term needs (Department of Health, 2005).

   Care co-ordination occasionally requires practitioners to be more accountable to colleagues from other disciplines – for instance, where a nominated care co-ordinator is accountable to the care manager who has budgetary responsibility for the overall care package. Another potential point of conflict is that, in practice, care co-ordination may result in a key worker replacing the work of a team, where the individual is not able to enlist wider team help (for example, if other members have their own heavy case loads). Thus clients may not be able to draw on a team of different experts with specialised skills.

Are teams cost-effective, efficient and effective?

The second commonplace assumption made about teamwork is that it is an efficient, effective and cost-effective way of allocating resources. Offering a co-ordinated package of care based on a division of labour between team members is useful, as it can eliminate unnecessary duplication of effort. Also, where a division of labour between members of the team is negotiated, the best (or cheapest) person for the job can be selected (for instance, the introduction of nurse-led units within hospitals). This economic rationale for teamwork fits well with the logic of marketisation and the reality of limited resources.

   Against this, it can be argued that teamwork may well prove inefficient and expensive, particularly where team members do not communicate adequately. For one thing, using a team approach can lead to unnecessary duplication. Øvretveit's (1997b) evaluation of the work of a community mental health team points out how some clients had many different duplicating review meetings (held by day centre staff, care co-ordinators, hostel staff, and so on).

   Another example is that of new service-users receiving multiple 'initial interviews' by every member of the team, so that the clients repeat the same basic information, explaining their problems several times over. In such situations, it is not uncommon for the patient to complain 'Don't you people talk to each other?' (Øvretveit 1997a: 9). Townsley, Watson and Abbott (2004) also found that within the context of working with disabled children, interprofessional working resulted in improved experiences, but that there was little evidence of a drop in the number of assessments carried out. Such duplication is not only a potential waste of time and resources, but can also be distressing for the service-users, as they feel that the professionals have not listened to previous accounts and that the different team members have not been adequately briefed.

   It can also be argued that teamwork is inefficient in that it requires so much extra work in the form of team meetings and strategic negotiations. It is not uncommon to hear staff complain that they do not have time to see their service-users! Further, the many accumulated hours spent trying to liaise and collaborate could arguably be more usefully spent in direct service-user contact. Thus the mechanics of teamwork may result in ineffective service delivery.

Do teams offer a positive experience?

The third claim made about teamwork is that it can be a positive experience for the team members themselves. The team offers each member a source of meaning and identity as well as learning opportunities, positive feedback and satisfying social interactions. In a stressful work situation where professionals struggle with difficult clients and inadequate resources, the team can be experienced as the one positive force which keeps members motivated. The team in this context empowers. Cohesive teams give individuals strength and confidence as they know that they have the team's backing and that responsibility is shared. In other words, strength is drawn from the group. However, the reverse can also sometimes apply (see Box 9.5). Team-member interactions can be unsupportive, or even negative, and power can be abused. Where there is an over-abundance of conflict and undue competition between members, the team becomes a source of problems as well as solutions, and political decision making can take precedence over clinical decision making (Finlay, 1999).

Box 9.5   Some research on social workers in teams

- Within the context of the Newborn Hearing Screening Programme (NHSP) in England, Young et al. (2005) carried out qualitative interviews with participants from education and social care services. All participants agreed that joint working within the NHSP was poorly developed. However, participants from education attributed this to role, value and skills, while those from social services argued this was due to conflicts of ethos and culture.

- Leipzig et al. (2002), reporting on a survey of medical, nursing and social work students participating in geriatrics interdisciplinary team training, found that medics rated the benefits of team working less highly than the other two disciplines. Futher, social work and nursing students consistently disagreed with medical students that a team's primary purpose was to assist physician decision making, and they did not agree with medical students that physicians had the right to alter patient care plans agreed by the team.

- Gould (2000) interviewed social workers within a national voluntary child-care agency to identify how practitioners and managers conceptualised learning within their organisation. Teams were viewed as providing very important opportunities for learning.

- Using focus groups and interviews, King and Ross (2003) explored the ways in which social and health care professionals constructed their identities. Pertinent issues included role ambiguity, role erosion and extension. Within joint working, challenges were presented by disparate personal meanings, organisational arrangements and public perceptions.

- Barbour et al. (2002) carried out three focus groups with professionals working with families with both parental mental health needs and child-care concerns. Professional differences that impacted on services included varied 'thresholds' and codes of practice. Some psychiatric diagnoses were felt to be of limited value and there was scepticism about the value of a keyworker system with this particular group of clients.

Different teams, different advantages

Teams, when they work well, can be a valuable vehicle for the delivery of effective treatment and care, but there is nothing inevitable about this process. Whether teams are a beneficial or destructive force depends on how they work in practice, given the particular situation, constraints and people involved. Moreover, different types of team have different values and limitations (see Table 9.2).

A *parallel* or *consultative* team allows professionals to practise autonomously and draws specifically on the expertise of different members. However, poor team communication can result in fragmented or contradictory interventions and unnecessary duplication. *Collaborative*, *co-ordinated* and *multidisciplinary* teams are likely to have a better co-ordinated division of labour, offering the possibility of more holistic care that addresses multiple needs. The leadership or facilitation role means that there are clear lines of accountability that can promote effective use of resources, but team relationships may be experienced as disempowering or unsupportive. Tensions within the team can also inhibit co-operation and impact negatively on service provision. An *interdisciplinary* or *integrative* team has the potential to empower its members, and service-users are likely to benefit from greater interdisciplinary respect, a totally integrated service delivery and possible involvement themselves as members of the team. On the negative side, interdisciplinary and integrative teams can be expensive, and decisions take longer to reach. There is also the possibility that team members may become self-absorbed, putting team concerns ahead of those of service-users.

Engaging in teamwork is always challenging. Rather than believing that teamwork is inevitably good, we need to be critical and question: (a) whether teamwork is the best way of delivering services in the first place; (b) which way of organising the teamwork will provide the optimum service to users; and (c) how the challenges of actually engaging in team collaboration can be faced.

The first step to minimising the costs and maximising the benefits of teamwork is to understand more about the dynamics of how the team is functioning – the subject of the next section.

3 Understanding divisions, problems and conflicts

Conflict is interwoven with interprofessional collaboration because there are deep-rooted social differences in the division of labour which has developed over the last 200 years in the health and welfare service.

(Loxley, 1997: 1)

Consider the scenario in Box 9.6, which exposes some of the divisions, problems and conflicts that can occur in a team.

Table 9.2   Benefits and limitations of different types of team

	Parallel/consultative teams	Collaborative/ co-ordinated/ multidisciplinary teams	Interdisciplinary/ integrative Teams
Potential benefits	Professionals have autonomy. Service-users can benefit from individual professional attention and expertise.	Co-ordinated division of labour facilitates more holistic care, addressing multiple needs. Lines of accountability and responsibility are clear.	Holistic and integrated care, with the service-user at the heart of services. Empowerment of and support for members (who may include service-users). Interdisciplinary respect and trust.
Potential limitations	Poor team communication, resulting in fragmented interventions and unnecessary duplication. Team members can be split and in conflict. Service-users may find the multiple approaches confusing and contradictory.	Team relationships can be experienced as disempowering and unsupportive. Tensions and inequalities can inhibit co-operation.	Team members may become self-absorbed and unduly focused on team relationships, putting these ahead of service-users' needs. Collaboration can be timely and expensive. Responsibility is diffuse and lines of accountability are unclear.

Box 9.6   Problems in a multidisciplinary team

The doctors and nurses on an acute admission ward want to discharge a patient (in part to release bed space). They argue that the patient is well enough to go home; however, the occupational therapist would like to carry out a home visit with the main carer to ensure that the home environment will enable the patient to live as independently and safely as possible. On the next ward round, the doctors consult with the nurses and they discuss the possibility of discharging this patient. The consultant asks the newly qualified occupational therapist whether the patient can function independently in terms of washing and dressing. She replies that on her limited assessment thus far he is independent, but that a fuller assessment of his needs is warranted. She has talked with the patient and wants to check whether some modifications within the patient's home, such as grab rails in the bathroom, would make the home safer. The occupational therapist wants to argue against discharging the patient too soon, but feels unable to assert herself directly with this senior consultant. The social worker at this point tries to back up the therapist and suggests that a discharge date later on in the week would allow time for the home visit. The consultant asks the patient whether he would like to leave the hospital today and whether a family member can pick him up.

(Continued)

(Continued)

After the ward round, the therapist and social worker let off some steam about lack of respect for their views within the team, and criticise the consultant's unduly authoritarian approach. The patient is discharged later that day. He lives alone and arrangements for activating some social support systems in the community have not been made. A week later the patient is readmitted with some injuries following a fall, which happened as he was trying to get out of the bath.

Several different problems confront this team. Conflicts between different professional values and team member priorities occur in a context of unequal status and power. At a 'micro' level of analysis these problems can be seen to arise because of a clash of values between individuals of professional groups (for example between the consultant and the therapist). Equally, problems may be due to the nature of the group dynamics as a whole (for example, the way the team engages in decision making may have become established as a norm). At a broader level of analysis, issues such as leader effectiveness, how the team functions as a system and how decision making is organised need to be examined. Finally, underlying 'macro' issues need to be explored, as the functioning of a team may have to do with professional and power issues, in the context of how health or social care is organised.

To understand what is happening in a team, it can be useful to examine three different and to some extent competing levels of analysis.

- The *group* in terms of interpersonal dynamics
- The *organisation* in terms of decision-making structures
- The *society* in terms of power and broader structural issues.

Group level of analysis

The roles played by different members can have a major impact on how a team functions. The characteristics of the leader, for example, can affect how effectively the group functions. The leader who is imposed upon a group may be less successful than the leader whom the group elects. As another example, the informal role of 'clown' can both enable and impair teamwork. Belbin (2004) identifies a number of different roles which he suggests can be found within successful management teams, including the company worker, chairman [*sic*], the shaper, the plant and the resource investigator. Additional roles which can contribute to the success of teams include that of monitor-evaluator, the team worker and the completer finisher. While other members may be useful contributors in terms of their personal qualities, Belbin maintains that these eight roles would be sufficient to form a comprehensive team.

Group dynamics can also be relevant at a more unconscious level. A team may put up psychological defences, such as stereotyping, denial, blaming and avoidance, to combat the anxieties and stresses of work. These defensive behaviours enable the practitioners to cope, but they may also be maladaptive and produce additional problems. Box 9.7 illustrates how defensive behaviour can get in the way of effective team work.

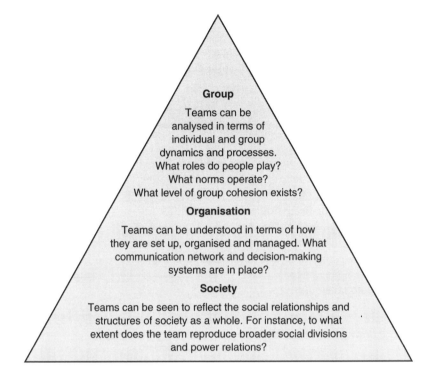

Figure 9.1   Three levels of analysis

Box 9.7   Example of conflict in a social work team

A team responsible for child protection meets fortnightly with a supervisor/team manager to discuss their work. The process of talking about the nature of the work (for instance, assessing levels of child abuse) and sharing their different experiences about how they handled situations was stressful to the team members. The social workers often felt 'exposed' and vulnerable. In one such tense group meeting, a member started to cite some heavily theoretical research. The other members quickly joined in with similar references. The discussion soon became academic and well distanced from the difficult emotions and feelings of inadequacies aroused by their work and the group itself. When the supervisor/team manager pointed out the group's use of intellectualisation to deny and avoid their painful emotions, the group members were forced to confront their own behaviour. This challenge enabled them to refocus on giving each other emotional support.

(*Source*: adapted from a case illustration cited in Hornby, 1993)

Organisational level of analysis

Problems at organisational level emerge when team members and their managers are not clear about their responsibilities and the team's division of labour. Øvretveit (1997c) argues that team leaders have a responsibility to ensure effective systems are in place and that there is an appropriate division of labour between members. He identifies (p. 50) common problems for team leaders and managers to look out for when they are reviewing a (collective responsibility) team, including the following:

- Team meeting problems – frequent absences, avoiding issues, too many issues which do not need team discussion, unclear decision-making processes, inadequate chairing.
- Emergency work driving out longer-term more effective work, or too much long-term work without review.
- No team influence over closure decisions, making it difficult to allocate new cases or work.
- No agreement over priorities, or priorities are not defined in specific terms to monitor whether they are being met.
- No forum for in-depth discussion of selected cases.
- Separate professional information and record systems, or difficulties getting information from others.
- Insufficient administration support and inadequate team base (no good coffee/meeting area).
- Leadership with no authority.

Society level of analysis

At a society level, teams are understood to reflect the relationships and structures of society as a whole. In particular, teams are seen to reproduce broader social divisions (for instance, to do with gender or ethnicity) and power relations. Practitioners in a team are likely to have different status, power, pay, experience and conditions of work – and each of these is a potential source of tension and is disempowering for team members. Cott (1998) suggests team structures commonly reflect social class distinctions, as high-status professionals assume responsibility and control and lower-status workers carry out the tasks, leading to a 'we decide, you do' division of labour. Similarly, hierarchical attitudes to gender may contrast the 'professional work' of men with the 'supportive activities' of women.

Competition among team members, arising in the context of marketisation (where practitioners compete with each other for contracts, for funds and even for their jobs) also leads to splits in the team. Competition can impact negatively as it may involve destructive sub-grouping, as sub-groups attempt to usurp power and exclude others, and negative stereotyping of the 'other' (for example, the characterisation of different professional groups according to one or two characteristics). The team is unlikely to function effectively in the face of such processes. Moreover, if practitioners are spending their time protecting their own territory and guarding their backs, they do so at the expense of thinking about service-users' needs.

4 Rising to the challenge of teamwork

Although there are many challenges to multi-agency working, the benefits are worth the energy and effort involved. Delivering the programme together led to the development of working practice based on common aims … and the overall effect of collaborative work in this way showed that the whole was, indeed, greater than the sum of its parts.

> (Marsh and Male, 2003, writing about the multi-agency Barnsley's Strengthening Families Programme)

Enabling a team to work together more positively involves working at different levels and drawing on a combination of strategies related to: (a) team building; (b) reviewing the team's organisation; and (c) challenging power structures.

Team building

An extensive range of literature details different staff development activities designed to promote a sense of 'team-ness' and to develop teamworking skills. Typically, 'time out' is recommended, where the teams put aside their daily responsibilities and carve out a focused space for some shared endeavour. The sharing involves whatever is appropriate to the team, be it a common meal, a day of staff development at a local hotel or bonding together on an Outward Bound programme. The aim of such activities is to develop a sense of team spirit through shared collaboration and participation. Individuals need to feel actively included and be given opportunities to contribute. They may also gain from learning new team skills, such as negotiation and effective leadership.

Another common team-building strategy is the use of 'sensitivity' groups. Here, the team meets on a regular basis to express and explore individuals' feelings and team issues. Sometimes an outside facilitator is brought in to challenge the team to look at its interpersonal dynamics and defensive practices. These types of group can initially be threatening, but are also empowering as members connect emotionally and offer mutual support. In Box 9.8, Hornby (1993) describes how discussion helped some groups of practitioners move from being defensive and isolated in their professional identities towards having a shared identity.

Box 9.8   A group discussion – sharing

In a discussion about families with problems and the responsibilities of practitioners, criticism was directed at the social workers in the local area office.

Area social worker: We don't always get the support we would wish, particularly from GPs.

Health visitor: You can't get out of it by blaming someone else.

Social worker [*angrily*]: Well, health visitors can visit and be seen as kind and helpful, and the social workers get turned into the 'baddies' because they have the power to take children away. You hide behind us.

Another social worker: Often in this group you have been hinting that we were not doing our job properly. You seem to think you know it all.

(Continued)

(Continued)

Health visitor [*after a short pause, and in an unexpectedly distressed voice*]: I don't know it all. I wish I did. Sometimes I feel I am no help at all to the families I work with.

[*Silence*]

Social worker: I feel just the same.
[A wave of fellow-feeling swept the group. The tone changed completely. Suddenly people were free to express doubts about their work. They spoke of cases which had gone from bad to worse or certainly had shown no signs of improvement.]
Someone: Sometimes I go home at the end of the day, wondering why I do this job. It all seems so hopeless.
Another: There are so many problems that are beyond us to put right.

[*Long silence*]

Health visitor [*who had sparked off the discussion*]: I feel better having said what I did, because I realise that I'm not the only one, and I do know that sometimes I can make a difference to a family.

Social worker: I know you can, from some of the cases of yours that have come my way.
Someone: Then perhaps we should look at what it is possible for us to do – given that we work in an inner-city area and we're none of us superhuman …

[*Laughter*]

(*Source*: Hornby, 1993: 171–2)

Reviewing the team's organisation

Effective teamwork demands that the team engages in regular evaluation of its process and outcomes. Is the service being delivered both appropriate and effective? Are the team members and service-users satisfied? What decision-making and conflict-resolution structures are in place? Evaluation must take into account the type and purpose of the teamwork involved. For instance, mutually satisfying team relationships will be less of a goal for a consultative team than for an integrative team.

Ideally, the team should regularly review how it functions in terms of the contributions individuals make to the whole. Members' roles and channels of communication need to be reviewed in the context of team goals. For example, the physiotherapists and occupational therapists in a team might decide a division of labour (to avoid duplication of effort) whereby the physiotherapists focus on patients' lower-limb function and mobility, while the occupational therapists focus on upper-limb and daily living activities.

It can be argued that the most important individual role is the work of the leader or leaders. What type of leadership is required to meet the team goals? Might it be useful to distinguish between different leader roles and allocate responsibilities according to individual member's expertise (see Box 9.9). What style of leadership is most appropriate – directive or democratic?

Beyond individual member roles, the team needs to explore opportunities for creating a spirit of joint enterprise. Examples could include collaborating on therapy or research projects, or engaging in interdisciplinary supervision. Joint management and recruitment strategies can also be useful in this context. For example, when a professional is being appointed to work in a multidisciplinary team, other members of the team could be present at the selection interview and participate in induction.

Box 9.9   Distinguishing between different leadership functions

- **team manager** – responsibility for the long-term development of the team and services offered to service-users
- **chairperson** – responsibility for chairing particular meetings
- **facilitator** – responsibility for enabling participation among team members
- **keyworker or care manager** – responsibility for co-ordinating services for specific client cases
- **medical/care director** – responsibility for overall medical treatment or care delivered

---

Challenging power structures

The first step to challenging power structures is for the team to be *reflexive* and consciously critical about how they go about their daily work. Where team relationships are problematic, the team needs to give itself time to reflect on what is happening and why. Is the conflict best understood at a micro or a macro level? How does the conflict impact on the team's functioning? What should be done about it? More specifically, team members may need to confront defensive, destructive, discriminatory and disempowering practice.

Davey et al. (2006) report on the use of a web-log as a tool to enable the six interdisciplinary members of the research team to explore self-reflection as part of an ethnographic research project exploring student learning experiences.

Collaboration: the key to working with 'difference'?

Where teams are concerned, conflicts are inevitable: by definition, teams involve 'difference'. It is difference that makes teamwork such a demanding and difficult task. Here, Loxley is arguing in favour of *collaboration* (not simply co-operation) between team members. She explains how collaboration means working across boundaries, and that this

> challenges the safe reductionist view, the adequacy of tunnel vision, the security of the territorial forces, the hard-won power and influence, the taken-for-granted nature of the perception. Collaboration requires communication across open boundaries, the willingness to take risks, the reciprocity of costs and gains.

(Loxley, 1997: 49–50)

Table 9.3   Two team styles

Concept of the individual	bounded	connected
Group process/style	formal adversarial 'explaining'	relaxed co-operative 'exploring'
Outcomes	resolution is imposed assumption of finality vindication and elation or defeat and despair	expectation of change enhanced commitment stronger bonds personal renewal

One answer to the question of how to work with difference is to learn to value or celebrate it. Difference can be a source of tension, but the greater the differences the more we stand to gain from the expertise of others. It is only on this basis that we can really work together. Davies has expanded on this using the concept of *reflective solidarity*:

> Each of us may arrive at a position we were not previously in – a position we could not have reached by dint of struggle on our own, or by dint of seeking support from those whose histories and perspectives are similar.

> (Davies, 1998: 51)

She argues that the jolt of challenge from difference 'gives expression to some of the most powerful and energising moments in social life' (1998: 52). She goes on to offer a vision of what it is to work collaboratively. Too often, she argues, we work with a notion of each other as bounded and fully knowledgeable individuals. Yet this can sometimes get in the way of real collaboration. She contrasts traditional team styles with more collaborative styles (see Table 9.3).

Anyone with experience of good teamwork will recognise this sense of learning from others. In a collaborative team, members have the opportunity to connect with each other. It is the challenge we pose to each other that enhances us, renewing us personally and stimulating us professionally. In this sense, the collective really can be seen to possess the potential to produce better solutions.

Conclusion

Teams have values and limitations. In practice, teamwork can be problematic, inefficient and even damaging. The process of engaging in team collaboration is always a challenge given the conflicts that can arise. It is the challenge of working with difference that all team members need to grasp. It requires a willingness to listen and a desire to hear what others are saying.

One of the shifts in practice in health and social care in the twenty-first century is increasingly that individual practitioners are simultaneously members of a number of different teams, which may have disparate aims, and contrasting styles. Advances in information technology have led to the growth of 'virtual teams' in which team members rarely if ever meet in person, but work collaboratively using the medium of the Internet. One such example is the writing of 'networked books' in which sometimes thousands of authors collaborate remotely.

Within such rapidly changing contexts, creativity, flexibility and good leadership are, arguably, even more important to ensure effective teamworking in health and social care. It is more pertinent today than ever before to ask ourselves: 'Are we up to the challenge?'

References

Barbour, R.S., Stanley, N., Penhale, B. and Holden, S. (2002) 'Assessing risk: professional perspectives on work involving mental health and child care services', *Journal of Interprofessional Care*, 16 (4): 323–34.

Barnes, D., Carpenter, J. and Dickinson, C. (2000) 'Interprofessional education for community mental health: attitudes to community care and professional stereotypes', *Social Work Education*, 19 (6): 565–83.

Belbin, R.M. (2004) *Management Teams: Why They Succeed or Fail.* Oxford: Butterworth Heinemann.

Boon, H., Verhoef, M., O'Hara, D. and Findlay, B. (2004) 'From parallel practice to integrative health care: a conceptual framework', *BMC Health Services Research*, 4. Available at www.biomedcentral.com/1472-6963/4/15 (accessed on 06.01.07).

Cott, C. (1998) 'Structure and meaning in multidisciplinary teamwork', *Sociology of Health and Illness,* 20: 848–73.

Davey, J., Kruger, S., Martin, L., McLoughlin, D., Roberts, S. and Williams, S. (2006) 'Ethnographic research partnerships: challenges within an interdisciplinary team at Edge Hill', SOLSTICE Conference, 03.05.06, Edge Hill University. Available at: www.edgehill.ac.uk/Sites/SOLSTICE/ResearchandDissemination/documents/SOLSTICEConference-Ethnographic May2006.pdf (accessed 06.01.07).

Davies, C. (1998) 'Care and the transformation of professionalism', in T. Knijn and S. Sevenhuijsen (eds), *Care, Citizenship and Social Cohesion: Towards a Gender Perspective.* Utrecht: Netherlands School for Social and Economic Policy Research.

Department for Education and Skills (2003) *Every Child Matters.* Available at: www.everychildmatters.gov.uk (accessed 06.01.07).

Department of Health (2005) *The National Service Framework for Long Term Conditions.* London: HMSO.

Department of Health (2006a) *A New Ambition for Old Age: Next Steps in Implementing the National Service Framework for Older People.* London: HMSO.

Department of Health (2006b) *Creating an Interprofessional Workforce Programme.* Available at: www.cipw.org.uk. (accessed 06.01.07).

Finlay, L. (1999) 'Safe haven and battleground: collaboration and conflict within the team', in C. Davies, L. Finlay and A. Bullman (eds), *Changing Practice in Health and Social Care.* London: Sage/Open University (K302 Reader 1).

Gould, N. (2000) 'Becoming a learning organisation: a social work example', *Social Work Education*, 19 (6): 585–96.

Hornby, S. (1993) *Collaborative Care: Interprofessional, Interagency and Interpersonal.* Oxford: Blackwell Scientific.

King, N. and Ross, A. (2003) 'Professional identities and interprofessional relations: evaluation of collaborative community schemes', *Social Work in Health Care*, 38 (2): 51–72.

Laming, H. (2003) *The Victoria Climbié Inquiry*. Cm 5730, London: HMSO.

Leipzig, R.M., Hyer, K.E.K., Wallenstein, S., Vezina, M.L., Fairchild, S., Cassel, C.K. and Howe, J.L. (2002) 'Attitudes toward working on interdisciplinary healthcare teams: a comparison by discipline', *Journal of the American Geriatrics Society*, 50 (6): 1141–8.

Loxley, A. (1997) *Collaboration in Health and Welfare: Working with Difference*. London: Jessica Kingsley.

Marsh, P. (2006) 'Promoting children's welfare by inter-professional practice and learning in social work and primary care', *Social Work Education*, 25 (2): 148–60.

Marsh, M. and Male, S. (2003) *Young Minds Magazine Chat Back*. Available at www.young-minds.org.uk/magazine/66/marsh.php (accessed 06.01.07).

Mind (2007) *A Brief Guide to Who's Who in Mental Health*, Available at www.mind.org.uk/ Information/Factsheets/History+of+mental+health/A+brief+guide+to+whos+who+in+mental+ health.htm (accessed 06.01.07).

O'Brien, S., Hammond, H. and McKinnon, M. (2003) *Report of the Caleb Ness Inquiry*. Edinburgh: Edinburgh and Lothians Child Protection Committee.

Øvretveit, J. (1997a) 'How to describe interprofessional working', in J. Øvretveit, P. Mathias and T. Thompson (eds), *Interprofessional Working for Health and Social Care*. Basingstoke and London: Macmillan.

Øvretveit, J. (1997b) 'Evaluating interprofessional working – a case example of a community mental health team', in J. Øvretveit, P. Mathias and T. Thompson (eds), *Interprofessional Working for Health and Social Care*. Basingstoke and London: Macmillan.

Øvretveit, J. (1997c) 'Planning and managing interprofessional working and teams', in J. Øvretveit, P. Mathias and T. Thompson (eds), *Interprofessional Working for Health and Social Care*. Basingstoke and London: Macmillan.

Payne, M. (2000) *Teamwork in Multi-professional Care*. Basingstoke: Palgrave Macmillan.

Townsley, R., Watson, D. and Abbott, D. (2004) 'Working partnerships? A critique of the process of multi-agency working in services to disabled children with complex health needs', *Journal of Integrated Care*, 12 (2): 24–34.

University of Reading (2007) *Promoting Inter-Professional Education Project*. Available at: www.pipe.ac.uk (accessed 06.01.07).

Young, A., McCracken, W., Tattersall, H. and Bamford, J. (2005) 'Interprofessional working in the context of newborn hearing screening: Education and Social Services compare challenges', *Journal of Interprofessional Care*, 19 (4): 386–95.

Chapter 10

Organisations and organisational change

Janet Seden

Introduction

Social workers usually work within organisations. The organisations that exist in health and social care can be very diverse, ranging from small voluntary organisations with one office and two or three staff, to large, complex organisations, such as NHS trusts. The social worker's relationship to the organisation also varies. For example, some people work in organisations with clear lines of management and clearly delineated organisational structures. Others are based in organisations containing more informal networks of people who meet from time to time. Independent social workers may relate to several different organisations from the outside and work to a series of contracts.

An organisation is commonly defined as a way of arranging a set of people and resources together to achieve certain goals. In health, social work and social care, local authorities remain the dominant organisation, together with NHS trusts, not-for-profit (voluntary) organisations and private agencies. Although, as will be argued in this chapter, organisations consist of individuals who can influence the culture and climate of the workplace, in reality the organisation is often experienced as a complex system which the individual seeks to understand in order to be effective.

Workplace experience can be very much dependent on the way an organisation is arranged and how management handles such important matters as leadership and management, change, ethics, diversity, information, budgets, health and safety, new technologies, employees, relationships with other organisations and, importantly, relationships with service-users and carers (Aldgate et al., 2007).

Understanding organisations

Whatever kind of organisation they are based in, social workers, to be effective in practice, must understand how the organisation works, and their own role within it in relation to the roles of colleagues. Each person needs to know how their own actions affect other people and the interfaces between their own specific tasks and the tasks of other practitioners, both within their own and partnership agencies. Failure to understand the opportunities, constraints and dilemmas that different aspects of organisational structure and culture present may mean a failure to obtain the best responses from the organisation and partner agencies for the person the social worker wants to help.

For example, in most organisations, arranging transport for a service-user to a day centre involves liaison with others and some paperwork. A misunderstanding of such arrangements could lead to someone being anxious and distressed because the transport does not arrive or, as in a much publicised case, a vulnerable person being taken to the wrong address and left outside, in the cold, with no support. Understanding organisational and inter-organisational arrangements is therefore very important for all social workers, and it is essential for service-users that their practitioners have a good grasp of organisational procedures and inter-agency working.

One of the biggest challenges for social workers at the beginning of the twenty-first century is to have confidence about their own role and what the organisational remit empowers them to do, while at the same time understanding the roles and contributions of others working with the same service-user groups. This can be complex, but the trick is perhaps to be clear about what you are able to contribute to any plan of work, what others might contribute, and to be sure that there is a plan to co-ordinate and review the work about which the service-users are fully knowledgeable, and with which all parties are as far as possible in agreement. Usually this means working across organisational boundaries or across interprofessional boundaries within a multi-disciplinary organisation.

An understanding of your role in an organisation, and the roles and responsibilities of colleagues in other agencies is essential knowledge for social workers in contemporary organisational contexts. In particular, social workers have to understand some organisational theory, so that they can analyse the impact of organisational systems on themselves and others. This also enables them to be critical and reflective about possible changes to organisations to improve services, and the impact of organisational changes on themselves and service-users.

The organisational context for care services

In this chapter, therefore, I explore briefly some aspects of the structures and cultures of the organisations that deliver care services, and consider the position of the social worker in relation to them. One key issue for any social worker is the extent to which they can influence the organisation in the interests of service-users, and a second is the extent to which organisational arrangements create unnecessary barriers for people who need services. A third critical issue is the extent to which the organisational arrangements enable and empower social workers to carry out their tasks, and the extent to which organisational procedures can make social workers' tasks more difficult or leave them feeling oppressed and disempowered by organisational barriers. The fast pace of organisational change can contribute to misunderstandings about roles and responsibilities and also lead to serious practice errors, for instance those identified in the Climbié report (Laming, 2003). Organisational change and how social workers respond to it is also a key theme of the *21st Century Social Work Review* in Scotland (Scottish Executive, 2006) and of this chapter.

Organisations are the context or environment for everything that social workers do. They are also complex, rarely staying the same for long. Organisational theorists have been quick to point out that organisations are full of ambiguities and variables which have to be read and understood and experienced (Handy, 1993; Morgan 1997). However, each organisation, at any point in time, is a system with formal ways of doing things (rules and structure) and informal ways of acting and behaving (culture). The people in the organisation will have varying degrees of power and control, to make decisions, use resources and carry out tasks. These elements – structure, culture, human and material resources – work together to create the workplace environment. An organisation is experienced as a living, dynamic and interactive place. This is shaped in turn by the organisation's relationship to external factors such as other organisations, the service-users, law, social policy and public opinion. Therefore some theories of organisation are next considered briefly:

- organisational structures
- organisational cultures
- images of organisation
- learning organisations
- power, influence and climate
- appreciative inquiry
- organisational change and interprofessional working

Organisational structures

Social services departments, hospitals and other welfare agencies are often bureaucracies with hierarchical structures. The basic shape of many organisations is often pyramidal, consisting of roles, usually represented on organisational charts as little boxes, occupied by individuals, with the head at the top, middle managers in between and frontline managers and their staff at the bottom. People often use 'bureaucratic' as a term of abuse when they meet organisational barriers to obtaining services, but a well-run bureaucracy can be effective and can clarify routes to obtaining help. Clear rules and procedures can help the people who implement them to know what their remit is and make processes visibly fair and accountability transparent.

Large organisations with clear procedures can provide a single point of access that makes it easier for people wanting services to make contact and to ask what their entitlements are. Having rules can be useful for making fair decisions. However, if there is no culture of discretion within them, large organisations can be inflexible, leaving professionals within them little autonomy, which can be difficult for other professionals and service-users to relate to (Lipsky, 1980; Hasenfeld, 1983; Coulshed and Mullender, 2001; Evans and Harris, 2004). Also, if rules and procedures become self-perpetuating, with layer upon layer of complex regulations, they can indeed become barriers to the fair and prompt delivery of services.

There are other kinds of organisational structure which are useful for social welfare. Residential care homes, for example, are organised more flexibly, with residents often taking responsibility for some of its functions themselves (Whitaker et al., 1998). In the voluntary sector there are organisational types that are very different from mainstream models – therapeutic communities, for instance, where there is no hierarchical management structure (Seden, 2003). Other collaborative or collective ways of working, established in women's refuges or by organisations run by their service-users, similarly operate in a very fluid way based on relationships and community meetings. This can cause difficulties for outsiders looking for a point of liaison and influence. A non-hierarchical organisation still needs to have ways of taking decisions and co-ordinating and allocating activities, but it may involve more people or a more diverse cross-section of people, and roles may not be fixed (Handy, 1993, 1995, 1999).

Organisational cultures

Organisations also have cultures. Culture can be defined as the underlying values, beliefs and principles that underpin an organisation's management system. In other words, it is the way things are done: the behaviours, the patterns of delivering services that exist in any organisation, agency, office or team (Seden, 2003). Whatever the organisational structure, culture develops from the shared experiences and traditions of the workforce. Therefore, while structure influences culture, two organisations with similar structures can have very different cultures. Charles Handy describes four organisational ideas or beliefs about the best way to organise services, and focuses on: *power*, *role*, *task* and *person* (1999: 183–91). The models are summarised in Box 10.1.

Box 10.1   Handy's Four Organisational Cultures

The power culture

This kind of organisational culture is represented as a spider's web with the key to the organisation being at the centre. Lines of responsibility stretch out from the centre and lines of trust link them. This type of organisation is centred on a leader and a group of like-minded people. The advantages of such organisations, which work on trust, is that they can respond immediately to change because there are very short lines of communication to the centre. This kind of organisation can thrive only if the group is small (fewer than twenty) and the person at the centre is making sound judgements. If the 'spider' at the centre of the web is weak or corrupt or makes poor appointments, the organisation can fail. This kind of structure is seen in smaller entrepreneurial social care agencies and can be recognised as the pattern of some social care teams both in field and residential care, the team leader being the 'spider' at the heart of the web.

(Continued)

The role culture

The structure here is a pyramid, with the roles set out in job boxes. This logical and orderly plan provides the roles and responsibilities needed to do the agency's work. It is a common structure for public agencies. Individuals take on a prescribed role. If the arrangement is not delivering the outcomes that are wanted, the structure will be changed to meet new priorities and the role of individuals reordered. These kinds of organisations are formally managed through procedures. It is an arrangement that offers predictability and certainty and is suitable for stable and unchanging tasks. The weakness is that it is not a flexible arrangement for responding quickly to change or exceptions to its rules. If the design is correct for the work, this can be a very efficient way of fulfilling administrative tasks.

The task culture

This is depicted as a net. The organisational idea is that of recruiting a team with certain abilities to suit a particular task. Each task gets the team and resources that are appropriate to what the organisation plans to achieve. This kind of co-operative group of professionals without much hierarchy works by planning and reviewing, and remaining open to new ideas and ways of doing things. A task organisation can be expensive because it needs to employ experts. Task cultures can be seen in projects and specialist teams within role organisations.

The person culture

While the other three models put organisational mission and purpose first and fit individuals into a grouping to carry it out, the person organisation brings individuals with talent into a group to work together. These groupings are rather loose coalitions of people with similar skills who work together, for example a GP practice or a social care consultancy. Often there will be minimal formal role organisation, and equality of status. This organisational culture allows for individuals to work in their own way and at their own pace in ways which might not succeed for the complex organisational responsibilities of a hospital, school or social services department.

Source: Henderson and Atkinson (eds), 117–18, adapted from Handy, pp.183–91 for *Managing Care in Context* (2003)

Each organisation, however, may be a mix of the four cultures. For example, role organisations can contain teams based on the other models. The critical issue is whether the organisational model is relevant to delivering the kind of service it is set up for (Mintzberg, 1981, 1992). For example, benefits agencies are often hierarchical role cultures and, given the lack of discretion that exists, it could be argued that this is the best organisational arrangement for administering payments.

Children's homes and other residential homes, however, may work best as combinations of task and person cultures, so that the young or older people can have a voice in how the unit is organised and in its developing culture. This is particularly important if the organisation is also someone's home (Reynolds and Peace, 2007). An organisation which is also someone's living space needs to reflect that reality, and the environment can be managed in a different way (Peace and Reynolds, 2003). Teams in social work are often task cultures situated within a role culture organisation. This gives a combination of flexibility and organisational clarity about lines of accountability. The combination of organisational clarity about roles and responsibility together with some flexibility of implementation may be the organisational shape most likely to be responsive to service-users, while at the same time being capable of transparency and accountability. This remains, however, a debatable topic.

Images of organisation

Both Handy (1993) and Morgan (1997) have claimed that while organisations can to an extent be *understood*, they are primarily *perceived* and *experienced* by the people who work in them. Gareth Morgan's work on 'imagisation' has been helpful in enabling people to think about their own images of their organisations. As Morgan (1997) and Mintzberg (1981) have argued, there is no ideal organisation. The most important factor is that organisational arrangements suit the purpose of the organisation. Morgan theorises that analysing 'images of organisation' promotes understanding of how organisations work. While recognising that the list below is not exhaustive, his eight images provide some ideas which can generate thinking about how we experience and perceive our own working environments. They are outlined in Box 10.2.

Box 10.2   Morgan's Images of Organisation

Machines

This refers to organisations that have machine-like structure and links to concepts such as: efficiency order, run like clockwork, standardised, maintained, inputs, outputs, measurement, control, design.

Organisms

This is another metaphor for organisations that links to concepts such as: living systems, ecology, adaptation, life-cycle, health and illness.

Brains

This is a metaphor for organisations that links to concepts such as: learning, information-processing, intelligence, feedback, knowledge networks, mind-sets and intellectualisation.

Cultures

This is a metaphor for organisations that links to concepts such as: society, values, beliefs, vision and mission, and quality.

(Continued)

Political systems

This is a metaphor for organisations that links to concepts such as: power, rights, hidden agendas, deals, authority, leaders, conflict-management, party line, censorship and gate-keeping.

Psychic prisons

This is a metaphor for organisations that links to concepts such as: conscious and unconscious processes, repression and regression, denial, projection, defence mechanisms, dysfunction and stress.

Flux and transformation

This is a metaphor for organisations that links to concepts such as: constant change, equilibrium, flow, self-organisation, chaos, complexity, emergent properties, paradox.

Instruments of domination

This is a metaphor for organisations that links to concepts such as: alienation, repression, imposing values, compliance, maintenance of power, force, discrimination, primary of corporate interest, and exploitation.

Source: Morgan (2006).

Morgan would be the first to suggest that in reality organisations may have aspects of all these images. Metaphors, after all, are simply a figurative way of describing something to help us to generate ideas which improve our understanding. In an interview published on the internet (www.imaginiz.com/provocative/metaphors/questions_html, accessed 27.09.06) Morgan is reported as saying:

I don't want people to think that the eight metaphors in Images are the only metaphors. I want people to develop metaphors of their own. So, in my new edition I specifically state that gender can be seen as a whole metaphor of its own, while continuing to focus on gender as aspects of the culture metaphor, the politics metaphor and what I have to say about the psychic prison metaphor.

This emphasis on encouraging people to use his method to understand, perceive and experience organisations is because metaphor may be used as a way of imaging and considering organisations, to promote learning both about how they function currently and about how they might adapt and change to new circumstances. The idea of a learning organisation and the theories associated with it are therefore also relevant to how social workers might understand and interact with their employing and partner organisations.

Learning organisations

Much current theorising about organisations is based on the concept of the learning organisation. This idea originated in business as a means of moving ahead of competitors. The theory suggests that those organisations which best adapt to changing external circumstances are most likely to improve their market share. It has been adopted by health, education and social work social care organisations that need to adapt to meet changing political and policy directives. The emphasis is on the organisation as a system that can adapt to changing external environments and changing demands (Reynolds, 2003).

When services are subject to frequent policy changes through modernising government, as in the early twenty-first century, this is an important idea. For example, organisations can become entrenched in bureaucratic procedures which mean that new members or new policy ideas are expected to fit within existing arrangements. This can make it difficult for new service-delivery mechanisms to work or, at the individual level, for the perspectives of service-users to be heard, let alone taken on board and responded to. This can particularly be the case when service-users and carers are invited to consultations, or on to management committees and interview panels (Seden and Ross, 2007). Managers of organisations therefore often have to learn how to make changes which may challenge organisational assumptions about power relations, or which avoid minority individuals or groups being marginalised or treated as tokens within the cultural mainstream of organisations (Malcolm, 2007). This may mean structural changes, for example sensitive planning of meeting times and user-friendly agendas.

The interest in learning organisations (Senge, 1990; Pearn et al., 1997; Gould, 2003) may be a direct response to the fast pace of change which legislative and policy change have brought to health, social care and social work since the 1990s, as the changes to the mixed economy of welfare made by the Thatcher governments were followed immediately by the innovation and modernisation agendas of New Labour. Accompanying these drives were notions of creating a 'competent workforce', where everyone within the organisation is committed to learning and development. Thus it is a response to the demands of managerialism, change and innovation. As Pine and Healey (2007: 75) put it:

> Current thinking recognises that change is inevitable and that organisations are open to developing the knowledge and skills of their staff will be best placed to respond flexibly and nimbly to the demands they face. This has implications for working practices, systems and structure, culture and environment, and challenges the very basis on which power in organisations is distributed and used.

Change to organisations is therefore likely to be a feature of every social worker's working life, therefore understanding some of the key issues about organisations will be necessary to survival. Power, influence and climate are part of that and are discussed next.

Power, influence and climate

In most organisations social workers will be immediately answerable, not just to service-users, but also to their supervisors and/or immediate first-line managers. Managers have power in most organisations and the best managers will work to provide a healthy and supportive working environment. The manager's role here is critical; they have authority within the terms of their appointment, but there is a range of ways of using it. Brody (1993) describes how managers can set the tone for a positive organisational climate. He suggests (1993: 25–33) that the following are important:

- **Job ownership**: employees are encouraged to care about their work and the way it is done. Managers create a climate where employees are expected to support each other in complex tasks. Managers aim to model and build relationships of trust between workers and foster the desire to build a better service.
- **The primacy of the consumer**: the organisation is friendly towards its service-users by answering telephone calls and letters promptly, conveying respect in their interactions with users. The service-users are treated as genuine partners by engaging them in activities that evaluate and develop services.
- **Work quality as central**: quality is a complex idea but Brody frames it in terms of consumer satisfaction. Are consumers made to feel welcome? Are their negative feelings and views attended to? Do they feel there is a high level of concern for their welfare?
- **Communicating the organisation's values**: managers and workers together are responsible for making sure that the values statement is communicated, shared, owned and practised through the agency.

In an organisational culture where there are such open and participatory models of management (Pine and Healey, 2007) both service-users and social workers can directly influence the way care is managed. Organisational structures that support and organisational cultures that enable are both in place. Without them it is difficult for social workers to maintain their ability to provide services for people and feel that the workplace is 'healthy' enough for them to have a sense of well-being at work and to carry out their tasks without undue stress and pressure. It is also important that service-users can gain access to organisational cultures and structures to influence service provision, to take part in consultation, to know how to complain and, in some organisations, to manage services (Seden and Ross, 2007). Such structures and cultures therefore need to be transparent and open to scrutiny by those who need them.

It is also important to note that, when practitioners are feeling pressured and stressed, they often take individual responsibility for their own stress, sometimes leading to poor performance and/or sickness. However, the health and well-being of those who work in an organisation are very often related to organisational practices (Elkin and Rosch, 1990; Arnold et al., 1998). While self-care does matter, organisations have legal responsibilities towards their employees and should ensure that their systems, structures and cultures offer support to help employees meet role expectations and also opportunities for professional development (Peel, 2003).

This is another reason for social work and care workers to understand the organisation. It may be that social workers and their colleagues may have to take action to argue for improvements in working conditions and the culture in their organisation. For example, are there arrangements to support staff who experience abuse, bullying, harassment or violence in the workplace? This is important not just for them but also for service-users, because social workers who are struggling with the way their work is organised or a negative workplace culture are not as effective with their caseloads as those who are better supported to carry out their tasks by a positive organisational climate, where they are supported and supervised effectively (Glisson and Hemmelgarn, 1998).

Some authors have argued that the climate of the organisation is more important than the structure, not just for the social workers, but also for the delivery of services. Glisson and Hemmelgarn (1998) have suggested that organisational change needs to be accompanied by a change in climate (including low conflict, co-operation, role clarity and personalisation) to produce better services. Their research into services for children found that improvement in the children's psychosocial well-being appeared to be directly related to work carried out from offices where there were the most positive working climates. This was because in the offices with the better climates the social workers were more focused on the personal relationships with service-users, not just on the processes of the work. Where employees had high levels of job satisfaction, this enhanced their ability to meet the children's needs.

Other research has emphasised the importance of positive relationships with social workers to better outcomes for children and their families (Prior et al., 1999; Department of Health, 2000). Glisson and Hemmelgarn also argued that inter-organisational co-ordination had a negative effect on service quality and no effect on outcomes. This finding challenges the wisdom of the focus on organisational co-ordination as a way of improving services and points to a different kind of solution – a focus on a change of climate, and an approach which 'reinvigorates social work's core values' (Scottish Executive, 2006: 3).

Social workers, therefore, need to be articulate with managers and others with delegated authority and power in their organisations about the impact of organisational arrangements on themselves, service-users and colleagues. The social worker is in a pivotal position between service-users and management, particularly if based in a team with other practitioners, to contribute to the creation of social work practices which do not make unnecessary barriers between managers and staff, and between staff and service-users.

It is also possible to challenge poor managerial practices that lead to discrimination and unfair distribution of resources. Front-line managers may welcome the contributions of their team in making the case to senior management on a range of issues from staffing needs to which services are most useful to the particular service-user groups. Often senior managers are making decisions at a distance from the day-to-day realities of practice (Kitchener et al., 2000; Causer and Exworthy, 2003) and it can be critical that the organisation responds to the views and knowledge of those working closest to the delivery of care. Another tool for understanding how to create this change is 'appreciative enquiry'.

Appreciative enquiry

Appreciative enquiry is a strengths-based approach to analysing what needs to change in a situation and to focusing on positive ways to problem-solve and make changes, similar to other solution-focused and strengths approaches. It begins from the assumption that there have been things that have worked well in the past. Therefore, stakeholders are asked to identify and explore those times when the organisation was working well. From this, a plan for the future can be outlined and a shared vision developed for practice. Pine and Healey (2007: 85, 86) describe the stages as outlined in Box 10.3.

Box 10.3   Stages of an appreciative enquiry

Definition

Decide what to learn about/enquire into in consultation with people in the organisation. This sets the focus of the enquiry and determines the specific questions on which people will be interviewed.

Discover/Explore and Understand

Conduct the enquiry, involving participants in interviews/sharing stories about the organisation at its best, and working together to draw out themes of success.

Dream/Imagine

Generalise from these themes to create a picture of how the organisation would look if these elements existed now or in the future. This is rooted in the participant's knowledge and experience of what the organisation has been, and could be, capable of being.

Design/Create

Develop ideas and practical steps about how to create this picture of the organisation now. Work out what needs to happen (people, structures, resources) next to achieve this in practice.

Delivery

Put these ideas into practice, building on what has been learned in the previous phases.

Source: Barnes (2007)

Appreciative enquiry, as theorised by Cooperrider et al. (1991) and others, has been much used in individual therapy, groupwork, personal coaching and business as a means of enabling people to build on their successes for future action. It has also been used as a means of action research in practice. It has proved helpful in enabling groups and teams to manage organisational change.

Organisational change and interprofessional working

The organisational shape for the delivery of social work and care service in England, Scotland, Wales and Northern Ireland develops and changes as governments and authorities who act for governments seek to modernise care services and deliver them as economically as they can. Since the 1990s the pace of change has been fast. Managers who were interviewed for the Open University course Managing Care (Henderson and Seden, 2000,

2004) said that 'change was the only certainty', and that they found themselves 'running to keep up' with the fast pace of change. As one person said: 'There were lots of new initiatives and everyone was feeling overloaded.'

As this chapter is written, the planned changes to organisations continue, and usually have the aim of making interprofessional collaboration easier, as it is argued that this gives better services to the people who need them. The drivers for organisational change are therefore often less about the shape of individual organisations and more about how organisations can learn to work together. Paradoxically, however, this can have the opposite effect, as the fast pace of change can derail professionals, leading them to feel less secure about their identities and professional roles. Hiscock and Pearson (1999), for example, in their study of the boundaries between health and social care identified that reorganisation can lead to professionals becoming preoccupied with the changes they are experiencing:

> The interviews revealed practitioners in both health and social services to be highly preoccupied with the form and fast pace of change **within** their own organization and immediate professional environment prompted by the introduction of market mechanisms and the associated drive for cost containment. The development of external links and joint working was therefore hardly a consideration.
>
> (Hiscock and Pearson, 1999: 156)

Three particular factors were of concern to the respondents: changing workloads, adjusting to different demands and expectations, and job insecurity. Henderson and Seden (2000, 2004) also found that the fast pace of change and moves to new organisational structure for delivering services led individuals to question their professional role and identity, and it required strong leadership from managers who could adapt to, and even enjoy, organisational change to support the new teams through transition.

> There isn't a shared language – a vocabulary to express what I had been trained to express in the way I had been trained to express it … Over time I don't think it's changed. I think I've got more used to it and can accommodate it more perhaps.
>
> (Practitioner)

> Managing multi-disciplinary teams is a big threat because you don't have understanding of their professional expertise or language.
>
> (Front line manager)

> I like innovating and hope the enthusiasm is contagious. It's important to build on the assets of the past and it's important to acknowledge the value of what people have done.
>
> (Practitioner)

Organisational change therefore can at best challenge and at worst deskill some people, and it is important to understand that this has a basis in the psychological make-up of human beings, for whom change can be seen as opportunity but also as a challenge and possibly a threat. Hopson and Adam's (1976) model of self-esteem in transition has often been used to analyse the stages that individuals experience when faced with change. These are:

1. **Immobilisation**: faced with change the person is shocked and disbelieving and feels like doing nothing.
2. **Minimisation**: the appreciation of the potential change is clearer, but the person tries to make the change fit with current realities and decides 'it won't affect me'.
3. **Depression**: at this point change is seen as inevitable but the reaction is anger, a feeling of loss of control and depression.
4. **Acceptance**: the inevitable is accepted but accompanied by uncertainty and the fear of failure.
5. **Testing out**: questions are asked about the proposed change and the individual begins to interact with the process.
6. **Searching for meaning**: the person accepts the change and begins to understand how it will work out for them.
7. **Internalisation**: the understanding of how to implement change is worked out and the person feels a renewed sense of self-esteem.

The value of this model for practitioners is that it helps them to appreciate that the threat to self-esteem is a usual, and predictable, reaction to change, and that by appreciating the psychological dimensions it is possible to work through the stages in relation to a particular change and regain a sense of control and purpose. Change can be difficult for everyone. This model is also useful to help to explain colleagues' and service-users' reactions to transition and change.

Working across organisational boundaries

Interprofessional collaboration and the delivery of service through inter-agency relationships will continue to be a challenge to social workers' and other professionals' sense of identity and role awareness. Despite new arrangements to join up services, it is likely that some of the barriers to inter-organisational collaboration as described by Hardy et al. (1992), shown in Box 10.4, will continue to challenge practitioners. These are:

Box 10.4   Five categories of barriers to inter-organisational co-ordination

Structural

- fragmentation of service responsibilities across inter-agency boundaries
- fragmentation of service responsibilities within agency boundaries

(Continued)

(Continued)

- inter-organisational complexity
- non-coterminosity of boundaries.

Procedural

- differences in planning horizons and cycles
- differences in budgetary cycles and procedures.

Financial

- differences in funding mechanisms and bases
- differences in the stocks and flows of [financial] resources.

Professional

- differences in ideologies and values
- professional self-interest
- threats to job security
- conflicting views about user interests and roles.

Status and legitimacy

- organisational self-interest
- concern for threats to autonomy and domain
- differences in legitimacy between elected and appointed agencies.

(Source: Hardy et al., 1992, cited by Hudson et al., 1999: 241)

Practitioners, who make assessments, intervene and provide services to the public for which they are accountable, need to be able to analyse where such barriers still exist and understand, or indeed develop, the mechanisms for overcoming them. Where new arrangements for joined-up organisations and budgets are in place, this may be easier. However, within organisations it is possible for sub-groups to exist and for there to be differences of perspective and power which are barriers to collaboration. Some of the barriers may be informal, or a result of poor professional relationships; others will be more structural. Either way, the cultures and structures of the organisations will need to develop in ways that enable co-operation and create a positive interprofessional climate, if services are to be more responsive to service-users.

Martin (2007: 281) has argued that the development of inter-agency services brings particular challenges to managers and service providers to develop partnerships, share philosophies and strategies and 'above all pool budgets'. While service-users have repeatedly said they want timely and effective services that improve their quality of life, it remains to be seen whether structural reorganisation will produce the desired outcome. However, there are indications of what makes for positive inter-agency working, which, according to Martin (2007), include: mutual gain through working together, including cost savings from shared resources, common purposes, for example promoting service-user choice, common goals, such as meeting the needs of a particular locality. Such changes, however, require careful planning and good leadership to become effective, as the people in organisations respond to the changes to their working practices. It also remains to be seen whether service-users will find these arrangements easy to access and feel more in control find it increasingly difficult to know who is leading the provision of the services for them (Postle and Beresford, 2007; Scourfield, 2007).

Future directions

The organisations that provide care are frequently in transition. It is impossible to predict exactly what will happen, but there will be more change in line with policy drivers from all four countries in the UK. For example, the development of Children's Trusts in England will lead to new kinds of interprofessional collaboration. As the twenty-first-century review in Scotland is implemented, there is a clear agenda to examine and develop the capacity to deliver personalised services and the capacity of the social work and care workforce. This also means building sustainable change through the redesign of services, organisational develop-ment and new organisational approaches building on the core values of social work.

It is important, therefore, that social workers seek to understand the shape of changing organisations and the implications for themselves, their colleagues and their service-users. Whatever the shape of the organisational structures and cultures and climates for deliver-ing care, practitioners have a role in understanding how to work within them and be influ-ential in improving practice. As organisations are developing and changing, practitioners have a significant contribution to make in building the kind of climate within organisations that leads to better outcomes for service-users by applying their core values to organisa-tions, their structures, cultures, human and material resources.

Acknowledgement

This chapter has been updated from Janet Seden, 'Managers and their organisations', Chapter 5 in Jeannette Henderson and Dorothy Atkinson (eds), *Managing Care in Context*. London: Routledge, 2003.

References

Aldgate, J., Healey, L., Malcolm, B., Pine, B., Rose, W. and Seden, J. (eds) (2007) *Enhancing Social Work Management: Theory and Best Practice from the UK and USA*. London: Jessica Kingsley.
Arnold, J., Cooper, C.L. and Robertson, I.T. (1998) *Work Psychology. Understanding Human Behaviour in the Workplace*. London: Financial Times and Pitman.

Barnes, J. (2007) 'Improving performance in social work through positive approaches to managing change', in J. Aldgate, L. Healy, B. Malcom, B. Pine, W. Rose and J. Seden (eds), *Enhacing Social Work Management*. London: Jessica Kingsley.

Brody, R. (1993) *Effectively Managing Human Service Organizations*. London: Sage.

Causer, G. and Exworthy, M. (2003) 'Professionals as managers across the public sector', in J. Reynolds, J. Henderson, J. Seden, J. Charlesworth and A. Bullman (eds), *The Managing Care Reader*. London: Routledge.

Laming, H. (2003) *The Victoria Climbié Inquiry*. CM 5730, London: HMSO.

Cooperrider, D., Fry, R., Barrett, F., Seiling, J. and Whitney, D. (eds) (1991) *Appreciative Inquiry and Organisational Transformation: Reports from the Field*. Slough: Greenwood Press.

Coulshed, V. and Mullender, A. (2001) *Management in Social Work* (2nd edn). Buckingham: Palgrave.

Department of Health (2000) *The Children Act Now*. London: HMSO.

Elkin, A.J. and Rosch, P.J. (1990) 'Promoting mental health in the workplace: the preventional side of stress management', *Occupational Medicine: State of the Art Review*, 5 (4): 739–54.

Evans, T. and Harris, J. (2004) 'Street-level bureaucracy, social work and the (exaggerated) death of discretion', *British Journal of Social Work*, 34: 871–95.

Glisson, A. and Hemmelgarn, A. (1998) 'The effects of organizational climate and interorganizational coordination on the quality and outcomes of children's services systems', *Child Abuse and Neglect*, 22 (5): 401–21.

Gould, N. (2003) 'Becoming a learning organisation: a social work example', in J. Reynolds, J. Henderson, J. Seden, J. Charlesworth and A. Bullman (eds), *The Managing Care Reader*. London: Routledge.

Handy, C. (1993 and 1999) *Understanding Organizations* (4th edn and 4th edn revised). Harmondsworth: Penguin.

Handy, C. (1995) *Inside Organisations*. London: BBC Books.

Hasenfeld, Y. (1983) *Human Services Organisations*. Englewood Cliffs, NJ: Prentice-Hall.

Henderson, J. and Atkinson, D. (2003) *Managing Care in Context*. London: Routledge.

Henderson, J. and Seden, J. (2000) 'What do we really want from social care managers? Aspirations and realities', paper presented to Dilemmas 2000 International Conference, 1–3 September, University of East London.

Henderson, J. and Seden, J. (2004) 'What do we want from social care managers? Aspirations and realities', in M. Dent, J. Chandler and J. Barry (eds), *Questioning the New Public Management*, Aldershot: Ashgate.

Hiscock, J. and Pearson, M. (1999) 'Looking inwards, looking outwards: dismantling the "Berlin wall" between health and social services?' *Social Policy and Administration*, 33 (2): 150–63.

Hopson, B. and Adams, J. (1976) 'Towards an understanding: defining some boundaries of transition dynamics', in J. Adams, J. Hayes and B. Hopson (eds), *Transition: Understanding and Managing Personal Change*. London: Martin Robertson.

Hudson, B., Hardy, B., Hewood, M. and Wistow, G. (1999) 'In pursuit of inter-agency collaboration in the public sector: what is the contribution of theory and research', *Public Management*, 1 (2): 235–60.

Kitchener, M., Kirkpatrick, I. and Whipp, R. (2000) 'Supervising professional practice under new public management: evidence from an invisible trade', *British Journal of Management*, 11 (3): 213–26.

Lipsky, M. (1980) *Street-Level Bureaucracy*. New York: Russell Sage Publications.

Malcolm, B.P. (2007) 'Managing diversity in social service settings', in J. Aldgate, L. Healey, B. Malcolm, B. Pine, W. Rose and J. Seden (eds), *Enhancing Social Work Management: Theory and Best Practice from the UK and the USA*. London: Jessica Kingsley.

Martin, V. (2007) 'Managing across inter-agency boundaries: a learning agenda for change', in J. Aldgate, L. Healey, B. Malcolm, B. Pine, W. Rose and J. Seden (eds), *Enhancing Social Work Management: Theory and Best Practice from the UK and the USA*. London: Jessica Kingsley.

Mintzberg, H. (1981) 'Organisation design: fashion or fit?', *Harvard Business Review* (January/February): 103–16.

Mintzberg, H. (1992) 'Structuring of organisations', in H. Mintzberg and J.B. Quinn (eds), *The Strategy Process*. London: Prentice-Hall.

Morgan, G. (1997) *Images of Organisation*. Thousand Oaks, CA: Sage.

Peace, S.M. and Reynolds, J. (2003) 'Managing environments', in J. Henderson and D. Atkinson (eds), *Managing Care in Context*. London: Routledge.

Pearn, M., Roderick, C. and Mulrooney, C. (1997) *Learning Organisations in Practice*. London: McGraw-Hill.

Peel, M. (2003) 'Managing professional development', in J. Seden and J. Reynolds (eds), *Managing Care in Practice*. London: Routledge.

Pine, B. and Healey, L.M. (2007) 'New leadership for the human services: involving and empowering staff through participatory management', in J. Aldgate, L. Healey, B. Malcolm, B. Pine, W. Rose and J. Seden (eds), *Enhancing Social Work Management: Theory and Best Practice from the UK and the USA*. London: Jessica Kingsley.

Postle, K. and Beresford, P. (2007) 'Capacity building and the reconception of political participation: a role for social care workers?', *British Journal of Social Work*, 37 (1): 143–58.

Prior, P., Lynch, M.A., Glaser, D. (1999) 'Responding to child sexual abuse, an evaluation of social work by children and their carers', *Child and Family Social Work*, Vol. 4, pp. 131–43.

Reynolds, J. (2003) 'Acting and reacting', in J. Seden and J. Reynolds (eds), *Managing Care in Practice*. London: Routledge.

Reynolds, J. and Peace, S. (2007) 'Managing care environments: reflections from research', in J. Aldgate, L. Healey, B. Malcolm, B. Pine, W. Rose and J. Seden (eds), *Enhancing Social Work Management: Theory and Best Practice from the UK and the USA*. London: Jessica Kingsley.

Scottish Executive (2006) *Changing Lives: Report of the 21st Century Social Work Review*. Edinburgh: Scottish Executive.

Scourfield, P. (2007) 'Social care and the modern citizen: client, consumer, service user, manager and entrepreneur', *British Journal of Social Work*, 37 (1): 107–20.

Seden, J. (2003) 'Managers and their organisations', in J. Henderson and D. Atkinson (eds), *Managing Care in Context*. London: Routledge.

Seden, J. and Ross, T. (2007) 'Active service user involvement in human services: lessons from practice', in J. Aldgate, L. Healey, B. Malcolm, B. Pine, W. Rose and J. Seden (eds), *Enhancing Social Work Management: Theory and Best Practice in the UK and the USA*. London: Jessica Kingsley.

Senge, P. M. (1990) *The Fifth Discipline: the Art and Practice of the Learning Organization*. London: Doubleday/Century Business.

Whitaker, D., Archer, L. and Hicks, L. (1998) *Working in Children's Homes: Challenges and Complexities*. Chichester: Wiley.

Chapter 11

Accountability

Maureen Eby and Alun Morgan

An accountable person does not undertake an action merely because someone in authority says to do so. Instead, the accountable person examines a situation, explores the various options available, demonstrates a knowledgeable understanding of the possible consequences of options and makes a decision for action which can be justified from a knowledge base.

(Marks-Maran, 1993: 123)

Accountability has always been central for health and social work practitioners. Yet there is an inherent tension between accountability to service-users via codes of practice, and accountability to the community as a whole that is reinforced by law and regulation. Most social workers and health care staff are employed as public officials. Thus they are accountable to the public; but this accountability was only defined formally by government in 1995 (Nolan, 1995), when it was included as one of the 'Seven Principles of Public Life', along with selflessness, objectivity, integrity, openness, honesty and leadership. Accountability is a principal feature of the value base for all professions in health and social care; for example, one of the key roles for qualifying social workers is to: 'manage and be accountable' (Training Organisation for Social Services, 2004: 12; Scottish Executive, 2003); and registered nurses are 'personally accountable' for their practice ('Nursing and midwifery code of professional conduct: standards for conduct, performance and ethics', NMC, 2004: 3).

  Being accountable is the process of being called to account to others for your actions and conduct: to be responsible, to answer for. The first step in this process is for the practitioner to learn and understand the requirements and the limits of their professional role and liability. This involves an appreciation of what is theirs to account for, and, in addition and importantly, to learn what can be said reasonably *not* to be their responsibility. This can be complex because the mechanisms for tracking accountability through organisational systems can be diffuse and complex – for example in multi-professional workplaces and complex management structures. Partnership working may involve moves away from linear and hierarchical line-management.

It is not easy to be confident in expressing accountability appropriately in contexts where practitioners feel under pressure and face diminishing resources and increasing workloads. In such conditions staff can face contradictory demands from service-users, their employers, their professional bodies, from government policy and scrutiny, and from the increasingly litigious climate in which services are delivered. Individual practitioners can become caught between their personal and legitimate sense of professional responsibility, and the requirements of the organisations and society to which they belong, including accountability demands from many other external organisations and communities of interest.

In this chapter we aim to explore some of these challenges. We look at how individual workers are held to account in their dealings with service-users and patients, being both monitored by their employer and regulated by their profession. The focus in this chapter is on the individual operating through four dimensions of accountability – social, ethical, legal and professional.

Social accountability

In everyday social interactions, individuals are accountable in a variety of ways; explaining the reason for being late to work; ensuring that all earnings are declared for tax; or conforming to the maximum speed limit on a motorway. Individuals either offer or are asked to give accounts to explain their actions in an effort to mitigate or alter another's opinion or perspective, or to recast their actions in another light. For example, Buttny (1993) offers seven accounts of the imagined act of someone seen striking another person with a hammer. When asked to give an account of this act it could at first, suggests Buttny, be said to have been an accident, as the other person got in the way of the hammer aimed at the nail. Alternatively it may have been inadvertent as the individual did not see the person while hitting the nail; or the individual using the hammer may have mistaken the person hit for someone else who previously had hit them. Perhaps, though, it was self-defence, as the individual thought the person was about to attack. Maybe, though, it was through provocation; or could it be that the individual was bullied into hitting the person? Yet another explanation could be that the individual with the hammer was suffering a severe psychosis with an impaired capacity to take appropriate responsibility for their actions.

Each one of Buttny's seven accounts recasts the original act. This illustrates the importance of unseen factors, such as motivation, contextual antecedents and the individual's intended outcome, within any account of liability, cause or of fault. In addition, the different accounts have different consequences. Whereas the first two might well result in an apology with forgiveness as an outcome, the account of provocation might well result in further retaliative action rather than a resolution. A flexible appreciation of social accountability, therefore, can ease the stresses and strains in society, as it 'lubricate[s] social relations by discursive means' (Buttny, 1993: 8).

Social accountability sets the parameters of acceptable behaviour and social etiquette. Social parameters change and evolve over time. However, every society, community and workplace has conventions and expectations, and not to comply with such local conventions may require an account to be provided for that non-compliance. That is, an account which explains or mitigates such non-compliance with a view to altering existing opinions or perspectives. Practitioners should seek an awareness of and to be able to work positively with the boundaries of social accountability.

Ethical accountability

Being accountable implies values such as honesty, duty and trust. Fowler and Levine-Ariff (1987: 48) argue that 'being answerable in this regard is a moral obligation and is derived from the nature of the implicit trust relationship between client and [the practitioner]'. But there could be a number of ways to approach such moral and ethical obligations when accounting for actions in practice. For example; a *duty-based* approach would focus on the duty of the worker to be accountable; while a *consequences-based* approach would highlight not the explanation or the individual but rather the consequences of how the person acted. Alternatively, a *virtue-based* approach would focus on the integrity of the accountable individual and express faith in that person's knowledge and judgement of what is the right explanation to give. A *principle-based* approach, on the other hand, would argue that truth-telling and honesty are the fundamental principles upon which to base an account. Finally, an *emotive approach* might well focus on fear, or perhaps some of the less rational elements surrounding any account of or explanations for action.

The impact of these different ethical difficulties and approaches, and their relationship to accountability affects not only the nature of an individual's explanation but also the response to that account. This is illustrated in Case Study 1, where a student social worker grapples with his duty as a worker and the potential consequences of his choices and actions for the service-user.

Case Study 1   David, a student social worker

A young mother was referred to a family centre because of feelings of social isolation. During a counselling session with her key worker (David, a student social worker), and while discussing budgeting and the problems caused by spending any time away from her daughter, the young mother revealed that she was claiming income support while still working nights as a cleaner. David's thoughts on hearing this were 'Should I ignore it? Or should I report this to the Benefits Agency? Do I have a duty to uphold the principle of confidentiality in this case?'

(Source: adapted from Banks, 1995: 145–6)

David is faced with an ethical dilemma. Is it his duty to inform his supervisor or the Benefits Agency about this situation? If so, what would be the consequences for the mother and her family? After all, it is actually a case of fraud which could incur a criminal conviction and fine. Does the mother assume that David will not disclose this information? What should he say to her? Should he respond at all? Did he clarify his role at the outset of the interaction? It is unlikely that he can remain neutral. Indeed, Clark (2006: 75) points out, 'value neutrality over many pressing contemporary social issues is … neither feasible nor desirable for human service professionals'. David has an ethical dilemma and may be unsure how to proceed: to say nothing, or to report what appears to be a criminal act. The questions raised relate to his professional duty and to the principle of confidentiality, and he is also dealing with questions of responsibility and autonomy – two concepts that are very closely linked with accountability.

Responsibility

Responsibility is the acceptance of a course of action as well as the acceptance that an individual should be willing to account for the nature and conduct of that action. Responsibilities can be seen as tasks that go with the job and, as such, are relatively unproblematic. Accounting for the nature and conduct of the task may be more problematic. For example, did David establish clear boundaries of confidentiality for his counselling relationship with the service-user? The service-user may have expected a higher level of confidentiality. It would have been David's responsibility to have clarified and obtained specific terms of reference for this particular piece of work with the service-user in advance.

David could stay silent and not bring these difficult issues into the open. French (1993) remarks: 'no wonder that avoidance of responsibility has become almost an art form, one that is learned and practised relatively early in life and honed to the end'; and Musil et al. (2004) report that there is evidence that some front-line social workers evolve patterns of behaviour that enable them to avoid the dilemmas provoked by their uncertain working conditions. In social work, staff supervision is normally the first place in which actions are accounted for and is vitally important in enabling front-line staff to have reflective distance from their service-users. Supervision provides an opportunity to explore options and account for actions in the context of ethical dilemma in a relatively safe and structured way.

The practice area of learning disability, particularly where service-users exhibit challenging behaviour, is described by Stevens (2006) as, 'a "moral web": a complex network of antecedents, behaviours and consequences'. Here, responsibility, once accepted, must be followed through in a sophisticated way. A responsible professional should not simply and unquestioningly complete a series of tasks relating to practical care of the learning disabled person; rather they would take steps to establish a commitment to understanding the causes and triggers for their service-users' challenging behaviours, along with a willingness to work patiently to develop helpful strategies for reducing the ensuing negative effects.

Robyn Holden, an Australian nurse teacher, criticises some nurses for hiding from and avoiding their broader responsibilities through 'compulsive, ritualistic behaviour' (Holden, 1991: 398). Holden suggests that practitioners who continue to adhere to ritualistic, regimented patterns of work do not learn to discriminate between, or to choose freely one course of action over another. Holden links responsibility with the freedom to choose. In her example, regimentation meant that nurses were denied such freedom. Batey and Lewis (1982: 14) warn:

> We must be careful not to confuse responsibility with the state of being responsible. While responsibility denotes a charge, being responsible or having a sense of responsibility is the acceptance of a charge. It denotes that one knows what the charge is and is willing to fulfil it.

Returning to David, who is faced not with rules and constraints – albeit with their inherent ambiguities and grey areas – but with what, for him, may be equally if not more anxiety-provoking: autonomy. That is, the apparent freedom to choose when, how, or indeed whether to intervene.

Autonomy

Personal responsibility as an attribute or a virtue denotes a sense of freedom to choose particular actions and how those actions will be carried out. Autonomy reflects the independence of an individual to make decisions based on his or her own abilities rather than on organisational position. Sometimes it is difficult for people within a given work situation to recognise autonomy, preferring instead to think of themselves as subject to others' control. But in reality all individuals have autonomy although this is distributed unequally. Depending on the terms of reference that may have been negotiated and agreed with the service-user, does David have the autonomy to ignore or act upon what the young mother said? Hall (1968) identifies two types of autonomy – structural and attitudinal:

> Structural autonomy exists when professional people are expected to use their judgement to determine the provision of client services in the context of their work. Attitudinal autonomy exists for people who believe themselves to be free to exercise judgement in decision making.

> (Hall, 1968, quoted in Duff, 1995: 53)

Arguably, David has both structural and attitudinal autonomy in this case. He could ignore what the young mother has said about working and not record it in case-file notes, indicating attitudinal autonomy. At the same time, David, acting responsibly, could have recorded additional information disclosed by the young mother that she had left her child unattended while at work. David would almost certainly have decided to report such information to his supervisor or line-manager. David would be exercising structural autonomy by using his judgement based on the ethical principle of non-maleficence (the obligation not to inflict harm intentionally) in the case of the child and also on the legal and local authority procedural guidelines for safeguarding children. In the first case, David would have chosen not to be accountable by not documenting in the notes the young mother's account about earning additional undisclosed income. In the second case, he would have chosen to be accountable by reporting the situation to officers in his authority with specific responsibility for safeguarding children.

Whistle-blowing – ethical accountability at work

Brammer (2007: 111) suggests that 'whistle blowing can in some circumstances be an appropriate response to concerns about bad practice and is a legitimate aspect of the social work role'. Whistle-blowing is the ancient art of bringing to light wrongdoing in any area of life (Eby, 1994a). It is the process of forcing the issue in accountability; the act of bringing to public attention abuses or dangers that jeopardise public safety, those that would not otherwise be publicised (Chadwick and Tadd, 1992). As Gerald Vinten writes:

[Whistle-blowing is] the unauthorised disclosure of information that an employee reasonably believes is evidence of the contravention of any law, rule or regulation, code of practice, or professional statement, or that involves mismanagement, corruption, abuse of authority or danger to public or worker health and safety.

(Vinten, 1994: 5)

In Vinten's words (1994: 10), the whistle-blower 'has only one sting to use, and using it may well kill off one's career'. Within health and social care there have been some very widely publicised whistle-blowers. Alison Taylor, for example, complained about abuses in children's homes in North Wales in the 1970s and 1980s, complaints that led subsequently to the Waterhouse inquiry in 1996. Alison was sacked but later received damages for unfair dismissal from an industrial tribunal (Cervi, 1996). Julia Wassell, the Women's Services Director at Broadmoor high-security psychiatric hospital in Berkshire, reported to her managers in 2001 serious allegations of rape, indecent assault and sexual harassment of women patients by some male patients. Her concerns, in her view, were not responded to adequately, despite there being a formal whistle-blowing policy at Broadmoor. Julia subsequently resigned, claiming constructive dismissal. In 2003 there was an out-of-court settlement in her favour.

Whistle-blowing is one solution to an ethical dilemma, and can be viewed principally in three ways. First, whistle-blowers can be seen as 'rats' undermining their company or organisation in a rush to leave the sinking ship, a ship that they themselves were apparently helping to sink. A second approach is to view whistle-blowers as tragic individuals; indeed, research has indicated that people suffer equally from not blowing the whistle as when they do (Hunt, 1995). In a small-scale study of thirty-five 'whistleblowers', Lennane concluded that;

although whistle blowing is important in protecting society, the typical organisational response causes severe and long-lasting health, financial and personal problems for whistleblowers and their families.

(Lennane, 1993: 670)

Thirdly, whistle-blowing can be an obligation, such as when there is potential serious harm to the public; when all other internal channels within the organisation have been exhausted and no acceptable response is offered; or when there is documentary evidence that would convince a reasonably impartial observer there is a serious public risk. Whistle-blowing may also be considered an obligation when an individual has good reason to believe that blowing the whistle publicly will bring about a necessary change.

In July 1998, the Public Interest Disclosure Act, the first whistle-blower's protection legislation, became law and came into force in July 1999. This Act protects employees from being dismissed or victimised when disclosing information in good faith and where they have reasonable grounds for their belief in what is disclosed. Disclosure by an employee will only be protected if it is made to the employer or to the person responsible for the matter; or to a Minister in the case of civil servants or their equivalent or to a designated regulatory body identified in Statutory Instrument 1999 No. 1549 (HMSO, 1999); or, in the course of obtaining legal advice. If whistle-blowers are subsequently victimised, as employees they can seek redress through industrial tribunals for compensation. In cases where dismissal is involved, individuals may also seek a re-employment order, enabling them to return to their former employment, should they wish to do so.

Legal accountability

Accountability is also enshrined in law through acts of parliament, case law and the various public mechanisms such as tribunals and inquiries. Practitioners face legal accountability as private citizens and in their workplace, in areas such as health and safety, or negligence (see Case Study 2).

Case Study 2   Manager of a residential home

The manager of a residential home was recently instructed by her employer, a multinational corporation, to cut costs and to implement a chill–cook system of meals to replace freshly prepared meals. Unfortunately, soon after implementing this new system, ten of the residents developed salmonella poisoning and the environmental health inspector is now asking for the name of the chill–cook meals supplier.

This residential care manager faces legal accountability if she is asked to explain the source of the food given to the residents of this residential home. Did the manager follow her company's policies in selecting this supplier? After all, selecting a supplier was the manager's responsibility. Did she undertake this task in a responsible manner by requesting references or inspecting the premises of the supplier prior to contract?

Let us assume that the chill–cook meals were not the source of salmonella. Rather, one of the care assistants brought in some home-made mayonnaise for residents' bedtime snacks. This care assistant was very newly appointed and had not yet undertaken the mandatory basic food hygiene course for all employees. Investigation determined that she had no idea that her home-made mayonnaise was contaminated. Yet the company policy which this employee had read before starting her care duties stated that home-made foods should not to be given to residents. Was this care assistant being responsible? Clearly not. Was she accountable? Yes, both to the manager of the residential home via her employment contract and to the environmental health inspector under health and safety law. If one of the residents died as a result of this incident, further action, possibly leading to a criminal charge, might well ensue.

This case study illustrates that an understanding of both authority and liability is crucial to legal accountability. Good practice, of course, would acknowledge and support the legal framework for accountability, but also promote organisational practice cultures that were open and trusting, so that hopefully the case of the care assistant bringing in her own mayonnaise could have been prevented in the early stages by a higher collective awareness of risk among the staff group.

Authority

Authority is 'the rightful [legitimate] power to fulfil a charge [responsibility]' (Batey and Lewis, 1982: 14) and derives from the *situation*, *expert knowledge* and *position* (Duff, 1995). Authority arising from the *situation* occurs when circumstances demand that action is taken quickly; say, to save life or to prevent harm. For example, in an emergency and in the absence of a doctor, a nurse can attempt cardiopulmonary resuscitation and even administer cardiac drugs, under suitable protocols, to ensure a rapid and life-saving response. Alternatively, a social worker may be given the authority by a court to remove a child from their home in a case of immediate danger, under the provisions of an emergency protection order (Hendrick, 1993; Hoggett, 1993).

Authority derived from *expert knowledge* is the basis of professional power and is awarded on the basis of prior academic achievement and, often, through statutory registration; while for authority stemming from *position*, power is derived from the organisational role an individual has or from the occupational grouping to which they belong. For example, the police have authority based not only on the legal system that creates a police force, but also on the trust given by the public to the police. It is when this trust breaks down that this form of authority is challenged. Health and social care workers do not always recognise fully within themselves this form of authority. Yet it is an important professional task for such workers to create and maintain appropriate trust and respect from service-users and from the public.

Professionals with the appropriate 'position' authority can deprive a person with mental health problems of their liberty – for example, if a person's condition is considered to be a risk to themselves or to others. Health and social care professionals in such circumstances have authority drawn from the specific *situation*, from their *expert knowledge*, and from the *position* they hold to specifically undertake this role. At the time of writing there is the likelihood that the provisions of the Mental Health Act 1983 are to be amended, to widen the professional background of those appointed to fulfil such a role from, as formerly, the Approved Social Worker (ASW) leading the assessment, to include nursing and other health staff under the more generic title of Approved Mental Health Professional (AMHP).

Liability

Liability identifies who is responsible for an action or decision. However, in a legal sense, liability is the obligation one individual incurs to another person or organisation as a result of harm or injury caused by the actions of that individual. This is illustrated by the following equation:

act (or omission) + causation + fault + protected interest + damage = liability

(Cooke, 1997: 4)

Within health care, liability is often associated with negligence, as described by Lord Atkin in the case of *Donoghue* v. *Stevenson* (1932):

You must take reasonable care to avoid acts or omissions which you can reasonably foresee would be likely to injure your neighbour.

(Cooke, 1997, p. 29)

Brammer (2007: 108) also refers to the *Donoghue* v. *Stevenson* (1932) case about the duty of care to one's neighbour, adding, 'it is also established that if a person is considered to be a professional or expert, this duty or standard will be applied more rigorously'.

Failure to take reasonable care may suggest negligence. There are three fundamental threshold conditions to establish whether negligence may have occurred. First, a duty of care must be owed; second, that duty of care must have been broken; and, third, the breach in the duty of care must have caused the damage (Eby, 1994b: 11). The standard used in determining whether there has been a breach in the duty of care is known as the Bolam Test, after the judgement in the case *Bolam* v. *Friern Hospital Management Committee* (1957). It was alleged in this case that the doctor administered electro-convulsive therapy to Mr Bolam without anaesthetic or muscle relaxants. Mr Bolam suffered a fractured jaw. In his judgement, Mr Justice McNair stated:

> The test is the standard of the ordinary skilled man exercising and professing to have that special skill. A man need not possess the highest expert skill ... it is sufficient if he exercises the ordinary skill of an ordinary competent man exercising that particular art. ... [A] doctor is not guilty of negligence if he has acted in accordance with a practice accepted as proper by a responsible body of medical men skilled in that particular art. ... Putting it the other way round, a doctor is not negligent, if he is acting in accordance with such a practice, merely because there is a body of opinion that takes a contrary view.

> (Eby, 1994c: 9)

The case of *Wilsher* v. *Essex Health Authority* (1986) involved the monitoring of oxygen in an infant, Martin Wilsher. A junior, inexperienced doctor, unsure whether he had inserted the monitoring catheter in the right place, asked his senior registrar to check. The senior registrar not only failed to notice that the oxygen-monitoring catheter was in a vein rather than an artery but also later reinserted another oxygen-monitoring catheter into the vein as well. As the medical staff thought Martin's oxygen levels were low, he was administered a high dose of oxygen. Although the allegation that the dosage of oxygen caused Martin's blindness failed to be upheld, this case is important because it has modified the Bolam Test, especially in situations of expanded role. As Lord Justice Glidewell stated:

> In my view, the law requires the trainee or learner to be judged by the same standard as his more experienced colleagues. If it did not, inexperience would frequently be urged as a defence to an action for professional negligence.

> (Tingle, 1998a: 54)

To illustrate, if a nurse increases his or her abilities and assumes the doctor's responsibilities, for example prescribing medication, then that nurse's prescribing is judged by the standard set by doctors, not that of other nurse prescribers. This also implies that in performing their responsibilities as a social worker, student social workers will judged by the same standard as their qualified colleagues. Inexperience may be cited as a mitigating factor but the service delivered to service-users cannot be of a lesser standard than that expected of a qualified practitioner.

There are three types of liability: *direct liability*, where an individual is injured not by another person but by defective equipment or product, or if the organisational system itself failed, resulting in injury; *personal liability*, where the liability is that which any individual has if someone is injured as a result of failing to meet the standard of care of the ordinary individual in any given situation; and *vicarious liability*, the liability an employer has as a result of the actions of its employees (Tingle, 1998b). Employees of the NHS, the private sector or local government working within health and social care settings face either direct or vicarious liability as illustrated by the case study of food poisoning in a residential home (Case Study 2).

In the example in Case Study 2, had the cook–chill meal system been the source of the salmonella poisoning, the meal supplier and possibly the residential home would have faced direct liability. However, since the salmonella poisoning was apparently the result of the staff's actions, vicarious liability would apply. It is highly unlikely that the care assistant would be personally sued under personal liability, as her financial worth would be far smaller than that of her employer. The employer would be liable for the acts through the vicarious liability of the manager and of the care assistant, although there might well be an argument that the care assistant was not covered by vicarious liability because she did not follow company policy. The care assistant, though, could plead mitigating circumstances since she had not done the basic food hygiene course. In this case, both the manager and the care assistant would have to account for what happened and why the situation and potential risk was not identified at an earlier stage.

Human Rights Act 1998

The Human Rights Act 1998 (HRA) incorporates the European Convention on Human Rights (ECHR) into domestic law in the United Kingdom. The HRA imposes a responsibility on public authorities, under section 6, making it unlawful for a public authority to act in a way that is incompatible with a Convention (ECHR) right as defined in the ECHR 'articles', unless as a result of primary legislation the public authority and their representatives could not have acted differently. ECHR articles with particular relevance to health care and social work include, for example: a prohibition against torture or inhuman or degrading treatment or punishment (Art. 3); the right to liberty and the security of the person (Art. 5); the right to a fair and public hearing (Art. 6); the right to respect for private and family life (Art. 8); and the right to freedom of expression (Art. 10).

Public authorities, including courts, tribunals, police, health authorities, social work agencies, and others, will inevitably through the course of their work take actions that may be construed as infringing the human rights of the individuals with whom they work. For example, a health visitor checking regularly on the development of a baby failing to thrive may find the child's parents asserting that their human right to family privacy was infringed as a result of the visits; or a person in an acute depressive phase of a bipolar disorder may argue that their human right to freedom of expression through suicide was denied when they were prevented from taking a self-administered lethal overdose of medication, by being detained and medicated safely in hospital.

The Human Rights Act addresses such potential challenges by requiring that any interference with an ECHR right, such as by a social worker or a health care worker, must be 'in accordance with the law, for a legitimate purpose, and proportionate' (Brammer, 2007: 129).

The Approved Mental Health Professional (AMHP), therefore, in the case of the person making a suicide attempt must:

- act within the remit of their relevant and current mental health legislation;
- be sure that attempting to save the person's life was a legitimate aim;
- satisfy themselves that making an order to enforce treatment was proportionate in the circumstances.

In practice, perhaps very few AMHPs would choose not to argue in favour of making an order for treatment in such a situation: but for some, especially if they had extensive previous knowledge of the person concerned, the scenario may present as a serious ethical dilemma.

Public mechanisms of legal accountability

Inquiries

Public inquiries are usually convened through government ministerial action. They are a means of providing a hearing to individuals and groups before a decision is made – for example, in the case of environmental matters in advance of major infrastructure projects such as airports. Public inquiries also allow investigation into why an event occurred: for example, the Fallon Inquiry (1999) into the alleged abuse of patients and children at Ashworth hospital; or the public independent 'Shipman' Inquiry (2005) into the circumstances surrounding the murder of patients by the GP Dr Harold Shipman. Inquiries are about finding out what has happened and often about allocating blame; but they also provide an opportunity for lessons to be learned for future practice.

Inquests

Inquests are judicial inquiries which set out to determine matters of fact. A coroner's inquest is a legal inquiry in England, Wales and Northern Ireland that takes place in the event of a sudden, violent or suspicious death, to determine the cause (Bird, 1983). Coroners' inquests can involve a jury but are not criminal proceedings. If an inquest finds that a particular person caused the death, indicating a homicide, the matter is passed to the Crown Prosecution Service (CPS). Other inquest verdicts may be death from natural causes, accidental death, or death by suicide; or the coroner may make recommendations (for example, about a dangerous product) to prevent similar deaths in future. In Scotland, the procedure for handling these types of cases is different from that for other UK countries. The coroners' work in Scotland is handled by the Procurator Fiscal and the police undertake investigations on the Fiscal's behalf (Knight, 1992).

Tribunals

A tribunal is a body that acts judicially and is appointed to adjudicate on disputed matters, perhaps between a citizen and a government department, or between individuals. Examples can include social security tribunals, or employment and industrial tribunals which hear disputes between employers and employees. The Care Standards Tribunal hears cases where there are disputes about the registration of care homes and independent schools, or about the inclusion of an individual's name on Department of Health lists in England and Wales of those considered unsuitable to work with children. The Mental Health (Care and Treatment) (Scotland) Act 2003 introduced a new system of mental health tribunals with authority to make decisions about long-term compulsory care and treatment of people in Scotland who have a mental health disorder. Under the Mental Health Act 1983 (England and Wales) with additional powers proposed in the Mental Health Bill 2005, a Mental Health Review Tribunal will be an independent judicial body with the power to order the discharge of a patient from detention for assessment and/or treatment.

Tribunals are usually presided over by a legally qualified chairperson, but they are largely composed of lay people and are less formal than courts of law. Tribunal decisions, while based on rules of law, often concern broad discretionary issues and require members to bring their own experience to bear in reaching their conclusions. Tribunals, rather than adhering to court procedures, observe instead the rules of natural justice and act within the limits of their jurisdiction and prescribed procedure (O'Donnell, 1996).

Professional accountability

The complexity that you have been considering so far is likely to have highlighted the usefulness of professional guidelines and bodies in health and social work. Professional accountability relies on individuals recognising that they are members of a profession and 'accepting that status, with the rights and responsibilities that go with it' (McGann, 1995: 18). Professional accountability is also informed significantly by the context of professional theory. Payne (2005: 27) suggests – mainly in relation to social work theory but it could also apply to other professions – that 'workers use theory within the politics of their daily practice to offer accountability to managers, politicians, clients and the public'. Theory in this regard helps frame professional action and provides guidance on the relevance and legitimacy of intervention; and while very few theories offer perfect 'blueprints' for action, workers who ignore or abandon theory are likely to find it hard to account adequately for their individual professional choices, or properly to understand the choices and behaviour of the organisations in which they are employed. In general, professional accountability relies on two interrelated concepts: ability and competence. Is the practitioner able and competent?

Ability

Ability is seen as 'the relevant knowledge, skills and values [required] to make decisions and to act' (Bergman, 1981: 54, quoted in Rodgers, 1995: 70). Without knowledge and/or skills, individuals would not be able to act in a purposeful way. It would be difficult to become a social worker or a nurse without the knowledge and skills needed. Values are also important in conveying the essence of the profession. But knowledge and skills are not static; they need updating to reflect current thinking. This responsibility of individuals to incorporate new knowledge and skills has been enshrined in social workers', nurses', and midwives' codes of practice, through which individuals are held responsible for maintaining their skills and abilities.

Competence

Competence is the capacity to perform a responsibility with appropriate knowledge and skill. However, performing such a responsibility involves the issues of scope and quality. As Eraut (1994: 167) states:

> The scope dimension [of competence] concerns what a person is competent in, the range of roles, tasks and situations for which their competence is established or may be reliably inferred. The quality dimension concerns judgements about the quality of that work on a continuum from being a novice, who is not yet competent in that particular task, to being an expert acknowledged by colleagues as having progressed well beyond the level of competence.

The *scope* of a practitioner's competence tends to expand over time through experience, skills training or through change of job. Moreover, time also tends to imply increased *quality* of competence as practitioners sharpen their knowledge and skills. Though service-users can reasonably expect to receive at the very least a competent service, rarely would they have the time to wait for professionals to perfectly hone their skills. Yet reality dictates that all practitioners will almost always be at differing levels of skills development. Service-users may identify with Mark Friedman's 'accountability by results' approach, as presented in his ambitiously titled book, *Trying Hard is Not Good Enough* (Friedman, 2005), in which he reminds and urges professionals to always consider the relevance of competence and accountability from the service-users' point of view. There is a variety of public mechanisms to regulate and ensure the ability and competence of practitioners.

Public mechanisms of professional accountability

Professional registration and conduct committees

Individual professionals are accountable and responsible to their statutory bodies and usually this accountability is regulated through the work of professional conduct committees. These committees can expect accountability from their registered members and decisions about a member's continued registration depend heavily on the quality of that accountability and the responsibilities involved. Most professions also have requirements for those persons registered to keep their registration up to date by completing additional training, and to expand their professional experience. Professional conduct committees cannot, however, impose financial liability on professionals, as they do not have the statutory power to impose a financial obligation – only a court currently has that power. What they can do in the most serious cases, though, is to remove a name from a register and effectively deny an individual the right to practise.

Working along the lines of a tribunal, there are professional conduct committees such as the NMC (Nursing and Midwifery Council), which looks at 'professional misconduct' in nursing. If cases are proven, these organisations may remove an individual's name from the register. For social workers to practise, registration is required with a UK nation specific 'care council'. Social workers are subsequently accountable for their conduct by the requirement to conform with the codes of conduct relating to the Social Care Register. A social care worker may be de-registered for a breach of the code of practice, whether or not the behaviour occurred during the working day. In 2006, for example, a social worker from Darlington was suspended from the register for two years for advertising herself as an escort via a website associated with prostitution. (http://www.gscc.org.uk/News+ nd+events/Media+releases/2006+archive/ – for this and other cases of de-registration by the GSCC, last accessed 20/02/2007).

Ombudsmen

The role of ombudsmen is to secure a satisfactory redress for complaints. They seek to remedy injustice and are not authorised to discipline those held responsible. Ombudsmen are 'the independent upholder[s] of the highest standards of efficient and fair administration' (Whyatt, 1961: 77, quoted in Allsop and Mulcahy, 1996: 56). There are several ombudsmen who oversee particular areas. Some of them, such as the Health Service Commissioner and the Commissioners for Local Administration, have a basis in statutory law; but others, such as the Banking Ombudsman and the Corporate Estate Agents Ombudsman, are private schemes established and funded by the relevant industry (Allsop and Mulcahy, 1996). The Local Government Ombudsmen investigate complaints of injustice arising from maladministration by local authorities and certain other public bodies; for example, education appeal committees, national parks authorities and fire authorities.

In January 2006 the Local Government Ombudsman's office reported on a case they had investigated recently concerning 'maladministration causing injustice' (LGO, 2006). The parents of a young man with severe physical and communication disabilities, who had been moved by the Council through a number of residential placements, complained that the Council had failed to meet their son's true needs and had failed to respond properly to the family's complaints on his behalf. Upon investigation, the Ombudsman upheld the complaint, finding maladministration causing injustice. A recommendation was made that the Council pay the young man £5,000 and pay his parents £2,000 in compensation. It was also recommended that the Council write to the young man directly, explaining the changes that had been made as a result of the complaint.

Inspection and regulation

Increasingly in recent years there have been many additional external third-party agencies established to inspect and regulate the work of social care and health. While systems such as these have been present for many years, increased privatisation and changes to management structures in public sector organisations have led successive governments to intensify their efforts to demonstrate that accountability can be proved by inspection and measurement, not simply assumed to be present, in services delivered by trained professionals.

Examples of such agencies include: the National Institute for Clinical Excellence (NICE); the Healthcare Commission; the Audit Commission; the Health and Safety Executive; the Mental Health Act Commission; the Commission for Equality and Human Rights; and the office of the Data Protection Registrar. Agencies such as these can at times respond to individual complaints or concerns from members of the public, but often they are engaged in monitoring the delivery of specific government programmes or policy initiatives in something of a 'policing' role. It is clear that the foreseeable future will include close inspection and regulation which, in all probability, is likely to increase (Walshe, 2002).

Conclusion

In this chapter we have focused on four dimensions of accountability – social, ethical, legal and professional – and how, as an individual, an employee and/or as a professional, accountability has impacted upon daily practice within health and social care. Accountable practice acknowledges elements of risk. This awareness will help in understanding the complexities of practice and this, in turn, will help practitioners to generate more informed decisions and to give an account of these decisions in the diverse contexts in which such an account is required.

References

Allsop, J. and Mulcahy, L. (1996) *Regulating Medical Work*. Buckingham: Open University Press.

Annandale, E. (1998) 'Working on the front line: risk culture and nursing in the new NHS', in M. Allott and M. Robb (eds), *Understanding Health and Social Care: An Introductory Reader*. London: Sage. pp. 279–86.

Banks, S. (1995) *Ethics and Values in Social Work*. Basingstoke: Macmillan and BASW.

Banks, S. and Williams, R. (2005). 'Accounting for ethical difficulties in social welfare work: issues, problems and dilemmas', *British Journal of Social Work*, 35: 1005–22.

Batey, M. and Lewis, F. (1982) 'Clarifying autonomy and accountability in nursing service: Part 1', *Journal of Nursing Administration*, 12 (9) (September): 13–18.

Bauman, Z. (1995) *Life in Fragments*. Cambridge: Polity Press.

Bauman, Z. (1996) 'On communitarians and human freedom: or how to square the circle', *Theory, Culture and Society*, 13 (2): 79–90.

Beck, U. (1992) *Risk Society: Towards a New Modernity*. London: Sage.

Bergman, R. (1981) 'Accountability – definition and dimensions', *International Nursing Review*, 28 (2): 53–9.

Bird, R. (1983) *Osborn's Concise Law Dictionary* (7th edn). London: Sweet & Maxwell.

Brammer, A. (2007) *Social Work Law* (2nd edn). Edinburgh: Pearson Education Ltd.

Brykczynska, G. (1995) 'Working with children: accountability and paediatric nursing', in R. Watson (ed.), *Accountability in Nursing Practice*. London: Chapman & Hall. pp. 147–60.

Buttny, R. (1993) *Social Accountability in Communication*. London: Sage.

Carson, D. (1990) 'Taking risks with patients – your assessment strategy', in *Professional Nurse: The Staff Nurse's Survival Guide*. London: Austen Cornish. pp. 83–7.

Cervi, B. (1996) 'Blasts from the past', *Community Care*, 1131 (1–7 August): 16–17.

Chadwick, R. and Tadd, W. (1992) *Ethics and Nursing Practice*. Basingstoke: Macmillan.

Clark, C. (2006) 'Moral Character in Social Work', *British Journal of Social Work*, 36: 75–89.

Cooke, J. (1997) *Law of Tort* (3rd edn). London: Pitman Publishing.

Davies, A. (2002) 'Structures and accountability', in L. Kendall and L. Harker (eds). *From Welfare to Wellbeing – the Future of Social Care*. London: Institute for Public Policy Research. pp. 94–121.

Department of Trade and Industry (1999) 'New protection for whistleblowers starts in July', Press Release P/99/480, 8 June. (http://www.nds.coi.gov.uk/coi/coipress.n...f19ec4c5bf38025678a 0052c550?OpenDocument – accessed 04.07.99).

Dowling, S, et al. (1996) 'Nurses taking on junior doctors' work: a confusion of accountability', *British Medical Journal*, 312 (11 May): 1211–14.

Duff, L. (1995) 'Standards of care, quality assurance and accountability', in R. Watson (ed.), *Accountability in Nursing Practice.* London: Chapman & Hall. pp. 49–69.

Eby, M. (1994a) 'Whistle blowing', in V. Tschudin (ed.), *Ethics: Conflicts of Interest.* London: Scutari Press. pp. 56–84.

Eby, M. (1994b) *The Law and Ethics of General Practice.* Beckenham: Publishing Initiatives.

Eby, M. (1994c) *Legal Issues in Nursing Practice.* Beckenham: Publishing Initiatives.

Eraut, M. (1994) *Developing Professional Knowledge and Competence.* London: Falmer Press.

Fallon, P, et al. (1999) *Report on the Committee of Inquiry into the Personality Disorder Unit, Ashworth Special Hospital*, vol. I, Cm 4194-II. London: HMSO.

Fowler, M. and Levine-Ariff, J. (1987) *Ethics at the Bedside.* Philadelphia, PA: J.B. Lippincott.

French, P. (1993) *Responsibility Matters.* Lawrence KS: Kansas University Press.

Friedman, M. (2005) *Trying Hard is Not Good Enough.* Crewe: Trafford Publishing.

Giddens, A. (1991) *The Consequences of Modernity.* Cambridge: Polity Press.

Giddens, A. (1994) *Beyond Left and Right.* Cambridge: Polity Press.

Gonzi, A., Hager, P. and Athanasou, J. (1993) *The Development of Competency-Based Assessment Strategies for the Professions*, National Office of Overseas Skills Recognition Research, Paper No. 8. Canberra: Australian Government Publishing Service.

Hacking, I. (1975) *The Emergence of Probability: A Philosophical Study of Early Ideas about Probability, Induction and Statistical Inference.* Cambridge: Cambridge University Press.

Hall, R.H. (1968) 'Professionalisation and bureaucratisation', *American Sociological Review*, 33: 92–104.

Hendrick, J. (1993) *Child Care Law for Health Professionals.* Oxford: Radcliffe Medical Press.

Heyman, B. (1998) *Risk, Health and Health Care: A Qualitative Approach.* London: Edward Arnold.

Higgs, P. (1998) 'Risk, governmentality and the reconceptualization of citizenship', in G. Scambler and P. Higgs (eds), *Modernity, Medicine and Health: Medical Sociology Towards 2000.* London: Routledge. pp. 176–97.

HMSO (1999) Statutory Instrument 1999 No. 1549. London: Her Majesty's Stationery Office.

Hoggett, B. (1993) *Parents and Children* (4th edn). London: Sweet & Maxwell.

Holden, R. (1991) 'Responsibility and autonomous nursing practice', *Journal of Advanced Nursing.* 16: 398–403.

Hunt, G. (1995) *Whistle blowing in the Health Service: Accountability, Law and Professional Practice.* London: Edward Arnold.

Jones, R. (1994) *Mental Health Act Manual* (4th edn). London: Sweet & Maxwell.

Kirkup, J. and Peev, G. (2006) '1.3m benefit fraud tip-offs end in only 4,000 convictions', *The Scotsman*, 31 August, p. 6.

Knight, B. (1992) *Legal Aspects of Medical Practice* (5th edn). Edinburgh: Churchill Livingstone.

Lennane, K. (1993) 'Whistle blowing: a health issue', *British Medical Journal*, 307 (11 September): 667–70.

LGO (2006), *Maladministration Causing Injustice*, Essex County Council (05/A/880), Office of the Local Government Ombudsmen. http://www.lgo.org.uk/socserv.htm (last accessed 28.12.06), reported 16 January 2006

Local Government Ombudsman (1997) *Digest of Cases.* London: HMSO.

Marks-Maran, D. (1993) 'Accountability', in V. Tschudin (ed.), *Ethics: Nurses and Patients.* London: Scutari Press. pp. 121–34.

McGann, S. (1995) 'The development of nursing as an accountable profession', in R. Watson (ed.), *Accountability in Nursing Practice.* London, Chapman & Hall. pp. 18–29.

Menzies, I. (1960) 'A case study in the functioning of social systems as a defence against anxiety: a report on a study of the nursing service of a general hospital', *Human Relations*, 13 (2): 95–121.

Musil, L., Kubalčíková, K., Hubíková, O. and Nečasová, M. (2004) 'Do social workers avoid the dilemmas of work with clients?' *European Journal of Social Work*, 7 (3) (November): 305–19.

Nolan, M.P. (1995) *Standards in Public Life: First Report of the Committee on Standards in Public Life*, Cm 2850. London: HMSO.

Nursing and Midwifery Council (2004) *Nursing and Midwifery Code of Professional Conduct: Standards to Conduct, Performance and Ethics*. London: Nursery and Midwifery Council.

O'Donnell, A. (1996) 'Legal and quasi-legal accountability', in R. Pyper (ed.), *Aspects of Accountability in the British System of Government*. Wirral, Merseyside: Tudor Business Publishing. pp. 82–118.

Payne, M. (2005) *Modern Social Work Theory*. Basingstoke: Palgrave Macmillan.

Rodgers, S. (1995) 'Accountability in primary nursing', in R. Watson (ed.), *Accountability in Nursing Practice*. London: Chapman & Hall. pp. 70–91.

Royal College of Nursing (RCN) (1998) *Guidance for Nurses on Clinical Governance*. London: RCN.

Scottish Executive (2003) *Standards in Social Work Education*. Edinburgh: Scottish Executive.

Shipman Inquiry (2005) The Sixth Report – Shipman: The Final Report, The Shipman Inquiry,

Skolbekken, J. (1995) 'The risk epidemic in medical journals', *Social Science and Medicine*, 40: 291–305.

Smith, R. (1999) 'Editor's choice: if in doubt, start an inquiry', *British Medical Journal*, 318 (27 February).

Standards in Social Work Education (SiSWE) (2003), Scottish Executive, http://www.scotland.gov.uk/Publications/2003/01/16202/17015

Stevens, M. (2006) 'Moral Positioning: Service User Experiences of Challenging Behaviour in Learning Disability Services', *British Journal of Social Work*, 36: 955–78.

Tingle, J. (1998a) 'Legal aspects of expanded role and clinical guidelines and protocols', in J. McHale, J. Tingle and J. Peysner (eds), *Law and Nursing*. Oxford: Butterworth Heinemann. pp. 49–60.

Tingle, J. (1998b) 'Nursing negligence: general issues', in J. McHale, J. Tingle and J. Peysner (eds), *Law and Nursing*. Oxford: Butterworth Heinemann. pp. 16–33.

Training Organisation for Social Services (2004) *The National Occupational Standards for Social Work*. Leeds: Training Organisation for Social Services.

United Kingdom Central Council for Nursing, Midwifery and Health Visiting (UKCC) (1996b) *Issues Arising from Professional Conduct Complaints*. London: UKCC.

United Kingdom Central Council for Nursing, Midwifery and Health Visiting (UKCC) (1998) *Statistical Analysis of the UKCC Professional Register 1 April 1997 to 31 March 1998*, vol. 5, *Professional Conduct Statistics* (July). London: UKCC.

Vinten, G. (1994) *Whistle Blowing: Subversion or Corporate Citizenship?* London: Paul Chapman.

Wagner, R. (1989) *Accountability in Education: A Philosophical Inquiry*. New York: Routledge.

Walshe, K. (2002) 'The rise of regulation in the NHS', *British Medical Journal*, 324 (20 April): 967–70.

Whyatt, J. (1961) *The Citizen and the Administration: The Redress of Grievances*. London: Stevens.

Winfield, M. (1994) 'Whistleblowers as corporate safety net', in G. Vinten (ed.), *Whistle Blowing: Subversion or Corporate Citizenship?*. London: Paul Chapman. pp. 21–32.

Chapter 12

Understanding the policy process

Celia Davies[1]

Everywhere I go, the senior people tell me of progress, of better working methods and value for money, of objectives achieved, of changes delivered. Everywhere I go, I also glimpse another world, a world inhabited by everyone else – a world of daily crisis, and concern, of staff under pressure and services struggling to deliver. Both worlds are real in the minds of those who inhabit them. Both worlds are supported by objective evidence. Both views are held sincerely.

(Jarrold, 1996, quoted in Hadley and Clough, 1996: 192)

This comment was prompted by the many visits to health care services and facilities that Ken Jarrold made in the mid-1990s as part of his responsibility as Director of Human Resources in the NHS Executive. It describes a profound gulf between different kinds of staff in the delivery of health care. The senior people (general managers and clinical directors) were telling him that the policy changes of the early 1990s were working. They were saying that the new health authorities and trusts in their relationships as purchasers and competitive providers had indeed generated entrepreneurial zeal, prompted new and better ways of working and overall been a spur to positive change and better value for money. Those delivering the service were telling him otherwise. These people felt on the receiving end of policy changes that left them under enormous pressure, starved of resources, barely coping, and suffering from stress and low morale.

The position is almost certainly more complex than this. Within the senior ranks, for example, it has been shown that the enthusiasts for the policy reforms of the early 1990s were more likely to be the new non-executive directors. The sceptics, on the other hand, were more likely to be managers who had had long years of service in a different tradition (Ferlie et al., 1996). The same set of studies also suggests divisions among professionals, with some keen to take on the new hybrid roles of clinical managers and directors and others deeply suspicious of the ideas associated with this. So what are we to make of such divisions and divided ideas about the nature and impact of policy?

---

[1]With thanks to Janet Seden for her section 'From paper policies to good practice'.

In this chapter I examine the policy process. First, some of the different answers that students of public policy have given to the question 'How does policy get made?' are considered. Second, the growing scope that new policy thinking is providing to help practitioners and others to develop and shape policies at local level is explored. We shall see that the old model – the one that presumed policy was a rational process, taking place at the top of organisations and requiring tight control of implementation – is being replaced. A new model is starting to emerge. It recognises policy as a complex and altogether messier process, with more participants, much experimentation and multiple feedback loops. In the era of transition from the Conservative governments of the 1980s and early 1990s to the policy changes that have been created under Labour, this is an important theme for all who work in health and social care.

Policy as 'rational decision making'?

It is a comforting kind of common sense to assume that new policies emerge out of a process of decision making that is essentially rational. Policy-makers set out the goals to be achieved and gather relevant information. In the light of the information, they select the best course of action to enable the goals to be met. Later they review progress and make adaptations. Such a model can be applied to governments, to organisations of all kinds, as well as to daily life. In a classic work, first published over forty years ago, American political scientist Herbert Simon questioned this. Real-world decision makers, he argued, are not 'maximisers' (selecting the best possible option from all that are available), but 'satisficers' (looking for a course of action that is good enough for the problem at hand). It was important to understand that people intended to act rationally, and they should probably be encouraged to do this – but 'bounded rationality' described their behaviour better (Simon, 1958).

The idea of the policy process as a set of rational steps remains. It is often portrayed as a cycle – looping round from an initial specification of the goal, through information gathering and so on, to an evaluation, which then sets the process in motion once again (Figure 12.1). The idea of an orderly and rational progression is still strong.

Questions can be asked about each one of these stages in the real world of public policy-making. Where do goals come from (step 1)? How do issues get on to the national agenda for policy-making in the first place? Political parties may identify them in their manifestos and proceed to follow through their manifesto commitments when elected to office. But this only raises further questions about how decisions were taken about what was to be a manifesto issue, and how other issues emerge and are rejected or selected during a term of office. Take, for example, the case of changes in maternity policy in the NHS that were heralded by the publication *Changing Childbirth* (DoH, 1993). Where did the pressures come from that resulted in the statements this policy contains about the need for greater choice and for a 'woman-centred approach'? Who listened to whom and why?

Then there is the question (step 2) of exactly what kinds of information are seen as relevant to be gathered and what process of information gathering over what time frame is seen as appropriate. *Changing Childbirth* is again a good example. There were influential lobbying bodies not only from the medical profession and from midwifery but also from organisations such as the National Childbirth Trust and the Association for Improvement

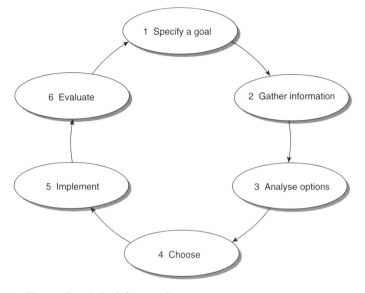

Figure 12.1   The rational decision cycle
(Source: adapted from Parsons, 1995: 77)

of Maternity Services. Who was on the committee and how alert they might have been to the government agenda of the time are also relevant to the shaping of policy (see Brooks, 1999). Asking such questions politicises the policy cycle, making it altogether less neatly rational and self-contained than the model suggests. It also allows comparisons over time. How, for example, does this older policy process compare with that around a more recent document prepared by the 'czar' concerned with potential service reconfiguration (Dott, 2007)?

Continuing to question the rational decision cycle, how are options analysed (step 3)? Today, formal techniques of expert option appraisal and policy analysis using statistical modelling are sometimes brought into play. However, these need to be seen as part of the information from which a choice is made rather than the mechanism for choice itself. To get at that (step 4), you might choose to listen to the debate in the House of Commons, or try to interview the civil servants. Sometimes, at least, you would want to prise open the closed doors of the Cabinet. 'Implement' (step 5) is less straightforward than it seems, as Box 12.1 demonstrates. Finally, different ways of evaluating (step 6) may produce very different notions of the next step.

Box 12.1   A classic study of policy implementation

In the early 1970s, two American political scientists studied the implementation of an economic development programme in Oakland, California. The aim was to establish permanent jobs for a long-term-unemployed minority ethnic workforce. The programme had involved

(Continued)

(Continued)

the construction and fitting of an aircraft hangar, bringing together employers and shaping their recruitment policies, and establishing a government-sponsored training programme for aircraft mechanics. A new agency was created to oversee this, substantial federal funds were allocated, local officials and employers agreed to participate. Why, then, with apparently everything in favour, were the results so poor? The authors trace in detail the different chains of decision making and where they had to mesh. They point out that a policy is not just about the first links in a complex causal chain, but all the subsequent ones too. And when circumstances change, adjustments and alterations need to be made. The authors set aside the idea that we need always to find the single point of implementation failure. In so complex a process, it is not necessarily the implementation but the ambition of the initial target-setting that is at fault. Policy and implementation, they argue, need to be brought more closely together. They offer the challenging observation that:

> our normal expectation should be that new programs will fail to get off the ground and that, at best, they will take considerable time to get started. The cards in this world are stacked against things happening, so much so that effort is required to make them move. The remarkable thing is that new programs work at all.

(Pressman and Wildavsky, 1973: 109)

In his memorably titled essay on 'the science of muddling through', Charles Lindblom (1959) argued that practical decision making involved something altogether less grandiose than a rational decision cycle. Policy developed, he suggested, through 'incrementalism': a policy 'is tried, altered, tried in its altered form, altered again and so forth' (Braybrooke and Lindblom, 1963). This at least had the advantage of testing the water and not making serious mistakes. The work of writers such as Simon, Lindblom, and Pressman and Wildavsky led others to see just how unrealistic it was to strive for control of implementation. To set out the conditions for 'perfect implementation' (see Box 12.2) is to show that they are never going to be met.

Box 12.2   The conditions for 'perfect implementation'

1. The circumstances external to the implementing agency do not impose crippling constraints.
2. Adequate time and sufficient resources are made available to the programme.
3. The required combination of resources is actually available.
4. The policy to be implemented is based on a valid theory of cause and effect.
5. The relationship between cause and effect is direct and there are few, if any, intervening links.

(Continued)

6. Dependency relationships are minimal.
7. There is understanding of, and agreement on, objectives.
8. Tasks are fully specified in correct sequence.
9. There is perfect communication and co-ordination.
10. Those in authority can demand and obtain perfect compliance.

(*Source*: adapted from Hogwood and Gunn, 1984, quoted in Hill, 1997: 130–31)

Is the rational decision-making model thoroughly discredited? Colebatch (1998), an Australian political scientist who has recently reviewed the concept of policy, is among many who feel that it must be kept in play but also kept in its place. Those working within the policy process do strive towards a process of appraising options. They do call for evidence and they seek to marshal it in systematic ways. They present policies as the outcome of such a rational process of appraisal even if their rationales are sometimes post hoc. Actors' understandings of themselves as working in this way must have a place in the analysis. But the overall process is more complex.

Colebatch offers a useful diagram blending a vertical and a horizontal dimension of the policy process (see Figure 12.2).

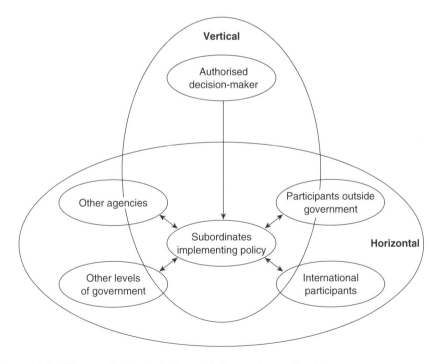

Figure 12.2   The vertical and horizontal dimensions of policy
(Source: Colebatch, 1998: 38)

The vertical dimension draws attention to the way in which those who are in legitimate positions of authority – particularly government ministers – transmit decisions downwards for implementation. The horizontal dimension refers to those outside the line of hierarchical authority who none the less are linked together in various ways and have an important role in mobilising opinion and lobbying. Both dimensions are part of the policy process. Each is linked to the other and the answer to the question of where policy is made involves both.

The point, Colebatch argues, is not to try to 'rescue' policy from the messy politics in which it is entangled, deleting the horizontal dimension and trying to ensure greater rationality in the vertical dimension. Instead, the job of policy analysis is to understand the multiple and sometimes conflicting facets of the policy process that contribute to multiple outcomes – some intended and some unintended. Colebatch urges those who would understand policy:

- to resist the idea of a single person or group of policy-makers – ask not, 'Who makes policy?' but 'Who participates in the policy?'
- to resist the notion of policy being made in a place (at the top) – ask not, 'Where are decisions taken?' but 'What networks, links and policy communities group around this issue?'
- to resist the idea of a single policy decision, which is the key determinant of practice – ask not, 'What is the policy framework for this setting?' but 'What is shaping behaviour in this practice setting?'

This suggests that the policy process is complex but is also necessarily provisional and fallible. If so, then the logic may well be to call for more not less participation. While it may be right to assume that considerable work is done to explore and evaluate policy options at senior level in the civil service or in policy division in a local authority or elsewhere, this work is only one input to the policy process. Should other inputs not be encouraged to broaden and deepen the policy?

We can begin to recognise that there are multiple stakeholders who have an interest in this process, and they should perhaps be more explicitly involved as policy is being decided. We might also observe that certain stakeholder groups sometimes need to be fostered and developed so that their voices can be heard. This is the theme of the next section.

Developing stakeholder thinking

A stakeholder has been defined as 'any group or individual that can affect or is affected by the achievement of an organisation's purpose' (Freeman, 1984, quoted in Winstanley et al., 1995: 20). Different stakeholders come into play in different areas of policy. We have already referred to some of the lobbying groups in the area of maternity policy. Stakeholders also sometimes form alliances in the policy process and exert strong influence by doing so. Stakeholder thinking can be used both to examine and contrast the way in which particular issues have been framed and discussed, and to ask who is included in and who is excluded from this and whether there is change over time. Stakeholders need to be seen as all those with an interest in an outcome and more or less power to affect it. It may be as well to remember here that the term 'stakeholder' derives from the practice of pioneers driving a stake into the ground to signify their ownership of new territory; they were sometimes oblivious to the indigenous population who might well have had a prior claim to the same land.

The stakeholder power matrix

Winstanley and her colleagues (1995) have developed what they call a 'stakeholder power matrix' and applied it to both NHS and local authority settings. They argue that there are two broad kinds of power. The first, which they call criteria power, is the power to define the aims and purposes of the service, to design the overall system of provision, set the performance criteria and carry out evaluations. Governments vest this power in particular departments and ministries or delegate it in varying proportions to local government or to appointed agencies. The second kind of power is operational power – this is the power of those who actually provide the service to decide how it should be done by allocating resources or deploying knowledge and skills in a particular way. These distinctions, the authors suggest, relate to the well-established theme of power as multi-dimensional, as being shaped not only by overt decisions but also by more covert methods.

Figure 12.3 allows the position of stakeholders to be plotted according to these kinds of power. Government as a stakeholder, for example, might be strong on defining purpose and setting systems in place but weak as far as operational controls are concerned. This makes it a stakeholder in quadrant A of the diagram, arm's length power, and represents the situation where the gap between the policy pronouncements and experience on the ground is particularly marked. However, if the government has mechanisms in place to ensure that its policy pronouncements are worked through in detail and the behaviour of service-providers and users is closely controlled, then it is in quadrant B. Where a group of service-provider stakeholders has a lot of day-to-day freedom to shape the service, however, they are in quadrant D, operational power. Where stakeholders have neither the power to set the purpose of the services nor the power to influence day-to-day operation, they are in quadrant C – disempowered. Both service-providers and service-users can sometimes fit into this quadrant.

> Within the NHS, for example, there is a current issue of whether the reforms have actually created the conditions in which patients, carers and lower levels of staff are moving out of this corner, and if so whether they are moving vertically, horizontally or diagonally.
>
> (Winstanley et al., 1995: 21)

Winstanley and her colleagues used this matrix to begin to analyse changes in local authority services and the NHS over time. They suggest that the Conservative governments of the 1980s and 1990s, for example, having created the purchaser–provider split, were committed to a central government move from quadrant B to quadrant A. Clients and patients, starting at the left-hand extreme of quadrant C, have perhaps made some small moves diagonally upwards – gaining a little more of both kinds of power, albeit indirectly

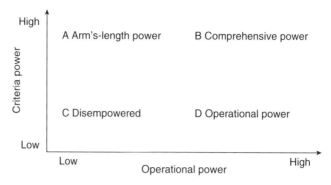

Figure 12.3   The stakeholder power matrix
(Source: Winstanley et al. 1995: 21)

through the operation of patient's charters and the requirements that service-purchasers and commissioners respond to consumer need.

Others with practical aims of bringing stakeholders into the policy process have used the stakeholder concept in a different way (see Box 12.3 for one example). Alternatively, Eden (1996) has described a procedure of gathering interested parties together, getting them to identify the different stakeholders in a policy arena and to map them as closer or further away from the centres of power. He then shows how this stakeholder-mapping exercise could be sketched as a set of concentric circles, with some groups in the inner circle and others in the middle or outer ones. Mapping of this sort enables participants to articulate for themselves the potential alliances that they could form in developing a new policy direction.

Box 12.3   Using stakeholder analysis – The Netherlands

The Dutch government is committed to finding ways of involving stakeholders in decisions. It sees itself as at the centre of a network of influence rather than at the top of a hierarchy taking authoritative decisions. Two key steps in creating a more interactive process are (a) making the different stakeholders explicit by brainstorming a list and (b) facilitating group working to ensure that knowledge is shared and mutual understanding is enhanced.

The following are examples of projects stemming from this philosophy.

1   Central government level – the development of a national environmental policy plan by one-day meetings with eighteen stakeholder groups given drafts of the preliminary chapters of the policy and asked to do a SWOT analysis (strengths, weaknesses, opportunities and threats) and then to develop their own draft of the next chapter on key issues.
2   Regional level – establishing a new policy for the Amsterdam–Rhine Canal by allowing four stakeholder groups, located in each corner of the room, time to develop a written

(Continued)

plan and then asking them to rotate to review and add comments to each of the other groups' plans in turn, ending with a revision of their original plans in the light of the comments.

3   Municipal level – developing a shared cultural policy between two municipalities by deliberately 'pairing' individuals from each municipality and giving them tasks to work on and present jointly to the whole group, rather than letting those from each municipality keep together as a group.

4   City ward level – establishing priorities for a day nursery policy by bringing together aldermen, civil servants, managers of day nurseries and day nursery leaders to identify a list of issues, then, with each member having four sticky-backed coloured dots to assign importance to issues, letting the ensuing dot count generate the priority listing for further work.

(*Source*: derived from de Jong, 1996)

De Jong (1996), working in the Netherlands, takes a different approach (as you saw in Box 12.3). He explains the Dutch government's commitment to get away from the familiar position where it is the civil servants who draft policies and where sending drafts out for consultation results in a series of position statements which the civil servants can then easily ignore. Instead, they devised several ways to help stakeholders identify issues and actually work together on priorities. This kind of approach, which could in principle be used at different levels of the policy process, enables new solutions to emerge and creates what has been called 'collaborative advantage' (see Huxham, 1996).

All these examples offer the potential not only of a much richer understanding of the policy process but also of its practical development beyond the model that sees it only as a set of rational calculations made by one group at one particular point in a hierarchical organisation.

Beyond stakeholder thinking?

If these are some of the benefits and potentials of stakeholder thinking, does it have weaknesses? Focusing on the interactions between the stakeholders who are actually present, or who are acknowledged by those who are present to be stakeholders, has its limitations.

First, there are often potential stakeholders on any specific issue who may not always be brought into a policy process. Concentrating on the stakeholders who come forward (even those who come forward to brainstorm who the stakeholders are) may thus serve to narrow the analysis and obscure particular perspectives on the issue. *Changing Childbirth* (DoH, 1993) provides an example in its treatment of women from black and minority ethnic groups. The document contains a broad statement about respecting the wishes of women from minority ethnic groups. But, to use the words of a later study concerning the experiences of Pakistani women with maternity services in Scotland, minority voices are often 'muted voices' (Bowes and Domokos, 1996) and imaginative and sensitive ways are needed to encourage them to be heard. Bowes and Domokos suggest that, even where there have been special service initiatives, these can construct South Asian women as 'a problem', rather than finding effective ways of working alongside them to determine what the issues are (see also Parsons et al., 1993). The consultation strategy of *Changing Childbirth* is relevant here. Efforts were made to gather minority group views in a survey and to hear perspectives from minority ethnic communities in a consensus conference, but the expert group used the usual process of issuing a general invitation for interested parties to state views, and waiting for groups to come forward. It did not actively encourage women to get together and create dialogue in the way that some forms of stakeholder analysis are now doing.

Secondly, identification as a stakeholder does not grant stakeholders power. Even where stakeholders are present, they may face difficulties in articulating their perspectives or in getting them heard. It is all too easy for a minority arguing for something new to be constrained by the weight of the traditional thinking of the majority, to struggle against incomprehension and against those who use their experience to put apparently insuperable obstacles in the way. Stakeholders may need to take forms of action other than – or as well as – participation in a policy process if they want their viewpoint to prevail. A stakeholder process thus runs the risk of failing to uncover the underlying values and ideologies and the interests that they serve; of not recognising taken-for-granted assumptions, the prior framing of issues that, left unchallenged, supports the status quo and means that a critical consideration of the full set of alternatives remains to be made.

Is it possible to use a stakeholder analysis to get to the heart of some of the strengths and weaknesses of a particular policy? Is it possible to use it to tease out some of the aspects of power that may otherwise remain hidden? A key way of doing this, we suggest, is through developing the concept of provenance, which can bring stakeholder thinking into alignment with the acknowledgement of the multiple and messy character of the policy process outlined on pp. 204–8. Dictionary definitions of 'provenance' explain that it refers to the source or origins of a phenomenon, and derives literally from the Latin, meaning 'coming forth'. Using this starting-point, Box 12.4 has a checklist of questions that might be asked of a particular policy initiative. Working with questions such as these is likely to reveal not just the obvious stakeholders but the factors influencing the powerful players, the groups who are missing and the issues that do not reach the agenda at all.

Local level – from policy implementation to policy development

Is there always a gap between policy and practice or at the least a tension between what is on paper and what happens in the real world? This section begins with a return to the question of 'implementation' of policy discussed on pp. 206–8. By seeing policy not as something that is given to people to implement but as something to be owned and developed by them, outcomes can be more positive. It may be that we have expected either too much or too little from policy pronouncements from the top.

Box 12.4   Examining the provenance of a policy – a summary checklist

1. **Primary purpose**
   What is the nature of this new idea? What are the problems it seeks to address? What is the vision that underlies it?

2. **Precedents**
   Where does the idea come from? (Does it borrow from another sector/another field of activity/another country?) Who initiated it? What are the assumptions that underpin it? What sets of values, principles and ideals are on display?

3. **Priorities**
   What pressure is there for a solution to this problem? How important is it – and for whom – to resolve this policy issue?

4. **Participants**
   Who are the existing stakeholders with an interest in this? What is their interest and what support are they giving/withholding? Who is most strongly championing it and why? How much access has each group got to the policy process and what is the likelihood that they will be heard?

5. **Processes and procedures**
   Who is to implement it? What training is being suggested? What financial resources are seen as required? What other support for development has been provided or assumed? What timetables are envisaged? How will resistance be responded to?

6. **Practicalities**
   What particular approvals will have to be obtained? Who needs to co-operate with whom to make this work? What resistances is it likely to encounter? Where will they come from? What form will resistance take? What other local agendas does it dovetail/clash with?

7. **Perversities**
   What are the unanticipated consequences (positive and negative) that this policy has had/will have? What by-products has it produced/will it produce for people not directly involved?

8. **Perspectives**
   (If hindsight is possible) in what sense was it a feature of its time? Did it link with other measures in ways not seen until later? Did it work as part of a wider agenda? Did it help build for the future?

Paper policies and daily practice

In a classic study published in 1980 in the USA, Michael Lipsky was concerned to explain how individuals – as citizens and as workers – experience public policies and how the aggregate of their actions comes to shape that policy. He argues:

> that public policy is not best understood as made in legislatures or top-floor suites of high-ranking administrators, because in important ways it is actually made in the crowded offices and daily encounters of street-level workers.

(Lipsky, 1980: xii)

Lipsky coined the term 'street-level bureaucrats' to refer to a wide array of employees, including teachers, social workers, police officers and others, who deal face-to-face with clients, making decisions to provide benefits or offer services. He recognises that they were working with a welter of policy documents, rules and guidelines, but observed that they often performed quite contrary to the rules. They favoured some clients over others and the effects of their behaviour at times actually minimised citizens' seeking of welfare benefits and services. To understand this, Lipsky argues, 'we need to know how the rules are experienced by workers in the organisation and to what other pressures they are subject' (1980: xi).

Street-level bureaucrats, Lipsky explains, come into their chosen area of work because of their high ideals, and have a strong commitment to the work they do. But they then face a harsh reality of high caseloads, huge classes, and so on. If they are not to drop out or burn out, they must find ways of dealing with this. Some practise a form of psychological withdrawal. Others genuinely see themselves as struggling to mitigate the worst effects of the system and work hard not to become cynical or withdrawn. They sincerely feel that they are doing their best under adverse circumstances. Yet their actions taken together serve to pervert the service ideal. Service-users are rarely in a position to challenge. They often lack the resources and understanding to question what is offered or not offered to them. If they do understand their rights and entitlements, they risk antagonising the workers by speaking out. If they organise collectively, they may get labelled as trouble-makers. Lipsky saw no point in trying to tighten the rules further: 'the fact is that we must have people making decisions and treating other citizens in the public services' (1980: xv). The solution must be sought, he felt, in the structure of the work and in reconstituting policy. Policies should state what they want workers to do and, where objectives are in conflict, documents should indicate what is to take priority. Agencies should be able to measure workers' performance, to make meaningful comparisons between them and have relevant incentives and sanctions. For more recent work, see Evans and Harris (2004) on Lipsky, and Schofield and Sausman (2004) on processes of policy 'implementation'.

How relevant is all this to the UK today? In some instances, policy documents are not so much subverted as ignored. Staff do not consider them as resources that might be of use in their day-to-day practice. And where staff are aware of policies, they may judge them to be unrealistic or irrelevant. Emma's story provides one case in point.

Case Study   Emma's story – policies and practices

Emma was a senior home care assistant working for a local authority in the south of England in 2000. She had been working in home care for less than two years. She was a single parent who had missed out on education and spent years at home. Now in her thirties, she was keen and enthusiastic about her job, anxious to gain qualifications, and to get on. She said 'yes' to just about any courses that were on offer. She was rapidly promoted. Emma talked eloquently about the dilemmas of home care work and the challenging situations she and her carers faced and the relentless pressures of the workload. Asked what policy documents guided her, she fell silent for a moment and asked whether she could go away and check. A raft of paper emerged. There was the ring-binder she could not remember when she had last opened. There was an array of leaflets summarising policies, giving information on local services. There was the paperwork from the training courses she had attended. When we looked at this we realised that quite a number of the training events she had attended were actually based on the policy documents in the folder. There were also, she said, two box files at work. She was going to take a look at them the next day – if, that is, she got a moment to do it.

So were any of the many policy documents she held really important to her practice? 'Moving and Handling', she said immediately and the course on diabetes. She could recognise that an elderly lady lying on the floor might be in a diabetic coma and she could advise the emergency services accordingly. These things were about building a knowledge base for carrying out her work. What about the local authority's policy on how to tackle difficult situations? 'Ah,' she said, 'sexual harassment'.

'One of my carers came to me and said she was not prepared to visit a particular elderly man again who was regularly exposing himself to her and masturbating in her presence. I agreed with her that she should not have to put up with that and went to my manager. She said "It's all part of the job, she should be able to handle it." I disagreed. In the end my carer was moved to a different patch. Someone else was brought in. Together we then looked for the written policy. There was one, but it was missing from the file.'

In some areas, however, policy has been developed in great detail, both centrally and locally. Child protection is an important example, where cases in the courts and 'trial by media' have resulted in much energy being devoted to policies and policy guidelines. But with what result?

Research across England and Wales in the mid-1990s indicated uneven development and continuing areas of confusion. The findings suggested that policies were still sometimes being imposed on practitioners rather than being developed with them (see Box 12.5). But things can be different, as the more recent examples in the next sub-section show.

Box 12.5   Policies in practice – child protection

Social workers in child protection report that policies can be of value in clarifying roles and reducing stress. However, a survey of 117 local authorities in England and Wales following the issuing of guidance on policies and procedures once a child's name has been entered in the child protection register found:

27 authorities had policies alone

37 had procedures alone

15 had no documentation at all.

Only two had policies, procedures and guidance, and only one of these had developed standards and an evaluation checklist.

The researchers found that plans for children were unclear, action time-scales varied, and the idea of core group responsibility was blurred. They listed a range of areas where policy and procedures needed to be developed to clarify workers' roles and responsibilities. Guidance, they argued, should be embedded in the real world, acknowledging the pressures being faced so that policies and procedures can become a benchmark for quality rather than a standard against which professionals fail.

(*Source*: adapted from Horwath and Calder, 1998)

From paper policies to good practice in children's services in England: a new assessment framework and a plan for integrated services

At the beginning of the twenty-first century, policies for children's services in England have developed fast. Aldgate et al. (2007) reported on the process of implementing *The Framework for the Assessment of Children in Need and their Families* (Department of Health et al., 2000) in one local authority (Browning Forest). Recognising the tensions inherent in change, they outline the key elements of process (2007: 285–8). These were:

- A critical interplay of factors (for example the proposed policy change fitting the direction managers had intended to take).
- High-level involvement of senior managers.
- Multiple steps to implementation identified for stakeholders.
- Leadership by management.
- Rising to the challenges of moving away from old ways of working.
- The ability of managers to mediate change.

They observed how making the journey from policy initiative through to its reality was a complex process, sometimes messy and not always seamless. The team of practitioners and especially middle managers were 'pivotal in the process' (2007: 289).

Another set of new policy initiatives for children's services were introduced from 2001 onwards, into which *The Framework for the Assessment of Children in Need and their Families* has been integrated. A child death, that of Victoria Climbié in 2000, and the subsequent report (Laming, 2003) became the rationale for the introduction of the government's next agenda for children's services, *Every Child Matters: Change for Children*. A spate of papers emerged from the Department for Education and Skills (DfES 2004a, 2004b) who were gradually taking responsibility for all children's services. This led to the Children Act 2004 which mandated for integrating children's services in local authorities through strategic partnerships. In particular, section 11 specified inter-agency collaboration for children in need under the 1989 Children Act.

Further legislation has followed. The Children Care Act 2006 is meant to 'transform' early years provision. Proposals for the Children Bill 2008 further set the scene for a childcare policy paradigm that aims to support children from their early years through to adulthood. The government's ten-year strategy envisages an interdisciplinary approach to child well-being, led by education as much as social workers or health, with the expectation that local authorities create children's trusts and children's centres. The whole approach is heavily outcomes focused. Other developments such the revised *Working Together to Safeguard Children* (DfES, 2006) and the *Integrated Children's System* (DoH, 2002, implemented in 2006) reinforce the drive towards good interdisciplinary action and information-sharing in child protection cases. The appointment of a children's commissioner might also mean that children's voices are better heard.

Although there are guidance documents, there is no particular blueprint as to how each area will respond to the expectation of creating children's trusts by 2008. Each local authority will need to work out how to bring local partners together to form a strategic partnership. The challenge for each area will again be 'implementation' – how to bring policy into practice at local level in the best way for children, their families and those who work with them. An example of an area which moved ahead early is Cambridgeshire. The social care magazine *Community Care* reported on their quest to integrate children's services (Sale, 2005). So, what did Cambridgeshire council need to do to bring policy from paper into practice? Box 12.6 summarises the process.

Box 12.6   Achieving a children's trust:

- The twenty-one partnership organisations were identified, including social services, district councils, primary care trusts and voluntary bodies.
- Four consultation documents were sent to stakeholders.
- Consultation meetings were held with children, young people, parents and carers.
- A two-year plan was set out.
- The transition plan was formally put to the council.
- Work to implement it was begun.

Source: Sale, 2005

This plan began at the horizontal level (Colebatch, 1998: 38, as shown in Figure 12.2). Only after much work at the horizontal level, in the shape of preparation meetings and consultations, was the written proposal for change taken to the vertical level. There, the authorised decision makers (the council) ratified the transition plan. It is also noticeable that Eric Robinson, the director of social services, had a clear vision for what needed to be achieved, and after the plan was formally agreed continued working to keep practitioners from all the different backgrounds – teachers, libraries, social services, health, leisure, youth offending teams, the fire service and many others – fully involved in the move to integration. He is quoted as saying:

> If you actually believe the rhetoric of building services round the needs of children and young people then you have to do something different to deliver that, otherwise it is all fine words and no action.
>
> (Sale, 2005: 31)

He understood that policy has to be made relevant to children, their families and the practitioners who want to work with them if policy change is to be effective in action, and that effective leadership works to bring people alongside the vision for change:

> This is about hearts and minds. These are public servants who came to do something different for children. What this debate is about is how they can do what they came into the job to do.
>
> (2005: 31)

There are multiple stakeholders, not least the service-users, involved in policy change, so implementation has to take account of diverging perspectives and the complexity of having to involve many participants. Some senior practitioners in Cambridgeshire also spoke to *Community Care* magazine and said:

> If we are successful with this then the children who are underachieving will achieve more. (Director of education, libraries and heritage)
>
> It is about slowly establishing trust and moving forwards at a pace people feel comfortable with, which isn't always easy. (Head of youth offending)
>
> It was a huge concept to imagine … On a personal level it is where am I going to be based, who am I going to be sitting next to? Social work is nothing if it's not about managing change. (Senior social worker, children and families support)
>
> (2005: 32–3)

Aldgate et al. (2007: 263) also highlighted the issues of involving everyone affected by change. Government's view of policy change is often wide-ranging and strategic, for example, 'to bring about radical reform of public services and improve the lives of children, young people and their families in this country'. Rose et al. comment that, as suggested earlier in this chapter, policy is not implemented top-down, but rather:

> Since the mid 1980s a more sophisticated understanding of the difficulties of introducing change in public service agencies can be detected among parts of the policy making community... policy design in different countries of the UK has drawn on the views of research and practice communities and the experiences of children and families.

> (2007: 265)

The vision that every child and young person is able to fulfil their full potential will only happen if policies, in any of the UK countries, are tested at local level and revised from feedback from children themselves, their families and practitioners. For adult services, which are also subject to continuous policy change, implementation will only be achieved through the involvement of all stakeholders, and careful attention to the complexities of involving all constituencies and the contingencies of day-to-day practice. Government guidance is increasingly recognising these elements of good practice and the necessity to make the process of policy implementation a loop rather than a line.

All this is a far cry from the notion that policies are devised at the top and implemented at local level. Policies that are nurtured in the way described here surely stand more chance of being relevant to a locality and gaining the commitment and support of staff.

Finally, the sheer complexity of the policy dilemmas being faced today means that there is a need to promote tentative approaches and accept a continual cycle of learning from service-users and practitioners. Clarke and Stewart (1997) long ago suggested that, for some local government issues, causal chains are hard to unravel and some problems hard to define. Solutions may be temporary and issues may need revisiting. They refer to these as 'wicked issues' – not meaning that they are bad, but rather that they are tricky and resistant to solution. Box 12.8 summarises their key points.

Box 12.8   How to deal with 'wicked issues'

1. DO NOT search for certainty; instead accept that understanding will be partial.
2. DO NOT think in a linear way; instead think holistically and look for interrelationships.
3. DO NOT be trapped by the obvious and conventional; accept different perspectives and approaches and tolerate not knowing.
4. DO NOT consult the usual people; instead draw in as wide an array of organisations and interests as possible and be open to 'outsiders' and their new attitudes and behaviours.
5. DO NOT go for the usual answers; instead be prepared to learn and encourage experiment, diversity and reflection.

(*Source*: adapted from Clarke and Stewart, 1997: 15–16)

As advocates of such approaches, Clarke and Stewart perhaps underplay the adjustments needed to make a reality of this. People need not just think differently but develop new skills, and perhaps make changes in fundamental aspects of their identities as managers and as practitioners to work in these new ways. After 1997, new policy documents came thick and fast – on the shape of the 'new NHS', on local government and community care, and on matters such as collaboration, quality and regulation. At the same time, there were calls for bids to win demonstration site status for health action zones, primary care groups and more besides. The pace of policy change has not slackened. Practitioners are thus increasingly finding themselves drawn into discussion about how to put flesh on the bones of policy and are asking how they, along with other stakeholders, can help policy development in their local areas. Will we see a real paradigm shift for the new century? Will the gulf that Ken Jarrold observed as he visited health services in the mid-1990s be bridged?

Conclusion

It is easy to regard policy as a given – a set of decisions made somewhere on high, handed down to those working in a local situation, often with little recognition of actual working conditions and scant regard for the specific nature of needs in a local area. This chapter has tried to show that there is another perspective – that of seeing policy as a process, encouraging involvement of different stakeholders in policy and facilitating the creation of feedback loops to allow learning and adjustment to occur. A critical practitioner needs to be both willing and able to take part in the policy process, acknowledging the multiple perspectives that people will bring, and welcoming opportunities to engage with policy development and make it relevant to and supportive of practice.

References

Aldgate, J., Healey, L., Malcolm, B., Pine, B., Rose, W. and Seden, J. (2007) *Enhancing Social Work Management, Theory and Best Practice from the UK and the USA*. London: Jessica Kingsley.

Bowes, A. and Domokos, T.M. (1996) 'Pakistani women and maternity care: raising muted voices', *Sociology of Health and Illness*, 18 (1): 45–65.

Braybrooke, D. and Lindblom, C. (1963) *The Strategy of Decision*. New York: Free Press.

Brooks, F. (1999) 'Changes in maternity policy – who, what and why?', in C. Davies, L. Finlay and A. Bullman (eds), *Changing Practice in Health and Social Care* (K302 Reader 1). London: Sage.

Brown, H. (1998) 'Implementing adult protection policies', *ESRC Seminar Series* (2 April), Milton Keynes, The Open University, School of Health and Social Welfare.

Brown, H. and Stein, J. (1998) 'Implementing adult protection policies in Kent and East Sussex', *Journal of Social Policy*, 27 (3): 371–96.

Clarke, M. and Stewart, J. (1997) *Handling the Wicked Issues: A Challenge for Government*. Birmingham: University of Birmingham, School of Public Policy.

Colebatch, H.K. (1998) *Policy*. Buckingham: Open University Press.

Department for Education and Skills (DfES) (2004a) *Every Child Matters: Change for Children*. London: HMSO.

Department for Education and Skills (DfES) (2004b) *Every Child Matters: The Next Steps*. London: HMSO.

Department of Health (DoH) (1993) *Changing Childbirth,* Part 1: Report of the Expert Maternity Group. London: HMSO.

Department of Health (DoH) (2002) *The Integrated Children's System*. London: Department of Health.

Department of Health (DoH) (2007) *Making it Better for Mother and Baby – Clinical Case for Change*. Report by Sheila Shribman, National Director for Children, Young People and Maternity Services. London: Department of Health.

Department of Health, Department for Education and Skills and the Home Office (2000) *The Framework for the Assessment of Children in Need and their Families*. London: HMSO.

Department of Health, Home Office and Department for Education and Skills (2006) *Working Together to Safeguard Children*. London: HMSO.

Eden, C. (1996) 'The stakeholder/collaborator strategy workshop', in C. Huxham (ed.), *Creating Collaborative Advantage*. London: Sage.

Evans, J. and Harris, J. (2004) 'Social work and the (exaggerated) death of discretion', *British Journal of Social Work*, 34 (6): 871–95.

Ferlie, E., Ashburner, L., Fitzgerald, L. and Pettigrew, A. (1996) *The New Public Management in Action*. Oxford: Oxford University Press.

Freeman, E. (1984) *Strategic Management: A Stakeholder Approach*. London: Pitman.

Hadley, R. and Clough, R. (1996) *Care in Chaos: Frustration and Challenge in Community Care*. London: Cassell.

Hill, M. (1997) The Policy Process in the Modern State (3rd edn). Hemel Hempstead: Prentice Hall/Harvester Wheatsheaf.

Hogwood, B.W. and Gunn, L. (1984) *Policy Analysis for the Real World*. Oxford: Oxford University Press.

Horwath, J. and Calder, M. (1998) 'Working together to protect children on the child protection register: myth or reality?', *British Journal of Social Work*, 28 (6): 879–95.

Huxham, C. (1996) *Creating Collaborative Advantage*. London: Sage.

de Jong, A. (1996) 'Inter-organizational collaboration in the policy preparation process', in C. Huxham (ed.), *Creating Collaborative Advantage*. London: Sage.

Laming, H. (2003) *The Victoria Climbié Inquiry*. Cm 5730, London: HMSO.

Lindblom, C. (1959) 'The science of "muddling through"', *Public Administration Review*, 19: 78–88.

Lipsky, M. (1980) *Street-Level Bureaucracy: Dilemmas of the Individual in Public Services*. New York: Russell Sage Foundation.

Parsons, L., Macfarlane, A. and Golding, J. (1993) 'Pregnancy, birth and maternity care', in W. Ahmad (ed.), *'Race' and Health in Contemporary Britain*. Buckingham: Open University Press, pp. 51–75.

Parsons, W. (1995) *Public Policy*. Aldershot: Edward Elgar.

Pressman, J. and Wildavsky, A. (1973) *Implementation*. Berkeley, CA: University of California Press.

Sale, A.U. (2005) 'We've got to be different', *Community Care* (27 January–2 February): 30–33.

Schofield, J. and Sausman, C. (2004) 'Symposium on implementing public policy: learning from theory and practice. Introduction', *Public Administration*, 82 (2): 235–48.

Simon, H. (1958) *Administrative Behaviour*. New York: Macmillan.

Winstanley, D., Sorabji, D. and Dawson, S. (1995) 'When the pieces don't fit a stakeholder power matrix to analyse public sector restructuring', *Public Money and Management*, 15 (2): 19–26.

Chapter 13

Continuing professional development: A critical approach

Barry Cooper

Introduction

The central argument in this chapter is both simple and challenging. I will propose that the attitudes of professional workers to their continuing professional development (CPD) is a strong indicator, if not a defining feature, of their approach to practice. This is not to maintain that the individual learner must carry the entire burden of post-qualification CPD. However, it is individuals who are expected to decide upon, initiate, maintain and complete their responsibilities for post-registration learning. Within the increasing profile of arguments for 'life-long learning' across all aspects of modern life, the individual learner is identified as a key mediator in creating knowledge through 'dialogues' that purposefully link the organisational contexts and settings of professional practice with the opportunities for continuing professional development. Dialogues with service-users and carers, as well as colleagues and supervisors, in particular, are crucial. Supervision is an important and underplayed aspect of CPD for health and social work practitioners. The chapter will include a critical examination of key rationales underpinning professional education in social care and an exploration of constructive arguments for dialogue with colleagues and managers to enhance creative notions of continuing professional 'capability'.

The emerging structures of what are currently called 'Post Registration Training and Learning' (PRTL) in social work (GSCC, 2006b) offer two main routes towards meeting CPD requirements in England.[1] Firstly, individuals can create evidence to meet the re-registration requirements for informal 'uncertified' learning and practice development.

---

[1] The frameworks in other nations of the UK may exhibit similarities and differences of emphasis but it is likely that some combination of these two main routes will offer most flexibility for post-registration requirements.

The minimum requirement to keep 'updated' is to show 'evidence' of fifteen days' PRTL over three years, in England. In Scotland, an important aspect of PRTL is the requirement on all newly qualified social workers to undertake specific training in the protection of children and vulnerable adults within the first year after qualification. This broad approach may be replicated in other nations of the UK. In nursing, the answer is considerably less at thirty-five hours, or about one week, in three years (NMC, 2006). These are hardly onerous expectations. Secondly, there will also be formal, 'certified', programmes of post-qualification study leading to higher education awards through HE institutions (HEIs). These will include far greater expectations and, consequently, offer opportunities for studies at a number of different graduate and post-graduate degree levels. Both of these routes to meeting the PRTL requirements highlight contrasting but also convergent implications for individual practitioners, their employing organisations and HEIs. The interplay of interests between individuals and institutions is an enduring feature of social work CPD and this chapter will examine some perspectives upon this relationship.

Higham and Rotheram (2005) maintain that three priorities are likely to dominate social work CPD: the use of research findings to inform knowledge-based practice; working together with colleagues from different disciplines; and working in partnership with service-users and carers. This is an important combination of priorities: increasing the focus on the nature of research and practice knowledge; sharpening the clarity of professional identity within flexible, inter-professional service settings; and creating power-sharing relationships with service-users through participative practices. These three, it can be argued, encapsulate the key challenges facing social work CPD in the future. However, this focus on social work needs to be seen in the context of wider professional developments towards structures of CPD and the promotion of life-long learning.

Arguments to ensure that professionals maintain and develop their skills and knowledge are part of much wider political developments that try to ensure greater accountability and quality of practices across the professions. The notion that professionals must be life-long learners, beyond initial qualification, is driven by wider educational developments (Fryer, 1999) as well as by the now well established marketisation demands of efficiency and consumerism in Higher Education (Neave, 1988). Within these large-scale developments, it is important for individuals and employing organisations to understand their different responsibilities and obligations. A broad definition of professional development is offered by Madden and Mitchell (1993: 3):

> the maintenance and enhancement of the knowledge, expertise and competence of professionals throughout their careers according to a plan formulated with regard to the needs of the professional, the employer, the profession and society.

In social work, the care councils for the nations of the UK have adopted codes of practice that apply to both individual practitioners and their employers. This emphasis upon employer responsibilities is new and the relationship between individuals and employing organisations will influence decisions about the pattern of CPD undertaken. The guidance allows much scope between the minimum requirements for re-registration evidence, on the one hand, and certified awards that offer structures of continued study and practice development. Understanding the implications of choices at different stages is an important factor in choosing pathways of CPD.

Focus on CPD: arguments for a radical approach

A landmark book in the field of CPD, by Houle (1981), predicted that structures of post-qualification and continuing development would grow to rival those of initial, pre-qualification education. Two more recent surveys and overviews of the last 20–25 years in Europe and the US have confirmed this prophecy of growth (OECD, 1995; Cervero, 2001). The OECD report, for example, appears to suggest that underlying the growth in CPD is 'a keenly felt awareness of the rapid and complex question of the obsolescence of knowledge' (OECD, 1995: 16). There are a number of key themes emerging from the literature. Firstly, that the field of CPD continues to be characterised by conflict and debate about ways in which CPD should be conceptualised, organised and delivered. Secondly, they chart significant changes in the relationship between the worlds of education and employment. Thirdly, that continuing education is being used more frequently to regulate professional practice. And finally, that the field continues to be in a state of transition, with no clear prospect of 'firming up' what forms of CPD may look like for the future.

These general themes are as germane to health care as they are to social care. However, I want to argue here that there is something about social work, work in the field of 'the social', that requires a more critical examination and analysis. Social work has been described as a unique activity invoking complex processes of power and ambiguity (Donzelot, 1988; Parton, 1998). The dynamic and negotiable nature of social work challenges the conceptions of knowledge used to explain and inform social interventions. Bickham (1998: 73) captures the essence of the challenge I am proposing through his assertion that the professions can only survive and thrive through radical reform of structures of CPD where efforts are made to 'break down the epistemological and pedagogical barriers separating knowledge construction and theory from actual professional practice'. For example, Celia Keeping's chapter earlier in this book discussed the role of the practitioner researcher, in which practitioners via research actively construct the knowledge base of social work. Research evidence for practice need not always be disseminated from the 'mountain-top'. Bickham's assertion reflects arguments for a situated knowledge for social work and repeats the case made unequivocally by Rein and White (1981: 37):

> The knowledge [that social work seeks] *must* be developed in the living situations that are confronted by the contemporary episodes in the field... [I]t is necessary to enlarge the notion of context to include not only the client's situation but the agency itself and more broadly the institutional setting of practice [original emphasis].

These institutional settings must include HEIs as well as service agency organisations. As Eraut (1994: 57) argues, HE has a major role to play in the transformation of CPD, but will only do so if it 'is prepared to extend its role from that of creator and transmitter of generalizable knowledge to that of enhancing the knowledge creation capacities of individuals and professional communities'.

The implications of this for individuals and institutions undertaking either informal or certified award-based programmes of CPD are profound. It means that individual practitioners have a responsibility to re-conceive their practice as transformative opportunities for knowledge creation across all aspects of service interactions with colleagues, carers and service-users. It also means that HE institutions have a responsibility to facilitate, encourage and pedagogically support both individuals and service agencies in these processes in order to capture, reflect upon and critically analyse practice developments.

In social work, this question of 'the knowledge base' has been particularly contested (see, for a recent example of current debates within the UK, Parton, 2000; Webb, 2001; Sheldon, 2001; Taylor and White, 2006). The debate shows social work to be 'ahead of the game' of issues addressed by the OECD report (1995). Interventions in 'the social' are fraught with uncertainty. The arena of 'expertise' and application within social fields has few obvious boundaries and those that can be established inevitably include behavioural factors of individual 'agency' that elude scientific certainty. This characteristic of epistemological uncertainty within social work practice undermines the modernist assumption about progress towards a body of knowledge that can be applied to an objectified world. It can be argued that a knowledge base for social work is an essentially moral one, negotiated and developed within and between the interactions of social actors, each of whom possesses human agency and free will. Knowledge of self and others within interactive social situations is therefore created or constructed rather than received. In this challenging context, emerging systems of CPD that support and 'professionally develop' social workers are necessarily implicated in these profound questions.

The most commonly given reason within the literature for the importance of CPD is the need for technical knowledge 'updating'. This notion of 'updating' has a 'common-sense' legitimacy that is especially difficult to question when applied to trying to keep up with changes in the names and configurations of different service resources, for example. Or, in an increasingly regulated world, updating has a role to play in keeping up to date with changes in the legislation that impact upon service obligations. Or, there is a clear need to keep updated with clinical procedures in medical interventions. The complexity of such knowledge of the material world, in an objectively verifiable reality, is changing rapidly and it is easy within these contexts to see how knowledge can become obsolescent.

Social realities are different. A constructionist perspective holds that there are few of these apparently solid certainties or objectivities to be found in the interactive and interpersonal realities that are the stock in trade of social workers. 'Updating' becomes an inappropriate and misleading descriptor for behavioural knowledge that is created through personal agency. Cervero (2001) questions the 'updating' model, and its assumption about the relationship between knowledge, professional learning and development, and practice, by arguing for a practice-centred approach. In doing so he draws upon the often cited work of Schon (1987). It is worth repeating the equally often cited metaphor employed by Schon as it vividly illustrates the core of the issue that we are exploring.

In the varied topography of professional practice, there is a high, hard ground overlooking a swamp. On the high ground, manageable problems lend themselves to solution through the application of research-based theory and technique. In the swampy lowland, messy, confusing problems defy technical solution. The irony of this situation is that the problems of the high ground tend to be relatively unimportant to individuals or society at large … while in the swamp lie the problems of greatest human concern.

(1987: 3)

Schon's metaphor is a particularly powerful one for social work. 'Messy, confusing problems' are on the everyday caseload and work agenda of practising social workers. Social work is a perfectly 'swampy' activity, in Schon's terms. The problems of social work are people-problems that regularly and conspicuously 'defy technical solution'. Schon's approach supports the argument that alternative approaches to 'real' problems within professional practice are needed. However, there are important implications for institutions involved in CPD, and particularly for the relationship between knowledge and practice in health care, social work and social care. It is to these issues we now turn.

'Competency' approaches: the debate

It is an advantage to all narrow wisdom and narrow morals, that their maxims have a plausible air; and, on a cursory view, appear equal to first principles. They are light and portable. They are as current as copper coin; and about as valuable. They serve equally the first capacities and the lowest; and they are, at least, as useful to the worst men as the best. Of this stamp is the cant of *Not men, but measures*; a sort of charm, by which many people get loose from every honourable engagement.

(Burke, 1770 (1981): 318; original emphasis)

Burke's vivid quote reflects the dangers of endeavours that are based upon the pre-eminence of measurement through reference to external sets of 'standards'. Such systems set themselves apart from the dynamics of relationships between people while assuming a spurious scientific respectability. At a time when 'performance cultures' are being increasingly invoked in social work and health care settings, the imposition of standards can suggest that staff are being measured and judged. But imposed frameworks can give rise to strong reactions, as the competency debate demonstrates. There are arguments in favour and against competency-based education and training (CBET) and I will be exploring some of these.

The most widely held understanding of the nature of CBET is where the aim is to set out a comprehensive set of task or behaviour descriptors that can be observed and assessed for satisfactory performance outcomes (Jessup, 1991). Melton (1994) locates the origin of this approach in behaviourism and functional analysis, which he identifies as being popular theoretical orientations in the 1960s and 1970s. The aim of the 'behavioural objectives' movement was, as the name implies, to set out 'what individuals should ultimately be able to do' (1994: 286). This emphasis upon observable and assessable behavioural outcomes has an obvious appeal to government. It offers the potential for a closer specification and control of professional activity that can, in theory at least, be tied into public policy aims.

The use of public funds to support professional training is a common argument in justification of this. In the UK, CBET was introduced to the world of work as part of government reforms of vocational education in the 1980s. These tried to address perceived 'skills shortages' in the workforce through an assumed link between higher levels of training and economic growth (Wolf, 1995). The National Council for Vocational Qualifications (NCVQ) was set up in 1986 with a mandate to develop a competence-based system for defining and assessing standards for *all* occupations. This move, to establish a unified system for vocational training through what Becher (1994) describes as the 'mother of all accrediting bodies', was an ambitious undertaking that, on one level, had laudable aims of transparency and veracity. As Lum (1999: 408) puts it,

> there must be something of value in an approach which is ostensibly directed towards a capacity or disposition to act in the world and which is concerned to make explicit and public the criteria by which we gain the measure of such capacities or dispositions.

In social work, the NVQ-approach continues to exert its influence upon practitioners and education providers alike through the ubiquity of 'National Occupational Standards' (TOPSS, 2002) in England and Wales, and the Scottish variation known as 'Standards in Social Work Education' (Scottish Executive, 2003). The same frameworks that attempt to control and codify practice can be found in the educational assessment schedules of occupational standards underpinning both pre- and post-qualification training in social work. Indeed, the regulatory bodies for social work in England have been consistently clear on this point for a number of years. Hence, these standards are claimed to both '*define and describe best practice* for social work staff at post-qualifying level' (TOPSS, 2002: 4, emphasis added), while at pre-qualifying level, 'The national occupational standards *define good practice* by defining the competence required for specific occupational roles' (GSCC, 2006a, emphasis added). In the revised post-qualification framework in England the continued bedrock rationale and influence of the competency approach remains clearly articulated, in that

> the PQ framework has been designed so that occupational standards form an integral part of it and progression through the Framework will depend on the assessment of practice competence. The GSCC will only approve PQ programmes that clearly specify the nature of the practice component and state clearly how practice competence will be assessed in line with specialist standards including national occupational standards.

(GSCC, 2004: paragraph 9)

Many of the commonly held criticisms of CBET in professional education programmes centre upon the widely held view that a functional analysis of concrete, observable tasks and behaviours is simply inappropriate for complex 'professional activities'; that it ignores the potential for professional judgement, takes no account of group processes and has no regard for the influence of social context or setting (Barnett, 1994; Eraut, 1994). Hager and Gonczi go so far as to cast 'very serious doubts about its relevance to work at any level' (1996: 248).

CBET – the case against

The core critique by Lum (1999) sets out to clarify and distinguish between competence as an educational aim, on the one hand, and competence as a construct that Lum infers from CBET's methodology and application in practice. Lum agrees with and quotes Barnett (1994: 71), in maintaining that 'there can be no objection *in principle* to the application of the terms (competence and outcomes) to educational processes' (1994: 71, original emphasis). The devil, however, as always, is in the detail. It is implied that CBET has (mis)appropriated the everyday usage of 'competence'. He argues that CBET tends to perpetuate a conflation between the means and ends of competence. Competence as an end in itself is like health, wealth and happiness – everybody is generally in favour of them. However, the CBET means of achieving the educational aim of competence is through their ubiquitous 'outcome statements'.

Outcome statements are the *sine qua non* of CBET. The pre-eminence afforded to these statements by CBET is based upon the assumption that competent action can be accurately defined. As Jessup, an early advocate of CBET, maintains with apparently unassailable logic, 'If you cannot say what you require, how can you develop it and how do you know when you have achieved it?' (1991: 134). Jessup goes on to make the CBET reliance upon outcome statements categorically clear:

> statements must accurately communicate their intent. For accurate communication of the outcomes of competence and attainment, a precision in the use of language in such statements will need to be established, approaching that of a science. The overall model stands or falls on how effectively we can state competence and attainment.
>
> (1991: 134)

A counter-argument would be that the CBET approach is bankrupt if, for any reason, competency outcomes cannot be precisely and accurately stated. Lum's analysis (1999) involves a crucial distinction between the prescriptive and the descriptive capacities of statements. The first of these, the prescriptive capacity of outcome statements, accounts for the political and managerial appeal of competency lists and CBET. The regulatory imposition of detailed outcome schedules upon the education and CPD of the professions tends to act as a lever upon the direction and priority activities of practitioners. This is the accountability function of prescribed CPD programmes leading to licensing and control by government through professional regulatory bodies such as the Nursing and Midwifery and Social Care Councils in the UK.

Lum's criticism of the descriptive capacity of outcome statements is possibly even stronger. Lum (1999) cites the work of Polanyi (1967) and Schon (1983) in positing the tacit nature of much of our knowledge. In other words, we know and are aware of far more than we are able to convey through language or descriptive statements of complex activities. The philosophical work of John Searle (1995) is used to argue for a key distinction – that is, between the 'brute facts' of the natural sciences and the socially constructed features of an agreed social reality. Competences, as a putative description of complex social activities, form part of this latter distinction. Searle's distinction allows for the existence of an objective, natural world that is analysed and described by modern science. However, performances of competence in health care, social work and social care practice may not be objectifiable. Practice contains features that Lum describes as 'observer-relative', which are,

> *entirely dependant upon human agreement*; in other words they constitute a reality which is socially constructed through processes of which we remain largely unaware. The addition of these observer-relative features does not add any new material objects to the world because the features added are ontologically subjective (e.g. a performance is only competent insofar as people regard it as such).

> (1999: 414, original emphasis)

Working from the assumption that competence is 'out there' to be discovered, the CBET approach inevitably follows a natural science causality and attempts to 'pin down' the exact nature of the competences through increasingly reductionist inventories and schedules of criteria and indicators. This approach is found in the same sets of 'standards' in social work which are claimed to describe and define good practice.

The second CBET assumption holds that it is possible for statements to describe, unequivocally, accurately and sufficiently, both subjective and objective features of the world. Searle's account of socially constructed reality relies upon his conception of intentionality (Searle, 1983). Intentionality implies and assumes human agency or intention as a first cause. Therefore one would not expect, from this position, to find a satisfactory understanding of competent performance 'out there' in the objective world. Intentionality involves the ability of individuals to conceive of and represent states of affairs in the world and to locate these, with others, against backgrounds of 'tacit' knowledge and inter-subjective agreements. Thus, it is Searle's notion of a tacit 'background' of knowledge that undermines the second assumption of CBET of sufficiently capturing the world through outcome statements alone.

Lum (1999) provides the simple example of three short sentences: 'Sally cut the cake', 'Bill cut the grass', and 'The tailor cut the cloth'. There is no ambiguity about the use of the word 'cut', but in each case we understand the verb differently according to our background knowledge about knives, lawnmowers and scissors, and what it is to cut these different things. From this analysis alone, we can understand that the background knowledge inherent within complex social situations, such as social work, healthcare, or virtually anything else, is scarcely likely to be conveyed 'unequivocally, accurately and sufficiently'. Notwithstanding this criticism, CBET has proliferated. It will be important to examine arguments in favour of the approach in order to understand some of the reasons for its success.

CBET – the case for

The response by some to the introduction of the concept of competence to education has been described as akin to the discovery of El Dorado (Norris, 1991).

O'Hagan (1996: 7) argues that the driver for CBET developments took place within a political and ideological context where the government saw public service and welfare industries as 'unenterprising and incompetent', and the higher education system as part of a systemic culture that sustained this incompetence through its vocational programmes. This shift of emphasis to one of 'action' and 'doing' was underpinned by central tenets of individual responsibility and accountability based upon evidence that were very much in tune with the espoused values and ethos of CBET.

Bridges (1996) makes the case for a more positive appraisal of a CBET approach. While recognising some of the criticisms of CBET, his case is based upon an acknowledgement of the meritocratic principles of what he calls 'practical competence' within a liberal education. A major plank of his argument rests upon the so-called 'transparency' of assessment, that

> opens the criteria to critical examination and debate, renders assessors accountable against public standards, empowers the assessed and … on this argument the competence movement is on the side of, if not of liberalism, then of liberation.

(1996: 369).

Bridges' case rests on two assumptions: first, that those frameworks can be legitimately prescribed by government or regulatory bodies; and second, that this broad recognition and acceptance of the positives of CBET does require 'a more generic and cognitively laden concept of personal and professional competence' (1996: 361). The defenders of CBET (Hodkinson, 1992; Walker, 1992; Bridges, 1996; Hager and Gonczi, 1996) often rely upon the argument that there are significant differences that flow from the diverse conceptions of 'competence' being employed.

The substantive argument for what they describe as an 'educationally sound conception of competence' is made by Hager and Beckett (1995: 1). This 'integrated' or 'holistic' approach to CBET is justified through an acceptance that the applicability and use of descriptive standards within professional activities are inevitably relational. In other words, the use of competency statements, in terms of judgements and assessments of task performance, will be affected by individual attributes, on the one hand, and by the influence of different situations and contexts on the other. This relational stance to competence leads the debate away from a barren behaviourism into the rich and fertile territory of 'situatedness' (Brown et al., 1989; Lave and Wenger, 1991; Billett, 1994). Hager and Beckett (1995) outline an argument for a socio-cultural process of 'cultural formation' in professional activities. This relational view of professional activity impacts upon judgements of competence. It reflects our earlier discussion of the argument put forward by Lum (1999), whereby assessments are socially constructed and agreed. In other words, as succinctly and pithily paraphrased by Hager and Beckett, ' "integrated competence" is what a profession's peer group says it is' (1995: 12).

There are clear implications of this stance for professional education and CPD. The integrated or holistic approach accepts the criticisms of outcome statements and standards that are present as CBET underpinnings to many of the professional frameworks. However, it puts them in perspective as one set of prescriptive guidelines. As such, they are not seen as descriptions of 'good practice realities' but, rather, as broad maps. The exact position of learners in referring to these maps should be open to discussion, negotiation and social agreement in particular contexts and among groups of peers participating in teaching and learning partnerships. This distinction between 'the map' and the contextual 'territory' of practice situations is a vital one to maintain and will be considered in the next sections.

Capability: distinguishing the map from the territory

There is a key distinction offered by an approach based upon capability; one that moves from the CBET concern with drawing ever more detailed and descriptive maps, to an approach that focuses upon the territory itself. In other words, the capability approach seems to recognise that professional practices are enacted by individual people, as part of social relationships, within complex situated environments. This approach starts from the recognition of reciprocal relationships between active individuals as part of an interactive environment and emanates from socio-cultural approaches to situated learning (Lave and Wenger, 1991).

The capability literature offers the potential for a more dynamic holism. It sets out to link 'knowing' with 'doing'; the traditional view of expertise, through command of a body of knowledge, with the ability to demonstrate expertise in action. The challenge for professional education and development in the twenty-first century, according to this view, is

> to move beyond considerations of knowledge and competence to helping people develop as capable practitioners equal to the challenges of fluid environments and unpredictable change, taking responsibility for their careers and their learning, and able to exercise the kind of practical judgement and systemic wisdom needed for a sustainable future.
>
> (O'Reilly et al., 1999: 1)

Lester (1999) employs a helpful illustrative metaphor to describe this fundamental change. He describes it as moving from 'map-reader to map-maker' and draws an important distinction between the 'map' or curricula, and the 'territory'. Lester argues that it is important not to confuse the two, as the former is only a set of externally prescribed criteria designed to establish and institutionally accredit a standard of 'fitness for purpose'. Such sets of schedules are vulnerable to attack on at least two fronts. First, they are open to the same accusations of reductionism levelled earlier at competency statements. Second, they can be questioned as to fitness for 'what purpose and whose purpose?' By contrast, the 'territory' is where the intervention in a social or interpersonal sphere takes place and the professional has to act within what is an existentially unique set of social circumstances. This intervention, by 'social field practitioners', into specific social situations is essentially a creative process where shared communications, understandings, agreements and plans of action are negotiated. These processes create knowledge and help create 'maps' of understanding and explanation. The ability of practitioners to make the transition from map-reader to map-maker can help characterise the necessary development between initial qualification training and extended CPD; or 'Novice to Expert' (Benner, 1984). While it may be minimally important for newly qualified practitioners to demonstrate proficiency in map-reading, there is no necessary connection of educational development between this ability and the confident exploration required to 'map uncharted territories and redraw the maps of known ones' (Lester, 1999: 46–7).

What is it about social work, or related social care work, that demands this degree of qualitative transition in its structures and processes of CPD? Social work practitioners are involved in trying to help find solutions to culturally defined problems of living. I have outlined some arguments for how 'social work problems' are uniquely complex in their location within the milieu of 'the social' at the boundaries of contested territories between public policies and private lives. The 'problem' itself, as a complex package of competing perspectives, rarely has an uncontested objective reality. The social work problem, therefore, needs to be defined. This definition needs to be socially negotiated and agreed, or, in many cases, its areas of disagreement agreed.

Maps of such agreements have to be created by social care practitioners through complex and often contested negotiation. As identified by Higham and Rotheram (2005) at the beginning of this chapter, this task frequently needs to occur in collaboration with multi-disciplinary colleagues and, increasingly, is expected to involve 'service-users' or lay members of the public. In order for this process to be 'holistic' and fully involve the necessary range of people, it needs to be participative within particular territories and situations. Lave and Wenger (1991: 51) argue that the necessary conception of such participation

> can be neither fully internalized as knowledge structures [within individual minds] nor fully externalised as instrumental artefacts or overarching activity structures. Participation is always based on situated negotiation and re-negotiation of meanings in the world. This implies that understanding and experience are in constant interaction – indeed are mutually constitutive.

Arguably then, competency frameworks are 'activity structures' which act at best as pre-qualification initiation into a professional discourse through familiarity with the jargon and cultural assumptions prevalent at different times. At institutional levels they facilitate educational assessment practices; and at public policy levels they have the ostensible aim of setting minimum standards that aim to militate against 'mistakes' in professional practice through a 'safety-net' approach to risk management. However, it is debatable whether even this is achievable at other than the most basic of levels.

Some of the misplaced attempts to achieve 'certainty' through external frameworks has probably now been recognised in professional education. The new social work degree-level qualification requires an initial first year 'apprenticeship' placement in order that very basic personal suitability or 'fitness for practice' can be assessed, *in situ*, within practice settings. From a perspective of promoting 'expertise' within CPD for social work it may be that such frameworks are actually counter-productive. As Lester (1999: 47) argues, 'an education in map-reading does not guarantee development of the abilities required for map-making, and may encourage limiting beliefs that blunt them'. If 'map-making professionalism' requires aptitudes and abilities of 'enquiry, critique, reflection and reconstruction' (1999: 47) then the means to such ends surely beg the question of how such processes are to be assessed. An argument to help 'break down the epistemological and pedagogical barriers separating knowledge construction and theory from actual professional practice' supports the Lave and Wenger (1991) conception of 'communities of practice', where the relationship between individuals and institutional contexts is based upon interactive processes of 'knowledgeability' – in other words, the combination of knowledge and skills required to operate successfully within communities of practice.

Supervision and consultation: dialogues for CPD

If CPD is about anything, it must be about practice. There has been a tendency in the literature for practice and education/training to be considered as different aspects of professional development. This has partly arisen through a historical tendency for practice and education to be located in the very different institutional arrangements of service agencies and colleges of higher education. However, the more recent priorities afforded to work-based or practice-based learning have recognised that CPD is enhanced by a necessary integration of social field interventions and academic appraisal through critical questioning of professional practices. Nonetheless, this relationship, between the demands and accountabilities of practice and the critical questioning of higher education within CPD, remains an uneasy alliance and a frequently contested integration. Supervision is a key area that illustrates these tensions. Jones (2004) clearly locates supervision and CPD within the nexus of power relations that routinely impact upon and define the potential for individuals and organisations to engage in the dynamics of learning. He identifies three core constellations of ideas that help to illustrate some of the tensions of supervision as a learning process: indeterminacy; accountabilities; and, reflexivity.

The 'indeterminacy' of knowledge about 'the social' was extensively explored earlier in this chapter. An acceptance of uncertainty and ambiguity (Parton, 1998) as a defining feature of social field interventions challenges the extent to which it is feasible to attempt to control or micro-manage practice through rules and procedures. A number of authors (Baldwin, 2000; Preston-Shoot, 2001; Evans and Harris, 2004) have argued that there still remains considerable scope for discretion by practitioners within, or perhaps even as a result of, increasingly rule-defined policies and procedures. The point is that even the most detailed of criteria still need to be interpreted by individuals within social processes of negotiation and agreement. For the individual practitioner, supervisory dialogues are an important part of this social process. As Jones puts it, 'the supervisor's role becomes one of facilitating learning networks within which practitioners can both receive *and generate new knowledge'* (2004: 20, emphasis added).

The 'generation of new knowledge', from the perspective of CPD learning, is a different way of describing the creative growth of new ways to explain and understand practitioners' conceptualisation of their roles, tasks and engagements with both colleagues as well as service-users. In other words, the processes of supervisory or consultative dialogues help to explore, develop and progress new perspectives and insights that inform the complexities of professional interventions in the lives of others. Individual reflections are important and, for most practitioners, an inevitable and ongoing source of internal exploration. However, individualistic conceptions of reflection have been criticised (Eby, 2000) as too restrictive. They are a necessary, but not a sufficient, condition for reflexive practice. Practitioners have to 'own' their judgements and justify their actions. Thus, an individual's grasp of situations forms a vital and necessary basis for dynamic processes of dialogues with a range of people, from service-users, carers, colleagues and supervisors, in order to engage in creative processes of professional development and learning. The linkage with supervision is particularly important as it connects practitioners to their employing organisations through the mounting profile of 'accountabilities'.

Accountability has become an increasingly important feature of professional practice and, for our conception of CPD, of *learning* about practice. However, within the power and knowledge networks of institutional interventions into peoples' lives, 'accountabilities' are complex, contested and often conflicting. The profile of accountability was raised within the government White Paper *Modernising Social Services* (DoH, 1998). It contains powerful, but ambiguous, messages of institutional reform through regulation. It demands the delivery of diversity through creative, individualised social work that, at the same time, is expected to take place within an increasingly normative network of institutional pressures for regulated consistency. Thus, 'the government judges that institutional change is essential to improve standards and public confidence' (DoH, 1998: 5.6); 'The government believes that [this] requires the regulatory framework for social care to be strengthened by regulating social care personnel for the first time' (5.7). There will be 'consistent action taken' 'to set enforceable standards of conduct and practice' (5.16). These will be published in 'codes' that will 'guide all staff and their employers in a common understanding of conduct and practice requirements' (5.16). This assumption, that a 'common understanding' will be achieved through the imposition of a set of external standards, is open to the same attack levelled at CBET earlier in this chapter. In other words, the critique, of a misplaced emphasis upon the efficacy of 'performance standards', is the same whether applied in professional practice or in education.

The assumed primacy of external, system controls over the individual can be further illustrated. 'Individual practitioners should be personally accountable for their own standards of conduct and practice based on the codes' (5.17). On the face of it we might not disagree with the point made. Of course, social workers and other social care staff must be accountable through the organisational systems that employ them. Significantly however, the 'author' of the quote did not add the word 'responsibility' to the word 'accountability'. Responsibility implies professional discretion but this quote only implies an external framework which appears to determine the actions of practitioners. However, the document is about making the case for modernisation through regulation and instrumental system changes. The critique that can be levelled at 'reform through regulation' is that it distorts the focus towards imposed frameworks and away from the existential realities of social relationships that create and sustain professional practices. These realities, including supervisory dialogues for CPD, are reflexive and essentially creative through the constant struggles to create sense within indeterminate contexts.

Reflexivity in practice and professional development, it is increasingly argued, helps recognition of the complexities linking individuals and institutions within the changing dynamics of power networks in social interventions (Fook et al., 2000; Healy, 2000; Parton and O'Byrne, 2000; Taylor and White, 2000). An understanding of reflexive processes helps to describe the responsible engagement by supervisor and practitioner within a learning partnership. Supervision for learning in such a partnership for CPD is characterised by dialogue and negotiation within multiple accountabilities. These processes of knowledge building within complex service networks have been helpfully described as the 'brokering of knowledge' (Muetzelfeldt et al., 2002). As Jones (2004: 21) argues:

The processes by which this brokerage occurs will at the same time be sustaining and constructing the operations of accountability. By retaining openness to multiple perspectives on accountability, the supervisor can be an agent in the proactive pursuit of transformative professional practices that maintain possibilities for critical engagement within the organisation and with service communities. Such openness is supported through the exercise of reflexivity.

Dialogues, by definition, are reciprocal processes of communication. The supervisor has an important facilitative role to play in encouraging awareness of reflexive practices and the integration of this into the practitioner's chosen route of CPD or, in the UK, post-registration teaching and learning. However, the *responsibility* for initiating direction and maintaining progress in both practice and CPD remains with the individual practitioner. The individual is the locus of practice engagements in social relationships and this remains the case for individuals' reconceptualisation of practices into processes of CPD.

Conclusion

It might have been expected that the rhetoric of the modernisation agenda of reform through regulation in health and social care (DoH, 1997; 1998) would have introduced high expectations of compulsory post-qualification CPD for professional practitioners. The reality, of three weeks in social care and one week in nursing every three years, appears disappointing. However, perhaps this pragmatic reality accepts the limits of regulatory compulsion while recognising that professionals have to choose their path of CPD. The flexibility of options offered, by minimum re-registration requirements on the one hand and a full range of post-qualification academic award programmes on the other hand, places the responsibility of choice squarely in a negotiation between individuals and their employing agencies. This is probably as it should be. Professional 'capability' is clearly located in the dynamics and cultures of social organisations. There is now, in social care, a clear 'codes of practice expectation' on both parties that opportunities and support should be offered and engagement with CPD initiated and maintained. It can be argued that the quality of choice in the routes of post-registration training and learning in social care (PRTL), or post-registration education and practice in nursing health care (PREP), is indicative of the quality of approaches to professional practices. Is professional practice a minimum-requirements activity? Or is professional practice an opportunity for life-long learning, challenge and growth? The responsibility for choice is yours.

References

Baldwin, M. (2000) 'Learning to practice with the tensions between professional discretion and agency procedure', in L. Napier and J. Fook (eds), *Breakthroughs in Practice: Theorising Critical Moments in Social Work*. London: Whiting & Birch.

Barnett, R. (1994) *The Limits of Competence*. Buckingham: Society for Research into Higher Education/Open University Press.

Becher, T. (1994) Introduction, in T. Becher (ed.), *Governments and Professional Education*. Buckingham: Society for Research into Higher Education/Open University Press.

Benner, P. (1984) *From Novice to Expert*. New York: Addison Wesley.

Bickham, A. (1998) 'The infusion and utilization of critical thinking skills in professional practice', in W.H. Young (ed.), *Continuing Professional Education in Transition: Visions for the Professions and New Strategies for Lifelong Learning*. Malabar, FL: Krieger.

Billett, S. (1994) 'Situated learning – a workplace experience', *Australian Journal of Adult and Community Education*, 34 (2): 112–30.

Bridges, D. (1996) 'Competence-based education and training: progress or villainy?' *Journal of Philosophy of Education*, 30 (3): 361–76.

Brown, J.S., Collins, A. and Duguid, P. (1989) 'Situated cognition and the culture of learning', *Educational Researcher*, 18 (1): 32–42.

Burke, E. (1770) 'Thoughts on the present discontents', in P. Langford (ed.) *The Writings and Speeches of Edmund Burke*. vol. II. New York: Oxford University Press (1981).

Cervero, R.M. (2001) 'Continuing professional education in transition, 1981–2000', *International Journal of Lifelong Learning*, 20 (1/2): 16–30.

Department of Health (DoH) (1997) *The New NHS, Modern, Dependable*. London: HMSO.

Department of Health (DoH) (1998) *Modernising Social Services*. London: HMSO.

Donzelot, J. (1988) 'The promotion of the social', *Economy and Society*, 17 (3): 395–427.

Eby, M.A. (2000) Understanding professional development, in A. Brechin, H. Brown and M.A. Eby (eds), *Critical Practice in Health and Social Care*. London: Sage.

Eraut, M. (1994) *Developing Professional Knowledge and Competence*. London: Falmer.

Evans, T. and Harris, J. (2004) 'Street-level bureaucracy, social work and the [exaggerated] death of discretion', *British Journal of Social Work*, 34: 871–95.

Fook, J., Martin R. and Hawkins, L. (2000) *Professional Expertise: Practice, Theory and Education for Working in Uncertainty*. London: Whiting and Birch.

Fryer, R.H. (1999) *Creating Learning Cultures: Next Steps in Achieving the Learning Age*. London: Nagcell.

GSCC (2004) *The Revised Post-Qualifying Framework for Social Work Education and Training*. London: General Social Care Council.

GSCC (2006a) http://www.gscc.org.uk/For+course+providers/Degree+resources/. General Social Care Council.

GSCC (2006b) *Post Registration Training and Learning (PRTL) Requirements for Registered Social Workers: Advice and Guidance on Good Practice*. London. General Social Care Council.

Hager, P. and Beckett, D. (1995) 'Philosophical underpinnings of the integrated theory of competence', *Educational Philosophy and Theory*, 27 (1): 1–24.

Hager, P. and Gonczi, A. (1996) 'Professions and competencies', in R. Edwards, A. Hanson and P. Raggett (eds), *Boundaries of Adult Learning*. London: Routledge/Open University. pp. 246–60.

Healy, K. (2000) *Social Work Practices. Contemporary Perspectives on Change*. London: Sage.

Higham, P. and Rotheram, R. (2005) 'Continuing professional development and education', in H. Burgess and I. Taylor (eds), *Effective Learning and Teaching in Social Policy and Social Work*. London: Routledge Falmer.

Hodkinson, P. (1992) 'Alternative models of competence in vocational education and training', *Journal of Further and Higher Education*, 16 (2): 30–39.

Houle, C.O. (1981) *Continuing Learning in the Professions*. London: Jossey-Bass.

Jessup, G. (1991) *Outcomes: NVQs and the Emerging Model of Education and Training*. London: Falmer.

Jones, M. (2004) 'Supervision, learning and transformative practices', in N. Gould and M. Baldwin (eds), *Social Work, Critical Reflection and the Learning Organisation*. Aldershot: Ashgate.

Lave, J. and Wenger, E. (1991) *Situated Learning*. Cambridge: Cambridge University Press.

Lester, S. (1999) 'From map-reader to map-maker: approaches to moving beyond knowledge and competence', in D. O'Reilly, L. Cunningham and S. Lester (eds), *Developing the Capable Practitioner: Professional Capability Through Higher Education*. London: Kogan Page. p. 45–53.

Lum, G. (1999) 'Where's the competence in competence-based education and training?' *Journal of Philosophy of Education*, 33 (3): 403–18.

Lum, G. (2003) 'Towards a richer conception of vocational preparation', *Journal of Philosophy of Education*, 37 (1): 1–15.

Madden, C.A. and Mitchell, V.A. (1993) *Professional Standards and Competence: A Survey of Continuing Education for the Professionals*. Bristol: Department for Continuing Education, University of Bristol.

Melton, F.R. (1994) 'Competences in perspective', *Educational Research*, 36 (3): 285–94.

Muetzelfeldt, M., Briskman, L. and Jones, M. (2002) 'Brokering knowledge: managing knowledge in a network of government and non-government human service delivery agencies', in: M. Considine (ed.), *Knowledge, Networks and Joined-up Government: Conference Proceedings*. Melbourne: University of Melbourne.

Neave, G. (1988) 'On the cultivation of quality, efficiency, and enterprise: an overview of recent trends in higher education in Europe, 1968–1988', *European Journal of Education*, 23 (1–2):

NMC (2006) *The PREP Handbook*. London: Nursing and Midwifery Council.

Norris, N. (1991) 'The trouble with competence', *Cambridge Journal of Education*, 21 (3): 331–41.

OECD (1995) *Continuing Professional Education of Highly Qualified Personnel*. Paris: Organisation for Economic Co-operation and Development.

O'Hagan, K. (1996) *Competence in Social Work Practice*. London: Jessica Kingsley.

O'Reilly D., Cunningham, L. and Lester, S. (1999) Introduction, in D. O, Reilly L. Cunningham, and S. Lester (eds), *Developing the Capable Practitioner: Professional Capability Through Higher Education*. London: Kogan Page.

Parton, N. (1998) 'Risk, advanced liberalism and child welfare: the need to rediscover uncertainty and ambiguity', *British Journal of Social Work*, 28 (1): 5–28.

Parton, N. (2000) 'Some thoughts on the relationship between theory and practice in and for social work', *British Journal of Social Work*, 30 (4): 449–63.

Parton, N. and O'Byrne, P. (2000) *Constructive Social Work*. London: Macmillan.

Polanyi, M. (1967) *The Tacit Dimension*. London: Routledge.

Preston-Shoot, M. (2001) 'Regulating the road of good intentions: observations on the relationship between policy, regulations and practice in social work', *Practice*, 13: 5–20.

Rein, M. and White, S.H. (1981) 'Knowledge for practice', *Social Service Review*, 55 (1): 1–41.

Schon, D. (1983) *The Reflective Practitioner: How Professionals Think in Action*. Aldershot: Ashgate.

Schon, D. (1987) *Educating the Reflective Practitioner*. London: Jossey-Bass.

Scottish Executive (2003) *Standards in Social Work Education*. Edinburgh: Scottish Executive.

Searle, J. (1983) *Intentionality*. Cambridge: Cambridge University Press.

Searle, J. (1995) *The Construction of Social Reality*. London: Allen Lane/Penguin.

Sheldon, B. (2001) 'The validity of evidence-based practice in social work: a reply to Stephen Webb', *British Journal of Social Work*, 31: 801–9.

Taylor, C. and White, S. (2000) *Practising Reflexivity in Health and Welfare. Making Knowledge*. Buckingham: Open University Press.

Taylor, C. and White, S. (2006) 'Knowledge and reasoning in social work: educating for humane judgement', *British Journal of Social Work*, 36 (6): 937–54.

TOPSS, (2002) *The National Occupational Standards for Social Work*. Leeds: Training Organisation for the Personal Social Services UK Partnership.

Walker, J.C. (1992) The Value of Competency Based Education, in: J. Hattie (ed.) *The Effects of Competency-based Education on Universities: Liberation or Enslavement?* Perth, University of Western Australia.

Webb, S.A. (2001) Some Considerations on the Validity of Evidence-based Practice in Social Work, *British Journal of Social Work*, Vol. 31, No. 1, pp. 57–79.

Wolf, A. (1995) *Competence-Based Assessment*. Buckingham: OUP.

Chapter 14

Social work in new policy contexts: Threats and opportunities

James Blewett

In recent years there have been major developments in social welfare policy in the UK which have had a significant impact on the role of social work. Current and planned policy developments in both children's and adult services, and the pace of the change involved, raise serious questions about the future of social work in respect of both roles and tasks. There have been several recent attempts by regional and central government in the UK to look at the role of social work within the wider social care workforce – *Options for Excellence* (DoH and DfES, 2006), the *21st Century Social Work Review* (Scottish Executive, 2006) and *A profession to value: Social Work in Wales* (ADSS Cymru Project, 2005). In this chapter I will explore the context and major features of this changing policy agenda, and attempt to answer some of the questions raised, including identifying the implications for the users of social work services and the social work practitioners who provide them.

Much of what has been written recently about the future of social work gives an impression of a profession in 'crisis' (Unison, 2004). I will consider some of the current threats to social work that support such a view but conclude that social work still has a unique and indeed crucially important contribution to offer to fellow citizens who find themselves in a range of challenging situations. Far from being a period of terminal decline, this decade could represent a period of great opportunity for social work to experience a reinvigoration and for the profession to confront and positively address some of the very real challenges ahead.

Social work and social policy

Social work concerns itself with a range of difficulties in individuals' lives which pose fundamental questions about the relationship between each individual and the state. Social work is thus shaped by the policy context in which it operates and therefore constitutes an inherently political profession. That is not to say that social work is inherently radical or progressive. However, it operates at the heart of the debate about the appropriate level of state involvement in the lives of individuals, including the supportive or coercive nature of the relationship which accompanies that involvement. Fox Harding (1997) recognised that social work as a profession can take a number of different positions along a continuum from voluntary service-user involvement to compulsory state intervention.

Dominelli (2002) and Payne (2006) identify three similar positions historically occupied in response to social welfare policy. Firstly, they recognise the *therapeutic* tradition in social work, whereby the practitioner is concerned with enabling the individual to problem solve, or at least come to terms with, the difficulties facing them in their lives. Secondly, there is what Payne terms the *social order* – which Dominelli terms the *maintenance* approach – whereby social work provides an important role in addressing social problems on behalf of the state. Within this perspective the practitioner as 'expert' provides information and practical help that enables individuals either to cope, or to deal adequately with problems in their lives. If the individual is unable to do this then the practitioner is able to intervene in the individual's life on behalf of the state through the legal frameworks provided, for example, by the Children Act 1989 or the Mental Health Act 1983. These interventions may take place within a framework of care but also within a framework of control. Lastly, both Payne and Dominelli identify the *transformational* or *emancipatory* tradition in social work, whereby the social worker recognises that in many respects they are attendants to the results of the failure of social policy. Social workers see their role as promoting social justice and take an overtly political stance, being closely linked to ideas of personal empowerment and advocacy. These three positions are not mutually exclusive and they are perhaps better conceptualised as three positions or perspectives between which practitioners may move, depending on the setting in which they are working and the nature of current policy imperatives.

Social work practitioners must reflect directly on the policy context in which social work is situated. However, before examining some aspects of the recent policy context for social work, it is worth considering two associated points about the nature of the relationship between policy and practice (Adams, 2002). Firstly, the interrelationship is not a linear one but rather 'complex' and indeed often messy. At any one time there will be a whole number of *different* policy initiatives and political messages impacting on agencies and the work of individual practitioners. On occasion some of these messages can be outright contradictory, but much more commonly there exists a tension between them. For example, the Schools White Paper (DfES, 2005b), with its emphasis on increased autonomy for schools to promote children's attainment, is potentially at odds with the emphasis within *Every Child Matters* (DfES, 2004a), on the promotion of integrated services for vulnerable children being delivered within and around schools. Secondly, even in the absence of an overt ideological tension between policy initiatives, social welfare organisations are complex systems and a range of unintended consequences can arise from the impact of different factors – including different and/or competing policy initiatives – on the service system at any one time. For example, a drive to speed up social work assessments at the point of intake can have unforeseen implications for longer-term teams when resources are shifted to the 'front end' of agencies.

Historical context of contemporary welfare policy

Before considering the main features of the contemporary New Labour policy context, it is helpful to examine their antecedents in the Conservative era. In many respects the agenda that emerged in that period, between 1979 and 1997, has continued to exert a significant influence over current policy and practice. The economic crises of the late 1970s destabilised the post-war consensus around the welfare state (Hendrick, 2003). In particular there was scepticism among politicians and policy-makers about the viability of a welfare system in which significant numbers of vulnerable people were being cared for by the state in residential settings. In 1977, for example, besides the high number of adults with disabilities and chronic mental health problems, there were 101,000 looked-after children (Parker et al., 1991), largely living in residential settings. This compares with today's figure of a little over 60,000 (DoH and DfES, 2006). Economic factors were increasingly questioned by professionals as well as by service-users, as being the appropriate sole determinants of decisions, which might in some cases mean the placement of people away from their own communities, whether this was appropriate or not.

Hence the Conservative government throughout the 1980s promoted a model of 'community care'. The drivers for this were threefold. Firstly, it reflected the emerging professional consensus about the need to remain within one's community; and secondly, a prevailing view about the most prudent use of resources in welfare. Thirdly, however, it reflected a deeply held ideological distrust of the state's involvement in citizens' private lives. Reflecting what Fox Harding (1997) termed a 'laissez-faire' perspective, the view from what was collectively termed the New Right was that the state should be 'rolled back' and that instead networks within the community, particularly the family, should care wherever possible for the vulnerable (Gladstone, 1995). There was therefore a somewhat 'ironic fit' between fiscal prudence and the rights of the individual for inclusion in the community.

Associated with this drive to shift the responsibility of care from the state to the community was a belief that the state monopolies of health and local authorities delivering personal social services were inflexible and inefficient, and like other areas of national life at the time would benefit from the introduction of the market (Pollitt, 1990). The NHS and Community Care Act 1990 therefore introduced the purchaser–provider split, which became increasingly dominant in adult social services and extremely influential in children's social services. In adult services many social workers shifted from a social work role to a care management role, in which the emphasis was on assessment and commissioning rather than the direct delivery of services. A further effect of the introduction of *the market* was the challenge to 'old' welfarist notions of welfare rights, and instead a shift to the idea of the user of services as *consumer* and/or *customer*. To support this shift a new managerialism began to emerge with a view to 'professionalising' the function of management in the sector (Harris, 2005).

In respect of the development of social work practice in this period, the implementation of the recommendations of the Seebohm Report (1968) had led to the creation of unified social services departments and by the early 1970s most social workers were working within generic settings. Stevenson (2005) argued that this was an important move forward for social work as it enabled the profession to begin to assert a coherent identity that was not specific to any one practice setting or service-user group. This generic approach was endorsed by the Barclay Report (1982), which constituted the last systematic attempt, before the current round of reviews, to examine the role of social work. As well as supporting the generic model Barclay also promoted a community social work model. However, over the subsequent twenty years this genericism was gradually eroded so that by the early 1990s social workers were usually working in highly specialised teams and increasingly in a wide range of voluntary and private sector settings, alongside what were by now seen as the 'traditional' local authority statutory settings. Recent structural change required by *Independence, Well-being and Choice* (DoH, 2005) and *Every Child Matters* (DfES, 2004a) and the associated Children Act 2004 has completed this move away from the generic model.

The move toward specialisation can be seen in part as a response to trends in legislation beginning with the Children Act 1989 and NHS and Community Care Act 1990, which drove adult and children's services in diverging directions. Stevenson (2005), however, also cites the influence of the growth of managerialism in which, in the context of significantly reduced resources provided by central government, performance was increasingly measured in terms of *outputs* rather than *outcomes*. A further factor which pushed social work into a more defensive posture was the impact of a series of child death tragedies. In the twenty years following the Maria Colwell Inquiry in 1973 there were at least a further forty such inquiries. The messages they delivered were remarkably and depressingly similar. They highlighted systemic breakdown in the multi-agency networks, which manifested role confusion and poor communication. However the inquiries were also very critical of individual social work practitioners, particularly for what was perceived as a failure to protect children because of an over-identification with the difficulties of the parents. The Cleveland Inquiry (1988) followed and reported on what was perceived as an excessive and ill-conceived response to suspected sexual abuse by social workers who were seen as too eager to intervene punitively in families' lives. There was a widely held perception among social workers that 'they were damned if they did and damned if they didn't', in terms of responding to concerns raised about children's welfare (Parton, 2005).

The result was that the concept of child protection increasingly dominated the public discourse regarding social work, and meant that social work agencies introduced increasingly bureaucratic procedural systems in order to minimise risk. By the early 1990s concerns were being raised, particularly in light of the challenges presented by the Children Act 1989, that local authorities were only prepared to provide preventative services where there were serious child protection issues and were ignoring their statutory responsibility to promote the welfare of children. These concerns crystallised around the publication of a cohort of influential research studies into the child protection system (DoH, 1995). These studies collectively asserted that there needed to be a refocusing of social work services toward more proactive and preventative work, a message that had implications for the profession that went beyond child care. A further (Conservative) government-commissioned research initiative around the implementation of the Children Act echoed these concerns and confirmed the existence of gate-keeping systems around early access to preventative services (DoH, 2001a; Tunstill and Aldgate, 2000).

Social policy under New Labour

Although Tony Blair and his government had been anxious not to raise what they considered to be unrealistic expectations, there was a strong feeling the future was much brighter for social work under New Labour than under the previous administration. However, it became clear very quickly that the government did not see social work services, particularly within local authority settings, as central to its agenda (Williams, 2001). In terms of this agenda there were a number of key components.

Integration with economic policy

In contrast to the Conservatives, the Labour government saw welfare reform as an integral component of its economic policy (HM Treasury, 1999). The government believed that the UK needed to *modernise* so that it was a high-skill, high-knowledge economy and this would enable it to compete on the world stage, particularly with emerging economies. A threat to this aim was the *social exclusion* of a significant proportion of the population. This concept extended beyond poverty to the fact that poverty could mean individuals were excluded from the economic life of the nation as either consumers or producers. Much of the welfare reform in the last ten years has not been simply about addressing society's moral responsibility toward vulnerable citizens but has been a cross-departmental desire to address the issue of social exclusion (Garrett, 2003).

Rights and responsibilities of citizens

There has been a strong emphasis on not only the rights that citizens possess but also their social responsibilities. The UK has adopted the European Convention of Human Rights with the Human Rights Act 1998, and extended the right to privacy via the Data Protection Act 1998. The government has articulated the belief that the state has a responsibility to enable socially excluded citizens to find paths toward social inclusion, and that this increasingly means employment. However, politicians have also made it clear that on the basis of people's civic responsibilities there should be an element of compulsion in taking up these sources of support. Jordan and Jordan (2000) have described this relationship between government and the more vulnerable citizens as 'tough love', and it has continued to be an important backdrop to contemporary social work practice. It has had many manifestations across public policy. Measures have included the penalisation of parents who fail to take up subsidised child care and subsequent employment opportunities; the attack on incapacity benefit with a veiled attack on the 'work-shy'; the punishment of parents who fail to ensure their children attend school; and the introduction of measures to control anti-social behaviour, most notably through anti-social behaviour orders (Hill, 2001).

Inadequate models of care services

There has been a continuing theme that the traditional models of delivering care services are inadequate, both in terms of their effectiveness but also in the experience that they provide for service-users. Services therefore need to be *modernised*. In particular, New

Labour has sought to extend the market model into all aspects of service delivery and further develop the mixed economy of care. They have combined this with the further development of a consumer model, built-in adult services increasingly on the notion of individualised care packages. Across adult and children's services has been structural reform that has sought to 'join up' services working with specific service-user groups. As a result the unified social services departments in which social work was prominent have been replaced by new configurations of services. In children's services, therefore, there has been a move toward integrating education and social care into unitary children's services departments. In adult services the integration process between health and social care that began in the 1990s has continued to be greatly extended.

Workforce reform

Across all service-user groups New Labour has identified the need to undertake workforce reform as an important part of the modernisation agenda. There was a strong sense that a workforce that had grown up in a culture of 'silo-based' practice, where services lacked cohesion, needed reforming. This was essential if the structural and organisational reforms that New Labour introduced were going to translate into more flexible and responsive services (DoH and DfES, 2006). Government has therefore sought to make inter-professional boundaries more diffuse, and required that professionals work more flexibly in terms of their roles. There was also a belief that 'high-status professionals' could constitute a blockage to progress by behaving in a territorial way and attempts have been made to shift responsibilities to less or unqualified staff. In education, for example, teachers' duties have shifted toward teaching assistants. In health, nurses have taken on tasks traditionally assigned to doctors; and in turn health care assistants have taken on tasks which, in the past, would have been carried out by nurses. In social care there has been an attempt to use differently qualified or unqualified staff to undertake the roles that would have been the preserve of registered social workers (Stanmore, 2006).

Regulation and inspection

New Labour saw itself as addressing perceived inertia, and identified reform of the regulatory and inspection regimes in the sector as the key to the success of its modernisation agenda. New funding has been provided by government but is closely tied to performance targets. Under New Labour there has been a proliferation of such targets and they have become a significant part of social work practitioners' working lives (Munro, 2004). The Care Standards Act 2000 created the General Social Care Council and introduced the protection of the title 'social worker'. There is now a requirement for, in the first instance, registration for social workers, but this will eventually apply to all social care staff in order to raise the standing of the profession and to protect standards. Skill sector councils have recently been divided along adult/children's lines with the creation of the Children's Workforce Development Council and Skills for Care. The Commission for Social Care Inspection, itself only created in 2004, is also in the process of splitting along similar lines, with part going to the Health Care Commission and part to OFSTED by 2009, when CSCI will be abolished.

Key developments in adult services

The organisational divergence between adult and children's services means that a number of developments will be more relevant to social workers in one sector than the other. In adult services the government has articulated its vision for adult social care most clearly in the White Paper, *Independence, Well-being and Choice* (DoH, 2005) and its health equivalent, *Our health, our care, our say* (DoH, 2006). These put forward a vision for social care based on individually tailored packages for care with an emphasis on direct payments. That is, they envisage funding being devolved to the service-users so that they can purchase their own services. There was also a move within the White Paper (DoH, 2005) to strengthen strategic partnerships between agencies, and the government has set seven outcomes for service-users against which the effectiveness of services should be measured. Direct payments have been seen as a key tool for improving the responsiveness of services by government since their introduction for younger disabled adults in 1997, and have now been extended to all users of adult services, as well as to the families of disabled children. Many commentators have welcomed them (Beresford et al., 2007) but they have not lacked critics, who argue they have often been difficult to administer and have placed a high degree of responsibility on service-users, who may be at a vulnerable point in their lives or have impaired capacity (CSCI, 2005).

The other body of key guidance that has sought to promote independence and choices is in the field of learning disability with *Valuing People* (DoH, 2001b), and introduces a person-centred approach with the aim of bringing to fruition the aspiration to 'normalisa-tion' articulated twenty years ago. The Valuing People Support Team (DoH, 2005) reported that there was considerable positive progress but recent reports by the Heath Care Commission (Commission for Health Audit and Inspection, 2007) highlight the fact that practice is extremely uneven and for many learning disabled people their enjoyment of full civil rights remains a distant aspiration.

Many of the other key policies with an impact on social work in adult social care have been in respect of the allocation of resources, particularly across the threshold between health and social care services. The government attempted to establish national criteria in *Fair Access to Care Services* (DoH, 2003). This set three levels at which local authorities could deliver services. However, this framework has highlighted the paucity of funding, particularly for older people. Dame Denise Platt, the chair of the CSCI (*Guardian*, 13/01/07) reported that local authorities were now beginning to restrict the offer of social care services to those in the most acute or 'critical' need. The necessity for a bath, for example, would only meet these criteria if its absence could be linked to a serious threat to health.

In the context of this scarcity of resources the relationship between social care and health can obviously become strained as the NHS attempts to push patients toward the social care sector. Despite the emphasis on joined-up collaborative working, the Delayed Discharge Act 2003 penalises local authorities that have been found to be 'blocking' beds in hospitals. Hospital social workers have often found themselves at the heart of this ten-sion as they have had to negotiate with NHS managers anxious to discharge patients as quickly as possible. At the same time they have also been accountable to social care man-agers trying to avoid having to provide care for people who are not yet ready to be cared for in the community; or who have health needs that cannot or will not be adequately met by social care services (Glasby and Lester, 2004).

Government has experienced major challenges to its planned reforms in the field of adult mental health and clarification of the role of social work has been at the heart of these difficulties (Rapaport, 2006). A draft mental health bill was dropped in 2005 following an outcry from service-users and professionals alike, and the government has now attempted again to reform the Mental Health Act 1983. These reforms strengthen the coercive elements of the Act with the notion of compulsory treatment for patients in the community. They also broaden the definition of mental illness to capture those with serious personality disorders. Most crucially for the purposes of this discussion there has been a proposal to extend the approved social worker role to encompass a wider range of approved mental health professionals. This has been controversial because the extension of the role to health professionals has been seen as compromising what has widely been regarded as the independent role of the approved social worker, who has been able to act as an important check and balance within the mental health system (Rapaport, 2006).

Key developments in children's services

In the past decade a plethora of new legalisation and policy guidance for children's services has been introduced to cover all areas of work carried out in this sector. Major initiatives have occurred in the fields of adoption, leaving care and youth justice. Most recently the government has published the *Care Matters* Green Paper (DfES, 2006a) with the aim of improving provision for looked-after children. The government's overall vision for children, however, is best captured in *Every Child Matters* (DfES, 2004a) and the Children Act 2004. Like adult services, this policy framework is built around five outcomes against which *all* children's progress is measured. Again like adult services, there is an emphasis on structural reform, which has led to the integration of children services – particularly with education but also with other services through children's trusts.

Whereas in adult services the stress has been on individualised care, in children's services the government has promoted early intervention and preventative services through area-based integrated services. Sure Start local programmes which featured targeted intensive family support have been effectively abandoned in favour of children's centres which are to provide early years' child care, and also to act as 'hubs' for the delivery of other services (Tunstill et al., 2006). The aim is that these hubs, which also include extended service schools, will facilitate the development of a far more cohesive workforce. To underpin this process the government has published a *Children's Workforce Strategy* (DfES, 2005a) and a *Common Core of Skills and Knowledge* (DfES, 2004b) which provides the foundation for all practice with children and families. Single or common assessment has been a theme across service-user groups, and in children's services a formal *Common Assessment Framework* has been launched already, linked to the newly enhanced systems for information-sharing (DfES, 2006).

The role of social workers within these new systems is not entirely clear. Their role is not identified specifically within the *Children's Workforce Strategy* (DoH, 2005a), and the latest edition of *Working Together to Safeguard Children* (DfES, 2006b) makes only brief reference to their role as lead professionals in cases of safeguarding. As has so often been the case, it was a child's death, that of Victoria Climbié, followed by a subsequent inquiry (Laming, 2003) that provoked a high-profile public debate about both standards within the profession and its future role. Laming attempted to avoid the vilification of the individual social work practitioner involved, but the well publicised impact on Lisa Arthurworrey was considerable and effectively ended her career. In fact, Laming attempted to link poor practice with systemic failure and highlighted poor management, and in particular weak supervision of front-line workers. He also attempted to preserve the link between the safeguarding of children with the promotion of their welfare more generally, and articulate a role for social work across the spectrum of need.

The challenges for social workers

The international definition of social work sets an ambitious agenda for the profession:

> The social work profession promotes social change, problem solving in human relationships and the empowerment and liberation of people to enhance well-being. Utilising theories of human behaviour and social systems, social work intervenes at the points where people interact with their environments. Principles of human rights and social justice are fundamental to social work.

> (http://www.ifsw.org/en/p38000208.html, accessed 13/12/06)

These aspirational aims are reflected in most other recent attempts to define the role of social work within the UK (Asquith et al., 2005; Brand et al., 2005; DfES and DoH, 2006). They reflect the tradition of social liberalism in which social work has generally sought to locate itself and see the role of social workers as improving the lives of vulnerable people in society, often in the context of discrimination and social injustice. To say the least, key features of the current policy context of social work in the UK make implementing this vision extremely challenging.

A diminished role for social work?

A striking feature of recent government publications, including *Independence, Well-being and Choice,* (DoH, 2005), *Every Child Matters* (DfES, 2004), *The Children's Workforce Strategy* (DfES, 2005a) and the latest draft Mental Health Bill is the absence of any reference to social work as *a profession*, or as having a particular role to play and/or tasks to undertake in the rapidly changing field of care services. That is not to say that other professions have high profiles. Instead, the emphasis within those strategy documents is much more on outcomes to be achieved and services to be delivered. Rather than focusing on individual professional roles (DfES, 2005a), the stress is on the homogeneity of the workforce and on the common knowledge base and skills sets in the children's or adult fields.

For all professions this strategy could present a challenge in terms of maintaining their professional identity: for social workers, however, it raises particular difficulties. While there will clearly be political periods in which professionals such as teachers or doctors are unhappy with aspects of government policy, in general these two professions have both enjoyed a 'good press' from government and seen their salary levels rise significantly. An often repeated policy aim is to 'employ more teachers, doctors, nurses, police officers…' (Stanmore, 2006). Social work has not been held in comparable regard and indeed has on occasions encountered outright hostility (Butler and Drakeford, 2005). The reasons for this attitude of ambivalence are complex. It is certainly not an inevitable phenomenon, as Stevenson noted from her involvement in the *British Journal of Social Work* in the early 1970s (2005). However, in the current context social work appears to represent those aspects of a liberal tradition in social policy which have been rejected by the current government (Jordan, 2004).

This sense of ideological unease with which social work is regarded is compounded by the complexity of the social work role. All of the activity undertaken by *caring professions* potentially involves complexity. Common to all groups are high levels of variation in the degree of sophistication with which practitioners undertake the task. However, the impact of this variation between individual workers is exacerbated in the context of social work by the inherent complexity and fluidity of the social work role. Asquith et al. (2005) describe the contested views of social work; and both Dominelli (2002) and Payne (2006) construct typologies of social work practice which are composed of very different tasks and roles. This theoretical breadth is in many ways an important social work strength. It reflects the ability of social work to be flexible and to adapt itself to different professional environments in a way that is perhaps unique. However, unless this strength is acknowledged by policy-makers and strategic managers it will remain at best invisible and at worst be seen to constrain the ability of the profession from advocating on behalf of itself.

Marginalisation of social work

Marginalisation of social work could occur if its main activity was to be confined to meeting acute need. One possible response to the quest for a specific role for social work is to argue that social workers are the obviously best-qualified group to work with situations involving the most acute need; and specifically those which invlove the *duty to protect*. This capability certainly plays to a dominant theme in public policy which is concerned about the management of risk (Beck, 1992). Indeed, social workers are well equipped to deal with such cases. They have the capacity to understand potential harm, whether it be to children or vulnerable adults in the context of a constellation of complex factors. In so doing, an assessment can be made about its impact, bearing in mind the legal framework and thresholds that surround such situations (Adams et al., 2005).

Social work, however, is more than simply implementing those clauses in the law which address protection, rather than those addressing the promotion of welfare more broadly. Moreover, the profession would be consigning itself to a very narrow and marginal position if it saw its only mandate as the legal framework (Preston-Shoot and Braye, 2006). It is all too easy for complexity to be equated with acute need or protection. In fact many cases where need is less acute nevertheless have layers of complexity that social work is well placed to understand and address. It is ironic that at a time when government guidance stresses the protection of vulnerable children is 'everyone's business' (DfES, 2006b), social work is in danger of being seen as the profession that has ownership of safeguarding children. *Every Child Matters* (DfES, 2004a) places an emphasis on early intervention and preventative work, and social work has a strong track record of fulfilling this role (Gardner, 2005). Indeed, social work's emphasis on developing and sustaining relationships means that it has been demonstrated as effective in engaging hard-to-reach service-users (Quinton, 2004; Tunstill et al., 2006).

Bureaucratisation and performance management

Many social workers currently report that one of the most difficult aspects of their jobs is the increasing levels of bureaucratisation (Statham et al., 2002). Such a culture can be deskilling and divert social workers away from the work that they value, usually the face-to-face engagement with social work service-users. Critical thinking and reflective practice can be curtailed when the working day is taken up with completing internally generated procedural processes (Munro, 2004). Some social workers have expressed a view that it is these bureaucratic procedures, and not simply shortage of time, which have undermined their use of professional judgement and decision making. For example, many social workers report the proliferation of panels that make decisions which in the past would have been made by first-line managers. In some cases these 'decisions' have involved paper reassessments of cases, and have recommended courses of action contrary to those identified by the practitioner and their first-line manager (Gupta and Blewett, 2007).

Some practitioners blame the influence of performance management for this process and certainly there has been a significant increase in the number of performance standards against which local care services are measured (Tilbury, 2004). Moreover, there have been very clear instances when these performance indicators have distorted social work practice and decision making (Munro, 2004). It would be unwise, however, to categorically dismiss performance indicators. They can represent an important mechanism for professional accountability and large sums of public money go into them. Rather, Allnock et al. (2006) argue that it is not so much the existence of performance indicators that can cause difficulty but whether those performance targets are the most appropriate. They need to be linked to outcomes for service-users rather than mechanically focused on bureaucratic outputs. The Care Programme Approach in mental health has been recognised as one instance of a relatively user-friendly bureaucratic process that works well for both service-user and practitioner (DoH, 2006).

One area in which these bureaucratic pressures have been particularly acutely felt is in the field of adult services where the care management model has prevailed, following the implementation of the Community Care Act 1990. Knapp et al. (2005) concluded from a national UK study that the care management role was often ill defined and very variable in both its nature and effectiveness. They reported that service-user satisfaction rates were often low, and in many ways, despite the associated difficulties, such attitudes have fuelled the move towards direct payments. The Single Assessment Process was meant to streamline the role. Tools were developed that sought to promote an outcome-based approach for practice. However, Qureshi (2002) argued that the 'Tools suggested to assist assessment are … designed, in my view, with more of an eye to consistent measurement than as a basis for consequent action.'

Limited resources

There is undoubtedly evidence of new investment in the care sector but long-term funding issues should not be underestimated. The recent move to providing care services only to adults in 'critical need' exemplifies the way in which aspirational language for any new initiative can be significantly undermined by a lack of resources. It is difficult to promote relationship-based approaches to practice, where personal empowerment lies at the centre, when practitioners are not even able to offer the most basic of services such as bathing or cooking. The aims of the funding undermine the realisation of such ambitious vision.

The erosion of poverty and social exclusion is a key government aim, but one of the striking features of the UK today is the enduring levels of poverty and deprivation (Palmer et al., 2006; UNICEF, 2007). Unless social work practice accommodates this reality as one of the starting points for practice, many of the plans to address the plight of the most vulnerable and excluded which have been outlined above will be discredited.

Meeting the challenges

If the picture were simply one of an under-resourced, disempowered profession, strangled by ever-increasing bureaucratic demands, stigmatised in the opinion of service-users, and lacking any clear role in the changing care sector, then this would indeed be bleak. However the future for social work is much more complex than this gloomy scenario. The basis for some cautious optimism is twofold. Firstly there is, despite the constraints alluded to above, considerable practice evidence that much excellent work is taking place. Encouragingly, some of the best evidence for this comes not from the professional forums but from those who are on the receiving end of social work practice. The recent study by Beresford et al. (2007) on the role of social work in palliative care contains examples of work by social workers who are providing an authoritative and sensitive service at a vulnerable point in people's lives. Morgan (2006) collated the views of children and young people who have experienced a social work service. Again, while examples of poor practice were identified, for the most part the young people were extremely positive about social workers. Even where the involvement of social workers is not a voluntary choice, examples abound of service-users who report a positive experience of social work intervention. CSCI (2006) for example reported on the views of parents whose children were in the child protection system. Many of these parents were positive about social work interventions which they saw as both supporting them as parents, as well as safeguarding their children. These views concur with earlier studies which collected views from the parents of children whose children were the subject of care proceedings; these parents were positive about the social work support received which they saw as fair, respectful and transparent (Freeman and Hunt, 1998; Braden et al., 1999). Rapaport (2006) also reported that despite the coercive elements of the approved social work role, service-users have been among the strongest supporters of it remaining discrete to social work.

The theme that recurs from all service-user perspectives is that *good social work is based upon the quality of the professional relationship*. While professionals in every discipline would see relationships as a core component of their role, social work goes one step further. The relationship between a social work practitioner and a service-user is itself seen as having a transformational significance (Ruch, 2005). That is not to say that the relationship is an end in itself, because user feedback also highlights the crucial importance of a combination of emotional support and practical help. Social work's link to social justice and the importance of advocacy and anti-oppressive frameworks have also been central to much of what is recognised as positive about social work. The values of social work have not fundamentally changed between the seminal work of Biestek (1961) and their contemporary expression in the professional codes (GSCC, 2002) and national occupational standards (TOPSS, 2001). These values have consistently stressed the centrality of relationship-based practice. However, as demonstrated throughout this discussion, there are factors in today's configuration of care services that militate against this. Therefore if social work is to remain and indeed become more credible and enjoy higher recognition it must find ways of operating in environments where the nature of its contribution is valued and promoted.

This tension between the potential of social work and the more prosaic reality of today's practice environments is currently provoking wide-ranging debate. As well as the government-sponsored reviews, other voices are beginning to proffer radical suggestions for the future of the profession. Legrand and Pettigrew (2006), for example, have proposed that social work be effectively privatised and delivered through local private practices. While this strategy aspires to offer a more localised and responsive service, its adoption would dangerously weaken the link with democratically accountable local services. Tunstill et al. (2005), Butler and Drakeford (2005) and Brand et al. (2005) have taken the opposing view in arguing that far from marginalising itself organisationally social work should seek to locate itself at the heart of the reconfiguration of services. Social work should not retreat into a defensive position as the expert profession in managing risk, but should argue its capacity to offer services across the spectrum of need. Indeed, it is particularly well placed to deliver a service at the preventative end of the spectrum where high quality support can be so effective, both for individuals but in a value-for-money sense too (Tunstill et al., 2006).

The early twenty-first century is a period of challenge for social work. That it is to say, it is a period in which social work has enormous opportunity but also a period in which it faces a significant threat to the integrity of the profession. The social work profession has a strong case to make. Its defenders can draw with confidence on considerable evidence from both research and service-user feedback in order to argue convincingly that social work makes a valuable contribution to the process of improving the lives of some of the most vulnerable members of society. However, in articulating this case the social work profession cannot simply rely on sympathetic policy-makers and politicians. The profession must find among its professional and trade union forums and its alliances with service-users a way of speaking with greater confidence and clarity than it has in the past, and succeed in painting an accurate picture of its achievements and potential.

References

Adams, R. (2002) *Social Policy for Social Work*. Basingstoke: Palgrave.
Adams, R., Dominelli, L. and Payne, M. (eds) (2002) *Critical Practice in Social Work*. Basingstoke: Palgrave.
Adams, R., Dominelli, L. and Payne, M. (eds) (2005) *Social Work Futures*. Basingstoke: Palgrave.

ADSS Cymru Project (2005) *Social Work in Wales: a Profession to Value*. Cardiff: ADSS.

Allnock, D., Akhurst, S. and Tunstill, J. (2006) 'Constructing and sustaining a Sure Start Local Programme Partnership: lessons for future inter-agency collaborations', *Journal of Children's Services*, 1 (3).

Asquith, S., Clark, C. and Waterhouse, L. (2005) *The Role of the Social Worker in the 21st Century*. Edinburgh: Scottish Executive.

Barclay, P.M. (1982) *Social Workers: Their Role and Tasks*. London: Bedford Square Press.

Beck, U. (1992) *Risk Society*. London: Sage.

Beresford, P., Adshead, L. and Croft, S. (2007) *Palliative care, social work and service users*. London: Jessica Kingsley.

Biestek, F.P. (1961) *The Casework Relationship*. London: Allen & Unwin.

Brand, D., Reith, T. and Statham, D. (2005) *Core Roles and Tasks of Social Workers. A Scoping Study for the GSCC*. London: General Social Care Council.

Brandon, M., Lewis, A., Thoburn, J. and Way, A. (1999) *Safeguarding Children with the Children Act 1989*. London: HMSO.

Butler, I. and Drakeford, M. (2005) 'Trusting in social work', *British Journal of Social Work*, 35: 639–53.

Cleveland Inquiry (1988) *Report of the Inquiry into Child Abuse in Cleveland 1987*. London: HMSO.

Commission for Healthcare Audit and Inspection (2007) *Investigation into the Service for People with Learning Disabilities Provided by Sutton and Merton Primary Care Trust*. London: Commission for Healthcare Audit and Inspection.

Commission for Social Care Inspection (CSCI) (2005) *Direct Payments: What Are the Barriers?* London: CSCI.

Commission for Social Care Inspection (CSCI) (2006) *Supporting Parents, Safeguarding Children*. London: CSCI.

Department for Education and Skills (DfES) (2004a) *Every Child Matters: Change for Children*. London: HMSO.

Department for Education and Skills (DfES) (2004b) *Common Core of Skills and Knowledge*. London: DfES.

Department for Education and Skills (DfES) (2005a) *The Children's Workforce Strategy: Building a World-Class Workforce for Children, Young People and Families*. London: HMSO.

Department for Education and Skills (DfES) (2005b). *Higher Standards, Better Schools for All – More Choice for Parents and Pupils*. London: HMSO.

Department for Education and Skills (DfES) (2006a) *Care Matters: Transforming the Lives of Children and Young People*. London: HMSO.

Department of Education and Skills (DfES) (2006b) *Working Together to Safeguard Children*. London: HMSO.

Department of Health (DoH) (1995) *Child Protection: Messages from Research*. London: HMSO.

Department of Health (DoH) (2001a) *Children Act Now*. London: HMSO.

Department of Health (DoH) (2001b) *Valuing People: A New Strategy for Learning Disability for the 21st Century*. London: HMSO.

Department of Health (DoH) (2003) *Fair Access to Care Services*. London: HMSO.

Department of Health (DoH) (2005) *Independence, Well-being and Choice: Our Vision for the Future of Social Care for Adults in England*. London: HMSO.

Department of Health (DoH) (2006) *Our health, our care, our say*, White Paper, London: HMSO.

Department of Health and Department for Education and Skills (DoH and DfES) (2006) *Options for Excellence: Building the Social Care Workforce of the Future*. London: HMSO.

Dominelli, L. (2002) 'Anti-oppressive practice in context', in R. Adams, L. Dominelli and M. Payne (eds), *Critical Practice in Social Work*. Basingstoke: Palgrave.

Fox Harding, L. (1997) *Perspectives in Child Care Policy*. London: Longman.

Freeman, P. and Hunt, J. (1998) *Parental Perspectives on Care Proceedings*. London: HMSO.

Gardner, R. (2005) *Supporting Families*. Chichester: Wiley.

Garrett. P.M. (2003) *Remaking Social Work with Children and Families: A Critical Discussion on the 'Modernisation' of Social Care*. London: Routledge.

General Social Care Council (GSCC) (2002) *Code of Practice for Social Care Workers and Code of Practice for Employers of Social Care Workers*. London: GSCC.

Gladstone, D. (ed.) (1995) *British Social Welfare: Past, Present and Future*. London: UCL Press.

Glasby, J. and Lester, H. (2004) 'Delayed hospital discharge and mental health: the policy implications of recent research', *Social Policy and Administration*, 38 (7).

Gupta, A. and Blewett, J. (2007) 'Change for children? The challenges and opportunities for the children's social work workforce', *Child and Family Social Work*.

Harris, J. (2005) 'Globalisation, neo-liberal managerialism and UK social work', in I. Ferguson and M. Lavalette (eds), *Globalisation, Global Justice and Social Work*. London: Routledge.

Hendrick, H. (2003) *Child Welfare: Historical Dimensions, Contemporary Debate*. Bristol: Policy Press.

Hill, M. (ed.) (2001) *Effective Ways of Working with Children and their Families*. London: Jessica Kingsley.

HM Treasury (1999) *Opportunity for All*. London: HMSO.

Jordan, B. (2004) 'Emancipatory social work? Opportunity or oxymoron', *British Journal of Social Work*, 34(1): 5–19.

Jordan, B. and Jordan, C. (2000) *Social Work and the Third Way*. London: SAGE.

Knapp, M., Fernande, Z. J., Kendall, J., Beecham, J., Northey, S. and Richardson, A. (2005) *Developing Social Care: The Current Position*. London: SCIE.

Laming, H. (2003) *The Report of the Inquiry into the Death of Victoria Climbié*, London: HMSO.

Legrand, J. and Pettigrew (2006) 'Child care would be better as a business', *Guardian*, 4.10.06.

Morgan, R. (2006) *About Social Workers: A Children's Views Report*. London: Commission for Social Care Inspection.

Munro, E. (2004) 'The impact of audit on social work practice', *British Journal of Social Work*, 34: 1077–97.

Palmer, G., MacInnes, T. and Kenway, P. (2006) *Monitoring Poverty and Social Exclusion*. London: The Joseph Rowntree Foundation.

Parker, R., Ward, H., Jackson, S., Aldgate, J. and Wedge, P. (1991) *Assessing Outcomes in Child Care*. London: HMSO.

Parton, N. (2005) *Safeguarding Childhood*. Basingstoke: Palgrave.

Payne, M. (2006) *What is Professional Social Work?* Bristol: Policy Press.

Pollitt, C. (1990) *Managerialism and the Public Services: The Anglo-American Experience*. Oxford: Blackwell.

Preston-Shoot, M. and Braye, S. (2006) 'The role of law in welfare reform: critical perspectives on the relationship between law and social work practice', *International Journal of Social Welfare*, 15 (1): 19–26.

Quinton, D. (2004) *Supporting Parents: Messages from Research*. London: Jessica Kingsley.

Qureshi, H. (2002) 'Social and political influences on services for older people in the United Kingdom in the late 20th century', *Journals of Gerontology Series A: Biological Sciences and Medical Sciences*, 57A, 11, M705–M711.

Rapaport, J. (2006) 'New roles in mental health: the creation of the approved mental health practitioner', *Journal of Integrated Care*, 14 (5) (October): 37–46.

Ruch, G. (2005) 'Holistic approaches to contemporary child care social work', *Child and Family Social Work*, 10: 111–23.

Scottish Executive (2006) *Changing Lives: Report of the 21st Century Social Work Review*. Edinburgh: Scottish Executive.

Seebohm, F. (1968) *Report of the Committee on Local Authority and Allied Social Services*. London: HMSO.

Stanmore, E. (2006) 'New roles in rehabilitation: the implications for nurses and other professionals', *Journal of Evaluation in Clinical Practice*, 12 (6): 656–64.

Statham, J., Candappa, M., Simon, A. and Owen, C. (2002) *Trends in Care: Exploring Reasons for the Increase in Children Looked After by Local Authorities*. London: Institute of Education.

Statham, J., Holtermann, S. and Winter, G. (2002) *Supporting Families: A Comparative Study of Outcomes and Costs of Services for Children in Need*. London: Institute of Education.

Stevenson, O. (2005) 'Genericism and specialization: the story since 1970', *British Journal of Social Work*. doi:10.1093/bjsw/bch298.

Tilbury, C. (2004) 'The influence of performance measurement on child welfare policy and practice', *British Journal of Social Work*, 34: 225–41.

Training Organisation for Personal Social Services (TOPSS) (2001) *National Occupational Standards for Social Work*. Rugby: TOPSS.

Tunstill, J., and Aldgate, J. (2000) *Services for Children in Need, from Policy to Practice*. London: The Stationery Office.

Tunstill, J., Aldgate J. and Hughes, M. (2006) *Improving Children's Service Networks*. London: Jessica Kingsley.

Tunstill, J., Meadows, P., Allnock, D., Akhurst, S., Chrysanthou, J., Garbers, C., Morley, A. and Van de Velde, T. (2005) *Implementing Sure Start Local Programmes: An In-depth Study*. London: DfES.

UNICEF (2007) 'Child poverty in perspective: an overview of child well-being in rich countries', *Innocenti Report Card* 7, UNICEF Innocenti Research Centre, Florence.

Unison (2004) 'The way forward for Scotland's Social Work', http://www.unison-scotland.org.uk/localgovt/socialwork/index.html.

Williams, F. (2001) 'In and beyond New Labour: towards a new political ethics of care', *Critical Social Policy*, 21 (4): 467–93.

Index